Home and Identity in Late Life

*International
Perspectives*

Graham D. Rowles, Ph.D., is Professor of Gerontology and Director of the Graduate Center for Gerontology at the University of Kentucky. He is a graduate of Bristol University (England) and has a Ph.D. from Clark University (Massachusetts). His research focuses on the experience of aging in different environmental contexts. A central theme of this work is exploration, employing qualitative methodologies, of the changing relationship between elderly people and their environment with advancing age, and the implications of this transition for health and well-being. He has conducted in-depth ethnographic research with elderly populations in urban (inner city), rural (Appalachian), and long-term care environments. His publications include *Prisoners of Space? Exploring the Geographical Experience of Older People,* four co-edited volumes on aspects of aging and the environment, and more than 50 book chapters and articles. Dr. Rowles is a Fellow of the Gerontological Society of America and the Association for Gerontology in Higher Education, serves on the editorial board of the *Journals of Gerontology (Social Sciences)* and is president of the Southern Gerontological Society.

Habib Chaudhury, PhD, is an Assistant Professor in Aging and the Built Environment in the Department of Gerontology at the Simon Fraser University, Vancouver, Canada. He holds a Ph.D. in Architecture/Environment-Behavior Studies from the University of Wisconsin-Milwaukee. He was a Fellow in the Institute on Aging and Environment at the University of Wisconsin-Milwaukee. Dr. Chaudhury's research interests include: Design and planning of housing and community for older adults, place-therapy for persons with dementia, self in dementia, design for people with dementia, health care environments and design for active living in older adults. He has conducted qualitative research with persons with dementia, family members and formal caregivers exploring the potential of "home" as a resource in a person-centered care approach. Dr. Chaudhury is also affiliated as a qualified health researcher with the Centre for Research on Personhood in Dementia at the University of British Columbia.

Home and Identity in Late Life

International Perspectives

Graham D. Rowles, PhD
Habib Chaudhury, PhD
Editors

 Springer Publishing Company

Springer Publishing Company, Inc.
11 West 42nd Street
New York, NY 10036

Acquisitions Editor: Sheri W. Sussman
Production Editor: Janice Stangel
Cover design by Joanne Honigman

05 06 07 08 09 / 5 4 3 2 1

Library of Congress Cataloging-in-Publication Data

Home and identity in late life international perspectives / edited by Graham D. Rowles & Habib Chaudhury.
    p. cm.
    Includes bibliographical references and index.
    ISBN 0-8261-2715-0 (hard cover)
    1. Older people—Dwellings—Psychological aspects—Cross-cultural studies.
2. Home—Psychological aspects—Cross-cultural studies. 3. Identity (Psychology) in old age—Cross-cultural studies. I. Rowles, Graham D. II. Chaudhury, Habib.
BF724.85.H65 2005
155.67—dc22
                                    2005008168

Printed in the United States of America by Sheridan Books.

We dedicate this volume to the memory of M. Powell Lawton, who touched so many lives and minds (including the editors of this volume) with his genius, insight, and humanity.

Contents

Part III: Disruptions of Home

Part IV: Creating and Recreating Home

Part V: Community Perspective on the Meaning of Home

Part VI: Leaving Home: Commentaries

Contributors

Elaine Caouette, MOAQ, is a practicing architect in Drummondville, Quebec, Canada.

Maria G. Cattell, Ph.D, is Research Associate at the Field Museum of Natural History in Chicago, Illinois.

Joan Dacher, Ph.D., is Director of the Palliative Care Program in the Community Hospice, Abany, New York.

Carole Després, Ph.D., is Professor at the Ecole d'architecture of the Universite Laval, Quebec, Canada.

Kim Dovey, Ph.D., is Professor of Architecture and Urban Design, University of Melbourne, Australia.

Jacquelyn Frank, Ph.D., is Associate Professor and Coordinator of Gerontology Programs in the School of Social Work at Illinois State University, Normal, Illinois.

Caroline Holland, Ph.D., is a Research Fellow in the School of Health and Social Welfare at the Open University, Milton Keynes, United Kingdom.

Amy F. Hosier, M.S., is the Charlotte Schmidlapp Fellow in the Graduate Center for Gerontology at the University of Kentucky, Lexington, Kentucky.

Leonie Kellaher, Ph.D., is Director of the Center for Environmental and Social Studies and Ageing at the University of North London, United Kingdom.

Fereshteh Ahmadi Lewin, Ph.D., is Associate Professor of Sociology in the Department of Sociology at Uppsala University and Senior Lecturer in the Department of Caring Sciences and Sociology at the University of Gavle, Sweden.

Sebastien Lord, M. Arch., a Research Associate with the interdisciplinary research group on the suburbs (GIRBa) at the Universite Laval, Quebec, Canada, is completing his doctoral dissertation at Ecole superieure d'amenagement du territoire et de developpement regional (ESAD).

Sanjoy Mazumdar, M.Arch.A.S., M.C.P., Ph.D, is Professor in the Department of Planning, Policy and Design, Department of Health Science and Policy, Department of Asian American Studies, and Program in Religious Studies at the University of California, Irvine.

Shampa Mazumdar, Ph.D. is Lecturer in the Department of Sociology at the University of California, Irvine.

Kate de Medeiros, M.S., is Research Associate and a doctoral candidate in the Center for Aging Studies at the University of Maryland, Baltimore County.

Carolyn Norris-Baker, Ph.D, is Professor and Director of the Kansas State University Center on Aging, Manhattan, Kansas.

Frank Oswald, Ph.D, is Senior Research Scientist and Deputy Chair of the Department of Social and Environmental Gerontology in the German Centre for Research on Ageing at the University of Heidelberg (DZFA), Germany.

Sheila M. Peace, Ph.D, is Senior Lecturer in the School of Health and Social Welfare at the Open University, Milton Keynes, United Kingdom.

Amos Rapoport is Distinguished Professor Emeritus, Department of Architecture, University of Wisconsin, Milwaukee.

Nora J. Rubinstein, Ph.D. is President of Place/Space Associates in Middletown Springs, Vermont.

Robert L. Rubinstein, Ph.D, is Professor of Anthropology in the Department of Sociology and Anthropology at the University of Maryland Baltimore County.

Cherry Russell, Ph.D, is Associate Professor in the School of Behavioural and Community Health Sciences, Faculty of Health Sciences, University of Sydney, Lidcombe, N.S.W., Australia.

Rick J. Scheidt, Ph.D., is Professor in the School of Family Studies and Human Services in the College of Human Ecology at Kansas State University in Manhattan, Kansas.

Edmund Sherman, Ph.D, is Professor Emeritus in the School of Social Welfare at the State University of New York, Albany, New York.

Maria D. Vesperi, Ph.D., is Professor of Anthropology in the Division of Social Sciences in New College of the University of South Florida, Sarasota, Florida.

John F. Watkins, Ph.D., is Associate Professor of Gerontology and Director of Graduate Studies at the University of Kentucky Graduate Center for Gerontology, Lexington, Kentucky.

Hans-Werner Wahl, Ph.D, is Professor of Social and Environmental Gerontology and Chair of the Department of Social and Environmental Gerontology at the German Centre for Research on Ageing at the University of Heidelberg (DZFA), Germany.

Preface

The seeds of this volume were planted at the 17th Congress of the International Association of Gerontology in Vancouver in July of 2001 during a conversation between the editors. Following numerous e-mails and telephone conversations with potential contributors, the silhouette of our edited collection began to take shape. Springer Publishing committed to the project at an early date but an array of unforeseen and unpredictable circumstances delayed completion of the work. Thus, we are both glad and relieved to reach the end of an editorial tunnel and see the light of the print version of the book.

Home and Identity in Late Life, the first comprehensive volume on the concept of home and aging in more than a decade, consists of original essays and research studies providing a contemporary perspective on the complex relationship between home and identity as this relates to well being in late life. Perspectives presented are myriad. They represent a diversity of geographical, philosophical and methodological lenses revealing the depth and richness of the human experience of home.

Key features of the book include a critical interdisciplinary focus, an international perspective (with contributions from five continents), introduction of novel theoretical perspectives on the meaning of home, detailed empirical research, and exploration of practical implications of developing deeper understanding of the concept of home for planning and designing residential environments for elders. Aging societies throughout the world are moving through unprecedented demographic transitions. Increasing numbers and proportions of elders are expressing a variety of needs, presenting new challenges and exploring new opportunities. Against this backdrop, both researchers and practitioners are investigating the possibilities and constraints of "aging in place" and are creatively planning and promoting ways of providing the opportunity for older adults to remain in their own familiar dwellings and communities. As part of this process, scholars are becoming increasingly attuned to the complexity of the relationship between elders and their environments and to the need to understand the meanings and values that underlie a sense of being "at home." This book provides avenues for deepening our understanding of the meaning of home and community that will be critical as we progress in such endeavors.

The volume is organized in six sections exploring key elements of home. An opening section establishes a context by providing a comprehensive interpretive review of the status of research on home and aging over the past decade. Section II consists of chapters providing a critical perspective on the meaning of home in different cultures. Chapters include an empirically based analysis of dimensions of the meaning of home (comparing the former East and West Germany), a critical analysis of the relationship of home to elders' sense of self and identity, an interpretation of the role of cherished possessions and memorabilia as elements in the creation of home, and a chapter illustrating the manner in which the arrangement and use of dwelling space in India is imbued with religious and sacred meanings. Section III considers the antithesis of home—homelessness. Threats to sustaining a sense of home are explored in chapters on political and social separation from home, estrangement from home associated with the immigrant experience, the poignant alienation from and ongoing quest to find home for the person with Alzheimer's disease, and the notion of homelessness considered from a life course perspective. Emphasizing a more explicitly dynamic perspective, Section IV focuses on processes of creating and recreating home in chapters that explore expressions of this theme in western Kenya, Sydney, Australia, and Quebec City, Canada. In section V, emphasis shifts to shared community perspectives on the meaning of home in chapters exploring the manner in which home is often equated with community in small towns in Kansas, ways in which elders' sense of home identity and well being in selected English settlements is intimately tied to locality, and the manner in which neighborhood design and planning in Quebec City is linked to the ability to sustain an ongoing sense of home in suburban environments. A final section, Section VI, consists of essays by three eminent scholars who were asked to review the volume and provide critical commentary. Each adds his or her unique perspective on the significance of home in old age.

This volume is designed for students, scholars, service professionals and policy-makers in gerontology, the social and behavioral sciences, and the health sciences. A particularly important audience is design and planning educators and professionals with a concern for creating residential environments that are sensitive to the lived experience of their occupants. Overall, our goal is to provide stimulation and food-for-thought for anybody interested in the interrelationships among human aging, home, community, and identity.

Deepest thanks to our talented contributors for their unrelenting commitment to this venture and for their gracious tolerance of sometimes picky and occasionally insistent editorial demands. We especially appreciate the conscientious hard work of Elizabeth 'Beth' Hunter who coordinated project correspondence with authors and assembling the manuscripts. Our sincere gratitude to Helvi Gold at Springer Publishing Company for being extraordinarily patient with the ever-shifting submission timeline of the manuscript. Finally, we offer a big thank you to our respective spouses, Ruth and Atiya, for enduring our frequent absences from home as we worked at our offices on this project.

Graham D. Rowles, Lexington, Kentucky
Habib Chaudhury, Vancouver, British Columbia

Acknowledgments

$\mathbf{W}$e have found a home for *Home and Identity in Late Life.* The seeds of this volume were planted at the World Aging Congress in Vancouver in July of 2001 during a conversation between the editors. Following numerous e-mails and telephone conversations with potential contributors, the silhouette of our edited collection began to take shape. Springer Publishing committed to the project at an early date but an array of unforeseen and unpredictable circumstances delayed completion of the work. Thus, we are both glad and relieved to reach the end of an editorial tunnel and see the light of the print version of the book. We believe this volume presents readers with an insightful collection of original essays and findings from empirical studies on home, self, and human aging. Perspectives presented are myriad. They represent a diversity of geographical and philosophical contexts and reveal the depth and richness of the human experience of home.

Deepest thanks to our talented contributors for their unrelenting commitment to this venture and for their gracious tolerance of sometimes picky and occasionally insistent editorial demands. We especially appreciate the conscientious hard work of Elizabeth 'Beth' Hunter who coordinated project correspondence with authors and assembling the manuscripts. Our sincere gratitude to Helvi Gold at Springer Publishing Company for being extraordinarily patient with the ever-shifting submission timeline of the manuscript. Finally, we offer a big thank you to our respective spouses, Ruth and Atiya, for enduring our frequent absences as we worked at our offices on this project. Yes, we will now be coming home!

Graham D. Rowles, Lexington, Kentucky
Habib Chaudhury, Vancouver, British Columbia

PART I

Coming Home

CHAPTER 1

Between the Shores of Recollection and Imagination: Self, Aging, and Home

Habib Chaudhury and Graham D. Rowles

"Home" is where we belong. It is in our experience, recollections, imagination, and aspirations. Home provides the physical and social context of life experience, burrows itself into the material reality of memories, and provides an axial core for our imagination. The experience of home environments, the relationship of this experience with self-identity, and the evolving meaning of home over the life course have received increased attention from researchers in recent decades. During the 1980s and early 1990s, several books and anthologies focused on aspects of the topic (see for example, Altman & Low, 1992; Altman & Werner, 1985; Marcus, 1995). It is now widely accepted that home provides a sense of identity, a locus of security, and a point of centering and orientation in relation to a chaotic world beyond the threshold. It is also increasingly acknowledged that a sense of being "at home" is related to health status and well-being and that disruption of this sense, through *in situ* environmental change (for example, change in an established neighborhood), relocation (either forced or voluntary), or through disruption of a more existential sense of being at one with the world, can

3

result in significant changes in well-being. In many cases, involuntary relocation and separation from a sense of identity has been shown to have pathological consequences and to lead to increases in rates of morbidity and mortality.

As knowledge in this growing multi- and interdisciplinary field proliferates, and as increasingly sophisticated theory and practical insights develop, it is important to synthesize fragmentary findings from different fields within a coherent contemporary perspective on the phenomenon of home. This volume provides such a perspective—a second-generation synthesis and interpretation of the field. Our contributors focus on the meaning of home to elders and the manner in which this meaning may be sustained, threatened, reconstituted, or otherwise modified in association with both normal and pathological changes associated with the experience of growing old. Adopting an international perspective that emphasizes the contrasting but complementary perspectives of different cultures, we include original contributions from leading contemporary scholars who seek to take us beyond the ad hoc findings of the past century.

OBJECTIVES

We have commissioned and organized the chapters that follow to accomplish five distinct but overlapping objectives. First, this volume seeks to provide a contemporary summary of recent conceptual scholarship and empirical research on the substance, meaning, and significance of the experience of home in later years. A second objective is to expand horizons of discourse by embracing international perspectives on home. Integral and parallel to such elaboration, is adoption of increasingly complex and nuanced perspectives that reflect the ongoing evolution of gerontology from a multidisciplinary to an interdisciplinary field (Bass & Ferraro, 2000). A third objective is to contribute novel theoretical perspectives on the meaning of home. By moving in these directions, the intent is to facilitate a fourth objective—creation and sharing of original perspectives that can guide future theoretical, substantive, and methodological inquiries. A final important objective is to explore practical implications of a deeper understanding of the meaning of home for improving the quality of life of our elders.

ORGANIZATION

The book is comprised of six sections. In this chapter, which constitutes Part I of the volume, **Coming Home,** we establish a framework for the chapters that follow by providing an in-depth review and overall perspective on complex interrelationships among place (environmental context), life history, and evolving personal identity that characterize the meaning of home. The chapter incorporates insights that have emerged during the past decade within the framework of a general model of "being at home" or "being in place" that we argue represents a fundamental human need. In addition, the chapter explores and summarizes what is known about practical and applied implications of developing deeper understanding of the meanings of home. The stage is set for a series of thematically organized chapters that amplify different aspects of the phenomenon.

Part II comprises chapters on the phenomenological **The Essence of Home**. A primary focus here is on presenting alternative conceptions of the meaning of home and identifying and distinguishing those themes that are universal and those that may be culturally or environmentally specific. Emphasis is placed on highlighting contrasting views of home in the context of the life course and as experienced by the elders of different cultures. The section begins with a review and synthesis of Western conceptualizations of meaning of home in old age, which have been suggested in environmental psychology and environmental gerontology, and presents empirical findings from Germany identifying a typology of dimensions of the meaning of home (Oswald and Wahl, Chapter 2). A particular focus is on comparative assessment of home in the former East Germany and West Germany in the context of reunification. The remainder of the section comprises contributions that focus in more detail on specific aspects of the meaning of home. In Chapter 3, Rubinstein and Medeiros contribute a philosophical interpretation of the relationship of a sense of home to self and identity. Sherman and Dacher (Chapter 4) consider the role of cherished possessions and memorabilia as elements of the creation and maintenance of home. Finally, in a detailed analysis of the arrangement and use of space in the residences of elderly Hindus in India and the manner in which the residence becomes the site of shrines that are integral to the conduct of daily life, Mazumdar and Mazumdar (Chapter 5) provide an exemplar of the deep religious meanings that may pervade a dwelling, making home a sacred place.

Having introduced the reader to different dimensions of the phenomenon, Part III, **Disruptions of Home**, focuses on antitheses of home. We explore threats to home as well as the absence or apparent absence of home. Rubinstein (Chapter 6) vividly captures our imagination of the experience of severance of home as a political, social and personal reality. The many facets of meaning of home for the diaspora come to light in this chapter. Issues of separation are exemplified in Lewin's exposition on the immigrant experience of home (Chapter 7). Lewin provides theoretical perspectives on the meaning of home for elderly immigrants and explores issues of habitation and integration of Turkish and Iranian immigrants in Sweden. A different form of alienation from home that frequently accompanies dementing illness and the potential for reconstruction of home are considered by Frank (Chapter 8) as she explores the relationships among the meaning of home, sense of self, and unsolicited outbursts involving the word "home" among people with Alzheimer's disease. Finally, Watkins and Hosier (Chapter 9) present and illustrate a theoretical perspective on the global phenomenon of homelessness that advocates moving beyond the limitations of an overly simplistic home/homeless dichotomy. Each chapter in this section focuses on the manner in which often-enforced modifications or variants of "mainstream" living result in the need for consideration of fundamentally different conceptions of home.

In Part IV we consider home in temporal context through explorations of the dynamic theme of **Creating and Recreating Home**. Cattell (Chapter 10) provides insightful perspective on the ways in which she gradually developed a sense of being at home as, over several decades of sojourns to western Kenya, she became assimilated within the perspective on home of the Samia. She demonstrates how the cultural expression of home and community and its link to places of origin is embedded in the cultural landscape of sub-Saharan Africa. At the same time, she illustrates ways in which traditional conceptions of home are being challenged by the increasing mobility and growing global perspective of younger generations in Kenyan society who are creating continuous rural–urban social fields and translocal communities. Considerations of home, identity, and belonging in later life for inner-city men are explored by Russell (Chapter 11). Picking up on the theme of homelessness, she presents data revealing how, over their life course, elderly men in urban Australian communities develop senses of home that reflect the characteristics of their life histories and affinity with a neighborhood or familiar area rather than a specific dwelling. Adopting an architectural perspective, the manner in which the meaning of home, following relocation from a community to a specialized communal residential environment, evolves in parallel with a lifelong residential trajectory is explored by Caouette (Chapter 12). Her in-depth multimethod study of 25 elders not only identifies themes in modifications of perceptions of home following relocation but also provides important insight into her participants' perceptions of potential future relocation to a nursing facility and their preferences regarding the design of such facilities.

Part V focuses on the relatively overlooked area of **Community Perspectives on the Meaning of Home**. Here, we move beyond the dwelling. Chapters are included on the manner in which sociological, historical, and anthropological aspects of community life, social conditioning, and shared expectations influence the formation and evolution of group identity and shared understandings of home in particular communities. The section considers ways in which shared aspects of community experience contribute to an emergent sense of communal territory and architecture and willingness to identify with, become attached to, and defend shared community space as a manifestation of home. Norris-Baker and Scheidt (Chapter 13) examine the interrelated concepts of place identity, place attachment, and place dependence in a discussion equating home with community. Their discussion of sustaining community, protecting community identity, reframing community, accepting a dying community, and letting go of community as manifest in the small towns of Kansas provides us with insight on home viewed on a larger scale. The meaning of home on the neighborhood and community level and its impact on identity and well-being of older adults is also explored by Peace, Holland, and Kellaher (Chapter 14) in their study of three English communities: one metropolitan, one small town/suburban, and one rural/village. Through focus groups and in-depth personal interviews with elders they are able to show how themes of belonging, insecurity, connectivity, and movement pervade appraisals of

community as home. Important questions are raised in their concluding comments regarding housing policy, community planning, and
supportive service delivery for older adults. In the final chapter of
this section, Després and Lord (Chapter 15), describing an extended
program of research in Quebec City, Canada, look into the topical
issue of aging suburbanites and planning of the suburbs. There is
plenty of food for thought, debate, and action in this chapter for city
planners, architects, and regional health care authorities concerned
with responding to the needs of older adults who would like to
continue to live in neighborhoods originally built with less environmentally vulnerable middle-aged populations in mind.

In the final section, Part VI, **Leaving Home: Commentaries**, we
have invited three eminent scholars to provide critical commentary
on the volume. Each commentator adds a unique perspective on
the topic. Amos Rapoport, a leading critic of the lexicon of terms
employed in existing research on home (Rapoport, 1995), provides
a challenging critique of basic underlying assumptions and emphasizes the continuing ambiguity of the concept. He contextualizes his
critique of the words "home" and "place" in terms of their value in
achieving the goals of this volume and asks if use of alternative words
might have been more effective. Kim Dovey, author of a seminal early
contribution to the literature on home (Dovey, 1985), provides a
counterpoint to Rapoport as he celebrates the paradox of home in
its potency and mystery in representing an experience of stability
and of a dynamic evolution over time. He also identifies common
themes in the various chapters of this volume. Maria Vesperi, an
anthropologist, journalist, and prolific writer, contributes a unique
interpretation of home against the backdrop of current demographic
transitions and social change that represents a look forward to the
need for an expanded view of home that will become increasingly
pertinent within the political economy of the future. In a concluding
reflection on the path we travel, we identify recurrent themes in the
book and suggest useful future research directions in an invitation
to continue probing ever more deeply into what it means to be
coming home.

WHY COMING HOME?

The title of this opening section, *Coming Home*, reflects two levels
of inspiration, one historical, the other substantive. Historically, it

connotes our editorial aspiration to present a second-generation collection of essays in the domain of home and aging research. It refers to the basic intention in assembling this volume of returning, coming home once more—collectively—to a topic that has been receiving attention from various disciplines as well as philosophical orientations but which in recent years has been characterized by diffuseness and divergence of perspectives. On a substantive level, "coming home" alludes to both the process and product of a fundamental human experience. *Coming Home* is about the experience of home within the context of aging and in relationship to what we believe to be a primary human aspiration—to seek and to find a place where we may feel at one with our self and our world. On this level, coming home refers to acknowledging the multiple levels of salience of the concept in our lives; from its role in facilitating physical and emotional well-being, through its contribution to maintaining the continuity of our self-identity, to resonance in a higher level of self-awareness and comfort that stems from having sought and found our place in the cosmos. As Maria Cattell (chapter 10) eloquently expresses this, coming home is an existential process of returning, both literally and figuratively to where we belong.

Home has physical, social, political, economic, and philosophical dimensions. The inherent richness of the topic has led to a burgeoning of scholarship in multiple disciplines. In recent years there have been efforts to reconceptualize emotional relationships with dwellings and places (e.g., Anthony, 1997; Fried, 2000; Hay, 1998; Hidalgo & Hernandez, 2001; Jorgensen & Stedman, 2001; Low, 2000; Manzo, 2003; Moore, 2000; Twigger-Ross & Uzzell, 1996). These attempts have added two somewhat neglected aspects of home or place experience to the discourse. There has been growing recognition of the diversity of places that may evoke a sense of home or belonging—the experience of identifying with community environments from an individual and group perspective, the self-identity associated with workplaces, and the meaning and experience of landscapes that can nurture emotional relationships. There is also increasing acknowledgment that the context of home may provoke a range of emotional experiences. In contrast with traditionally positive conceptualizations, home may evoke ambivalent or negative emotions; for example, when family abuse takes place in the privacy of home. Home may also become a contested territory in terms of a public–private dichotomy when it is also the place of work; for example, in the context of an increasing volume of telecommuting.

Although the literature is becoming more sophisticated and multifaceted, ambiguity in the meaning of home persists. Is the expression "meaning of home" redundant in its approach when the word "home" already refers to the "meaning" of "house" or "dwelling"? Rapoport (1995), in a thought-provoking critique, raises fundamental questions about the usefulness of the term "home" and the phrase "meaning of home" in environment–behavior research. His arguments, reinforced in his commentary (Chapter 16), point out, among other concerns, the lack of consistency among researchers in use of the term "home" with a tendency toward variation based on disciplinary orientation and personal preference, the inherent difficulty of construing "home" as referring to both an object and a subject–object relationship, and limitations in the use of the term "home" in cross-cultural research.

Although we do not intend to directly "counter" Rapoport's (1995) critical perspective, we present three observations on the inchoate concept of "home." First, we believe that the emergence of multidisciplinary and interdisciplinary perspectives on "home" expresses one of the strengths of the concept. Although it is true that "home" can be construed as having a fairly diverse range of meanings, this diversity of expressed meanings can help us better appreciate the unique contributions of particular disciplinary or scholarly orientations in amplifying the construct. Second, there have been attempts to conceptualize emotional relationships with home environments from various perspectives (e.g., Rowles, 1983; Rubinstein & Parmelee, 1992). Given the complexity and diversity of experience and meaning of home, we need to embrace this plurality of theoretical frameworks, and at the same time strive toward creating bridges across these frameworks to attain a richer and more comprehensive understanding of the phenomenon. Third, the *experiential* foundation of the concept "home" makes it a highly potent concept from both a substantive and methodological perspective. The semantic core of the term immediately captures the popular imagination (it transcends such mundane terms as "setting," "house," "residence," "apartment," and "accommodation"). People relate to "home" because of its close relevance to their own life experiences and everyday usage on a level far transcending merely a physical structure. Precisely because of this emotional resonance, "home" captures the diversity, complexity, and richness of an essential aspect of being in the world. Notwithstanding the ambiguity of its plural meanings, the notion of home provides a rich potential for experiential understanding of human behavior and affect in environmental context. In seeking to build on this potential, we present four conceptual positions.

TRANSCENDING TEMPORALITY THROUGH MEMORIES OF HOME

This position explores parallels between "memory" and "home" in their function of bringing unity in diversity. In the landscape of memories of home, recollection and imagination are intertwined like land and water. Here the term "recollection" refers to recall of the perceived objective experience of a given individual, whereas "imagination" refers to the subjective interpretation of that "objective" experience. Recollection of meaningful homes as a personally reflexive or as a socially shared reminiscence activity is common among elders. In the process of remembering, we selectively recall events, locations, emotions, and people in a manner that provides continuity in our sense of self (Burr & Butt, 2000). The elements of "recollection" and "imagination" have temporal dimensions. At the time of the original occurrence of an event, the historical reality (somewhat akin to what might be captured on a video camera) serves as the reference frame for "recollection." On the other hand, each individual's experience is laden with subjective valence or "imagination." Let us fast forward to a time subsequent to the original event. As the individual remembers the event, recollection and imagination are once again at interplay in recreating the original experience. This recreation of the experience is filtered through physical, psychological, and social changes that may have occurred in the person's life during the intervening time. Especially with the loss of social roles, retirement, physical frailty, and environmental changes, for many older adults the past experience of home may hold different meanings. For example, a 10-year-old boy's play in the family home's backyard with his sister would be remembered in a particular way a day after, in another way when he is a young man in college away from home, and again in a very different way when he is 85 years old and living in a nursing facility. In one sense, memory performs not only the feat of interdependent fusion of recollection and imagination, but also allows a dynamic evolution over time based on the subjective experience and idiosyncratic life circumstance transitions that occur over the life span. The evolution of memory over time is by nature a product of the individual's own evolution.

Similar to the integrating function of memory, "home" ties together diverse life experiences occurring in a given time as well as at different times. Home provides the cognitive–affective structure that shapes and anchors life events spanning temporal boundaries. Resilience to temporal influences is aided by the reality of the physical environment. As self is arguably tied to bodily reality, so, too, is our life experience anchored in the physical reality of places. And home serves as a central place in most life experiences. Home represents a physical setting that remains a witness over time to changing social interaction patterns, personal triumphs and tragedies, lifestyle adjustments, beliefs, and preferences. The diversity in these aspects in a given time, as well as their changing nature over time, permeates the experience of home. The centrality of home in life experience provides a fulcrum, a vantage point—physically, cognitively, and emotionally—from which to view life experiences in different places that are not home. The power of home as a reference point extends into the territory of memory, where home has the potential of acting as the mnemonic anchor for life experiences. From this perspective, memory and home are both vehicles for transcending the flux of time and becoming grounded in temporal unity. To remember particular places from our past or to remember by means of place, we can intensify our power of remembering as a journey that passes through and transcends time and space. The promise of temporal synthesis in memories of homes is multiplied by the process of imagination of home that allows the creation of a reality beyond the present temporal reality, and at the same time the temporal context of the particular remembered or imagined geographic/spatial home reinforces the reference of the present time.

HOME AND AN ENDURING-EVOLVING SELF

Based on the work of James (1890) and Mead (1934) on dual aspects of the self—"I" and "Me," this position looks at the enduring and evolving nature of the self in the context of the experience and meanings of home. The object of self, as signified by "Me," primarily relates to historical experiences associated with home, whereas the subject of self, as signified by "I," relates to creative endeavors of the self. Such endeavors are grounded in "as experienced" reality but they also reach out toward the horizons of imagination. This process provides maintenance of the self and, at the same time, opportunities for rediscovering and recreating the self. Although it is acknowledged that home contributes to the formation and preservation of identity (e.g., Lalli, 1992; Marcus, 1995; Proshansky, Fabian, & Kaminoff, 1983), understanding of the processes through which the self becomes integrally associated with home remains limited.

One useful approach in understanding the process is considering "social identification" (Hogg & Abrams, 1988) and "place identification." Hogg and Abrams (1988) refer to "social identification" as identity dependent on social categories such as nationality, gender, and occupation. Traditionally, this conceptual approach does not take into account environmental contexts, such as residences, in processes of identity construction. On the other hand, a few approaches (e.g., Marcus, 1995; Rowles, 1983, Rubinstein & Parmelee, 1992) focusing specifically on place or, in some instances, home, recognize the significance of social identification in the construction and maintenance of place or home-oriented identities. In fact, "home" and "place" are fundamentally sociophysical concepts. The transformation of spaces in home and community into personally meaningful places occurs, for the most part, through socialization of the spaces over time. The physical environment is given meaning through personal engagement. We argue that identity formation in relationship with home experience is a social process irrespective of the level of involvement of "others." Life experience of the self is strongly influenced by interaction with an "other," whether that other is one's fellow human beings or the residential environment.

Home experience provides the tools for both enduring and evolving possibilities for the self. Homes serve as referents for past life experience. They remind us, both as individuals and groups, of our past. This continuous reminding feeds into the enduring nature of our selves, preserves self-identity, and provides the critical thread for continuity into the future. The process is signified by the "Me" aspect of the self being nourished, validated, and strengthened. The other aspect of home experience relates to the evolving nature of the self. In addition to being sustained, aspects of the self may discontinue as a result of changes in life circumstances, e.g., moving into a care facility symbolizes loss of home for an elder. However, the perceived and real effect of such external change in life circumstances is mediated through the "I" of the self. It is contingent on the creative power of the "I" that may consider a change in residential environments as catastrophic, manageable, and liberating or somewhere in between. There is a dynamic dialogue between the "I" and "Me" in which these two aspects of the self are preserved, discontinued, or recreated. Self-reflexivity is fundamental in this interplay of "I" and "Me" in maintenance of the identity, and at the same time is open to possibilities of self-adaptation and self-recreation. The process characterizes potential adaptation to new environments through recreation or redefinition of one's preferences, beliefs, or values.

CONTEXTUALIZING HOME

In order to understand the fuller and richer meanings of home, there is a great need for acknowledging the interrelationship of home with other places. The meaning of home is not only a product of individual, social, and cultural experience, but also of the experience of macro environments and "places" beyond home. Sociocultural issues and their implications for the experience of diverse places that are "not home" affect the meaning of home. In general, public and institutional environments have been studied with focus on the activities or behaviors, ignoring their sociocultural "meaning" aspects (Groat, 1995). On the other hand, macro-level environments have been addressed from sociopolitical perspectives that have, in general, overlooked the interconnective nature of home as a place with other places and the larger cultural landscape (e.g., Agnew & Duncan, 1989). Experiences of place at the scale of neighborhoods/communities, cities, regions, and countries are varied and multifaceted. Social, cultural, and political dimensions of these experiences vary at each level in relation to the level of engagement and interaction. More important, these experiences are interlocked with the meanings ascribed to an individual's home. For example, aspects of emotional attachment to one's neighborhood (or lack thereof) are likely to mediate one's attachment to home. On the flip side of this argument, the meaning of home affects the meaning of other places. In sum, juxtaposition of the experience of home with experience of a range of other places creates a symbiotic relationship between the meanings of home and other places.

This position could be couched in the dialectic of private versus public, homelike versus institutional, or self versus other. For many older adults, the dialectic can be experienced first hand in care environments that are "homes" for the balance of their lives. Residential care environments such as assisted living and long-term care facilities strive to create a homelike physical and social environment within an organizational/institutional framework. To what extent are these places institutional or homelike for the individuals living there? In what ways do they symbolize or deny the homes or communities the elders have left behind? Can we really recreate the personal homes left behind in the collective or communal homes into which many elders move? These are questions that relate back to the issue of the interrelationship of the meanings of diverse places.

THE DEEPER CALL

Among the various dimensions of meanings of home identified by scholars, the relationship of home experience and self is the most theoretically challenging. Experience of home is associated with defining, maintaining, and recreating self-identity. We need to explore beyond this approach and consider more symbolic and elusive possibilities in meanings of home. If the experience of and emotional relationship with home shapes the evolution of self, the process raises a number of questions. Is the human relationship with home an intrinsic experience finding expression in a multitude of shapes and forms across various cultural contexts? Is home necessarily and invariably place-based? What is the deeper nature of making home or being "at home"? Do the positive or negative valences of home experience help or hinder self-evolution? We pose these questions not as a preface to presenting answers, but rather as directions for ongoing discussion and debate. Questions like these require thoughtful consideration of intersections among complex philosophical issues and diverse levels of experience. They require us to revisit our ontological and epistemological presuppositions of the human condition and experiential reality.

In order to understand the deeper meaning of home, it is important to explore the nature of our understanding of the self and more specifically, the self in aging (Kaufman, 1986). The resilience and transformation of the self is a contested terrain (Cartensen & Freund, 1994; McHugh, 2000), and a discussion on that topic is beyond the scope of this chapter. If we shift the focus toward an individual level and consider the personal experience of aging, we can acknowledge the diversity among individuals in the enduring qualities and evolving nature of the self. A person's consciousness of his or her life experiences in the light of growing older enhances awareness of autobiographical aging. The process is inherently self-reflective and potentially self-evaluative. It involves allusion to a self that is beyond the self as we know it. There is a longing for a spiritual home. Remembrance at a deeper level prompts us to exploration of a level of home that is beyond that which is solely experientially based. This exploration characterizes what we believe to be an innate urge for transcending the ego-self and reaching out to the higher-self or soul—that is at the essence of being human. The homes we create are reflections of that recollection and transcendence. The self has been conceptualized as *embodied* and *emplaced* and the close relationship of self with the body and place has been the subject of discussion (e.g., McHugh, 2000). We argue that it is useful to consider the self in parallel to the integrated continua of *embodied* and *disembodied*, and *emplaced* and *displaced*. The disembodied and displaced aspects do not implicate a disconnect between the self with body and place, but rather a self that evolves to a realization that becomes aware of its connection with a spiritual home or transcendent higher-self. An evolving emotional relationship with home, with all its nuances, is a process that helps move the self toward self-realization. In effect, the process shapes our journey and our "coming home."

REFERENCES

Agnew, J. A., & Duncan, J. S. (Eds.). (1989). *The power of place: Bringing together geographical and sociological imaginations.* Winchester, MA: Unwin Hyman.

Altman, I., & Low, S. M. (Eds.). (1992). *Place attachment: Human behavior and the environment: Advances in theory and research* (Vol. 2). New York: Plenum Press.

Altman, I., & Werner C. (Eds.). (1985). *Home environments. Human behavior and environment advances in theory and research* (Vol. 8). New York: Plenum Press.

Anthony, K. (1997). Bitter homes and gardens: The meanings of homes to families of divorce. *Journal of Architectural and Planning Research, 14,* 1–19.

Bass, S. A., & Ferraro, K. F. (2000). Gerontology education in transition: Considering disciplinary and paradigmatic evolution. *The Gerontologist, 40*(1), 97–106.

Burr, V., & Butt, T. (2000). Psychological distress and postmodern thought. In D. Fee (Ed.), *Pathology and the postmodern: Mental illness as discourse and experience* (pp. 116–140). London: Sage.

Carstensen, L. L., & Freund, A. M. (1994). The resilience of the aging self. *Developmental review, 14,* 81–92.

Dovey, K. (1985). Home and homelessness. In I. Altman & C. M. Werner (Eds.), *Home environments* (pp. 33–64). New York: Plenum Press.

Fried, M. (2000). Continuities and discontinuities of place. *Journal of Environmental Psychology, 20,* 193–205.

Groat, L. (1995). Introduction: Place, esthetics and home. In L. Groat (Ed.), *Giving places meaning.* London: Academic Press.

Hay, B. (1998). Sense of place in developmental context. *Journal of Environmental Psychology, 18,* 5–29.

Hidalgo, M., & Hernandez, B. (2001). Place attachment: Conceptual and empirical questions. *Journal of Environmental Psychology, 21,* 273–281.

Hogg, M. A., & Abrams, D. (1988). *Social identification.* London: Routledge.

James, W. (1890). *The principles of psychology.* New York: Holt.

Jorgensen, B., & Stedman, R. (2001). Sense of place as an attachment: Lakeshore owners' attitudes toward their properties, *Journal of Environmental Psychology, 21,* 233–248.

Kaufman, S. (1986). *The ageless self: The sources of meaning in later life.* New York: Meridian.

Lalli, M. (1992). Urban-related identity: Theory, measurement and empirical findings. *Journal of Environmental Psychology, 12,* 285–303.

Low, S. (2000). *On the plaza: The politics of public space and culture.* Austin, TX: University of Texas Press.

Manzo, L. C. (2003). Beyond house and haven: Toward a revisioning of emotional relationships with places. *Journal of Environmental Psychology, 23,* 47–61.

Marcus, C. C. (1995). *House as a mirror of self.* Berkeley, CA: Conari Press.

McHugh, K. E. (2000). The "ageless self"? Emplacement of identities in Sun Belt retirement communities. *Journal of Aging Studies, 14*(1), 103–115.

Mead, G. H. (1934). *Mind, self and society.* Chicago: University of Chicago Press.

Moore, J. (2000). Placing home in context. *Journal of Environmental Psychology, 20,* 207–218.

Proshansky, H. M., Fabian, A. K., & Kaminoff, R. (1983). Place identity: Physical world socialization of the self. *Journal of Environmental Psychology, 3,* 57–83.

Rapoport, A. (1995). A critical look at the concept "home". In D. N. Benjamin (Ed.), *The home: Words, interpretations, meanings, and environments* (pp. 25–52). Aldershot, England: Avebury.

Rowles, G. D. (1983). Place and personal identity in old age: Observations from Appalachia. *Journal of Environmental Psychology, 3*, 299–313.

Rubinstein, R. L., & Parmelee, P. A. (1992). Attachment to place and the representation of the life course by the elderly. In I. Altman & S. M. Low (Eds.), *Place attachment: Human behavior and the environment: Advances in theory and research* (pp. 139–163). New York: Plenum Press.

Twigger-Ross, C. L., & Uzzell, D. L. (1996). Place and identity processes. *Journal of Environmental Psychology, 16*, 205–220.

PART II

The Essence of Home

CHAPTER 2

Dimensions of the Meaning of Home in Later Life

Frank Oswald and Hans-Werner Wahl

The meaning of home in later life provides a perfect example of how strongly "objective" contextual factors and "subjective" representations are linked as people age. Although a considerable body of research has been published on the meaning of home among elders, the literature is still plagued by pronounced conceptual and empirical diversity. This makes it difficult for a broader audience to appreciate what has already been achieved by researchers in this field and hinders an understanding of what "aging in place" is all about. With this in mind, the first aim of this chapter is to clarify basic issues, namely: the relationship of house and home, and the need to understand the meaning of home within a life-span developmental context. The second aim is to review and synthesize major conceptualizations of meaning of home in old age, which have been suggested in environmental psychology and environmental gerontology. The third aim is to present a selection of our own empirical findings concerned with the meaning of home in old age.

SETTING THE STAGE

House and Home

A dwelling can generally be characterized as a physical unit, a defined space for its residents providing shelter and protection for domestic activities and concealment, and an entity separating private from public domains (Flade, 1993; Lawrence, 1987; Rapoport, 1995). Although the home has been a topic of scientific interest for decades in several disciplines (for overviews see, for example, Després, 1991; Moore, 2000; Saup, 1993; Sommerville, 1997), the key question, "What makes a house a home?" has not yet been answered (Lawrence, 1987, 2002). It is widely acknowledged that the home is "physically, psychologically, and socially constructed in both 'real' and 'ideal' forms "(Sommerville, 1997, p. 226). The home has also been described as an "extension of the self through places" (Fuhrer & Kaiser, 1992, p. 105), or as "that spatially localized, temporally defined . . . physical frame and conceptual system for the ordering, transformation and interpretation of the physical and abstract aspects of domestic daily life "(Benjamin, 1995, p. 158). Addressing the meaning of home focuses attention on the relationship between the objective sociophysical setting and subjective evaluations, goals, values, emotions, and observable or potential behaviors that people pursue. Thus, the meaning of home on the most general level links the person with his or her environment. There are many meaning-related terms to be found in the literature, such as "at-homeness," "placefulness," or "place/community/settlement identity" (Feldman, 1990, 1996; Lalli, 1992; Proshansky, Fabian, & Kaminoff, 1983; Relph, 1976; Rubinstein & Parmelee, 1992; Tuan, 1980). To bring more order into the complexity of place-related meaning systems, Rapoport suggests a differentiation of high-level, middle-level, and lower-level meanings of the built environment (1988, 1995). Whereas high-level meanings involve global worldviews and philosophical systems, middle-level meanings emphasize latent functions of the environment such as identity, status, wealth, and power. Lower-level meanings cover detailed functions such as privacy, accessibility, movement, and seating arrangements (Coolen, 2002; Rapoport, 1988, 1995). In this chapter we focus on middle and lower-level meanings.

SETTING THE MEANING OF HOME IN LATER LIFE IN A LIFE SPAN CONTEXT

From a life span perspective, development is a process from birth to death and is closely related to the sociophysical context in every life phase (Baltes, 1987). From birth on, persons interact with their social and physical environment, leading to a meaningful representation of the self within the environment (Oswald & Wahl, 2003). Within his *Ecology of Human Development,* Bronfenbrenner (1979, 1999) defines development primarily as the ongoing interaction between persons and their environment over time. Development becomes especially critical during ecological transitions, such as moving from family life to peer-group life, from school to the world of work, or from the labor force to retirement (Bronfenbrenner, 1999). It is assumed that the transaction between person and sociophysical environment becomes increasingly complex from childhood to adulthood. This driving force toward increasing complexity brings with it a challenge to each developing individual. He or she must find a balance between basic needs for a secure, safe, and stable base on the one hand and higher-order needs for exploration, stimulation, and environmental mastery on the other hand. Complexity also arises from an increasing action range (e.g., the individual's progressive ability to crawl, walk, leave home, ride a bus alone, and later, drive or even fly to different parts of the globe). Hence, the individual is given the opportunity to exploit newly "conquered" segments of the environment with the home in its center. Different theorists, working from the same general person–environment transaction view of human development, have emphasized different aspects of the meaning of home throughout the life span. Among them are the exploratory behaviors inherent to childhood play (Muchow & Muchow, 1935), territoriality such as occupation and ownership in adulthood (Altman, 1975), and age-related types of bonding in later life, such as autobiographical insideness (the sense of belonging to and having one's life expressed within a place that can stem from life long residence) (Rowles, 1983). Interestingly, the meaning of home is associated with ambiguous feelings throughout life. A child's home environment can be secure, supportive, and self-affirming, yet at the same time disruptive, frustrating, or frightening. This is especially true in later life. An elder's home might be a comforting, familiar place despite the fact that it is becoming burdensome to maintain and unsafe (and therefore a source of anxiety).

DEVELOPMENTAL DYNAMICS IN LATE ADULTHOOD AND THE MEANING OF HOME

As people age, the immediate home environment becomes more important for many reasons. Three of these are addressed in the text that follows. Acknowledging the growing importance of the home is critical for understanding its role and variety of meanings in the later years.

Sociostructural Antecedents of the Meaning of Home in Old Age

The vast majority of older adults in Western countries live independently in the community and not in institutions. For example, in the United States. and Germany, about 95% of people aged 65 years and older live in private households (Bundesministerium für Familie Senioren Frauen und Jugend [Federal Ministry for Family Affairs, Senior Citizens, Women and Youth], 2001; U.S. Bureau of the Census, 1996). Although the likelihood of living in a nursing home increases with age and the number of alternative purpose-built homes is on the rise in modern societies, the vast majority of older adults live in ordinary dwellings. Most either live alone or with a partner. To consider these typical types of household composition is important with respect to understanding social aspects of the meaning of home. Elders are relatively adept at staying put in one place, and the share of single persons 85 years and over living alone has increased over the last few decades (Bundesministerium für Familie Senioren Frauen und Jugend [Federal Ministry for Family Affairs, Senior Citizens, Women and Youth], 2001; Himes, 2001). Time spent living in a certain place of residence might have an impact on the meaning of home. For instance, German data from a national survey of about 4,000 persons showed that participants between 70 and 85 years of age had lived an average of 31.6 years in the same apartment and 50.3 years in the same town (Motel, Künemund, & Bode, 2000). Placing emphasis on the sociostructural givens for community-dwelling elders should not entail neglecting the meaning of home in institutions for elders; however, this is not the focus of this chapter.

Everyday Life Dynamics as Antecedents of the Meaning of Home in Old Age

The immediate home environment is the primary living space in old age; both in terms of the time older people spend in this space and its locale as the place where many activities occur. It is a well-documented finding that aging coincides with a reduction in action range, especially during very old age (Baltes, Maas, Wilms, & Borchelt, 1999; Moss & Lawton, 1982). Older people spend more time at home than do younger people. Indeed, recent data suggest that elders (65 years and older) spend on average 80% of their daytime at home (Baltes et al., 1999; Küster, 1998). Observational data have also shown an age-related tendency for environmental centralization inside the house, especially around the most favored places at home. These places, which can be found among both healthy and impaired elders, typically are "set up" to be comfortable, afford a good view outside, and are located close to many necessary and preferred items used in daily life (Rowles, 1981). Such places become "control centers" or "living centers" within the residence and probably serve adaptive functions such as maintaining and enhancing control and comfort over the immediate environment (Lawton, 1985; Oswald, 1996; Rubinstein & Parmelee, 1992).

Health- and Environment-Related Antecedents of the Meaning of Home in Old Age

The home acquires new meaning in old age because it serves to compensate for the reduced functional capacity of the aging individual, especially in very old age. To maintain autonomy and to avoid institutionalization, either environmental changes or behavioral adaptations must generally occur. Research based on the "environmental docility" hypothesis (Lawton, 1987; Lawton & Nahemow, 1973; Lawton & Simon, 1968) has shown a strong correlation between reduced environmental competence, such as vision loss or mobility impairment, and objective living arrangements (Wahl, Oswald, & Zimprich, 1999; Wahl, Schilling, Oswald, & Heyl, 1999). Consequently, research and application often reduce questions regarding the meaning of home to whether or not the home environment is accessible or usable (Steinfeld & Danford, 1999). The relationship between loss of competence and the meaning of home in a broader sense, however, has received comparatively little attention. For example, the stimulation provided by the home environment and its relationship to "environmental proactivity" should be considered (Lawton, 1989a, 1989b). Thus, the individual's meaning of home may reflect behavioral adaptations and modifications of the home environment to stay independent as well as the cognitive representation of a lifestyle, developed over years (Lehr, 2000; Thomae, 1988). Different patterns in the meaning of home possibly also reflect differences in coping processes in the face of environment-related impairments (Carp & Carp, 1984; Oswald & Wahl, 2001; Wahl, Oswald, et al., 1999).

Finally, the meaning of home plays an important role as an element in the process of relocation to another place of residence; it may reflect the outcome of coping processes in the face of environmental changes. Relocation in old age covers moving from home to home, from home into assisted living facilities or into institutions. This may occur both when the individual is in good health and when he or she is facing competence losses. The meaning assigned to a home influences the decision to move and moving into a new home initiates a process of reestablishing meaning in the new place through living there (Rowles & Ravdal, 2001; Rowles & Watkins, 2003). To consider the manifold meanings inherent in a move, it is useful to focus on the increasing proportion of older adults moving voluntarily. Many of these elders do not move merely to fulfill basic needs for continuing independence; rather, they strive to fulfill preferences and wishes and thus actively seek new and meaningful options in the years of life remaining (Carp & Carp, 1984; Oswald, Schilling, Wahl, & Gäng, 2002). A large number of persons relocated from one dwelling to another in eastern Germany after reunification in 1989. Most of these people improved their living conditions. Little is known about the meaning these elders were able to invest in their new homes after these transitions, and how their meaning of home compared to that of elders in western Germany who remained in relatively stable environmental conditions (see results later in the chapter). Another modern reality is that many elders have different homes for different seasons, sometimes maintaining dual residence over decades. Living in such a "circle of migration" (McHugh & Mings, 1996) affects the structure and temporal dynamics of the meaning of home.

THEORETICAL PERSPECTIVES ON THE MEANING OF HOME

Although a number of disciplines have contributed to our understanding of the meaning of home (Després, 1991; Miller, 2001; Moore,

2000; Sommerville, 1997), the concept has been largely developed by concentrated theoretical and empirical studies in environmental psychology and environmental gerontology. Although environmental psychology does not usually address aging issues, it nevertheless provides important insights that are relevant for a diversity of ages. The boundaries of each field are not distinct, and many studies could be assigned to either discipline.

Environmental Psychology Perspectives

An early effort to understand the variety of meanings assigned to the home was provided by Hayward (1975). According to Hayward, the meaning of home may embrace home as a *physical structure*, as a *territory*, as a *locus in space*, as *self and self-identity*, and as a *social and cultural unit*. Later attempts to define the meaning of home built on broader theoretical models, such as the theory of place (Canter, 1977), place identity theory (Proshansky, 1978), or place attachment theory (Schumaker & Taylor, 1983). Several studies in environmental psychology emphasize identity-related aspects of place (Altman & Low, 1992; Després, 1991; Howell, 1983; Neisser, 1988). Based on data from persons between childhood and late adulthood, Markus (1995) was able to extract three main functions of home: (1) *gaining cognitive and behavioral control* over space; (2) *manipulating, molding, or decorating space* in order to create a setting of physical comfort and well-being; and (3) *perceiving continuity* with significant places and people of the past. Using a more complex rubric, Zingmark and colleagues, in a study with participants aged 2 to 102 years, focused on the meaning of home throughout the life span. Key themes identified included *safety, rootedness, joy, privacy, togetherness, recognition*, and *control* (Zingmark, Norberg, & Sandman, 1995). Feldman (1996) analyzed the development of relationships between residential mobility and the meaning of home on a larger scale, at the level of an entire settlement. She empirically evaluated frequencies of indicators of bonding to different types of settlements among adult residents 25 to 65 years of age. These indicators included: *emotional aspects*, like "embeddedness" or "a sense of belonging in, being part of, and feeling at home." The indicators also included *cognitive aspects* of bonding, like "unity of identities," or "a joining of the identity of self . . . to the physical setting of the past, present, and future residential environs." Finally, indicators of bonding included *behavioral aspects* of bonding like "centeredness," "home place as a focal point of one's experiential space, a point of departure and return" and bonding related to the physical and social environment itself, reflected in a sense of "community," or "a sense of being involved with and tied to a geographical based social group" (Feldman, 1996, p. 426). The majority of participants indicated a desire to remain in a comparable type of locale in the future. Feldman's work suggests that the meaning of home is an enduring phenomenon with a number of relatively stable dimensions.

In another study, Harris, Brown, and Werner (1996) empirically analyzed the relationship between privacy regulation and the meaning of home in a group of persons aged between 19 and 69 years of age. Components of home-based meaning included *emotional* dimensions such as "positive evaluations" or "global feelings of attachment to . . . the home," *cognitive* dimensions conveying "identity," *behavioral* dimensions, such as "activity," and *social and physical* dimensions of home, such as "connection" (Harris et al., 1996, p. 289).

Beyond examining key concepts of home, recently there has been a tendency toward a context-sensitive focus on the meaning of home in different cultures (Miller, 2001), among subgroups such as homeless people, and among different age cohorts such as older adults. These studies tend to address also darker tensions within the essence of the experience of home (Moore, 2002). Such tensions include incarceration in a prison, house arrest, or when a person is unable to leave their house because of severe mobility impairment or other manifestations of loss of competence.

Major conclusions that can be drawn from environmental psychology are that individuals experience the meaning of home in a variety of domains and that the meaning of home involves a transactional relationship between persons and their environment that evolves over time leading to *behavioral, emotional,* and *cognitive* bonding within a meaningful *physical* and *social* setting.

Environmental Gerontology Perspectives

Judith Sixsmith empirically reduced a broad collection of meaning of home-related statements into three different modes of everyday home experience: the *physical home*, the *social home*, and the *per-*

sonal home (Sixsmith, 1986). The physical home mainly involves household facilities, everyday modern conveniences, style of architecture, and living accommodations that afford opportunities for activities. The social home mainly consists of relationships with others within a shared space. The personal home can be viewed as an extension of oneself, of one's own desires, feelings, hopes, and actions. Thus, home is "a central emotional and sometimes physical reference point in a person's life" (Sixsmith, 1986, p. 290).

Lawton emphasizes three basic environmental functions with relevance for understanding the meaning of home in later life: *maintenance, stimulation,* and *support* (Lawton, 1989b). Maintenance covers a "series of repetitive, well-practiced behaviors in relation to the environment" (Lawton, 1989b, p. 36), of which the subject may be unaware and that may be taken for granted. Stimulation represents "a departure from the usual, a novel array of stimuli, a problem to solve," which requires the person to respond emotionally, cognitively, or behaviorally (p. 37). Finally, support is characterized "by relative lack of variation and (. . .) by easy availability of the resources necessary to maintain life" (p. 38).

Rowles applied Relph's concept of insideness (1976) to the meaning of home in old age. Based on in-depth interviews, he suggests that the notion of an elder's sense of insideness within a place is central to understanding what home means for older people (Rowles, 1983; Rowles & Ravdal, 2001). There are three elements to insideness. *Physical insideness* or intimacy is characterized by familiarity and habitual routines of habitation within the home setting that enable the individual "to wear the setting like a glove" (Rowles, 1983, p. 114). *Social insideness* or immersion arises from everyday social exchanges and the creation and maintenance of social roles within a neighborhood over a long period of time. A third aspect of insideness in old age is *autobiographical insideness.* This "stems from the temporal legacy of having lived one's life in the environment. . . . Place becomes a landscape of memories, providing a sense of identity."

Anthropologist Robert Rubinstein (1989) proposed a similar tripartite model of psychological processes linking person to place and subsequent outcomes although he uses a somewhat different terminology. The *social-centered process* includes social norms and relationships to other persons, the *person-centered process* concerns the expression of one's life course in features of the environment, and the *body-centered-process* includes the "ongoing relationship of the body to the environmental features that surround it," often culminating in environmental centralization (Rubinstein, 1989, p. 47). Within the person-centered processes, bonding can be increasingly strong, culminating in personalization, and embodiment, i.e., the subjective merging of the individual and environmental features in which boundaries are blurred.

Environmental psychology and gerontology have not produced major differences in defining the meaning of home. Both fields suggest that the meaning of home among older adults is related to aspects of *physical, social* and *personal* bonding, on *behavioral, cognitive* and *emotional* levels. Because older adults have often lived a long period of time within the same residence, cognitive and emotional aspects of the meaning of home are often strongly linked to biography. Such links may be manifest through processes of reflecting on a past symbolically represented in certain places and cherished objects within the home. The same can be true for behavioral aspects of meaning, where familiarity and routines have been developed over time. The effect of environment-related competence losses or the need to cope with objective environmental changes may lead the individual to develop an idiosyncratic meaning of home.

SYNTHESIZING MAJOR APPROACHES TO UNDERSTANDING THE MEANING OF HOME IN OLD AGE

Using theoretical insights gleaned from environmental psychology and gerontology, we present a categorization of the domains of meaning of home including types of physical, social and personal bonding (Figure 2.1). Reasons for providing this categorization are: (1) to incorporate well-replicated empirical findings in environmental psychology and gerontology with respect to the meaning of home in old age; (2) to reduce existing conceptual diversity to a useful minimum; (3) to differentiate among psychologically relevant kinds of meaning, especially in terms of personal, i.e., behavioral, cognitive and emotional bonding; (4) to provide a set of distinct evidence-based categories with the intent to stimulate comparative and ex-

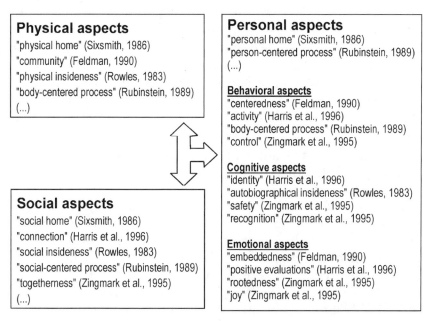

Physical aspects
"physical home" (Sixsmith, 1986)
"community" (Feldman, 1990)
"physical insideness" (Rowles, 1983)
"body-centered process" (Rubinstein, 1989)
(...)

Personal aspects
"personal home" (Sixsmith, 1986)
"person-centered process" (Rubinstein, 1989)
(...)

Behavioral aspects
"centeredness" (Feldman, 1990)
"activity" (Harris et al., 1996)
"body-centered process" (Rubinstein, 1989)
"control" (Zingmark et al., 1995)

Cognitive aspects
"identity" (Harris et al., 1996)
"autobiographical insideness" (Rowles, 1983)
"safety" (Zingmark et al., 1995)
"recognition" (Zingmark et al., 1995)

Social aspects
"social home" (Sixsmith, 1986)
"connection" (Harris et al., 1996)
"social insideness" (Rowles, 1983)
"social-centered process" (Rubinstein, 1989)
"togetherness" (Zingmark et al., 1995)
(...)

Emotional aspects
"embeddedness" (Feldman, 1990)
"positive evaluations" (Harris et al., 1996)
"rootedness" (Zingmark et al., 1995)
"joy" (Zingmark et al., 1995)

FIGURE 2.1   Heuristic framework on domains of meaning of home in old age.

planatory research; (5) to explicitly emphasize interrelations among the different domains; and (6) to encourage empirical replications that might confirm this heuristic framework. In the following section, empirical findings on the meaning of home are presented, emphasizing the impact of competence losses and environmental change.

FINDINGS FROM RESEARCH ON THE MEANING OF HOME IN OLD AGE

Several scales and questionnaires have been developed to measure the meaning of home. These include the "Urban Identity Scale" (Lalli, 1992), the "Attachment Scale" (Twigger, 1995; Twigger-Ross & Uzzell, 1996), the "Neighbourhood Attachment Scale" (Bonnes et al., 1997), and the "Rootedness Scale" (McAndrew, 1998). Our own research program on the meaning of home aims to empirically contribute to the theoretical traditions synthesized in Figure 2.1 by means of replication and extension using a qualitative (semistructured, exploratory method. First, we consider group comparisons among elders to illustrate the impact of personal (health, gender) differences. In a second study we focus on environmental differences in the meaning of home by comparing elders from East and West Germany. In addition to describing group differences, our findings reflect coping processes as part of person-environmental transactions in old age.

Variation in the Meanings of Home in Old Age: The Role of Health and Gender

In the first study (Study 1), we focused on data from community-dwelling older adults living at home in comparable living arrangements but suffering from significant competence losses that limited their access to the external environment. One hundred and twenty-six elders between the ages of 61 and 92 took part in the study. One third of the participants were in good health, one third suffered from severe mobility impairment, and one third was blind (Oswald & Wahl, 2001). Data are based on in-depth interviews that were tape-recorded and transcribed. During a multiphase coding procedure, different meaning categories were established. Each statement was coded into categories with satisfying reliability (Cohen's Kappa: 0.77–0.83). We expected to confirm the validity of the meaning-of-home constructs presented in Figure 2.1. However, the initial hierarchical model with three domains of meaning was adapted into a set of five equal categories all on the same level of abstraction. This was necessary because descriptions of meaning of home in the category "personal bonding" were made on the level of behavioral, cognitive and emotional aspects but not on the global level. We were able to empirically confirm 13 detailed and five global categories (see text that follows) based on 1,804 statements. Beyond replication, a second research aim was to assess whether patterns of meaning of home would differ among healthy and impaired older adults. Five global meaning categories similar to the ones suggested in major conceptual models (Figure 2.1) were empirically confirmed. These categories were: (1) "Physical," focusing on the experience of housing conditions such as experience of the residential area, access and furnishing; (2) "Behavioral," related to the everyday behavior of the person at home and to proactive ways of manipulating or rearranging items in the home; (3) "Cognitive," representing state-ments of cognitive, especially biographical bonding to the home, such as the experience of familiarity and insideness; (4) "Emotional," expressing emotional bonding including the experience of privacy, safety, pleasure, and stimulation; and (5) "Social," consisting of state-ments expressing relationships with fellow-lodgers, neighbors, or visitors. Comparison among participants showed different patterns of meanings among healthy, mobility-impaired and blind participants (Figure 2.2).

The frequency with which physical aspects were named was significantly lower among the mobility impaired compared to the healthy, and lowest among the blind. Healthy participants were more appreciative of the location, access and amenity aspects of the home. Cognitive aspects were reported significantly more often among the mobility impaired compared to the healthy participants, but were most frequent among the blind. Mobility impaired participants em-

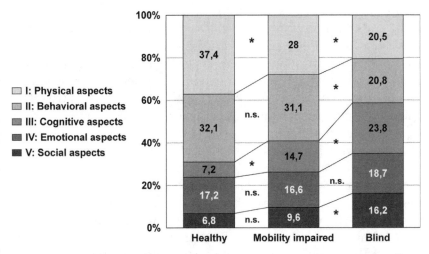

FIGURE 2.2   Relative frequencies of meaning of home domains for healthy, mobility-impaired, and blind older adults.

Note. Evaluation of verbal transcripts and tapes, based on 1,804 statements of $N = 126$ subjects. Mean number of statements per person amounted to 14.3. Multivariate MANOVA procedure for five domains was conducted to test differences between subgroups (Wilk's Lambda $= .707$; $F = 4.40$ (10, 232); $p < .05 = *$; explained variance: 29.3%). To show differences in detail, univariate simple contrasts were computed for each category between healthy and mobility impaired, as well as between mobility impaired and blind subjects.

phasized the cognitive and biographical significance of the home. As far as behavioral and social aspects were concerned, no significant differences between healthy and mobility impaired elders were found, but the blind had lower frequencies in the behavioral domain and higher frequencies in the social domain compared to the mobility impaired group. About the same share of statements were made with regard to emotional themes in all three groups.

How might these results be interpreted? Beyond confirmation of the variety of meaning of home domains, differences among the subgroups may be attributed to adaptive mechanisms. Following Carp and Carp's (1984) differentiation of environmental functions, the distinction between a *complementary* and a *congruent* style of environmental coping is useful. Whereas in the complementary style the environment acts by some means or other prosthetically on failing personal competencies, in the *congruent* style environmental attributes that enhance the match between environmental resources and personal needs are serving best. In detail, for some needs, "favorable outcomes are associated with environmental functions that complement existing skills when they begin to decline. The environment adds to or acts prosthetically on failing personal competencies" (Lawton, 1998, p. 7). Other needs "are best served by environmental attributes that enhance the match between environmental resources and personal needs. Congruence thus heightens the possibilities of growth, enrichment and positive satisfaction emerging from person-environment transactions" (Lawton, 1999, p. 7). In this study different patterns of meanings might reflect ways of coping with loss of competence at home in a *complementary* style (Carp & Carp, 1984). Different meaning patterns may serve to accommodate different kinds of competence loss by emphasizing those aspects of the home that are still accessible. Visually impaired participants, for example, concentrated on their social and cognitive sphere and ignored behavioral and physical aspects of the home, whereas the meaning patterns of the mobility impaired participants included behavioral aspects of meaning to a much greater extent. This was possibly a result of the fact that visually impaired elders were more affected in maintaining everyday life indoors compared to mobility impaired and healthy elders.

Gender differences were also observed. Although men and women were comparable in their physical, social, and cognitive bonding with home, differences were observed in the behavioral and the emotional domains. Women more often mentioned behavioral domains compared to men regardless of their health, whereas men (especially healthy ones) more often mentioned emotional domains compared to women. These patterns may reflect historically based gender roles in these cohorts of older adults, where women, for the most part, stayed at home and men went out to work. Consequently, old women, in contrast to their spouses, would have become familiar with the territory via everyday behavior and less in terms of feelings of privacy and retreat.

Meaning of Home and Societal Transformation

Reunification of East and West Germany provided the opportunity to use a "natural experiment" to compare groups of older adults with different experiences in housing and with different levels of perceived changes in their housing conditions. In East Germany, the quality of housing improved rapidly after 1989. As a result, the focus of a second study (Study 2) was on community-dwelling older adults living at home, all relatively healthy and of the same age but living in different environmental settings (East versus West Germany). A salient distinction between the regions concerns the prevalence of relocation (West Germany 5% versus East Germany 25%) and reconstruction (West Germany 23% versus East Germany 56%) (Oswald, 2003). As hypothesized earlier, it was anticipated that environmental changes would be social-structural antecedents of changes in the meaning of home. We expected to confirm the validity of the meaning-of-home constructs identified previously and to observe different patterns of meaning of home among elders in East and West Germany. Findings were based on in-depth interviews of a total of 227 highly competent elders drawn from the birth cohort from 1930 to 1932 (between 66 and 69 years old at the time of the research; Oswald, 2003). Half of this sample was drawn from the former East Germany and half from the former West Germany. Fifty percent of the respondents were women. Again, statements were coded into categories with satisfying reliability (congruence in relative frequencies: 89.3%). Group differences were calculated using multivariate analysis of variance (MANOVA) and analysis of variance (ANOVA) procedures. Comparisons between participants from East and West

Germany show differences in the domains of physical, behavioral, and emotional dimensions of the meaning of home (see Table 2.1).

Within the domain of physical aspects of the meaning of home, "amenities and furnishing" were far more frequently mentioned in East Germany than in West Germany. Those who experienced recent environmental change more often also mentioned physical dimensions of meaning more frequently. Mention of behavioral dimensions of the meaning of home, especially "everyday indoor activities" was more prevalent among participants from West Germany than East Germany. Those who experienced residential stability, i.e., the West Germans, more often mentioned everyday indoor behavior. Within the emotional domain, there was differentiation between more inward-oriented themes of "privacy, safety, retreat" and more outward-oriented themes of "stimulation, pleasure, excitement." Privacy and retreat were more relevant in West Germany, whereas stimulation and excitement were more important in East Germany. The importance of cognitive and social aspects of the meaning of home did not differ between the two regions.

These results again confirm the variety of meanings of home. Differences between the two groups in patterns of meanings may also reflect ways of coping with environmental stress at home in a *congruent* style, emphasizing environmental attributes that enhance the match between changed environmental resources and personal needs (Carp & Carp, 1984). Considering an essential difference between East and West Germany, specifically the tremendous amount of environmental change experienced in the former region, interesting differences appear. Each group emphasized those aspects of the meaning of home that conformed most closely to their current housing situation. Those who perceived many objective changes in their housing conditions showed a need to adapt within the new physical setting but they were also more stimulated and excited by it. Those who perceived more environmental stability did not need to cope with housing and thus focused on indoor behavior and the experience of privacy and retreat. In more general terms, the German natural experiment of reunification supports the argument that gross societal transformations may be echoed in quite a detailed manner in person–environment transactions in the context of home. Meanings-of-home analyses have the potential to mirror such macro dynamics on the individual micro level. However, although perceived

TABLE 2.1   Relative Frequencies of Meaning-of-Home Domains for Older Adults in East and West Germany

Domains of meaning of home (M, SD)	West Germany (n = 114)	East Germany (n = 113)	Differences
I: Physical aspects			
(1) Residential area and quality of neighborhood	0.82 (0.59)	1.01 (0.43)	**
(2) Accessibility to the outdoor environment	0.63 (0.67)	0.65 (0.53)	n.s.
(3) Amenities, furnishing	1.09 (0.28)	1.23 (0.53)	*
II: Behavioral aspects			
(4) Everyday indoor activities	0.95 (0.66)	0.68 (0.60)	***
(5) Proactive environmental manipulation	0.96 (0.62)	1.06 (0.57)	n.s.
III: Cognitive aspects			
(6) Perceived autonomy	0.36 (0.65)	0.26 (0.58)	n.s.
(7) Familiarity, maintenance, routine	1.00 (0.50)	1.09 (0.47)	n.s.
(8) Reminiscence, insideness, planning	0.25 (0.54)	0.15 (0.38)	n.s.
(9) Identity	0.11 (0.35)	0.11 (0.43)	n.s.
IV: Emotional aspects			
(10) Privacy, safety, retreat	1.32 (0.52)	1.17 (0.44)	*
(11) Stimulation, pleasure, excitement	0.99 (0.62)	1.21 (0.66)	**
V: Social aspects			
(12) Relation to fellow-lodger	0.65 (0.62)	0.61 (0.66)	n.s.
(13) Visitors, neighbors	0.75 (0.74)	0.71 (0.65)	n.s.

Note. Data from $N = 227$ subjects from the Interdisciplinary Longitudinal Study on Adult Development (ILSE), birth cohort 1930–1932, supported by the German Federal Ministry of Family, Senior Citizens, Women and Youth and the Baden-Württemberg Ministry of Science, Research and Art grant Ref. 314-1722-102/16. Results are based on expert ratings from 0 = nonexistent, 1 = existent, 2 = important aspect of meaning. ANOVA procedure for 13 domains was conducted to test differences between subgroups ($\alpha_{Bon} = .05/2 = .025*$; $.01/2 = .005**$; $.001/2 = .0005***$ [categories II and V]; $\alpha_{Bon} = .05/3 = .017*$; $.01/3 = .003**$; $.001/3 = .0003***$ [category I]; $\alpha_{Bon} = .05/4 = .0125*$; $.01/4 = .0025**$; $.001/4 = .00025***$ [category III]). To consider multiple correlations of domains, discriminant function analyses were conducted ($F = 3.22$, $p < .001$), approving important categories for group differences (Gansera-Baumann, 2002).

stability of the home could be regarded as an indicator for objective environmental stability, it should not be misunderstood as a synonym for immobility or inflexibility in later life in general. Housing in a broader sense may thus cover stable living conditions and various activities as well as dimensions of experience.

FUTURE PERSPECTIVES ON THE ROLE OF MEANING OF HOME

The aim of this chapter was to clarify the concept of the meaning of home and the dynamics of person–environment relationships in old age, to develop a conceptualization of the meaning of home in old age based on existing data in the field, and to elucidate this conceptualization with empirical data from our own research program. Specifically, we sought to illustrate the complexity of the meaning of home in the context of personal (i.e., declining health and reduced competence) and environmental (i.e., changing housing conditions or relocation) challenges. We have tried to sketch the social-structural, everyday-life and health-related antecedents of the meaning of home, such as the typical household composition of community-dwelling elders, their proclivity to live in their homes for a long period of time, the reduction of their action range, and their need for supportive environments in the case of reductions in competence. Each of these themes has been considered in the housing literature; however, the subjective meanings attached to these developmental patterns and changing circumstances has been largely neglected, even though such meanings may be important triggers of adaptive and proactive behavior.

A global categorization of meaning domains was presented based on theoretical assumptions and empirical studies from environmental psychology and environmental gerontology. Replicated findings suggest a content-oriented set of categories, emphasizing physical, social, and personal, that is, behavioral, cognitive, and emotional aspects of the meaning of home. Data from two empirical studies validated the conceptualization and showed differences among elders facing competence losses (e.g., vision loss) and elders facing environmental changes (e.g., relocation). In the first study, elders with different levels of loss of competence emphasized those aspects of meaning that still had personal relevance. Elders in the second study emphasized those aspects of meaning that corresponded to changes in their housing situation. Comparative results on different patterns of meanings among subgroups could be interpreted in terms of different adaptive mechanisms, either a complementary (Study 1) or a congruent (Study 2) coping style (Carp & Carp, 1984).

Both the research and applied aspects of this topic are likely to be challenged by evolving societal circumstances. We anticipate an ever-changing role of home environments in old age as a result of new mobility patterns and the emergence of different housing styles. It can be anticipated that meaning of home issues will affect future aging differently for relatively healthy elders in their "third age" in comparison with those who are increasingly vulnerable in their "fourth" age (Baltes & Smith, 1999). Among elders in their "third" age (in general, persons younger than 80 years of age), because of increased levels of mobility, links between indoor and outdoor environments have a much greater significance than in the past. Consequently, consideration of meaningful bonding to the environment must embrace an empirical linking of meanings for an array of spaces radiating away from the dwelling: from favorite objects, to favorite places at home, to the home itself, to specific outdoor settings in the immediate neighborhood, and to large-scale settings including the community and region. This will become increasingly important given new types of indoor and outdoor person–environmental interactions (e.g., the Internet), advances in technology, the increasing mobility of older adults, and the larger impact of the environment on the life of elders in general (Wahl, 2001).

New patterns of the meaning of home could be considered by planners and architects in a two-fold manner: to foster positive bonding with home and to reduce dysfunctional attachment whenever it may appear. For elders in their "fourth" age (in general, persons who are 80 years of age or older) findings on the meaning of home may contribute to everyday problem solving and enhancing or maintaining quality of life. There is a need to examine the role of the meaning of home in the lives of the very old who face an accumulation of environmental difficulties, such as reduced action range, losses of environmental competence, and the proliferation of environmental barriers. Knowledge about the potential of the home environment to generate meanings that enhance autonomy becomes increasingly relevant given the increasing numbers of older persons living alone in the community (Himes, 2001). Analysis of factors that might mediate or moderate the meaning of home, such as housing-related control beliefs, will become more important in this regard (Oswald et al., 2003). Future meaning of home research in very old age might profitably focus also on special groups of elders, for example, individuals with dementia and their relatives, to analyze the link between coping styles and patterns of meaning that may be harnessed in order to further enhance autonomy (Gitlin et al., 2001). Finally, from a methodological point of view, studies with a longitudinal focus are needed to clarify the time-related dynamics of adaptive mechanisms linking the meaning of home to well-being. In sum, meaning of home research has the potential not only to further gerontology scholarship on changing person–environment relations as people age but also to directly improve the quality of life of aging individuals through the employment of emerging findings in the field of practice.

REFERENCES

Altman, I. (1975). *The environment and social behavior: Privacy, personal space, territory, and crowding.* Monterey (CA): Brooks/Cole.

Altman, I., & Low, S. M. (Eds.). (1992). *Place attachment* (Vol. 12). New York: Plenum Press.

Baltes, M. M., Maas, I., Wilms, H.-U., & Borchelt, M. (1999). Everyday competence in old and very old age: Theoretical considerations and empirical findings. In P. B. Baltes & K. U. Mayer (Eds.), *The Berlin Aging Study* (pp. 384–402). Cambridge, UK: Cambridge University Press.

Baltes, P. B. (1987). Theoretical propositions of life-span developmental psychology: On the dynamics between growth and decline. *Developmental Psychology, 23,* 611–626.

Baltes, P. B., & Smith, J. (1999). Multilevel and systemic analyses of old age: Theoretical and empirical evidence for a Fourth Age. In V. L. Bentson & K. W. Schaie (Eds.), *Handbook of theories of aging* (pp. 153–173). New York: Springer Publishing Co.

Benjamin, D. (1995). Afterword. In D. N. Benjamin, D. Stea, & D. Saile (Eds.), *The home: Words, interpretations, meanings, and environments.* Aldershot: Avebury.

Bonnes, M., Bonaiuto, M., Aiello, A., Perugini, M., & Ercolani, A. P. (1997). A transactional perspective on residential satisfaction. In C. Després & D. Piché (Eds.), *Housing surveys: Advances in theory and methods* (pp. 75–88). Québec, Canada: CRAD Université Laval.

Bronfenbrenner, U. (1979). *The ecology of human development: Experiments by nature and design.* Cambridge, MA: Harvard University Press.

Bronfenbrenner, U. (1999). Environments in developmental perspective: Theoretical and operational models. In S. L. Friedman & T. D. Wachs (Eds.), *Measuring environment across the life span* (pp. 3–28). Washington, DC: American Psychological Association.

Bundesministerium für Familie Senioren Frauen und Jugend (BMFSFJ) [Federal Ministry for Family Affairs, Senior Citizens, Women and Youth]. (Ed.). (2001). *Dritter Bericht zur Lage der älteren Generation in der Bundesrepublik Deutschland: Alter und Gesellschaft* [Third report on the situation of older people. Ageing and society]. Berlin: BMFSFJ.

Canter, D. V. (1977). *The psychology of place.* London: Architectural Press.

Carp, F. M., & Carp, A. (1984). A complementary/congruence model of well-being or mental health for the community elderly. In I. Altman, M. P. Lawton, & J. F. Wohlwill (Eds.), *Human behavior and environment, Vol. 7: Elderly people and the environment* (pp. 279–336). New York: Plenum Press.

Coolen, H. (2002, July). *Meaning structures of preferences for aspects of a dwelling: A conceptual and methodological framework.* Paper presented at the 17th Conference of the International Association for People-Environment Studies (IAPS), A Coruña, Spain.

Després, C. (1991). The meaning of home: Literature review and directions for future research and theoretical development. *Journal of Architectural and Planning Research, 8,* 96–155.

Feldman, R. C. (1990). Settlement-identity: Psychological bonds with home places in a mobile society. *Environment & Behavior, 22*(2), 183–229.

Feldman, R. C. (1996). Constancy and change in attachments to types of settlements. *Environment & Behavior, 28,* 419–445.

Flade, A. (1993). Wohnen und Wohnbedürfnisse im Blickpunkt. [Emphasizing housing and housing needs.] In H. J. Harloff (Ed.), *Psychologie des Wohnungs- und Siedlungsbaus. Psychologie im Dienste von Architektur und Stadtplanung* (pp. 45–55). Göttingen: Verlag für angewandte Psychologie.

Fuhrer, U., & Kaiser, F. G. (1992). Bindung an das Zuhause: Die emotionalen Ursachen [Attachment to the home place: The emotional bases]. *Zeitschrift für Sozialpsychologie, 23,* 105–118.

Gansera-Baumann, B. (2002). *Subjektive Wohnbedeutung in Ost- und Westdeutschland und Aspekte der Persönlichkeit: Ergebnisse der Interdisziplinären Längsschnittstudie des Erwachsenenalters (ILSE).* [Meaning of home and personality in East and West Germany. Findings from the ILSE study.] Unpublished master's thesis, University of Heidelberg, Heidelberg, Germany.

Gitlin, L. N., Corcoran, M., Winter, L., Boyce, A., & Hauck, W. W. (2001). A randomized controlled trial of a home environmental intervention: Effect on efficacy and upset in caregivers and on daily function of persons with dementia. *The Gerontologist, 41*(1), 4–22.

Harris, P. B., Brown, B. B., & Werner, C. M. (1996). Privacy regulation and place attachment: Predicting attachments to a student family housing facility. *Journal of Environmental Psychology, 16,* 287–301.

Hayward, G. (1975). Home as an environmental and psychological concept. *Landscape, 20,* 2–9.

Himes, C. L. (2001). Elderly Americans. *Population Bulletin, 56,* 4.

Howell, S. C. (1983). The meaning of place in old age. In G. D. Rowles & R. J. Ohta (Eds.), *Aging and milieu. Environmental perspectives on growing old* (pp. 97–107). New York: Academic Press.

Küster, C. (1998). Zeitverwendung und Wohnen im Alter. [Use of time and housing in old age.] In Deutsches Zentrum für Altersfragen (Ed.), *Wohnbedürfnisse, Zeitverwendung und soziale Netzwerke älterer Menschen. Expertisenband 1 zum Zweiten Altenbericht der Bundesregierung.* [Housing needs, use of time, and social networks of older adults.] Frankfurt am Main: Campus.

Lalli, M. (1992). Urban-related identity: Theory, measurement, and empirical findings. *Journal of Environmental Psychology, 12,* 285–303.

Lawrence, R. (1987). What makes a house a home? *Environment & Behavior, 19,* 154–168.

Lawrence, R. (2002, July). *What makes a house a home? Reconsidered.* Paper presented at the 17th Conference of the International Association for People-Environment Studies (IAPS), A Coruña, Spain.

Lawton, M. P. (1985). The elderly in context: Perspectives from environmental psychology and gerontology. *Environment & Behavior, 17,* 501–519.

Lawton, M. P. (1987). Environment and the need satisfaction of the aging. In L. L. Carstensen & B. A. Edelstein (Eds.), *Handbook of clinical gerontology* (pp. 33–40). New York: Pergamon Press.

Lawton, M. P. (1989a). Environmental proactivity in older people. In V. L. Bengtson & K. W. Schaie (Eds.), *The course of later life* (pp. 15–23). New York: Springer Publishing Co.

Lawton, M. P. (1989b). Three functions of the residential environment. In L. A. Pastalan & M. E. Cowart (Eds.), *Lifestyles and housing of older adults: The Florida experience* (pp. 35–50). New York: Haworth.

Lawton, M. P. (1998). Environment and aging: Theory revisited. In R. J. Scheidt & P. G. Windley (Eds.), *Environment and aging theory. A focus on housing* (pp. 1–31). Westport, CT: Greenwood Press.

Lawton, M. P., & Nahemow, L. (1973). Ecology and the aging process. In C. Eisdorfer & M. P. Lawton (Eds.), *The psychology of adult development and aging* (pp. 619–674). Washington, DC: American Psychological Association.

Lawton, M. P., & Simon, B. B. (1968). The ecology of social relationships in housing for the elderly. *The Gerontologist, 8,* 108–115.

Lehr, U. (2000). Psychologie des Alterns (9. Aufl.) [Psychology of aging]. Heidelberg, Wiebelsheim: Quelle & Meyer.

Marcus, C. C. (1995). *House as a mirror of self. Exploring the deeper meaning of home.* Berkeley, CA: Conari Press.

McAndrew, F. T. (1998). The measurement of 'rootedness' and the prediction of attachment to home-towns in college students. *Journal of Environmental Psychology, 18,* 409–417.

McHugh, K. E., & Mings, R. C. (1996). The circle of migration: Attachment to place in aging. *Annals of the Association of American Geographers, 86,* 530–550.

Miller, D. (Ed.). (2001). *Home possessions: Material culture behind closed doors.* Oxford: Berg.

Moore, J. (2000). Placing home in context. *Journal of Environmental Psychology, 20,* 207–217.

Moore, J. (2002, July). *Making home work: The challenge of meaning-making in non-traditional contexts.* Paper presented at the 17th Conference of the International Association for People-Environment Studies (iaps), A Coruña, Spain.

Moss, M. S., & Lawton, M. P. (1982). Time budgets of older people: A window on four lifestyles. *Journal of Gerontology, 37,* 115–123.

Motel, A., Künemund, H., & Bode, C. (2000). Wohnen und Wohnumfeld älterer Menschen. [Housing and living arrangements of older adults.] In M. Kohli & H. Künemund (Eds.), *Die zweite Lebenshälfte—Gesellschaftliche Lage und Partizipation im Spiegel des Alters-Survey* [The second half of life—Societal stage and participation in the light of the Alters-Survey (pp. 124–175)]. Opladen: Leske & Budrich.

Muchow, M., & Muchow, H. H. (1935). *Der Lebensraum des Großstadtkindes* [Living space of urban children]. Hamburg: Riegel.

Neisser, U. (1988). Five kinds of self-knowledge. *Philosophical Psychology, 1,* 35–59.

Oswald, F. (1996). *Hier bin ich zu Hause. Zur Bedeutung des Wohnens: Eine empirische Studie mit gesunden und gehbeeinträchtigten Älteren.* [On the meaning of home: An empirical study with healthy and mobility impaired elders]. Regensburg: Roderer.

Oswald, F. (2003). Linking subjective housing needs to objective living conditions among older adults in Germany. In K. W. Schaie, H.-W. Wahl, H. Mollenkopf, & F. Oswald (Eds.), *Aging Independently: Living arrangements and mobility* (pp. 130–147). New York: Springer Publishing Co.

Oswald, F., Schilling, O., Wahl, H.-W., & Gäng, K. (2002). Trouble in paradise? Reasons to relocate and objective environmental changes among well-off older adults. *Journal of Environmental Psychology, 22,* 273–288.

Oswald, F., & Wahl, H.-W. (2001). Housing in old age: Conceptual remarks and empirical data on place attachment. *IAPS Bulletin of People–Environment Studies, 19,* 8–12.

Oswald, F., & Wahl, H.-W. (2003). Place attachment across the life span. In J. R. Miller, R. M. Lerner, L. B. Schiamberg, & P. M. Anderson (Eds.), *Human ecology: An encyclopedia of children, families, communities, and environments.* Santa Barbara, CA: ABC-Clio.

Oswald, F., Wahl, H.-W., Martin, M., & Mollenkopf, H. (2003). Toward measuring proactivity in person-environment transactions in late adulthood: The housing-related Control Beliefs Questionnaire. *Journal of Housing for the Elderly, 17*(1/2), 135–150.

Proshansky, H. M. (1978). The city and self-identity. *Environment & Behavior, 10,* 147–169.

Proshansky, H. M., Fabian, A. K., & Kaminoff, R. (1983). Place-identity. *Journal of Environmental Psychology, 3,* 57–83.

Rapoport, A. (1988). Levels of meaning in the built environment. In F. Poyatos (Ed.), *Cross-cultural perspectives in nonverbal communication* (pp. 317–336). Toronto: Hogrefe.

Rapoport, A. (1995). A critical look at the concept home. In D. N. Benjamin, D. Stea, & D. Saile (Eds.), *The home: Words, interpretations, meanings, and environments* (pp. 25–53). Aldershot: Avebury.

Relph, E. (1976). *Place and placelessness*. London: Pion.

Rowles, G. D. (1981). The surveillance zone as meaningful space for the aged. *The Gerontologist, 21,* 304–311.

Rowles, G. D. (1983). Geographical dimensions of social support in rural Appalachia. In G. D. Rowles & R. J. Ohta (Eds.), *Aging and milieu: Environmental perspectives on growing old* (pp. 111–130). New York: Academic Press.

Rowles, G. D., & Ravdal, H. (2001). Aging, place and meaning in the face of changing circumstances. In R. Weiss & S. Bass (Eds.), *Challenges of the third age: Meaning and purpose in later life* (pp. 81–114). New York: Oxford University Press.

Rowles, G. D., & Watkins, J. F. (2003). History, habit, heart and hearth: On making spaces into places. In K. W. Schaie, H.-W. Wahl, H. Mollenkopf, & F. Oswald (Eds.), *Aging in the community: Living arrangements and mobility* (pp. 77–96). New York: Springer Publishing Co.

Rubinstein, R. L. (1989). The home environments of older people: A description of the psychosocial processes linking person to place. *Journals of Gerontology: Social Sciences, 44,* S45–S53.

Rubinstein, R. L., & Parmelee, P. A. (1992). Attachment to place and representation of life course by the elderly. In I. Altman & S. M. Low (Eds.), *Place attachment: Human behavior and environment* (Vol. 12, pp. 139–163). New York: Plenum Press.

Saup, W. (1993). *Alter und Umwelt. Eine Einführung in die ökologische Gerontologie.* [Age and Environment. An introduction to Environmental Gerontology.] Stuttgart: Kohlhammer.

Schumaker, S. A., & Taylor, R. B. (1983). Toward a clarification of people place relationship: A model of attachment to place. In N. R. Feimer & E. S. Geller (Eds.), *Environmental psychology: Direction and perspectives*. New York: Praeger.

Sixsmith, J. A. (1986). The meaning of home: An exploratory study in environmental experience. *Journal of Environmental Psychology, 6,* 281–298.

Sommerville, P. (1997). The social construction of home. *Journal of Architectural and Planning Research, 14,* 227–245.

Steinfeld, E., & Danford, G. S. (Eds.). (1999). *Enabling environments. Measuring the impact of environment on disability and rehabilitation*. New York: Plenum Press.

Thomae, H. (1988). *Das Individuum und seine Welt. Eine Persönlichkeitstheorie* (2nd Edition). [The individual in its world. A theory of personality.] Göttingen: Hogrefe.

Tuan, Y. F. (1980). Rootedness versus sense of place. *Landscape, 24,* 3–7.

Twigger, C. (1995). *Developing a model of attachment to place.* Paper presented at the IV European Congress of Psychology, Athens, Greece.

Twigger-Ross, C. L., & Uzzell, D. L. (1996). Place and identity process. *Journal of Environmental Psychology, 16,* 205–220.

U.S. Bureau of the Census. (1996). *Current population reports, Special studies, P23-10, 65+ in the United States.* Washington, DC: U.S. Government Printing Office.

Wahl, H.-W. (2001). Environmental influences on aging and behavior. In J. E. Birren & K. W. Schaie (Eds.), *Handbook of the psychology of aging* (5th ed., pp. 215–237). San Diego, CA: Academic Press.

Wahl, H.-W., Oswald, F., & Zimprich, D. (1999). Everyday competence in visually impaired older adults: A case for person-environment perspectives. *The Gerontologist, 39*, 140–149.

Wahl, H.-W., Schilling, O., Oswald, F., & Heyl, V. (1999). Psychosocial consequences of age-related visual impairment: Comparison with mobility-impaired older adults and long-term outcome. *Journal of Gerontology: Psychological Sciences, 54B*, P304–P316.

Zingmark, K., Norberg, A., & Sandman, P.-O. (1995). The experience of being at home throughout the life span. Investigation of persons aged from 2 to 102. *International Journal of Aging and Human Development, 41*, 47–62.

CHAPTER 3

Home, Self, and Identity

Robert L. Rubinstein and Kate de Medeiros

The goal of this chapter is to examine the construction of the self in later life, its relationship to the notion of identity, and in particular its relationship to the home environment, a world both of and outside the person. By home, we have in mind elements including the residence itself, personal objects, and microenvironments therein; home as memory; and home routines or rituals. Key to our chapter is the idea of narrative—telling something to somebody—in the broadest sense. This "somebody" could include not only others, but also the elder himself or herself. Here we will identify different narrative forms or codes by which the self is expressed, identity is enhanced, and relations with the external world are established and maintained. We begin by examining the concept of the self, and the myriad of ways in which it is used, including the concept of the narrated self. We then move to the territory between the self and its immediate surrounds, the intrasubjective territory of self and object. In this domain (of objects, attachments, microenvironments, and the residence itself), the self is not only represented and narrated, but also these elements can become one with the self. We consider the concept of identity, both externally imposed and internally constructed, within this context. Finally, we deal briefly with the relationship of the self and the outer world with place attachment and the long-term care continuum. In all instances we tie our approach to examples of environmental experience in later life.

THE SELF

The "self" is a fundamental yet illusive term. Differences in definitions of the self across various academic traditions, combined with an explosive outgrowth of discipline-specific research (e.g., in anthropology, linguistics, philosophy, architecture and design, history, psychology, and sociology), have led to a rich but fragmented set of perspectives on the self (Peacock & Holland, 1993). Three questions provide a framework from which to consider self across disciplines: What comprises the self or how is self defined? What are the "essential" components of the self? And, what are the ways in which the self is known and made known, the architecture of the "she" or "he" and the "I," the "me," and the "mine"?

Defining the Self

The self has been described both as a dynamic, reflexive, symbolic, mediating agent and as an object or container, composed of other parts of the person such as personality and identity. Definitions of the self as an agent include the self as "the interpreter of experience" (Kaufman, 1986, p. 14), "that part of consciousness that comes into play when a human being begins to take herself as an object" (Wikan, 1995, p. 265), and "the part of the personality that mediates between environmental demands (reality), conscience (superego), and instinctual needs (id)" (Morris & Maisto, 1988). The self thus assumes an audience or an "other" and thus is always being narrated. From these perspectives, the self is an active entity that crosses the boundaries of the internal and external, and therefore engages in both subject and object/environment relations.

Unlike the active role played by the self as agent, definitions of the self as object describe the self as a type of storage closet for components of the person. Definitions here include the self as "the entire person from a psychological perspective" (McCrae & Costa, 1990, p. 161), and those "attributes or dispositions which constitute essential 'identity components'" (Brandtstädter & Greve, 1994, p.

53). In contrast, Herzog and Markus (1999) suggest a definition of self that combines the ideas of agent and object. They define self as "a multifaceted, dynamic system of interpretive structures that mediates behavior" (p. 228). This definition seems best suited for a discussion of home environments and the aged because it nominates the self as both interpreter and mediator within the storehouse of experiences, memories, and perceptions. This presupposes the ability to reflect outwardly, while, at the same time, incorporating or reflecting internally, the external. It defines a person–environment process.

Essential Components of the Self

Theories by Kashima et al. (1995) and Linde (1993) describe four dimensions of the self: distinctness of one person's self from another person's self (individualistic), reflexivity (or relational), self as collective, and continuity over time. These are significant for the aging self, identity, and environmental relations. Culturally, the construction of the self varies. In Western individualism or "individuality" we find perhaps its most extreme form in postmodern American individualism (Lutz, 1996; O'Nell, 1998). In contrast to the many communally oriented societies, this is a system of the self, based on individual agency, distinctiveness, and separateness, which are important cultural characteristics.

The relational or reflexive aspect of self refers to "the ability to relate to oneself externally, as an object or as an other" or that part of a self that functions as "one self among many similar selves, so that it can be reflected on, or related to another" (Linde, 1993, pp. 105, 120). This would also include environment and object. The reflexive property of the self enables one to interpret personal experience, develop direction toward or redefine goals, and to promote the self through expression or action (Atchley, 1999). This reflexive component can also allow for the assignment of meaning to environments, for the projection of the self into environments, and for the counterprojection of the self contained in environments back into the person, especially when the self weakens or fragments in later life.

The property of self-as-collective places the self within a larger cultural context (Kashima et al., 1995). Miner and Montoro-Rodriguez

(1999) describe the collective influences on the self as the "sociocultural grounding of self," or factors within a society or culture, such as a meaning system, social and economic conditions and hierarchies, and physical health, which influence one's perception of the self.

Linde's (1993) criterion of continuity for the self over time is an idea that also has been extensively explored (Ewing, 1990; Kaufman, 1986). In a related way, continuity theory in gerontology may suggest that throughout their development, people use adaptive strategies for decision making, finding meaning, and establishing coherence for their past experiences (Atchley, 1999). Ultimately, the self undergoes a continual process of construction, interpretation, and reconstruction of memory and meaning to create an internal sense of continuity over time, a present-day self (Brandtstädter & Greve, 1994). This is not to say that there is a single self that remains relatively unchanged over a lifetime. Rather, as Ewing (1990) and others argue, the experience of self is constantly changing but one reorders events to create one's own retrospective consistency at any given point in time.

The third framework, the "he or she," describes the ways in which the self is made known to the older person herself and himself and to others. In a sense, knowledge of the self is similar to identity in that it is concerned with who one really is and how one presents himself or herself to the outer world. Although one could argue that every interaction with another person or an object involves a presentation of the self, and that there are many ways the self is expressed, we will narrow our discussion to a very brief review of two study types: narratives and studies of presentation in object and environmental relations (Kaufman, 1986; Rubinstein, 1987).

The Narrated Self

We mentioned earlier that narrative has played an important role in investigations into the self. Definitions of narrative range from Becker's (1997) broad understanding of narrative as the stories people use to present their experiences or to tell about themselves, to Labov and Waletsjym's (1967) more precise criteria of clauses describing past experiencing in sequence of occurrence leading to a metaphoric or symbolic significance of object. We have also suggested that various media including those that surround the self (objects, home) and enact the self (behavioral routines) are forms other than speech that narrate the self. Research informants have been candid at identifying such media as communicative aspects of the self, relating to important life events and to the meaningfulness of lived experiences (Kaufman, 1986; Mishler, 1986; Rubinstein, 1987). Yet, narrative as an expression of the aging self does have limitations. These include a possible decrease in some abilities to use language for expression (e.g., abstract thought) with age (Kemper, 1992) and potential discipline-based bias in analyzing narrative themes (Hazan & Raz, 1997).

If it is the case that there is any decreased ability to express abstract thoughts through language with advanced old age, it does not mean the individual no longer thinks abstractly. Rather, the codes of language have interfered with expression (Kemper, 1992). Some degree of expression may be taken over by metaphor, cliché, writing, and art. Such language theory opens a way of looking at how narrative may be unable to fully capture the nature of experience that the embodiment of thought through home object may be able to convey. As noted, objects in a general sense may act as complements, proxies, augmentations, reminders, and representations of the self. They are not a meta-language, but work with speech. Speech is objectivated in that it is outside the person, but for us it lacks tangibility. These other narrative media have tangibility, but lack the full expressiveness of speech or are subject to different types of expression (for example, as home furnishing and organization follow social conventions).

In addition to any changes in a person's ability to express the self through language, disciplinary bias may affect the outside observer's ability to interpret themes and meanings within the narrative. Hazan and Raz (1997), for example, suggest that the structures of narratives of old age are based on a middle-aged construction of what constitutes aging, so that "the old speaker's world is hence too often obscured by the discourse of aging" (p. 266). They argue that theories (e.g., life course, life cycle, disengagement) and popular folk tales and stories of aging have formed a cultural script (master narrative) through which local narratives are told and interpreted, a script that does not necessarily reflect the depth of meaning and experience of the old. They add "metaphor, being a symbolic vehicle designed to connect different worlds by means of some analogy, becomes impossible" (p. 265). It may be through the metaphoric or metonymic connection of object and meaning that the home environment becomes especially revealing in the expression of self (cf. Kenyon, Birren, & Schroots, 1991).

The narrative perspective suggests that elements of the self, internally, and the presented self, externally, are always in dialogue with some entity (e.g., another person, one's self, an intended reader, and so on), telling that entity (real or imagined) about who one is and what one thinks. This would suggest that not only do internal components of the self narrate to one another, but also that the self, itself, is narrating externally. Becker (1997) describes narrative as "the stories that people tell about themselves" (p. 25). Narratives, including oral interviews and stories written by elders, have been one approach to understanding the presented self. Narrative approaches allow subjects to use language (and other symbols) to string together details from their past in a unified way, providing insight into how they have made sense out of isolated events or their lives as a whole.

The second study category, object relations, refers to physical symbols as expressions of the self. Words, objects, small environments, and the home itself are distinctive forms for expressing, communicating, and reminding the self. Rubinstein (1987) describes objects as "expressive media" that transcend the verbal and are capable of expressing meaning about the self in the larger social context, the self in relation to other individuals, and the internalized self.

Expressions of Self in the Home Environment

The Cartesian West represents an extreme position in the cultural dualism found in the separation of subject from object. The psychological *merger* of a person with a thing or a place is considered an illness in Western culture. This is not necessarily the case in non-Western cultures in which persons or their bodies "merge" in culturally specific contexts with both substances and things (Panoff, 1968). Nevertheless it is clear that in Western cultures, persons may use "objects" narratively as mediators, either to express (but be separate from) the self or to buttress it (for example, in placing important objects in a nursing home room as a reminders of the self). In the folk experience of aging persons, the equating or "merger" of person and home or person and object may be more significant, as has been ethnographically found (Rubinstein, Kilbride, & Nagy, 1992). This is not to say that a person cannot distinguish person from object, but rather that objects or environments take on new and heightened meanings (Rubinstein, 1995). Thus, in a sense, object relations may become subject relations of a sort in later life.

As discussed, the self is mediator, interpreter, and collector of experiences; grounded in a social context; adaptive to create continuity; unique to each person; reflexive; and expressed in a variety of narrative ways. As one reaches old age, changes in social, economic, and health status often lead to greater dependence on the home environment, especially with advanced old age. The actual, nonfantasy-life world may shrink, as may sources of satisfaction. The connection between the body and the world around it may heighten. Conversely, if the elder enters long-term care during this period, transitions, length of residence, ability to meaningfully adapt, and cognitive function may all change. There appear to be no studies that examine the relationship of environmental meaning specifically to the demented self, although we know anecdotally that cognitive performance and awareness may decline if one is removed from a familiar environment, for example, in the transition from home to nursing home.

Formal studies examining expression of the aging self in the home environment and in objects have been limited. A recent literature review on the aging self revealed, not surprisingly, that most of the current journal articles on the aging self focus on either the presentation of self in narratives, or on changes in performance on various cognitive and personality measures. Published work on the environment and aging has focused on architecture, design and home modifications, technological advances, housing patterns, and others issues related to the physical challenges of aging and environment (Charness, Parks, & Sabel, 2001).

The presentation of self through home (regardless of age) has been explored in a number of key articles and volumes (Boschetti, 1985; Dovey, 1985; Lawton, 1980; Rapoport, 1985; Rowles, 1978; Windley, 1982). Implications of these for the aging self and its relation to home environment include consideration of the way the older individuals narrate and reflect on their experience of self. Therein, greater dependence on home may occur simultaneously with re- duced external contacts and increased focus on internality. Narra- tively, personal objects, symbols, personal routines, and the home itself may increasingly complement language as a vehicle for express- ing the self (Rubinstein, 1989).

IDENTITY

Earlier work, including classic scholarship in sociology and other disciplines, has addressed the role of the social context of identity through social roles and identity management. Here, we will address the differences between and implications of both externally imposed and internally constructed identities. We will also examine their relationship to the larger context of self and home in later life (Rubin- stein, 1989).

Externally Imposed Identity

Identity may be understood as a component of the larger self. Whit- bourne (1999), from a psychological perspective, describes domains of identity such as the body, cognition, personality, intimacy, gen- erativity, and ego integrity. Whitbourne's model of identity is circular (tautologous). Overall identity leads to the interpretation of events relative to identity, which leads to a change in one's identity based on experience, which leads back to overall identity. In her model, identity is primarily internal and person-centered within the larger cultural framework. The individual responds to experiences, which in turn affects his or her inner concept of identity. Yet, in contrast to the psychological idea of an internal identity, philosopher Hilde Nelson (1991) points to the power of identity as an externally im- posed construct through a master cultural narrative.

Master narratives have also been called "folk models," "semantic networks," or "cultural templates." These are the complex, inter- locked sets of ideas that accompany themes in our dominant ideolo- gies that, consciously and unconsciously, suggest the nature of the world. For example, the master narrative of "being old" in American culture brings with it a set of ideas on sexuality, beauty, agency, competence, the body—and many other topics—that go with it. Thus, a master narrative is a preestablished, interlocked set of cultural definitions for a particular group, set of behaviors, or characteristics. Habitual narratives concern elements such as gender, race, socioeconomic status, or age. By virtue of belonging to a group, whether by choice or default, one or more (social) identities can be imposed on the person. Conflict may therefore arise between how the individual wishes to be identified and how the outside observer identifies him or her. Some work on aging and the home has found discordances between external reality and subjective meaning (Rubinstein et al., 1992). Thus, master narratives of family and life course are also found in neighborhood, house form, home amenities, and internal domestic organization and furnishing, as well as the body (see text that follows).

Internally Constructed Identity

Some work has examined the inner core of personal identity, which for elders may be experienced in the private sphere of the home. At home, as many elders note, "a person can be him- or herself." Identity is tied to comfortable bodily feelings; familiarity with home elements; the construction of personal daily routines; objects and symbols that may induce memories; and identity through body, that is, through emplaced embodiment (Casey, 1993; Clarke, 2001; Hurd, 1999). This focus on internal identity may be particularly important to persons who suffer from chronic illnesses or who are recovering from acute illnesses. In the case of the former, the home may take on a utility as a "second skin," and the inner domain expanded as the self is narrated through objects that reflect and reflect back onto the infirm person.

To explore the self as projected or represented through home objects, routine behaviors, and home microenvironments, we will look at some key ideas from work on the narrated self to see how objects, like language, may also express meaning in old age. We will look at ways in which people assign meaning to home objects and the role that the concept of identity plays in shaping the external and internal self.

The Self and the Outer World

Personal Meaning and Object Relations

Previously, the first author has outlined three processes through which people link environmental meaning to features of the home: a social-centered, a person-centered, and a body-centered process (Rubinstein, 1989). Personal objects (e.g., wheel chairs, beds), physical arrangement of rooms, personal possessions (e.g., photographs, mementos), routines, furniture, and other features of the home become ways in which people mediate and interpret their experiences through an overriding social order, through private meaning systems grounded within a particular social context, and through "entexturing" or fine-tuning objects within the home to accommodate the textural needs of the body (e.g., light, sound, comfort, ambiance) (Rubinstein, 1989, p. S50). In a sense, following Bourdieu (1977), the self reproduces itself, its structures and important identities through daily activities and contextual meanings. When the self encounters its own decline through illness or decreased abilities, this arrangement must be simplified through a greater focus on the core aspects of the self.

The idea of an overriding social order, or social-centered process, refers to the way in which an individual uses culturally defined notions of space and appropriate arrangement to construct his or her home space (Rubinstein, 1989). For example, items such as a welcome mat, a couch and coffee table, or a matching bedroom suite could all be attributed to an American sense of home decorum as opposed to a Japanese home, which may have different objects in different arrangement (Kondo, 1990). Individual choices of where to place specific objects (e.g., a couch) within an overriding cultural definition of organized space (e.g., a living room) may differ from person to person. Yet, the individual still lives within a cultural template (folk model or master narrative), which is individually modified.

Private meaning systems (person-centered processes) are more concerned with the importance that objects within the home have with regard to personhood as opposed to a greater social expectation (Rubinstein, 1989). Through personalization (the projection of one's self and identity into objects), extension (the conscious use of objects to represent important aspects of the self), and embodiment (a degree of merging between self-representation and object), the individual acts inseparably from objects.

Classic literature on identity, place, and aging has recently been expanded to include identity embodied through place (McHugh, 2000). As the last resort of the self, bodies (though body-centered processes) are of special significance in the relation of self and environment and display meaningful relationships, as an object, to surrounding environmental features. Bodily concerns include physical comfort, practical placement of home items to meet physical challenges or needs (e.g., positioning the chair closer to the television, moving the bedroom to the main floor), and routine activities within the home that help the individual navigate and manage both living space and time (e.g., cleaning, reading). As Casey (1993, p. xv) notes, "Place is the phenomenal particularization of 'being-in-the-world.' The same may clearly be said for the body."

External Domains and Residential Space

At the large-scale level, the relationship of the self to external domains is strongly affected by key social variables (SES [socioeconomic status], area of residence, age, gender, and ethnicity). These are forms of cultural master narratives that tell about the person to others and to the person as well. Also, these cultural master narratives sharply influence the creation of residential space, neighborhood selection, house form, layout, and other elements of residence. Both an urban row house in a run-down neighborhood and a large "McMansion" in a newly developed far suburb are also examples of narrative, speaking in a variety of channels about the nature of the person in social context (Cooper Marcus, 1992; Duncan, 1985).

As has long been noted, among the most successful neighborhoods for the daily praxis of the aged are those intimate settings that are amenity rich and walkable. Because most American elders now live in suburbs—the world made for cars—the relationship between the self and the external is now mediated by cars, which may be thought of as another language of the self—albeit one that not only degrades the self and costs money, but also one that does not easily adapt to changes in motor or cognitive skills (Maxwell, 2001). As Rowles (1978) showed in a classic work, attachment to far places is selective. In a sense, far places that are not currently reachable in old age, although real, also meld with memories and biography so that a place and a time may also meld (cf. Basso, 1996).

The Self in the Long-Term Care Trajectory

Little work has been undertaken on the self, identity, and the environment in the long-term care transition. Residential movement from home to assisted living to nursing home to hospital inevitably involves some process of divestment, a "sloughing off" of personal objects and, in the sense developed here, a clear reduction in narrative channels. To a degree, this movement may represent a "disemplacement"; these may be places that are not places (Brown & Perkins, 1992; Relph, 1976). Although formally these are settings that make a better fit of competence with environmental press, they are increasingly places where persons may be refugees from their own bodies, moving on from place to place as the body declines (Kalymun, 1983; Saegert & McCarthy, 1998). For this transition, we may identify two types of codes of self-expression: invested and contingent. Investment of the self in an environment, through the investment code, refers to the use of most or all narrative means and channels and, similarly, multiple sources of feedback to the self. This is the kind of idiomatic self-communication that takes place in the home, and is based on a feeling of safety, bodily and personal comforts, refuge, and other types of positive security. Elders will sometimes use the metaphor "like a port in a storm" to describe this level of comfort. A contingent investment, through the contingent code, represents a less-than-full, compromised, or temporary investment in a setting in which any sense of personal or bodily comfort must make peace with rules and restrictions that come from the outside (for example, rules of an institution).

CONCLUSIONS

In this chapter, we have outlined a set of relationships among the self, the home environment (and its objectified contents), and identity in later life. We have examined a variety of definitions of the self and have focused on essential aspects of the self, self-knowledge and a sense of personal continuity over time. Moving from the self, we have examined some issues in the relationship of subject and object in later life and have briefly discussed their implications for the home environment and its relationship to the self. We next examined the notion of identity, a part of the self that is more socially oriented, in essence answering the questions, consciously or unconsciously: Who am I to myself and to others? In better understanding identity and its relationship to the home, we focused on the idea of cultural "master narratives" that structure so much of our thought about persons, selves, and identities. These led to issues of how identity is structured internally, not only in relation to the home environment but also to the body as well. In relation to master narratives, we examined ways in which the self is narrated or unspoken. We then mentioned some issues around personal meaning, objects, and "object relations." Finally, we moved from the self and its immediate surrounds to the relationship of the self and external domains, and, in particular, issues in attachment, personal investment, and object within the long-term care continuum.

Some may argue that there is little of concern here because older people move and change residences often without much active consideration of "the self" and "identity." This view fails to take into account the reality that most people do not consider their homes to be "just space," but rather turn them into "places," that is, settings with personal significance. Culturally, homes are not (or should not be) "cold," but rather "warm." We would argue that regardless of the preceding view, selves are communicated through narrative in the broadest sense and one important channel for this communication is the home. Although homes "say something" to outsiders, they also say something to the possessor, and this something may increase in agency with age.

The importance of understanding self-identity becomes especially salient in the context of older adults moving from their homes into long-term care facilities. The move is a threat to personhood and it is critical that care settings provide a responsive context for the preservation and continuity of selfhood. Self-identity is intimately related to place-identity and support of place-identity would be a worthwhile goal.

REFERENCES

Atchley, R. C. (1999). *Continuity and adaptation in aging.* Baltimore, MD: Johns Hopkins University Press.

Basso, K. H. (1996). *Wisdom sits in places: Landscape and language among the Western Apache.* Albuquerque: University of New Mexico Press.

Becker, G. (1997). *Disrupted lives: How people create meaning in a chaotic world.* Berkeley, CA: University of California Press.

Boschetti, M. (1985). Emotional attachment to homes past to present: Continuity of experience and integrity. In D. Saile (Ed.), *Architecture in cultural change: Essays in built forms and culture research* (pp. 31–44). Lawrence, KS: School of Architecture and Urban Design.

Bourdieu, P. (1977). *Outline of a theory of practice.* New York: Cambridge University Press.

Brandtstädter, J., & Greve, W. (1994). The aging self: Stabilizing and protective processes. *Developmental Review, 14,* 52–80.

Brown, B. B., & Perkins, D. D. (1992). Disruptions in place attachment. In I. Altman & S. M. Low (Eds.), *Place attachment. Human behavior and environment: Advances in theory and research* (Vol. 12., pp. 279–304). New York: Plenum Press.

Casey, E. S. (1993). *The fate of place: A philosophical history.* Berkeley, CA: University of California Press.

Charness, N., Parks, D. C., & Sabel, B. A. (2001). *Community, technology and aging: Opportunities and challenges for the future.* New York: Springer Publishing Co.

Clarke, L. H. (2001). Older women's bodies and the self: The construction of identity in later life. *Canadian Review of Sociology and Anthropology, 38,* 441–464.

Cooper Marcus, C. (1992). Environmental memories. In I. Altman & S. M. Low (Eds.), *Place attachment. Human behavior and environment: Advances in theory and research* (Vol. 12, pp. 87–112). New York: Plenum Press.

Dovey, K. (1985). The concept of home. In I. Altman & C. Werner (Eds.), *Home environments. Human behavior and environment: Advances in theory and research* (Vol. 8., pp. 115–137). New York: Plenum Press.

Duncan, (1985). The house as a symbol of social structure: Notes on the language of objects among collectivistic groups. In I. Altman & C. Werner (Eds.), *Home environments. Human behavior and environment: Advances in theory and research* (Vol. 8, pp.138–162). New York: Plenum Press.

Ewing, K. (1990). The illusion of wholeness: Culture, self and the experience of inconsistency. *Ethos, 18,* 251–278.

Hazan, H., & Raz, A. E. (1997). The authorized self: How middle age defines old age in the postmodern. *Semiotica, 113,* 257–276.

Herzog, A. R., & Markus, H. R. (1999). The self-concept in life span and aging research. In V. Bengston & K. Warner Schaie (Eds.), *Handbook of theories on aging* (pp. 227–252). New York: Springer Publishing Co.

Hurd, L. C. (1999). We're not old! Older women's negotiations of aging and oldness. *Journal of Aging Studies, 13,* 419–430.

Kalymun, M. (1983). Factors influencing elderly women's decisions concerning living room items during relocation. *EDRA (Environmental Design Research Association), 14,* 75–83.

Kashima, Y., Yamaguchi, S., Kim, U., Choi, Sang-Chi, Gelfand, M., & Yuki, M. (1995). Culture, gender and self: A perspective from individualism-collectivism research. *Journal of Personality and Social Psychology, 68,* 925–937.

Kaufman, S. (1986). *The ageless self: Sources of meaning in late life.* Madison, WI: University of Wisconsin Press.

Kemper, S. (1992). Language and aging. In F. M. Craik & T. A. Salthouse (Eds.), *The handbook of aging and cognition* (pp. 213–270). Hillsdale, NJ: Lawrence Erlbaum.

Kenyon, G., Birren, J. E., & Schroots, J. J. F. (1991). *Metaphors of aging in the sciences and humanities.* New York: Springer Publishing Co.

Kondo, D. (1990). *Crafting selves: Power, gender, and discourses of identity in a Japanese workplace.* Chicago: University of Chicago Press.

Labov, W., & Waletsjym, J. (1967). Oral versions of personal experience. In J. Helm (Ed.), *Essays on Verbal and Visual Arts.* American Ethnological Society, University of Washington Press.

Lawton, M. P. (1980). *Environment and aging.* Monterey: Brooks/Cole.

Linde, C. (1993). *Life stories: The creation of coherence.* New York: Oxford University Press.

Lutz, C. A. (1996). *Unnatural emotions: Everyday sentiments on a Micronesian atoll and their challenge to western theory.* Chicago: University of Chicago Press.

Maxwell, S. (2001). Negotiations of care use in everyday life. In D. Miller (Ed.), *Car cultures* (pp. 203–222). New York: Berg.

McCrae, R. R., & Costa, P. T., Jr. (1990). *Personality in adulthood.* New York: Guilford Press.

McHugh, K. (2000). The 'ageless self'? Emplacement of identities in Sun Belt retirement communities. *Journal of Aging Studies, 14,* 103–116.

Miner, S., & Montoro-Rodriguez, J. (1999). Intersections of society, family and self among Hispanics in middle and later life. In C. Ryff & V. Marshall (Eds.), *The self and society in aging processes* (pp. 423–452). New York: Springer Publishing Co.

Mishler, E. (1986). *Research interviewing: Context and narrative.* Cambridge, MA: Harvard University Press.

Morris, C., & Maisto, A. (1988). (Eds.). *Psychology: An introduction* (10th ed.). Upper Saddle River, NJ: Prentice Hall.

Nelson, H. L. (1991). *Damaged identities, Narrative repair.* Ithaca, NY: Cornell University Press.

O'Nell, T. D. (1998). *Disciplined hearts: History, identity and depression in an American Indian community.* Berkeley: University of California Press.

Panoff, M. (1968). The notion of the double self among the Maenge. *Journal of the Polynesian Society, 77,* 275–295.

Peacock, J., & Holland, D. (1993). The narrated self: Life stories in process. *Ethos, 21,* 367–383.

Rapoport, A. (1985). Thinking about home environments: A conceptual framework. In I. Altman & C. Werner (Eds.), *Home environments. Human behavior and environment: Advances in theory and research* (Vol. 8., pp. 255–286). New York: Plenum Press.

Relph, E. (1976). *Place and placelessness.* London: Pion.

Rowles, G. D. (1978). *Prisoners of space? Exploring the geographical experience of older people.* Boulder, CO: Westview Press.

Rubinstein, R. (1987). The significance of personal objects to older people. *Journal of Aging Studies, 1,* 225–238.

Rubinstein, R. (1989). The home environments of older people: A description of the psychosocial processes linking person to place. *Journals of Gerontology: Social Sciences, 44*(2), S45–53.

Rubinstein, R. (1995). The engagement of life history and the life review among the aged: A research case study. *Journal of Aging Studies, 9,* 187–203.

Rubinstein, R., Kilbride, J., & Nagy, S. (1992). *Elders living alone: Frailty and the perception of choice.* Hawthorne, NY: Aldine de Gruyter.

Saegert, S., & McCarthy, D. E. (1998). Gender and housing for the elderly: Sorting through the accumulations of a lifetime. In R. J. Scheidt & P. G. Windley (Eds.), *Environment and aging theory: A focus on housing* (pp. 61–87). Westport, CT: Greenwood Press.

Whitbourne, S. K. (1999). Identity and adaptation to the aging process. In C. Ryff & V. Marshall (Eds.), *The self and society in aging processes* (pp. 122–149). New York: Springer Publishing Co.

Wikan, U. (1995). The self in a world of urgency and necessity. *Ethos, 23,* 259–285.

Windley, P. (1982). Environmental dispositions: A theoretical and methodological alternative. In M. P. Lawton, P. G. Windley, & T. O. Byerts (Eds.), *Aging and the environment: Theoretical approaches* (pp. 60–68). New York: Springer Publishing Co.

CHAPTER 4

Cherished Objects and the Home: Their Meaning and Roles in Late Life

Edmund Sherman and Joan Dacher

There is a natural, almost symbiotic relationship between cherished possessions and the home in late life. The image that comes to mind is of the home as the fitting place for objects that have been collected and cherished over the course of a lifetime. When one studies the variety of these objects and their meaning to their owners it becomes apparent that they play a number of key roles in late life.

This became evident in an interview survey about cherished objects with 94 older adults (60 years and older), 62 of whom were living in their own homes and 32 in a nursing home (Sherman & Newman, 1977–78). The kind of home made a difference in the number, types, and the significance of objects reported. It is useful to review salient findings of that survey to obtain an overview of the subject area and, after reviewing more recent findings on cherished objects, to consider their implications for practice, theory, and further research.

CHERISHED OBJECTS:
MEANINGS AND ATTRIBUTES

The key question put to respondents in the survey was: "Is there one personal possession you value above all others?" This became the working definition of a "most cherished" object. More than four of every five respondents were readily able to identify such an object. Almost half (48%) were able to identify a next most cherished possession, although it took them somewhat more time to do so. The highest number of cherished possessions identified was seven. Invariably, the respondents were able to point to or retrieve the most cherished possession within their home setting without hesitation. Possessions identified ranged from objects as small as a piece of jewelry (ring, pin, etc.) to those as large as the residence itself. They fell into several categories: religious items (bibles, torahs, rosaries, prayer books, etc.), symbolic jewelry, personal performance items, photographs, consumer items, and other. Symbolic jewelry refers to items given by or associated with a significant other or with significant events in the respondent's life. Jewelry that was cherished primarily for its material value was classified under consumer items.

Photographs were the most frequently identified type of object, making up a quarter of all types listed. Personal performance items included musical instruments, art materials, or objects that denoted a creative or personal performance-related function in the life of the respondent. Consumer items included entertainment objects such as televisions, radios, and books. Finally, the "other" category contained items that could not be classified in the prior categories including such things as documents (military discharge papers, birth certificate, etc.), pets, residences, and enabling items such as eye glasses, hearing aids, and canes. It should be noted that the one person who identified her home as her most cherished possession was living in her own home at the time of the interview, although there was one nursing home respondent who commented ruefully that her home *had* been her most cherished possession.

The personal meaning of the identified items invariably referred to either self or significant others: these referents had the following frequency: self (25), child (18), spouse (15), parents (5), grandchild (4), friend (1), grandparent (1), aunt (1), other relative (1), and other nonrelative (1). When these referents were cross-tabulated with type of cherished objects certain clusters became apparent. Religious objects, personal performance items, consumer items, and the "other" category were more frequently associated with self than significant others, whereas symbolic jewelry most often had a spouse as referent and photographs were most frequently associated with children. The range and poignancy of meanings and associations of the objects with their referents are too great to do justice to here, but the following brief examples convey a flavor of their richness:

> *Female respondent* (object: photos of her children)—"They mean I was a woman. I had children and built my life around them. Happy memories."

> *Female respondent* (object: ring)—"It was my mother's wedding ring. She gave it to me before she died."

> *Male respondent* (object: violin)—"I am a musician and the violin means everything to me."

> *Female respondent* (object: her oil painting)—"Painting keeps my mind off the nursing home."

An equal proportion (four fifths) of men and women were able to identify a most cherished object. There were significant differences in the type of object identified, with more consumer items identified by men and more photographs and symbolic jewelry identified by women. When respondents over 75 years of age were compared to those under 75, significantly more of them (30%) could identify *no* cherished object as compared to only 8% of the younger respondents. *Lack* of a most cherished object turned out to be a significant factor in terms of the morale of the respondents, as measured by the Life Satisfaction Index A (Neugarten, Havighurst, & Tobin, 1961). Lower life satisfaction scores of the older respondents have to be viewed in light of the fact that significantly more of them resided in the nursing home than did the younger respondents. Looked at more closely, on a case-by-case basis and in terms of *where* they resided, it was clear that in a number of cases, lack of a cherished object was associated with the absence of one's own home.

These findings suggest that the meaning of home and its objects comes into dramatic focus with the prospect or reality of loss of home. The move from one's own home in late life into long-term, institutional care often means moving into a place bereft of the meaningful objects that surround one in the home. The almost symbiotic bond between home and objects is severed.

OBJECTS AND THE HOME

Prior to the first study of cherished objects, Myrna Lewis and Robert Butler (1974) wrote that objects provide a sense of continuity, comfort, and security to the extent that fear of their loss is a frequent preoccupation among older persons. Earlier, Carp's study of relocation of older adults to Victoria Plaza demonstrated that "the surrender of furniture and other possessions was important, not only because the objects were missed, both as items in themselves and as reminders of the family events associated with them, but also because their absence and the substitution of cheaper and less distinguished furnishings was a continual reminder of general loss of status" (Carp, 1966, p. 89). Simone de Beauvoir went further and claimed that ownership of certain possessions served as a guarantee of "ontological security" for the older person by assuring a sense of "identity against those who would see him as nothing but an object" (de Beauvoir, 1973, p. 699). Viktor Frankl (1955) also noted the profound existential meaning of having all personal possessions taken away from concentration camp inmates in World War II: Their loss severed all visible external links inmates had with their former lives.

Erving Goffman (1961) also pointed out that when placed in total institutions such as mental hospitals, certain personal possessions become essential for maintaining a sense of self. He observed that clothing and cosmetics were like "identity kits," which allowed their owners to present a "usual" image of themselves to others. Objects can perform roles as diverse as maintaining a sense of self, of identity, and ontological security as well as provide a reassuring sense of continuity during environmental relocation. Findings from the initial interview survey suggested that certain personal possessions could serve as "transitional objects" for older adults in much the same sense that Winnicott (1971) found that certain objects assisted children in dealing with the developmental process of separation and individuation early in life.

Although it is clear that the home serves as a natural repository for cherished possessions, the home itself may be the most cherished object. As noted earlier, the one person who identified her home as her most cherished object was living in her own house at the time. It is possible that more respondents might have identified their homes as most cherished if the interviews had not been conducted *within* their homes, perhaps making them oblivious to their surrounding environment as a possible object in its own right. There is no way of knowing in retrospect whether this was true. This was made abundantly clear in the case of one woman in a nursing home who readily identified a photograph of her former home as her most cherished possession. This 81-year-old respondent immediately pointed to the photograph, which was in a prominent place in a small standup frame on top of her dresser in a semi-private room of the nursing home. The colored photograph revealed a small, modest, one-story brick house with ample green lawn, bushes, and flowers on a corner lot in a suburban neighborhood. The house looked solid, clean, and very well cared for. Taking the photograph in her hand, this woman became quite nostalgic and said:

> My husband and I spent the happiest years of our lives in that house. It meant a great deal to us, and every time I look at this [photograph] I know I'll never forget those times. We had that house for thirty years, and the funny part of it is that we bought it as an investment. . . . We were going to make certain improvements in it and then sell it at a profit because the housing market was very strong then. Instead, we fell in love with it and came to the point where wouldn't dream of selling it.

She then went on to provide a lively rich narrative about the three decades she and her husband spent in the house. She was obviously energized by the photograph and the memories it evoked, illustrating another role and dimension of the meaning of cherished objects—as reminiscentia.

REMINISCENTIA: MEMORIAL AND RECONSTRUCTIVE ROLES OF OBJECTS

The term "reminiscentia" was used by Edward Casey (1987) in his illuminating phenomenological study of memory, entitled *Remember-*

ing, in referring to objects "that act as *inducers* of reminiscence" (p. 110) and that possess the special aptitude for arousing a reminiscent frame of mind. Gerontological practitioners who have recognized the therapeutic value of fostering reminiscence in older adults have known this for decades and have accordingly used memorabilia to stimulate reminiscence in their practice in both community and institutional settings (Weiner, Brok, & Snadowsky, 1987). The memorabilia used in this practice are not necessarily the most cherished objects, but are more often chosen to fit topics selected for specific group reminiscence sessions.

In order to see what kinds of memorabilia tend to evoke reminiscence, the senior author conducted a study that sheds light on the role of cherished objects in remembering and their effects on late-life morale (Sherman, 1991). One hundred persons ranging in age from 60 to 102 were surveyed by questionnaire and follow-up interviews. Because the sample was drawn from four senior service centers all of the respondents were living in their own homes rather than in long-term care facilities. The questionnaire was designed to elicit responses on objects identified as memorabilia, those memorabilia that were identified as cherished objects, and the frequency and types of reminiscence in which the respondents engaged. Questions were posed in the following order:

1. What kinds of objects or memorabilia (books, photos, jewelry, etc.) tend to set you to reminiscing more than others?

2. Please list and describe any personal possession(s) or object(s) that is particularly special to you or that you cherish more than any others.

3. Why does the object(s) have such special meaning to you?

The order of questions was to determine, first, the kinds of objects that served a memory-evoking function in triggering remembrances and, second, to determine which of these items were viewed as cherished objects. No prior assumptions were made that the memorabilia identified would necessarily include, or be the same as, cherished objects. This turned out to be the case. The most cherished objects were *not* generally the first memorabilia items identified. All but four people could identify at least one memorabilia object that tended to set off reminiscing more than others, and three fifths of the respondents readily identified at least two pieces of such memorabilia. In contrast, 12 people could not identify a most cherished possession, and less than half could identify two or more. A total of 184 memorabilia items and 127 cherished objects were identified. There were differences in the relative frequency with which certain items were selected as memorabilia as distinguished from cherished objects. For example, photographs were the most frequently identified as both memorabilia and cherished possession. They made up over two fifths of the memorabilia items identified but less than one quarter of the cherished objects. Photographs were the predominant memorabilia identified but jewelry was almost as frequently identified as a most cherished possession.

There was great commonality and overlap in the findings about memorabilia and cherished objects. People who could identify more than one piece of memorabilia were more likely to identify more than one cherished possession. Significantly fewer cherished objects and memorabilia items were identified by the older respondents (persons 80 years of age and older) and some patterns by gender were revealed. Women more frequently identified photographs and jewelry as both memorabilia and cherished objects than did men, and they tended to identify more cherished objects than men. Women also attributed significantly more person-related meanings to cherished objects than did men, who were more likely to cherish an object because it related to their personal values, embodied their ideals, or had intrinsic value.

Because the study was undertaken to explore the relationship between objects and reminiscence, a set of structured questionnaire items on reminiscence developed by Romaniuk and Romaniuk (1981) were employed. These authors had discovered three basic types of reminiscence: (1) pleasure/image enhancement, (2) problem solving, and (3) life review. Pleasure/image enhancement reminiscence was undertaken because: "memories are pleasant, and help to pass the time of day," "to be amusing and entertaining," and "to inform people about the successes and accomplishments in my life." Uses of problem-solving reminiscence were: "to cope with a loss in my family," "to make plans for the future," and "to deal with some difficulty I am experiencing." The life-review type involved using reminiscence: "to solve something in my past which is troubling me," "to arrive at a better understanding of my past life and myself," and "to determine life's meaning."

Considering these different types of reminiscence, it becomes apparent that they either evoke or are associated with somewhat different feelings or moods. The pleasurable nature of the first type would seem naturally to be associated with more pleasant and positive feelings than the other two. Indeed, the Affect–Balance Scale (Bradburn, 1965) revealed a significant positive relationship between the numbers of memorabilia identified and the pleasure/image-enhancement type of reminiscence. The more memorabilia identified the more people engaged in this pleasurable type of reminiscence. Memorabilia, therefore, had a significant relationship to morale; the more memorabilia the higher the affect–balance score. Although only four people did not identify a piece of memorabilia, three of these individuals recorded the lowest of all the morale scores.

Cherished objects showed a somewhat different pattern of relationships with reminiscence and morale. There was a significant relationship between the number of cherished objects and problem-solving reminiscence. Postquestionnaire interviews indicated that some respondents used cherished objects in coping with losses or other problems they were currently experiencing, or expecting to experience. This became evident in statements like: "It (the object) reminds me that I've been through this before and that I can make it" and "It gives me courage."

Cherished objects did not show as strong a positive correlation with morale as memorabilia, perhaps because they tended more often to be associated with problem-solving or life-review types of reminiscence that are not always pleasurable. However, a chi-square test showed a strong and significant association between the Affect–Balance Scale and the *lack* of a most cherished possession. This is consistent with findings from the initial objects study, which showed that lack of a most cherished object was associated with low life satisfaction (Sherman & Newman, 1977–1978).

A key finding from the second study is that the home is important as a repository for cherished possessions and memorabilia but is not apt to be identified as a most cherished object in its own right. Only 2 of the 100 respondents identified their home as their most cherished object. However, it was very evident from the interviews that their homes were not only highly valued and intimate repositories of cherished objects and memorabilia but were full of memories related to their own history and the meaning with which they imbued their lives. Cherished objects, for the most part, were not among the objects immediately identified as reminiscentia (i.e.,

among those objects or memorabilia that readily evoke reminiscence). Most cherished items were identified for reasons other than
their capacity to induce reminiscence but when they were chosen
for that reason they seemed to serve a reconstructive function. Such
cherished possessions readily triggered memories and life narratives
that other memorabilia did not seem to evoke. For example, one
woman who identified her wedding ring as her most cherished possession said: "It doesn't just remind me of him [deceased husband],
it starts a whole chain of memories that help me put things about
our past together." Overall, the findings that emerged in this second
study about relationships between objects, age, gender, and morale
seem consistent with prior research on both cherished objects and
reminiscence (Csikszentmihalyi & Rochberg-Halton, 1981; Sherman,
1991; Sherman & Newman, 1977–1978). That cherished objects and
memorabilia in general were readily identified by the large majority
of respondents in both studies and that lack of cherished objects
is associated with significantly lower morale and life satisfaction is
testament to the place of objects in the lives of older persons.

RECENT PERSPECTIVES

More recent literature on cherished objects is sparse but expanding.
The significance and association of treasured objects with the well-
being of older adults continues to be well-supported. Kampter (1991)
examined the meanings and functions of possessions across the life
span. Age-related changes identified in this study parallel Erikson's
developmental stages; the propensity of possessions to serve as
reminiscentia and markers of personal history is demonstrated to
be related to the late-life task of achieving ego-integrity.

Interest in cherished objects has extended to the health profes-
sions. Writing in an occupational therapy text, Jackson (1996) reported that among elders with disabilities who lived successfully
within their communities, objects of meaning were held as symbols
of a meaningful life. As used by the respondents, cherished possessions were displayed in prominent spaces within the home for others
to view; such objects played a significant role in breaking down
barriers among friends and neighbors and inviting connections.

Livingstone and Lunt (1991) considered people's experience of
ownership and possessions as a function of their stage in the life

cycle and generation. Within this economic and social framework, the cultural climate in which one is socialized has an effect on the experience of ownership. Attachment to objects extends beyond the phenomenological to the instrumental; it becomes a reflection and function of attitudes toward necessities, spending, debt, identity, and pleasure.

Tobin (1996) observed that cherished objects have value both for self-continuity and generational continuity. Objects are described as "bequests" to oneself, particularly when they evoke memories of a person who is deceased. Viewed in the context of legacy, valued objects provide for the continuity of generations; they become markers of coherence and embeddedness in family. In a photo-elicitation study of elder's objects of identity, Whitmore (2001) concluded that objects offered study participants two types of identity continuity: they served as concrete and enduring representations of achievements and relationships and were external embodiments of personal goals and feelings.

Extant research clearly confirms the importance of a cherished possession as more than a mere memento; rather, such an item is a link to personal identity and evocative of life's events. The reference point for cherished objects is the home, the lived space of the older adult. The significance of objects within the context of home is that it is the objects themselves that lend meaning to the dwelling. Through the objects it contains, a space is imbued with significance. This is a dynamic and nonlinear process completed over the course of the life cycle rather than during one particular stage of life (Csikszentmihalyi & Rochberg-Halton, 1981; Kampter, 1991; Rowles, Oswald, & Hunter, 2003). Cherished objects are *experienced* as meaningful rather than merely known to be meaningful; hence their usefulness as reminiscentia (Sherman, 1991). In turn the home is experienced as more than a dwelling. If, as suggested by Whitmore (2001, p. 59), objects are "embedded with the essence of life's experiences," then this idea may be expanded to include the home or dwelling.

The rich and expanding body of data on cherished possessions may have important implications for practice. Outside of a body of literature on reminiscence therapy and relocation (generally to a nursing care facility), cherished objects are rarely referred to in practice-oriented publications. When consideration is given to the topic, much of what is currently recommended to health care practitioners (nurses, social workers, physical therapists, and occupational therapists, among others) with regard to incorporating cherished objects into work with older adults is speculative and assumptive. Of particular relevance may be the role and use of cherished possessions in providing anticipatory guidance, assisting older adults to age in place, the delivery of end-of-life care in the home, and sustaining a well-balanced environment.

ANTICIPATORY GUIDANCE

Asking older adults to identify possessions they want to retain as they age under various scenarios may be the most practical way to apply empirical knowledge to practice and assist individuals in garnering the benefits of their most treasured possessions. There are many circumstances under which identifying a cherished object may be so stressful as to render the task impossible. The most notable of these is when the older adult must enter a nursing home. Although Wapner, Demick, and Redondo's (1990) research provided only limited support to the belief that cherished possessions are instrumental in adaptation to a nursing home, it has increasingly come to be considered best practice in long-term care to allow residents to take into the nursing home their prized possessions. Support for this practice arises, in part, from an effort to minimize the institutional nature of the nursing home (where the designation "home" is often a misnomer) as well as to allow the resident a sense of continuity with what was left behind. This sense of continuity is thought to aid in relocation adaptation.

Although it is believed that the older adult should make the determination of what to bring into the new environment, in reality, it is more likely to be a family member making these critical choices, or a well-intended social worker or nurse. More often than not nursing home admission constitutes a crisis for the older adult, with ill health and recent hospitalization frequently lending to the experience of duress. Significantly, the individual entering the nursing home is likely to have some loss of cognitive capacity or a dementia. Under these circumstances, without advanced planning, the choice of objects is likely to reflect the sensibilities of a family member rather than the preference of the elder. The same can be said for situations in which an individual with dementia remains at home and attempts are made to sustain a rich and meaningful environment.

One of the authors (Dacher's) personal clinical experience working in the community with individuals with dementia has shown that attempts to promote well-being through an enhanced environment are more likely to be born of creativity or intuition on the part of the clinician than knowledge of individual preference. When these attempts are seemingly successful, the indicators for success and failure (generally behaviors) are broad and subject themselves to interpretation. Although preferences indicated before a diagnosis of dementia may not be enduring, engaging in this dialogue increases the likelihood that meaningful choices will be made. In circumstances where family members are asked to participate in lieu of the individual, there is always the risk that the objects identified are those *they* hope will have meaning; such choices are quite possibly a reflection of the family member's own need in a time of crisis. The extent to which this occurs is not known, and the potential benefits of promoting guidance and participation on the part of the older adult are yet to be realized.

A practice model that supports anticipatory guidance for older adults in all realms is both challenging and compelling from the perspective of the older adult and the practitioner. As evidenced by research on advanced directives, most individuals do not plan for the eventualities of aging (Hopp, 2000). In turn, health care practitioners are often reluctant and ill-prepared to discuss difficult topics such as dementia and death. Yet, a strong research-based argument can be made in favor of asking individuals to identify objects of importance and moving beyond the speculative nature of current practice. An inquiry as simple as, "If you had to leave your home what cherished possessions would you take with you?" could provide guidance. In the case of an absence of any cherished object, the practitioner will have an indicator of the baseline well-being of the individual and may be presented with an opportunity for intervention. Such a model would lie outside of the confines of the traditional medical model and perhaps be placed within a model of integrative care that is more sensitive to the nuances of persons' lives within lived space.

AGING IN PLACE

Aging in place or remaining in one's own home and community despite growing frailty implies that the individual will allow modification of his or her environment to improve person–environment fit (Pastalan, 1990; Silverstone & Horowitz, 1992). Aging in place is based on concepts of preference and self-determination: It is grounded in the preservation of identity and recognition of the perceived value of home. Home modifications described in the literature tend to be focused on the physical needs and abilities of the individual and are most likely implemented to promote home safety and optimal physical functioning. Practice in the community to support aging in place is oriented toward the same—physical and functional well-being supercede other considerations. Among home care workers ingrained practice behavior guides what one does on entering a home for the first time: Look for the red flags of hazard and remove them, no questions asked! Gilson (1997) cautions the social worker to remain focused on client-centered goals rather than the tasks of accommodation and adjustment when they encounter the individual who persistently refuses home modification and chooses to age in place on his or her own terms.

Fear of environmental hazard is great. Consequently, homes are frequently identified as potentially dangerous, threatening, and in need of alteration. This is especially evidenced in the literature describing fall prevention in the home, where environmental hazard is noted to contribute to risk, as in the literature promoted by the National Center for Injury Prevention and Control (Preboth, 2000). Practice wisdom among home care professionals advises making a home risk free to the greatest extent possible, the focus being on the physical characteristics of the home devoid of any other context including how the environment is experienced by the older adult. These risks are certainly profound. Carter, Campbell, Sanson-Fisher, Redman, and Gillespie (1997) found that among the homes of a population of older adults in Australia only one home in five was hazard free. But rather than regard this as in indicator of high risk, they acknowledge the lack of benchmarks as to what constitutes a hazardous home.

The extent to which the home is considered ripe for alteration in the name of safety and physical function and the need to support aging in place with necessary alterations is not in question. When the alternative environment for aging is the nursing home or assistive living facility, home often remains the most desirable alternative. Although the literature on aging in place refers to the value of home in theory there is little information to support a practice of active identification and preservation of the essential components that give meaning to home. In part this may be attributed to the prevailing belief that it is the ability to remain in the space itself that is important and beneficial, rather than the elements (or objects) that are contained in and constitute the space. Indeed, one may ask if the very notion of aging in place is called into question when significant alterations are made to the home environment without first establishing a context for assessing how the space is experienced by the older adult.

HOME, ILLNESS, AND THE END OF LIFE

The emerging trend for terminally ill persons to remain at home and receive care in familiar and comforting surroundings creates yet another possibility for considering the importance of cherished objects in practice. Although such circumstances for care are often designed to be palliative rather than highly medically interventional, the fact remains that the home itself may be transformed from a known environment to one that is more like a hospital both in appearance and in the manner in which it is experienced.

Physical comfort may be supported with hospital beds, commodes, oxygen, and intravenous equipment; to accommodate this furniture, objects are displaced, sometimes with no more thought than to get them out of the way! Amidst the restructuring of the home the person who is dying may find that elements of the environment that are personally most important are now far removed. Under such circumstances it is useful to be reminded of how critical personal possessions may be for the individual facing the end of life. The ritualistic function of personal objects in reiterating a person's core meanings, identities, and roles offers an opportunity for therapeutic intervention (Rubinstein, 1987). Applying the notion that certain possessions guarantee "ontological security" (de Beauvoir, 1973, p. 699) is especially promising because one of the greatest risks for dying individuals is to lose their core identity as they become the disease they suffer from. The continuing presence of cherished objects offers the individual an opportunity for reminiscence and support for ego-integrity, a means of continuing to invite connections, even in the face of an inevitable end. The benefits extend to caregivers as they are presented with evidence of a life that extends beyond the context of the disease. There is a need to challenge the current interpretation of what is needed and what it means to provide an effective environment for end-of-life care at home.

COMPONENTS OF A WELL-BALANCED ENVIRONMENT

As the perspective of what constitutes healthy aging is increasingly defined through the lens of physical function and productivity, a case can be made for extending the findings of the research on cherished objects and identifying their role as a component or marker of healthy aging. Less overt than physical prowess and perhaps less socially valued, attachment to cherished objects is clearly identified as a marker of well-being for older adults. The value of this is not to be underestimated in the face of increasing longevity and the certainty of concomitant physical limitations.

A well-balanced environment for aging is inclusive of many elements. Such a place may promote place attachment, offer the presence of special possessions that, despite not offering an obvious benefit toward promoting physical function or home safety, are highly valued, contain elements of universal and safe design, and facilitate a sense of control by the older adult. Although safety is critical to long-term survival in the community, an enriched experience of the home requires more. The case of a 76-year-old woman who returned to her home following rehabilitation for bilateral hip replacement offers some insight to the importance of cherished objects in giving meaning to the home, even when that space is constantly shrinking (Dacher, 1997). Faced with relocation from an 11-room farmhouse to a 20 × 20 foot cottage this person was able to focus on all that her new space contained rather than all that was lost. She names the space her "Dowager's Cottage" as if to commemorate a space filled with her beloved bed, photos, books and games; all evidence of a life to which she remains connected. Her connection to the space through each item is evidenced by the way she picks up an object and explains its significance; the pure physicality of her relationship to each item speaks louder than the words themselves. Within this context cherished possessions are markers of morale while simultaneously enhancing it. Each is an important element of a well-balanced environment for aging.

CONCLUSIONS

Research on cherished objects, once applied to practice, offers an opportunity for practitioners to become progressive and rethink traditional ways of looking at markers of healthy aging, preparing for old age, aging in place, and creating a balanced environment for aging. Further research is needed, particularly in the areas of anticipatory guidance for individuals with dementia and creating an appropriate and enriched environment for end-of-life care at home. Finally, we need to develop practice models that consider ways to make practitioners aware of this body of research and its potential for application to practice.

REFERENCES

Bradburn, N. M. (1965). *The structure of well being.* Chicago: Aldine.

Carp, G. (1966). *A future for the aged: Victoria Plaza and its residents.* Austin, TX: University of Texas Press.

Carter, S., Campbell, E., Sanson-Fisher, R., Redman, S., & Gillespie, W. (1997). Environmental hazards in the homes of older people. *Age and Aging, 26,* 195–204.

Casey, E. S. (1987). *Remembering: A phenomenological study.* Bloomington, IN: University of Indiana Press.

Csikszentmihalyi, M., & Rochberg-Halton, E. (1981). *The meaning of things: Domestic symbols and the self.* New York: Cambridge University Press.

Dacher, J. (1997). Older women's narratives of aging, disability, and participation in a rehabilitation program: A phenomenological study of lived experience. Doctoral dissertation, State University of New York at Albany.

de Beauvoir, S. (1973). *The coming of age.* New York: Warner.

Frankl, V. (1955). *The doctor and the soul.* New York: Bantam Books.

Gilson, S. (1997). When people with pre-existing disabilities age in place: Implications for social work practice. *Health and Social Work, 22,* 290–298.

Goffman, E. (1961). *Asylums: Essays on the social situation of mental patients and other inmates.* Garden City, NY: Anchor Books.

Hopp, F. (2002). Preferences for surrogate decision makers, informal communication and advance directives among community-dwelling elders: Results from a national study. *Gerontologist, 40*, 449–457.

Jackson, J. (1996). Living a meaningful existence in old age. In R. Zemke & F. Clark (Eds.), *Occupational science the evolving discipline.* Philadelphia: F. A. Davis.

Kampter, N. (1991). Personal possessions and their meanings: A life-span perspective. *Journal of Social Behavior and Personality, 6*, 209–228.

Lewis, M. J., & Butler, R. N. (1974) Life review therapy: Putting memories to work in individual and group psychotherapy. *Geriatrics, 29*, 165–169, 172–173.

Livingstone, S., & Lunt, P. (1991). Generational and life cycle differences in experiences of ownership. *Journal of Social Behavior and Personality, 6*, 229–242.

Neugarten, B., Havighurst, R., & Tobin, S. (1961). The measurement of life satisfaction. *Journal of Gerontology, 16*, 134–143.

Pastalan, L. (1990). Aging in place: The role of housing and social supports, *Journal of Housing for the Elderly, 6*, ix–xii.

Preboth, M. (2000). Brochure on the prevention of falls in the elderly. *American Family Physician, 62*, 886.

Romaniuk, M., & Romaniuk, J. G. (1981). Looking back: An analysis of reminiscence functions and triggers. *Experimental Aging Research, 7*, 477–489.

Rowles, G. D., Oswald, F., & Hunter, E. G. (2003). Interior living environments in old age. In H-W. Wahl, R. J. Scheidt, & P. G. Windley (Eds.), *Annual review of gerontology and geriatrics* (Vol. 23, pp.167–194). New York: Springer Publishing Co.

Rubinstein, R. (1987). The significance of personal objects to older people. *Journal of Aging Studies, 1*, 225–238.

Sherman, E. (1991). Reminiscentia: Cherished objects as memorabilia in late-life reminiscence. *International Journal of Aging and Human Development, 33*, 89–100.

Sherman, E., & Newman, E. S. (1977–1978). The meaning of cherished possessions for the elderly. *International Journal of Aging and Human Development, 8*, 181–192.

Silverstone, B. M., & Horowitz, A. (1992). Aging in place: The role of families. *Generations, 16*, 27–30.

Tobin, S. (1996). Cherished possessions: The meaning of things. *Generations, 20*, 46–49.

Wapner, S., Demick, J., & Redondo, J. P. (1990). Cherished possessions and adaptation of older people to nursing homes. *International Journal of Aging and Human Development, 31*, 219–235.

Weiner, M. B., Brok, A. J., & Snadowsky, A. M. (1987) *Working with the aged: Practical approaches in the institution and community.* Englewood Cliffs, NJ: Prentice-Hall.

Whitmore, H.(2001). Value that marketing cannot manufacture: Cherished possessions as links to identity and wisdom. *Generations, 25*, 57–63.

Winnicott, D. W. (1971). *Playing and reality.* New York: Basic Books.

CHAPTER 5

Home in the Context of Religion for Elderly Hindus in India

Sanjoy Mazumdar and Shampa Mazumdar

The meaning of home in the lives of people has been the subject of extensive scholarly inquiry (Altman & Werner, 1985; Dovey, 1985; Hummon, 1989; Marcus, 1974, 1992; Rowles, 1983). According to Relph (1976, p. 43):

> [T]here is for virtually everyone a deep association with and consciousness of the places where we were born and grew up, where we live now or where we have had particularly moving experiences. This association seems to constitute a vital source of both individual and cultural identity and security.

There is "bonding," "connectedness," and "rootedness" between "person and place" and between "dweller and dwelling" (Relph, 1976; Tuan, 1987, pp. 280–281). Spaces within the home are "appropriated" and "personalized" (Dovey, 1985; Korosec-Serfaty, 1985); objects are invested with symbolic meaning connected with past memories and experiences (Belk, 1992; Csikszentmihalyi & Rochberg-Halton, 1981).

> Precisely because of their highly personal nature, however, such domestic symbols may be particularly important: they have the

capacity and bear the strain of carrying the individual's personal sense of self through time—of providing a symbolic life line to a continuous sense of identity (Hummon, 1989, p. 219).

MEANING OF HOME THROUGH THE LIFE COURSE

Several authors have examined the links between attachment and emotional connections to home for those early in the life course, namely, children (see, for example, Chawla, 1992; Marcus, 1992). The focus of Marcus's (1992, p. 89) study was attachment and emotional connections to childhood homes and how "childhood memories of certain places" act as a "kind of psychic anchor reminding us of where we came from, of what we once were or of how the environment nurtured us when family dynamics were strained."

The experience and meaning of home for teenagers and youth has not received as much attention (for exceptions see Korosec-Serfaty, 1985; Korpela, 1992), and so not much is known about their connections with their home environments.

Attachment to place for elders and how such attachment gets "intimately linked to a preservation of a sense of personal identity" is explored by Rowles (1983, p. 300; 1984), who points out that home is the "fulcrum" of the world for elders and they "cognitively differentiate the physical environment into zones of decreasing intensity of involvement away from their homes" (Rowles, 1984, p. 143). "Emotional attachment," according to Rowles (1984, p. 146) is "closely linked to the concept of *insideness*" which involves:

> First, a sense of physical insideness, of being almost psychologically melded into the environment, results from an intimacy with its physical configuration stemming from the rhythm and routine of using the space over many years. . . . Second, emotional attachment to proximate space is enhanced by a social insideness that evolves not only from everyday social exchanges and relationships but also from a sense of being known well and knowing others. . . . Third, and most important, places assume meaning as foci of an autobiographical insideness grounded in personal history. (Rowles, 1984, pp. 146–147).

Connections between place and elders have been studied also by Rubinstein and Parmelee (1992) and Sugihara and Evans (2000).

Rubinstein and Parmelee (1992, p. 140) suggest that the attachment of elders to places of the past helps to "keep the past alive" and maintain "a sense of continuity," whereas "attachment to a current place may act as a buffer, a means of retaining a positive self image" as well as a means of asserting independence.

The concept of life course is not new[1] and though not directly related to progression in age, is implicit in descriptions of connections to environments of particular age-related sets, such as children, youth, adults, or elders, as exemplified in the previous descriptions. The bulk of the literature in environmental design research has either focused explicitly on the connections to places for adults or neglected to specify the point in the life course of the study population (Feldman, 1990; Mazumdar & Mazumdar, 1993; Proshansky, Fabian, & Kaminoff, 1983). Such studies have failed to point out how people–place connections are likely to change over the life course. Though studies are scant, the life course idea has been explicitly used by a few researchers of elders and space (Rubinstein & Parmelee, 1992). We shall return to this concept later.

ELDERS AND RELIGION

The literature on elders and religion reveals that religion is important to older people (Ainlay & Smith, 1984; Gray & Moberg, 1977; Hooyman & Kiyak, 1988; Mindel & Vaughan, 1978). Gray and Moberg (1977, p. 74) point out that to elders "their faith gives them happiness and comfort, contributing to their personal adjustment and life satisfaction, and it apparently reduces the fear of death" (see also Becker, 2002). Hooyman and Kiyak (1988, p. 422) report that "[a]cross the life span, church and synagogue attendance is lowest among those in their thirties, peaks in the late fifties to early sixties (with approximately 60 percent of this age group attending), and begins to decline in the late sixties or early seventies." This decline in church attendance, attributed primarily to health and transportation difficulties (Gray & Moberg, 1977; Hooyman & Kiyak, 1988), does not indicate an overall decline in religiosity (Hooyman & Kiyak, 1988; Hunsberger, 1985).

Examination of engagement in activities of organized religion is only one way to understand religiosity. Although participation in organized religion declines with age after 60, religiosity is reinforced and continually expressed through personal practices, such as "regular listening to church services and other religious broadcasts on radio and television, reading from the Bible at least weekly, prayer, meditation, and other personal and private devotional activities" (Gray & Moberg, 1977, p. 63). The many dimensions of religious participation are pointed out in the text that follows:

> Religious behaviors can be examined in terms of three factors: (1) participation in religious organizations, (2) the personal meaning of religion and religious activities within the home, and (3) the contribution of religion to individuals' adjustment to the aging process and their confrontation with death and dying (Hooyman & Kiyak, 1988, p. 422).

These important points are sometimes neglected in the study of religiosity. Indeed, church-going activities have received much research attention. However, it is useful to distinguish between organized and institutionalized religion and noninstitutional religion. Often neglected in the preceding approach are religions without a formal church hierarchy and ones that emphasize home-based practice (Mazumdar & Mazumdar, 1993, 1997a, 1997b). It is essential to differentiate between community-oriented religion enacted in the presence of a congregation in congregational public sacred spaces (such as churches, mosques, temples, and synagogues), and personal, home-based religion, which is individual and/or familial, involving family altars, shrines, and icons. This is not equivalent to a distinction between formal and informal religion because formal religion can be home-based (Mazumdar & Mazumdar, 1993; Pavlides & Hesser, 1989) and informal religious activities can be performed in the presence of a congregation in public sacred space (Mazumdar & Mazumdar, 1997c). Even though several researchers have pointed out that the home forms an important setting for religious lives (Mazumdar, 1998; Mazumdar & Mazumdar, 1993, 1994a, 1994b, 1997a, 1997b, 1997d; McDannell, 1986; Pavlides & Hesser, 1989), practice of religion at a personal level and in the home has been overlooked. How religion affects the architecture of the home has been covered for Hindu homes (Mazumdar & Mazumdar, 1994b, 1997d), Christian homes (McDannell, 1986; Pavlides & Hesser, 1989), Islamic/Muslim homes (Mazumdar & Mazumdar, 1994a), and Zoroastrian homes (Mazumdar & Mazumdar, 1997a). How home as sacred space and as the locus of sacred artifacts, rituals, and events defines and moulds the experiences of elders has also been neglected (Eliade, 1959; Raglan, 1964; Rapoport, 1982).

ELDERS, RELIGION, AND HOME

Using the conceptual lens of home as setting for the practice of religion and religious activities, and home as sacred space and repository of sacred artifacts (see also Mazumdar & Mazumdar, 1993, 1994b, 1999) we wish to understand home in the context of religion in the lives of elders. We focus on the private, domestic, personal, and devotional aspect of the religious lives of elders through a study of the Hindu home in India. We seek to understand how religious ideas, practices, rituals, and prayer influence the lives of elders, and give them meaning, purpose and acceptance of their life course.[2] In the following section we describe the relationship between home, religion, and the elder in the case of Hindus[3] in India.

HOME, RELIGION, AND THE HINDU ELDER IN INDIA

Religion and the Hindu Elder

Religion takes on special significance in the lives of elder Hindus in several ways. From a philosophical standpoint, Hinduism establishes a close relationship between religion and aging. Hindu philosophy conceptualizes and views life ideally as being composed of four important *ashramas*, that is, "life stages" or "life stations" (Radhakrishnan, 1927, p. 59). In the life-stage conceptualization and philosophical schema of Hinduism, though age is an important consideration, it is the role associated with that stage in life that is critical. Each stage has associated roles and tasks in which a Hindu is expected to engage (Bhaskarananda, 1994, p. 29). Both males and females are encouraged and expected to have different relationships with the environment, space, home, family, and society at the different life stages.

Life Stages in Hinduism

The first major life stage is that of *Brahmacharya* or student. It is associated with childhood and youth, is the student stage and is dedicated to education and study. In this stage, people are not expected to have major responsibilities except for learning and gaining knowledge and skills. In this stage a person is expected to explore the environment, learn from parents and elders about appropriate relationships, and form their own relationships.

The second stage is that of *Grihastha (Garhasthya)*,[4] a householder or family person. Commonly associated with young adults, in this stage Hindu men and women engage in marriage, procreation, work, worldliness, acquisition of material property, and seek material success. Home–family relationships as well as work–work relationships are of primary importance. This is the stage of intense and direct bonds between people and environmental components, of attachments to places, things, and worldly possessions. However, this stage is not seen as degrading: "Marriage is not so much a concession to human weakness as a means of spiritual growth" (Radhakrishnan, 1927, p. 60).

Vanaprasthya, the third stage is that of a retired person or contemplator. This station is commonly engaged during late adulthood to early old age, and involves retirement, reflection, contemplation, and slow withdrawal from the worldly focus of the previous stage. As Hindus approach middle age and their children marry and have their own children, it is considered time to gradually engage in spiritual and religious growth, prayer, meditation, and pilgrimage, and slowly disengage from worldly pursuits. This is a "period of retreat for the loosening of the social bonds" (Radhakrishnan, 1927, p. 59). Intense attachment to things and personal possessions and ownership bonds are slowly reduced. It is not uncommon for those at this stage to give their belongings to their children. Many obtain vicarious pleasure from observing their children enjoying what they once enjoyed. Some go on pilgrimages, experiencing the multifaceted sites of Hindu sacred geography ranging from natural phenomena, such as the Ganges in Benaras, where they take ritual purificatory baths, to praying at the majestic and/or significant temples of Puri and Kanyakumari, or birthplaces of holy men and women, such as Ramakrishna Paramahansa, Sarada Ma, Swami Vivekananda, and others.

Sannyasa, the fourth stage is that of a monk or ascetic. This is a stage of disengagement. Expected later in old age, this station emphasizes disengagement from the material world and increasingly deep engagement of the spiritual. This, in part, involves renunciation of dependence on materials things. More important, "renunciation is the surrendering of the notions of I and mine, and not the giving up of the work enjoined by the scriptures" points out Radhakrishnan (1927, p. 65). The elder is expected to submerge the ego, the I, and the me in the context of the home, the family, and society. They recognize the role and the *ashramas* of the next generation and their needs and claim to the expectations of that stage. Some elders retire, sell their property, and relocate to a sacred city; Benaras is a favorite destination. Here, they spend their time immersed in the sacred sights, sounds, and rituals of the city, awaiting their death with dignity and/or preparing themselves for "spiritual liberation" (Bhaskarananda, 1994, p. 36; Eck, 1981). Other elders remain at home but make significant lifestyle changes, adopting a minimalist perspective, minimizing their needs, desires, food, dress, and expenses. They are expected to hand over the management of day-to-day domestic affairs to the next generation and retire to a life of frugality, humility, prayer, and meditation. Achieving these idolized stations is fraught with difficulties of disengagement and renunciation and not without failures (Vatuk, 1980). The spirit of the stages, especially the latter two, is contained in the following explanation:

> Hinduism does not mistake tolerance for indifference. It affirms that while all revelations refer to reality, they are not equally true to it. Hinduism requires every man to think steadily on life's mystery until he reaches the highest revelation. While the lesser forms are tolerated in the interests of those who cannot suddenly transcend them, there is all through an insistence on the larger idea and the purer worship. Hinduism does not believe in forcing up the pace of development. (Radhakrishnan, 1927, p. 36)

This personal search for the "highest revelation" is the important driving force, though it is moderated by a sense of different levels and forms of achievement based on one's stage and developed capacity, which affects the major variations in the different stages. Radhakrishnan also points to the nature of the religion, the role of self-examination and self-development, and personal meditation.

These expectations apply to both men and women. From the perspective of enactment of rituals, however, women's activities change with age. For Hindu women, menopause signals a change in ritual status. Menstrual and postpartum discharges are considered ritually unclean and so menstruating and postpartum women do not participate in sacred rituals. They do not go to temple, nor do they take care of their domestic shrines during those days. Menopause frees a Hindu woman from these restrictions, making it possible for her to continue ritual duties and responsibilities without interruption and even take on additional ones. She no longer has to disengage from religion for a while every month.

Cultural mores change with station in life, particularly for women. Traditionally, religious and cultural mores imposed several social restrictions on widows (Mazumdar & Mazumdar, 2002). On becoming a widow a woman could no longer have an active social life, at least in public, which meant that her mobility outside the home was circumscribed. Rather, she was encouraged to further disengage and spend more time on selfless pursuits. Religion, religious ritual, discourse, prayer, fasting, and meditation took on additional importance for them. Much of this continues, though many have chosen to change from tradition.

Elder Hindus: Custodians of Faith

Hindu elders are the primary custodians of domestic religion, its sacred spaces, artifacts, festivals, and rituals. Though temples are many, and temple visits are important, Hinduism is essentially a noncongregational religion unlike Judaism, Christianity, and Islam. Hindus are not required to participate in prescribed congregational prayer on mandated days and times. Home-based, private religion takes precedence over temple-based, public religion, and constitutes the core of a Hindu's beliefs, practices, and identity.

Unlike in the earlier life stages, religion plays an increasingly important role in the lives of elder Hindus. They spend time in meditation, self-examination and in attempting to achieve personal salvation and oneness with God. They place greater emphasis on enacting religious requirements as completely and properly as possible. Regular prayer and ritual activities take on greater significance. As described in the following text, this involves creation of sacred space, maintenance of sacred space, cultivation of sacred plants, and performance of sacred rituals.

Creation of Sacred Space—Characteristics and Content

Located in the Hindu home is the *pooja* (shrine/worship) space as exemplified in the following: "We have a special *puja* room—room in the house for worship" (Pandurang, 1972, p. 45; see also Mazumdar & Mazumdar, 1993), and "On the ground floor of mother's establishment was our *pooja* room" (Mazumdar, 1977, p. 32). This in effect becomes the temple of the home (Raglan, 1964), and makes the home a sacred space.

The *pooja* area is the most sacred space within the Hindu house (Mazumdar & Mazumdar, 1993, 1994b, 1999). In old and large family houses, the family shrine is located in a separate room. It is usually located in a secluded space where the chances of ritual contamination and defilement are reduced. The room at the top of the stairs is a preferred space as it is the highest place in the house. In smaller and more modern houses, some households locate their *pooja* space in the kitchen, bedroom, alcove, corner, or closet (Mazumdar & Mazumdar, 1994b, 1997d, 2003).

The *pooja* area is where the household deities are enshrined. Each family honors its own primary deity (*kuladeva*). The *pooja* area is also the repository of the family's religious and sacred artifacts, as evident in the following descriptions: "Lord Venkateshwara's picture occupies the place of honor because he has a special position in our house, but we also keep statues of other gods in the cabinet in the corner" (Pandurang, 1972, p. 45). And: "On its faded saffron walls were pictures by Ravi Varma [a renowned artist], colour prints of various gods and goddesses with gilt frames tarnished by time" (Mazumdar, 1977, p. 32).

In the *pooja* room are kept ritual objects and artifacts used in daily prayer and meditation. There are brass and silver lamps, incense sticks, incense holders, *shankha* (conch shell), a stone slab and sandalwood for making fresh sandalwood paste, prayer beads, a basket for holding fresh picked flowers, silver and copper vessels for making ritual offerings (Mazumdar, 1977; Mazumdar & Mazumdar, 1993, p. 237).

Maintenance of Sacred Space—Activities

Hindus believe that the *pooja* room should be maintained clean. Maintaining ritual cleanliness requires its contents to be meticulously cleaned daily in order to maintain its ritually pure status. Specifically, this includes dusting and wiping clean the altar and ritual objects, cleaning and swabbing the floor with water, removing incense, ash, and wilted flowers; discarding the old wicks and oil or *ghee* in brass and silver lamps, polishing the lamp using tamarind pulp, and adding fresh wicks and oil or *ghee* (see Mazumdar & Mazumdar, 1994b). During daily prayers fresh flowers are offered and incense and lamps are lit.

Maintenance of the ritually pure condition is aided by behavioral rules involving cleanliness: "No one was allowed to enter this sacred room with unclean clothes, and leather footwear had to be left outside the doors" (Mazumdar, 1977, p. 32). In addition to maintaining sacred space in a ritually clean state, the tasks also include taking care of the space, performing sacred rituals, and acquiring and transmitting religious knowledge.

Maintenance and upkeep of the *pooja* area in a ritually clean state requires daily attention and care. The female elder of the household is primarily responsible for maintenance of the *pooja* area, a task to which, aided by junior members, she dedicates her time and energy. Family elders, thus, perform important ritual tasks assigned to priests in temples.

Cultivation of Sacred Plants—Activities

In the Hindu home, practice of religion requires the daily offering of fresh flowers and fruits, and involves the selection, planting, and nurturance of ritually significant flowers, fruits, shrubs, plants, and trees. Hindu elders take active interest in the care and upkeep of their gardens, often personally tending to specific plants. Flowers used in daily prayers/offerings, such as roses, hibiscus, marigolds, gardenias, and different varieties of jasmine, are planted and grown. The following is a description of a garden:

> *Dadu* (maternal grandfather) and *Didima* (maternal grandmother) had planted many different plants that were used in *pooja*. There

were radiant red and pink *jobas* (hibiscus), the very fragrant *beli phool* (pikake), *gandhoraj* (gardenia), and *genda phool* (marigold). There were many varieties of red roses which were *Dadu*'s pride and joy and which he tended to every evening. There also were oleander trees, plumeria trees, and the delicate orange-stemmed *sheuli* whose blossoms heralded the autumn festival of Durga *pooja*. Every morning, *Didima*, after her purificatory bath, would go into the garden to pick fresh flowers for her daily *pooja*. Walking barefeet, holding her ornate brass *shaaji* (flower container) she would go from plant to plant in search of the best freshly opened blooms. She particularly liked finding double-petaled pink *jobas*. Flowers had to be picked off the plant; those lying on the ground were not used in *pooja*. (AEN)[5]

The plant most commonly found in Hindu households is the sacred *tulsi* (or *tulasi*) (*Ocymum Sanctum*) plant. In some households it is placed on a raised platform to set it apart from the more common and to avoid it becoming polluted. Several rituals involve this plant:

> [P]ious old men and women water the plant after their bath every-day, sip a little water from its root, decorate their forehead with a bit of its sacred clay. . . . Every evening a candle (prepared out of torn cloth and soaked with oil) is lit (Das, 1965, p. 25).

These rituals involving sacred plants may vary:

> After the *puja* for Lord Venkateshwara I do a *tulasi puja* every morning. The *tulasi* is a sacred plant. We have one—the one I worship—in a pot next to the kitchen, and another in the garden. When I do the *tulasi puja* I fold my hands and turn two, five or nine times to the right. . . . After circling, I take a leaf of *tulasi* together with some water (Pandurang, 1972, p. 46).

Other trees considered sacred and planted in Hindu households are mango, coconut, banana, and *Asvatta* (*Ficus Religiosa*). Mango leaves are used in many sacred rituals, especially on auspicious occasions, such as birth, marriage, and festival days:

> [M]ango leaves are strung above the front door, the door into the kitchen, and the door of the *puja* room. They are left until the next festival, but no matter how long it is the leaves always seem to add a clean fresh atmosphere to the house (Pandurang, 1972, p. 47).

Some trees such as the *neem* (margosa) are planted for their medicinal properties.

> The oil extracted from the fruit of *Neem* tree, possesses much medicinal value. The temperature of the patient goes down if the oil is applied to his head and the lower part of the feet. Its flowers have the properties of blood purification when used as syrup. The soap made out of it cures skin disease and its toothpaste is used for cleansing the teeth (Upadhyaya, 1965, p. 6).

Because of their experiential knowledge of plants family elders play an important role in making decisions about which varieties to cultivate and for what purpose, be it ritual, medicinal, or environmental.

PERFORMANCE OF SACRED RITUALS

The Hindu household is the setting for the enactment of many sacred rituals. These can be categorized into two sets: personal individualized rituals and communal congregational rituals.

Personal Individualized Rituals

The rituals performed in the *pooja* area constitute the core of daily prayer and worship. In Hinduism, deities enshrined in the *pooja* area are treated as revered guests and the *pooja* rituals include symbolic hospitality rituals (Eck, 1981; Ramaswamy & Ramaswamy, 1993). These are personal and individual prayers and rituals. Each family member performs prayers at the family altar on a daily basis.

Though each person performs his/her personal set of rituals, it is the family elder who is in charge of the elaborate, daily *pooja*s for the family. This involves following an ordered sequence of steps using all senses—sight (*darsan* or viewing the deity), touch (cleaning the altar), smell (offering colorful and fragrant flowers), sound (ringing bells and chanting mantras), and taste (eating consecrated food, *prasaad*) (Eck, 1981, p. 9).

In some Hindu households it is the matriarch (the elder female) who is not only the principal caretaker of the *pooja* area but also responsible for the performance of this entire set of *pooja* rituals. It involves bathing or cleaning the deities, anointing them with tumeric, vermillion and sandalwood paste, offering fresh flowers, and *prasaad* (food and water), lighting *dhoop* (incense), *deewa* (lamps), and singing *bhajans* (devotional songs). The matriarch may also meditate using prayer beads and/or read from the sacred scriptures. Her *pooja* rituals now complete she does *pranaam* (body prostration) and then distributes *prasaad* (consecrated food) to family members (Eck, 1981; Ramaswamy & Ramaswamy, 1993).

In other households the male head of household (often the elder male) performs the daily *pooja* rituals.

> In the morning the heart is pure and uncontaminated by the worries of the day, so this is the time we offer our prayers. I prepare the *puja* room the night before for my husband. He is the master of the house and he does the most elaborate *puja*—it takes him nearly half an hour each day. He offers flowers, lights, lamps of ghee, and recites the 108 names of Lord Venkateshwara (Pandurang, 1972, p. 45).

In addition to the *poojas* performed daily, on certain days of the week special *poojas* are conducted to honor specific deities.

> On Tuesdays and Fridays I pray to Lakshmi the goddess of wealth, as well as to Lord Venkateshwara. Only women worship her in our family (Pandurang, 1972, p. 46).

An ethnographic study found similar practices in Bengali households:

> On Tuesdays, Thursdays, and Saturdays, one does the weekly worship of various deities: Narayan, Laksmi, and Soni. The Thursday worship, that of Laksmi, is performed by most households in which there are married women. Though the worship is quite simple, preparation for it requires time and effort: The worship room must be cleaned and the deity washed, garlanded, and dressed before the ritual is actually performed (Fruzzetti, 1982, p. 101).

Most of these *poojas* performed at home rely on the ritual expertise of family elders and do not usually require the specialized services of religious functionaries and intermediaries such as *purohits* (priests).

Congregational Rituals

Congregational domestic rituals transcend the boundaries of immediate family and bring together extended kin, friends, and neighbors
(Mazumdar & Mazumdar, 1999). One such religious event is Satya
Narayan Pooja, celebrated periodically in individual homes. The
following is an example:

> Satya Narayan Pooja was celebrated in Didima's house. This re-
> quired elaborate planning, organization, preparation, and clean-
> ing. First, *Didima* consulted the family *purohit* (priest) to select a
> ritually appropriate time and date. The *purohit* supplied her with
> a list of ritual items and artifacts needed for the *pooja*. Second,
> she invited her extended family (those who lived in the same
> town), friends, and neighbors to join her in this collective prayer.
> Third, using the list provided by the priest she later completed
> the purchases by going to several stores. Fourth, on the scheduled
> day, *Didima* prepared the setting, transforming ordinary space
> into ritually appropriate space. The living room was used for this
> purpose. The furniture was rearranged and some of it removed
> to make room for the invited congregation to sit on the floor and
> participate in the prayers. The room was swept clean and mopped.
> After the cleaning, *Didima* set up a shrine for *pooja*. Fifth, she
> prepared and arranged the items needed in the *pooja*. She washed
> the fruits thoroughly, cut or sliced them, and meticulously ar-
> ranged them on special plates reserved solely for such religious
> events. She prepared special sweets and put them on a separate
> plate. Flowers, leaves, and *dhurva* grass blades were arranged as
> required. She organized all other offerings and ritual items, such
> as lamps, incense, water containers, *ganga jal* (water from the
> river Ganges), camphor, *shankha* (conch shell) in front of the
> shrine. On completing all tasks for preparation she waited for the
> priest and guests to arrive (AEN).

Congregational religious events also include *pooja* to other deities such as Durga, Lakshmi (goddess of wealth) and Saraswati (goddess of knowledge). Several congregational religious events have
heavier or exclusive participation by one set of people, such as
females. Some life-cycle rituals, in particular those related to birth
and marriage, are celebrated at home and emphasize the important
role of the women's community. In Bengal, it is the role of women
to conduct the greeting and departing rituals involved in marriage
ceremonies. These are called *stri achar*s (women's rituals) and do

not require the assistance of priests (Fruzzetti, 1982; Mazumdar & Mazumdar, 1999; Mazumdar, 1977).

LEARNING AND TEACHING THE SACRED

Learning the Sacred

As Hindu men and women age they devote more time to learning about religion and engaging in spiritual pursuits. To do this, some choose a *guru*, a religious teacher and mentor, who instructs, informs, and interprets religion for his/her disciple. The initiate often visits his/her *guru* to obtain *diksha* (knowledge or wisdom), acquire proficiency in ritual, dogma, and philosophy, to learn special *mantras* (prayers), to ask for clarification, and to listen to religious discourse. Others search for knowledge on their own, attending lectures, reading scriptures, such as the *Bhagavad Gita* and its interpretations, and biographies of important religious teachers, saints, and philosophers.

> *Didima* did not have a guru. But she was a voracious reader. She spent many hours in the afternoon and/or evening reading the complete works of Swami Vivekananda (AEN).

Meditation is an integral part of Hinduism. Through meditation an individual acquires self-control, self-discipline, and self-knowledge. It becomes a spiritual pursuit for many. Meditation helps them find answers to important questions, such as the meaning of life. For elders, meditation becomes a significant part of their religious growth and maturity and helps in the *Vanaprastha* stage "to let go" and become disattached to material things:

> As my father grew older, he spent more and more time in trying to understand the meaning of life and preparing for after-life. This led him to teach himself meditation. At first it was difficult for him to sit still and empty his mind for an extended period of time. He would often get up after 10–15 minutes. Slowly, over time, he could meditate for an hour and around the time of his death at the age of 69 he could meditate for 2 to 2.5 hours. When asked why he meditated, his simple answer was "to prepare myself for peaceful death" (AEN).

Teaching the Sacred

Elders play a vital role in the formal and informal transmission of religious knowledge. This is in part due to the organizational structure of Hinduism, which is markedly different from the Judeo-Christian tradition with regard to formalized religious instruction. In Hinduism, there is no equivalent of religious or Sunday School and so children are not sent to religious school to attend formalized religious classes on a regular basis. Temple-based Hinduism in India does not incorporate religious instruction as an important component of its mission and goal. Rather, home-based learning is the most significant agency of religious socialization.

In the Hindu home, family elders become teachers and their teachings are multidisciplinary and multifaceted, ranging from philosophy and ethics to Hindu dietary restrictions and hygiene. This includes teaching about the sacredness of the *pooja* space, rules such as those related to the sacred and profane, purity and pollution, teaching about the care and maintenance of the *pooja* area, rituals such as the requirement for a morning purificatory bath before prayer. Shudha Mazumdar (1977, p. 31) describes learning this daily routine in her family home:

> First, there is the visit to the toilet followed by a bath. Then, dressed in clean clothes, comes prayers or meditation and only after this is it possible to eat. This then became my morning routine at the age of eight and I have never deviated from it.

Elders also teach the sequential steps involved in ritual acts (such as cleaning of the altar, arranging and cleaning of ritual objects, culmination of prayer through body prostration) as well as the norms of appropriate behavior when in the *pooja* area (such as leaving shoes outside, little talk, correct body language and posture during prayer and meditation). They also impart the less tangible, including attitude and Zeitgeist, such as that individual prayer and reflection is an important part of a Hindu's daily life.

Family elders teach through stories, positive reinforcement, occasional reprimands, and by example. They encourage young children to come and join them in *pooja* by assigning to them active participatory roles, such as picking flowers, helping to arrange and clean the *pooja* area, making sandal wood paste, ringing bells and singing devotional songs. They encourage and initiate older children to perform their own rituals, and as they grow in maturity, to take on more independent roles, set up their own shrine, adopt a deity, and perform their own rituals without supervision.

> In *Didima*'s house, next to her altar, I had set up my own miniature shrine which I tended to. I would put flowers, light incense and say my prayers (AEN).

They teach children about Hindu dietary regulations, such as the proscriptions against eating beef, and in strict vegetarian households the avoidance of chicken, lamb, goat, fish, and eggs.

Hindu family elders also teach respect for the environment, for trees, plants, shrubs, and flowers. Plants are respected and seen as living, and so Hindus avoid cutting down sacred trees (Aiyyar, 1982).

> "I will always remember *Didima*'s admonition when I plucked a flower in the evening. She would say: "flowers and plants sleep at night. You should not disturb them" (AEN).[6]

Elders inculcate respect through their own personal involvement in the care of the environment and through the performance of related rituals. An example of a plant related ritual is *tulsi brata*: "The *tulsi brata* teaches the child how to care for the bush of sweet basil that is so dearly cherished in every Hindu home" (Mazumdar, 1977, p. 29).

Elders also teach by imparting their experiential knowledge. Examples are the healing and medicinal properties of plants, such as the antiinflammatory properties of turmeric, the disease fighting (for gums, for example) capability of *neem* (margosa) leaves, the aid in digestion of fennel and coriander, the benefits to the eye from eating spinach and so on.

When elders feed crows, pigeons, and ants, and describe the Hindu doctrine of *ahimsa*, also practiced in Buddhism, children learn respect for animals and valuable lessons in ecology, harmony, and *ahimsa*. In many Hindu households *alpona* or *rangoli*—intricate ritualized patterns—are executed daily at the front threshold. These are made of rice flour and are seen not only as auspicious signs, as invitation to the gods to enter the house, but also as *bhutayajna* that is, offering of food (rice flour) to tiny creatures, such as ants and other insects (Ramaswamy & Ramaswamy, 1993). Ants and other insects consume the rice flour during the day and the pattern disappears to be remade the next day.

Finally, family elders are storytellers and impart religious/moral/ethical instruction to children. Elders buy them religious story books, take them to religious plays, musicals, and dance dramas. They read to children from Hindu texts such as the *Ramayana*, the *Mahabharata*, and the *Puranas*. They tell stories and parables from the texts as well as from their personal lives. Through all these strategies, elders foster and nurture a Hindu identity and sense of self. For the children, the elders in the home become the primary instructors of religion, as there is little direct instruction from priests or religious teachers.

CONCLUSIONS

Several major themes with implications for the literature on aging as well as that on environment behavior studies emerge from this research. First, this chapter points to the importance of the concept of *ashrama* or "stage of life" and the related social, cultural, and religious idealized and normative expectations of people as they age (Radhakrishnan, 1927, p. 59). In these stages certain expectations, duties, and obligations are important; children and youth must study, young adults ought to marry, take care of family, acquire property, and develop attachments to family and earthly things, elders must retire from work, and take up spiritual aspirations. According to this scheme, it would be inappropriate, perhaps even deviant, for a Hindu at the *sannyasa* station to marry and have children, or for a *brahmacharya* stage person to retire.[7] Major deviations, when they happen, become anomalies that society has difficulty dealing with (for example, child widows, Mazumdar & Mazumdar, 2002). Part of aging is transitioning from one stage to another and engaging different roles; to Hindus, retirement does not necessarily have the negative connotations of marginalization and loss of identity.

Acceptance of these stages implies, at least according to the roles fostered by religion, that for Hindus meanings of and attachment to space, place, and things will change over the life span. In the *brahmacharya* stage there is an emphasis on the development of personal experiences and social attachment. The *grihastha* stage is where the most intense attachments exist. In the *vanaprastha* stage one carries out one's role of teaching others and starts the disengagement process. Finally, in the *sannyasa* stage a person completes transfer of these social roles and responsibilities to the next generation, accepts a reduced minor role, and attempts to reach a higher understanding of the meaning of life through personal sacrifice and reduction of desire for material things, though this does not imply an end to one's personal attachments.

These life stages, though related to age, are not equivalent to the idea of life course, discussed earlier. The concept of life course envisions a deterministic, linear, time-based sequential flow of phases, except for unusual occurrences. Some have seen it as having four segments, namely, childhood and youth, young adulthood, middle age, and old age (Chew & McCleary, 1994, p. 242). Transition from one segment to another is automatic and time influenced. In contrast, the role associated with an *ashrama* or life stage is not automatic and requires active engagement. The age at which a person engages a stage varies. It is common to find people at the same age (for example, a high school graduating class) engaged in different stations (e.g., many may be at the *grihastha* stage though some may already be at the *vanaprastha* stage).[8] Had it been chronologically structured this variation would not have been possible. These stages enable and encourage engagement, attachment, passing on to others, disengagement, and transition from one stage to the next.

The notion of disengagement and reengagement for Hindu elders described here is important for a number of reasons. In the literature on aging, two major theories have achieved much attention: activity theory and disengagement theory. The latter, more relevant here, was proposed by Cumming and Henry (1961). In its original formulation this theory was presented as describing an intrinsic developmental process, valid for all aging men and women, regardless of particular social or cultural milieu (Vatuk, 1980, p. 137; Cumming & Henry, 1961, p. 17). The two ought not to be confused. Beside the obvious question of whether the Cumming and Henry (1961) proposal came earlier or the Hindu view (cf. Radhakrishnan, 1927), there are differences in formulation, emphasis, whether developmental or stations engagement oriented, and nature. Our focus here is on roles, stages, relationships, personal growth in the spiritual area, and disengagement from attachment to social roles, family, home, space and objects.

Of interest to the subject of elders and the home environment is the important role played by religion in mediating this relationship. Hinduism, the religion, sees this relationship as complex and does not perceive the relations to be polarized as either one of attachment and meaningfulness or lack of attachment. It expects changes in the nature and intensity of the relations with the physical environment depending on a person's station in life. Also evident is the acceptance of an individual's personal attachment though the emphasis is on the social valuation over the personal. Hindu religious ideology encourages engagement and attachment formation and later some disengagement from the material, from acquisitions, possessions, gain, desire, and needs. Yet, disengagement on retirement is only partial. One is simultaneously encouraged to engage in the spiritual and the religious, to seek knowledge and understanding of the deeper meaning of existence, to teach and demonstrate, and to prepare oneself for the ultimate passage from one life to the next. While awaiting the end of this journey the *sannyasa* stage elder is expected to adopt a lifestyle of simplicity, modesty, frugality, praying, fasting, meditating, gardening, teaching, and leaving to the next generation a rich cultural heritage.

Also of importance is the concept that roles, both socially given and legitimized by religion, affect the ways individual elders view and interact with space. In the literature, homes are seen as spaces where individuals form connections and attachments unaffected by social, cultural, and religious mores (Rapoport, 1975; Marcus, 1974). The concept of socially or culturally provided roles for individuals is not new. But, how this affects the ways in which the role-takers view, construct, and use space has not received much attention especially for home environments (work environments are exceptions) (Pratt, 1981).

From the perspective of the physical component of home we note the following. The saliency of the home, or its parts, does not remain constant over the span of a person's life, nor does attachment. The home, especially the *pooja* area, begins for children as a neutral space and grows in meaning and saliency as they learn the importance of the spaces for the practice of religion at home. This reverence increases as persons at the *grihastha* stage develop and care for their own *kuladeva*. In the *vanaprastha* stage, the role requires teaching and transferring of the conduct of role-related activities to the next generation, though personal attachment and activities continue. In the *sannyasa* stage only personal activities continue as social roles have already been transferred. Yet, there is an increase in personal spiritual growth, while memories of attachment at earlier stages continue to be cherished, similar to that pointed out by Rubinstein and Parmelee (1992). In these ways the attachment to and meaning of home evolves and changes over the life span for Hindus and remains dynamic rather than static.

Notably, home is not just a place where family relationships are born, nurtured, and sustained. Religion imbues it with much deeper meaning and in doing so gives elders a very significant role to play even in retirement. Home is sacred space, the *pooja* room is the temple (Eliade, 1959; Raglan, 1964) and the family elder is the specialist who knows the rules, sequence, and rituals of *pooja*. He/she is the caretaker of the deities, the custodian of the *pooja* space, and the guardian of the family's ritual obligations and responsibilities. Home is religious school, and the family elder is the teacher, instructing, socializing, and molding children's beliefs and identity through stories, ritual, art and devotional music. Home is like a garden, and the elder is the master landscaper, knowledgeable of the seasons, times for planting and pruning, and ritual significance and medicinal properties of flowers, herbs, fruits and leaves. Home is a place of higher learning and philosophy and the family elder is a student of religion building further on his/her earlier knowledge. Home is a canvas of art and the family elder executes elaborate patterns of art, while at the same time teaching and preparing the next generation and thus ensuring ritual continuity. Home thus embraces many layers of the elder's identity with religion, becoming an important anchor of their retired lives.

In the environmental-design literature home has been seen primarily as an individual or family setting (Altman & Werner, 1985; Duncan & Duncan, 1976; Marcus, 1974). It has not been viewed as influenced by larger social forces or institutions, such as religion (for exceptions see Mazumdar, 1998; Mazumdar & Mazumdar, 1994a, 1994b, 1997a, 1997b, 1997d; McDannell, 1986; Pratt, 1981; Rapoport, 1969, 1982; Saile, 1985). One attempt to disentangle space and place, collective and individual sees it this way:

> On the collective level, there is space: relatively undifferentiated territory largely outside the meaningful purview of the individual. On the individual level, place is space to which a person has assigned meaning. For example, a typical row house in a Northeastern city is, on the collective level, simply a *house form*: generally old and working class, a good use of precious urban land, and largely undifferentiated from the row houses on either side of it. But a peek inside may reveal that for its occupants, that row house is home: a richly endowed place full of memories and personal meanings (Rubinstein & Parmelee, 1992, p. 144).

From our study, it appears that society can play a strong role in the creation of place and affect the meaning attributed to it. Though individuals can create their places and have their own individual attachments, society provides an important substructure for it. Thus, the individual does not make decisions in a completely unaffected or unfettered way, but is instead influenced by social mores, and as we have pointed out, sometimes, the individual's view is strongly shaped by society right from the beginning. In this view, a person's individuality and freedom to make self-choices itself may be socially governed. Moreover, when the relationships between elders and their physical environments are examined in the context of home, culture and religion have largely been neglected (Altman, Lawton, & Wohlwill, 1984). Thus, the literature has taken an a-religious perspective. In contrast, we have pointed to the importance of considering society, culture, and religion.

Partly as a result of this neglect in the environmental-design literature, even though several have pointed to the increasing turn to religion by elders (Gray & Moberg, 1977; Hooyman & Kiyak, 1988; Hunsberger, 1985), designers and builders in the United States, and perhaps even other countries, have not internalized the notion of homes as sites for the conduct of religion and beliefs, nor considered them as sacred spaces. As this essay points out, this may neglect the psychological, social, and spiritual dimensions of home for Hindu elders in the United States. It seems likely that other elderly immigrants from South East Asia (from Vietnam, Cambodia, Thailand, and Japan) might be facing similar circumstances of having to live in inappropriately designed homes.

The importance of culture in the study of elders and space is made salient by this chapter. Studies of elders have tended to view them as relatively homogenous and, as Rapoport (1975) has pointed out, have neglected to examine cultural considerations and cross-cultural variations. We have pointed out how one cultural group in the elder population views aging and the emphasis they place on roles.

This study delineated the interrelationships between elders and the physical environments of their homes by focusing on one religion—Hinduism. Practices of Hinduism vary significantly in different parts of India and so no claim is made here that this account is "representative" or applicable to all Hindus. Religion might play an important role in the home lives of elders of other religions and may affect their meaning of home to them in significant ways that merit further exploration.

NOTES

1. Its use in related fields is more frequent, such as the examination of how motivations and opportunities for suicide differ over the life course (Chew & McCleary, 1994).

2. This chapter is based on several sources of information or "data." It is best classified as nonempirical, relying on secondary sources, such as autobiographical writings as these were found to provide rich information. It also includes autoethnographic notes (see Hayano, 1979; Jones, 1970) and recollections.

3. Our study focuses primarily on Hindu men and women in India born in the early part of the twentieth century and/or latter part of the nineteenth century.

4. We have used phonetically accurate spellings. *Grihastha* and *Garhasthya* are alternate spellings used in the literature perhaps due to language, dialect, and translation variations. Other examples are *tulsi* and *tulasi, pooja* and *puja.*

5. AEN refers to authoethnographic notes by Shampa Mazumdar.

6. J. C. Bose is said to have demonstrated that plants have life and react to pain and emotions, though not all scientists of his time accepted his experimental results. Later science gave credence to his work (see also http://www.tuc.nrao.edu/~demerson/bose/bose.html—checked 17 March 2005).

7. As with any ideal system, not every member can be expected to achieve the ideals set forth (Vatuk, 1980), and the system of *ashrama*s too can be

misused by participants and others. Here our focus has been on enunciating how religion, roles, age, and space are viewed in Hinduism and by Hindus.

8. For further clarification of the complex topic of *ashramas*, in contradistinction to simple chronological age, please see the cited works of Radhakrishnan (1927) and Bhaskarananda (1994).

REFERENCES

Ainlay, S. C., & Smith, D. R. (1984). Aging and religious participation. *Journal of Gerontology, 39*, 357–364.

Aiyyar, P. V. (1982). *South Indian customs*. New Delhi, India: Asian Educational Service.

Altman, I., Lawton, M. P., & Wohlwill, J. (Eds.). (1984). *Elderly people and the environment*. New York: Plenum Press.

Altman, I., & Werner, C. (Eds.). (1985). *Home environments*. New York: Plenum Press.

Becker, G. (2002). Dying away from home: Quandaries of migration for elders in two ethnic groups. *Journal of Gerontology, 57B*(2), 579–595.

Belk, R. W. (1992). Attachment to possessions. In I. Altman & S. Low (Eds.), *Place attachment* (pp. 37–55). New York: Plenum Press.

Bhaskarananda, S. (1994). *The essentials of Hinduism*. Seattle, WA: Viveka Press.

Chawla, L. (1992). Childhood place attachments. In I. Altman & S. Low (Eds.), *Place attachment* (pp. 63–86). New York: Plenum Press.

Chew, K. S. Y., & McCleary, R. (1994). A life course theory of suicide risk. *Suicide and Life Threatening Behavior, 24*, 234–244.

Csikszentmihalyi, M., & Rochberg-Halton, E. (1981). *The meaning of things: Domestic symbols and the self*. Cambridge, UK: Cambridge University Press.

Cumming, E., & Henry, W. E. (1961). *Growing old: The process of disengagement*. New York: Basic Books.

Das, K. (1965). The plant in Orissan folklore. In S. G. Sankar (Ed.), *Tree symbol worship in India: A new survey of a pattern of folk religion* (pp. 25–34). Calcutta, India: Indian Publications.

Dovey, K. (1985). Home and homelessness. In I. Altman & C. Werner (Eds.), *Home environments* (pp. 33–64). New York: Plenum Press.

Duncan, J., & Duncan, N. G. (1976). Housing as a presentation of self and the structure of social networks. In G. Moore & R. Golledge (Eds.), *Environmental knowing: Theories, research, and methods* (pp. 247–253). Stroudsbourg, PA: Dowden, Hutchinson & Ross.

Eck, D. L. (1981). *Darsan: Seeing the divine image in India*. Chambersburg, PA: Anima Books.

Eliade, M. (1958). *Patterns in comparative religion*. New York: Harcourt, Brace and World.

Eliade, M. (1959). *The sacred and the profane: The nature of religion*. New York: Crossroad.

Feldman, R. M. (1990). Settlement identity: Psychological bonds with home places in a mobile society. *Environment and Behavior, 22,* 183–229.

Fruzzetti, L. M. (1982). *The gift of a virgin: Women, marriage and ritual in a Bengali society.* New Brunswick, NJ: Rutgers University Press.

Gray, R. M., & Moberg, D. O. (1977). *The church and the older person* (rev. ed.). Grand Rapids, MI: William B. Eerdmans.

Hayano, D. (1979). Auto-ethnography: Paradigm, problems and prospects. *Human Organization, 38*(1), 99–104.

Hooyman, N. R., & Kiyak, A. H. (1988). *Social gerontology: A multidisciplinary perspective.* Boston: Allyn and Bacon.

Hummon, D. M. (1989). House, home and identity in contemporary American culture. In S. M. Low & E. Chambers (Eds.), *Housing, culture and design: A comparative perspective* (pp. 207–228). Philadelphia: University of Pennsylvania Press.

Hunsberger, B. (1985). Religion, age, life satisfaction, and perceived sources for religiousness: A study of older persons. *Journal of Gerontology, 40,* 615–620.

Jones, D. J. (1970). Towards a native anthropology.*Human Organization, 29,* 251–259.

Korosec-Serfaty, P. (1985). Experiences and the use of dwellings. In I. Altman & C. M. Werner (Eds.), *Home environments* (pp. 65–86). New York: Plenum Press.

Korpela, K. (1992). Adolescents' favourite places and environmental self-regulation. *Journal of Environmental Psychology, 12,* 249–258.

Marcus, C. C. (1974). The house as symbol of self. In J. Lang, C. Burnette, W. Moleski, & D. Vachon (Eds.), *Designing for human behavior: Architecture in behavioral sciences* (pp. 130–146). Stroudsburg, PA: Dowden, Hutchinson & Ross.

Marcus, C. C. (1992). Environmental memories. In I. Altman & S. Low (Eds.), *Place attachment* (pp. 87–112). New York: Plenum Press.

Mazumdar, S. (1977). *A pattern of life: The memoirs of an Indian woman.* New Delhi, India: South Asia Books.

Mazumdar, S. (1998). Religion and housing. In W. Van Vliet (Ed.), *The encyclopedia of housing* (pp. 464–465). Thousand Oaks, CA: Sage.

Mazumdar, S., & Mazumdar, S. (1993). Sacred space and place attachment. *Journal of Environment Psychology, 13,* 231–242.

Mazumdar, S., & Mazumdar, S. (1994a). Societal values and architecture: A socio-physical model of the interrelationships, *Journal of Architectural and Planning Research, 11*(1), 66–90.

Mazumdar, S., & Mazumdar, S. (1994b). Of gods and homes: Sacred space in the Hindu house. *Environments, 22*(2), 41–49.

Mazumdar, S., & Mazumdar, S. (1997a). Religious traditions and domestic architecture: A comparative analysis of Zoroastrian and Islamic houses in Iran. *Journal of Architectural and Planning Research, 14,* 181–208.

Mazumdar, S., & Mazumdar, S. (1997b). Religion and beliefs. In P. Oliver (Ed.), *Encyclopedia of vernacular architecture of the world* (pp. 102–104). London: Cambridge University Press.

Mazumdar, S., & Mazumdar, S. (1997c). Temples and sanctuaries. In P. Oliver (Ed.), *Encyclopedia of vernacular architecture of the world* (pp. 720–722). London: Cambridge University Press.

Mazumdar, S., & Mazumdar, S. (1997d). Sacred/profane space: Hindu. In P. Oliver (Ed.), *Encyclopedia of vernacular architecture of the world* (pp. 1.VII.6.j: 603–604) London: Cambridge University Press.

Mazumdar, S., & Mazumdar, S. (1999). 'Women's significant spaces': Religion, space and community. *Journal of Environmental Psychology, 19*, 159–170.

Mazumdar, S., & Mazumdar, S. (2002). Silent resistance: A Hindu child widow's lived experience. In A. Sharma & K. K. Young (Eds.), *The annual review of women in world religions* (pp. 93–121). Albany, NY: State University of New York Press.

Mazumdar, S., & Mazumdar, S. (2003). Creating the sacred: Altars in the Hindu American home. In J.N. Iwamura & P. Spickard (Eds.), *Revealing the sacred in Asian and Pacific America* (pp. 143–157). New York: Routledge.

McDannell, C. (1986). *The Christian home in Victorian America 1840–1900.* Bloomington, IN: Indiana University Press.

Mindel, C., & Vaughan, C. E. (1978). A multidimensional approach to religiosity and disengagement. *Journal of Gerontology, 33,* 103–108.

Pandurang, B. (1972). Our family gods. In M. Cormack (Ed.), *Voices from India* (pp. 44–47). New York: Praeger.

Pavlides, E., & Hesser, J. (1989). Sacred space, ritual and the traditional Greek house. In N. AlSayyad & J-P. Bourdier (Eds.), *Dwellings, settlements and tradition: Cross-cultural perspectives* (pp. 275–293). Lanham, MD: University Press of America.

Pratt, G. (1981). The house as an expression of social worlds. In J. Duncan (Ed.), *Housing and identity: Cross-cultural perspectives* (pp. 135–180). London: Croom Helm.

Proshansky, H. M., Fabian, A. K., & Kaminoff, R. (1983). Place identity: Physical world socialization of the self, *Journal of Environmental Psychology, 3*, 57–83.

Radhakrishnan, S. (1927) *The Hindu view of life.* London: George Allen & Unwin.

Raglan, F. R. S. (1964). *The temple and the house.* New York: W. W. Norton.

Ramaswamy, S., & Ramaswamy, S. (1993). *Vedic heritage.* Saylorsburg, PA: Arsha Vidya Gururkulam.

Rapoport, A. (1969). *House form and culture.* Englewood Cliffs, NJ: Prentice Hall.

Rapoport, A. (1975). Aging-environment theory: A summary. In P. Windley, T. Byerts, & F. G. Ernst (Eds.), *Theory development and aging* (pp. 263–282). Washington, DC: Gerontological Society.

Rapoport, A. (1982). Sacred places, sacred occasions and sacred environments. *Architectural Design, 9*(10), 75–82.

Relph, E. (1976). *Place and placelessness.* London: Pion.

Rowles, G. D. (1983). Place and personal identity in old age: Observations from Appalachia. *Journal of Environmental Psychology, 3*, 299–313.

Rowles, G. D. (1984). Aging in rural environments. In I. Altman, M. P. Lawton, & J. Wohlwill (Eds.), *Elderly people and the environment* (pp. 129–157). New York: Plenum Press.

Rubinstein, R. L., & Parmelee, P. A. (1992). Attachment to place and the representation of the life course by the elderly. In I. Altman & S. Low (Eds.), *Place attachment* (pp. 139–163). New York: Plenum Press.

Saile, D. G. (1985). The ritual establishment of home. In I. Altman & C. Werner (Eds.), *Home environments* (pp. 87–111). New York: Plenum Press.

Sugihara, S., & Evans, G. W. (2000). Place attachment and social support at continuing care retirement communities. *Environment and Behavior, 32,* 400–409.

Tuan, Y-F. (1987). American space, Chinese place. In H. Knepler & M. Knepler (Eds.), *Crossing cultures* (pp. 280–281). New York: Macmillan.

Upadhyaya, K. D. (1965). Indian botanical folklore. In S. G. Sankar (Ed.), *Tree symbol worship in India: A new survey of a pattern of folk religion* (pp. 1–18). Calcutta, India: Indian Publications.

Vatuk, S. (1980). Withdrawal and disengagement as a cultural response to aging in India. In C. L. Fry (Ed.), *Aging in culture and society: Comparative viewpoints and strategies.* New York: Praeger.

PART III

Disruptions of Home

Chapter 6

Psychic Homelands and the Imagination of Place: A Literary Perspective

Nora J. Rubinstein

> I had come a refugee from the Russian pogroms, aflame with dreams of America. I did not find America in the sweatshops, much less in the schools and colleges. But for hundreds of years the persecuted races all over the world were nurtured on hopes of America . . . the far-off 'golden country'. And so, though my faith in this so-called America was shattered, yet underneath, in the sap and roots of my soul, burned the deathless faith that America is, must be, somehow, somewhere.
>
> —(Yezierska, 1991, p. 110)

THE GROUND: WHERE ARE OUR PLACES OF BELONGING? WHAT ARE THE IMAGES OF DESIRE?

To begin a chapter in a book on "*coming home*" is like crossing a familiar threshold and being greeted by friends on common ground. It seems easy at first: there is the usual street, the ritual greeting, the language spoken with its rhythms and elisions for intimates, but mostly, when we come home, we come to a place where we belong, or so it seems; or so we have been told it should be. Or so it once was.

But belonging is not always easy.[1] It presumes some continuity with what was once there—a recognition, and something that's harder to define—a slight softening of the shoulders, as though in expectation of sitting down to reminisce. But if belonging presumes recognition and reminiscence, the opposite is not always true, and I have begun to wonder what happens when the link between them is severed by aging and dementia, by war and exile, and by the desire for journey itself. Recognition does not guarantee the desire to return. Reminiscence does not pre-suppose admittance. What then is the need to reminisce? Robert Coles has written that without memory we are everyone, and I would amend it: without memory we are everywhere, or nowhere—no place of birth, no route to work, no Sunday nights with children asleep in the back of the car on the way home. Without memory, all places are equal and alien. We are confined to an eternal "now"—a moment, and then another. We can not learn, for knowledge is a product of analogy: "just as it was," "better than," "safer," "familiar." Without these, there is no heritage, tradition, ritual or culture. We have no identity as we stand on this alien ground. How will society treat us so displaced—as refugees and exiles, as the orphans of memory? We have seen the answer in pogroms and ethnocide, and in institutions that warehouse the elderly as though they were objects to be arranged beside garden paths like potted plants.

In a book that explores aging, we must ask what the life course has taught us about "place," what home is for those who have spent more years becoming who they are, or perhaps we may say, becoming *where* they are. How different then is the *feeling* of dislocation of the nursing home than that of the refugee camp, without the familiar possessions or rituals to pace the day?

In a book on coming home, we must ask what it has meant to be "away." We must also ask what it is to imagine the return. To arrive. To belong. Or to be barred by frontiers and policy that spins on the color of our skin, or the way we believe, or our father's father's birthplace; or by the frailty of our bodies or minds. We must learn from those who imagine a "home" that is different from what they have known because it has changed—or they have. Sometimes, there is no way back home, no way to belong except in imagination, and what is left is loss, a longing for something that can not exist. But there are also times when reminiscence and fantasy morph and merge, when past and future interpenetrate, when imagination and longing may enrich us, protect us, save us, and that interpenetration may be a creative act.

If this chapter begins with many questions, it will end without perfect answers. Between the two is a journey with many ancestral models, from Thomas More's *Utopia* (1516; 1965) to Suarez's (1999) portrait of Polish and Croatian immigrants finding home away from home in Chicago. It is about the desire for a place where we feel we belong, or more accurately, the image we carry in our minds of such a place. It is about the manner in which that image grows from memory, or a vague sense of misfit, or fantasy, to become something we cherish, an intention, a need. An act. Its most critical quality is the sense of longing that defines it; its most significant impact is on the way we live in the present. This image or "psychic homeland" may make it easier to live as we do, believing that someday we will "come home," or it may make every moment spent in "exile," a torture. It may share characteristics with the imagined or desired places of others and be at the heart of nationalism and xenophobia, but its essence is a personal longing. Therefore, if we are to understand the manner in which we imagine and desire place, we must empower the personal, explore our own odyssey, and learn from those of others.

THE THRESHOLD: THE PERSONAL

I have been teaching myself about this longing for many years. For most of my adolescence, I was drawn to Ireland for reasons I can not explain by blood or history. I listened to the music and the rhythms of Irish speakers as though I were an adopted child finding a birth parent; there was an exotic familiarity that felt like "home." When I went to Ireland for the first time after college, there was a sense of having opened the door and having crossed a familiar threshold to a place I knew, though I had never been there. There was something integral about it and something satisfying in its pursuit. I went to Ireland for vacations several times, and while I made no effort to find a job there or live a situated life, there was something in the identification that gave me a kind of center. It is possible that it was just enough to keep me complacent where I was.

I don't know when that changed. It was, perhaps, as another more immediate longing took its place, a different kind of desire; one that grew out of loss. I lived in Vermont for only a few years;

long enough to know its high meadows and feel its hills etched in the muscles of my thighs; long enough to learn the language of sugaring and sound of snow. Then, when the house I was living in was sold, I moved back to a beach house on flat land where I had spent all the summers of my life. Its wood floors were patterned with bare-foot-print echoes of my first steps fifty summers before. I knew the rhythmic squeak of wagon wheels and gridded shadows on my hands, cast by a low Spring sun through window screens, but there was, deep within me, a voice that said, sometimes softly, "take me home." It was Vermont's high mountain meadows I saw when I closed my eyes.

Some of us have heard this from our parents, some in nursing homes, some lost in their own mental labyrinth, ever planning long past Christmas meals, or searching for something that was never under the mattress. We have been greeted by messages on an answering machine, when we have just returned from visiting them. "Where are you?" they ask. "When are you coming to see me? I have been taken prisoner," they say. "Come and take me home." And from some, who remain with spouse or children, at an oilcloth covered kitchen table or in their own beds, we hear the same refrain, "Come and take me home." We want to exclaim: "But you *are* at home!" It is not the tablecloth or pillows that matter of course, but something deeper than possessions, some blend of the imagined and remembered—a long-dead parent's face, that sense of ritual and control that paced the day, and more we can not know. They may be searching for some sense of who they were then, and there.

If they feel solitary, too often disconnected, they are not alone in their sense of loss, or more accurately perhaps, in the chimeras[2] they seek. We have heard this from others—from the immigrants, "footsteps dragging with exhaustion," there is that dream of a "golden country," and from the displaced, the ethnically "cleansed," the emigrants who await the *revolucion*: "take me home." For those displaced by war or ethnic slaughter, the homes they dream of returning to are long gone. For many, the nation-state and even the landscape is gone. Looking out their window, they would see nothing but the ruins of memory—no neighbors, no plowed fields. Do they simply leave the old place images behind and move on—or does their very dismemberment make the images, like phantom limbs, seem more real? For the orphaned children of Cambodia's Killing

Fields, of Rwanda, of Bosnia, of civil wars throughout the world,[3] there are no families, no schools, no rituals. There is no way to return to the trust that each day will dawn in an uneventful manner. So what "illusion or fabrication of the mind" can draw them toward a belief in the future, when belief itself is challenged nearly beyond repair? In a world with increasing numbers of displaced people, where the connections to past places are twisted and broken, the need for a psychic homeland—an internal narrative of a place to which they can retreat, if only in fantasy, seems to be valuable, or healthy, even necessary. If as environment professionals, we have been weaned on the belief that identity and behavior are indelibly linked to place and time, how are we to address these fractures of place and self, this "metaphysical loss of home"?[4]

INTRODUCTIONS AND GREETINGS: ASSUMPTIONS AND DEFINITIONS

I begin the journey with certain assumptions: first, that there is an indivisible link between place and person, and second, that place imagination is as important as place memory. We are defined, in part, by the environments through which we have passed. We are urban or rural, sedentary or mobile, and we see and interpret the landscape through a filter shaped by that experience. If now such analysis is rarely questioned, research still looks mostly to the individual's present and past to understand environmental attitudes and actions. We have explored the origins and meaning of home—our memories of kitchens and tree forts, and the manner in which they influence the places we live today.[5] We have explored our preferences for landscape qualities and their source in experience and culture.[6] We have described the love of these real places as "place attachment," born of sanctuary, or memories of courtship, or transcendent experience of nature. We have become webbed within our communities and are identified as New Yorkers or Parisians, brick layers or soccer moms, hunters or shamans, and we have called this "place identity."[7] But there are few studies that focus on those who still search for places of belonging with which they can identify, for a psychic homeland in reified or non-reified spaces, for the vicarious or idealized, for the fantasy itself. There is little that acknowledges the impact that dreaming a place can have on the communities where we live or those we long for. There is still less that supports the desire itself—not for a grounded place in time, but for the journey. Riley (1992) has suggested we are "restrained" as social scientists, not comfortable with imagination and desire.

THE LITERATURE

Imagination, Fantasy and Projection

There are exceptions. There are crucial contributions by historians and political scientists on nationalism, experts in children's environments and authors of fiction, and the strong voice with which landscape professionals speak to this issue. Lowenthal (1972) included fantasy as one of the elements that defines the relationship between humans and landscape, and Sopher (1979), Riley (1992) and others have outlined the manner in which imagination and symbol underlie the character of the ordinary landscape. Their work redefines the landscape from some bounded, ecologically defined, economically measurable place, to a vessel for projection and emotion. Riley suggested that the landscape imagined has more power than that experienced concretely, and notes that this is particularly important for the elderly, incapacitated and sick.

Graham Rowles' seminal book on aging provided a crucial corrective to the widespread generalization that as seniors become less physically mobile, they are intellectually imprisoned. Rowles wrote, "In fantasy, the individual is liberated. Physiological decline, ill health, economic constraints, social alienation, or environmental barriers provide no limitation. The only boundaries are those imposed by autobiography, personality, and the limits of imagination" (1978, p. 181). He proposed the existence of both "reflective" or reminiscent fantasy and "projective" or future-oriented fantasy in which elders are able to participate through "vicarious immersion" in places far removed from the daily realm. He notes however, that the general emphasis is on past places rather than the imagined future. It is not clear what the impact of privileging the past may be (as though our elders were incapable of dreaming), but if in fantasy we are liberated, then our emphasis solely on life review may further confine those who are already physiologically constrained.

The Darker Side of Imagination

Social Groups

If imagination of place can be liberating, it can also be a dangerous tool. Sopher (1979, p. 36) has argued that the "myth of a future homeland" may be sustaining for some groups, and he alludes to the notion of a "once and future home" among the Jews of the Diaspora. However Yehoshua (cited in Hoffman, 1999, p. 55) maintained that over 1800 years of Diaspora, Jews avoided settling in Palestine, to avoid turning myth into home, and to avoid taking responsibility for building a society. Hoffman has claimed that exile "allows people to conceive of themselves as perpetually Other. . . . It allows them to imagine the sources and causes of predicaments as located outside, in a hostile or oppressive environment rather than within" (p. 55). The impact of such "projection" on social and political marginalization has been little analyzed in the environmental literature, but if psychological notions of projection can be applied to social groups, the impacts may be measured in the strengthening of the bonds within the group, a more powerful dichotomy between "us" and "them," and the increase in inter-ethnic hostilities.

Certainly many other groups have been displaced since Sopher focused on the Diaspora. The United Nations High Commission on Refugees is responsible for more than 20 million displaced people with approximately 2.7 million of them under 18 years of age, and just under 400,000 over age 60.[8] This new category reflects increasing concern with the needs of older refugees and, presumably, an increase in their numbers. With return to their countries of origin a UNHCR goal, and the likelihood that a significant percentage of the displaced imagine a return, resettlement elsewhere is a less desirable option, but often the only one that is available. While some refugees have opted to remain in refugee camps rather than accept such a solution, others have found themselves attempting to build new lives in new places. The Native Americans who were resettled to unpopulated reservations in the 19th Century built a totemic relationship with these new lands, but others have found their place images in conflict with those already settled on, or native to the land. Ryden (1993) suggests, that maps reflect such conflict given that they are products of, and magnets for, imagination, and were "once drawn, and even today are interpreted, according not only to what is objectively out there but also to what we wish were out there, or hope to find out there" (p. 24). Rowles has noted a parallel with geosophy, suggesting that the settlement of many areas has been constrained by our images of the environment and its potential to become a home. He suggests that the upper Midwest was once construed as the "Great American Desert" by Easterners, and the belief in the "bad airs" or "miasma" that would accompany residence in the Central Valley of California, for a time, limited settlement of these areas (G. Rowles, April 2004, personal communication).

Nationalism and Projection

If the imagination of place has had power at the level of the ethnic or social group, it has had a still darker impact on nations, when the imagined homeland has become a rationale for civil war and ethnic annihilation. Nowhere was this clearer than during the Second World War when the Nazis used the image of "homeland" to embody the character of the proposed Aryan nation. Landscapes were manicured to represent a particular esthetic (Wolschke-Bulmahn, 1992), and the population considered the term key to its national birthright. In fact, the notion of *Heimat* was so closely linked with the horrors of the Third Reich, that only recently has a generation of environmentally aware German youth reclaimed the word to describe and restore folklore, music and poetry (1999). Morley and Robbins (1990; 1996) wrote: " . . . *Heimat* is an ominous utopia . . . linked to strong feelings, mostly remembrances and longing. *Heimat* always evokes in me the feeling of something lost or very far away, something which one cannot easily find or find again . . . It seems to me that one has a more precise idea of Heimat the further one is away from it" (p. 459). There are clear parallels with the psychic homeland as a place of origin, yearning, and as a place of 'impossible return.'

There are similar concerns with the manner in which the word "homeland" was perverted by the apartheid government in South Africa, to confine blacks to lands to which they had little connection, while restricting their access to the cities where many of them had spent their adult lives as workers (Schlemmer, 1972). The term served an economic purpose and evoked a benevolent familial and tribal homeland that never existed. In a fascinating article, written before the end of apartheid, South African born writer Kenneth Parker (1993) suggested that apart from its connotation as a place of repression for blacks, homeland also evoked the legitimacy of borders imposed by colonial powers and then reified by the newly nationalizing states. The mapping of a homeland thus becomes a tool for control and for consolidating power. Parker rejected the very notion of his own exile, saying,

> . . . The real tensions for 'Third-World' writers [are] between, on the one hand, natal, cultural, and ethnic identifications, and, on the other, participation in the . . . Western dominated . . . worlds where the writers live and work. . . . That is, to the obligation . . . that these writers 'dream the homeland' is added the burden that they also carry the banner for the dreams of other spaces as well. Bluntly . . . they are the new slaves, sold to dream the dreams for postcolonial African leaders. (pp. 68–69)

This co-optation of the dreamed or imagined home has parallels in American policies toward Native Americans who, having been re-settled on lands to which they had no ethno-historical ties, were then forced to fight with mining interests, to retain these lands at the risk of an even more complete ethnocide. The 2001 use of the term "homeland security" by the Bush Administration in the wake of the 9-11 terror attacks against the United States was ironic in light of these conflicts. While some suggested that the historic burdens of the term "homeland" were too great, others vaunted its use as a rallying cry at a time when Americans were being persuaded to see themselves as the last bastion against terrorism, and Arab Americans were arrested on the basis of their national identity alone. Homeland then is understood here, to subsume some of the more xenophobic and dystopic elements of racial and ethnic projection, as well as a "eutopic"[9] notion of a place of sanctuary and prosperity. In this chapter, the term is chosen to be as inclusive as possible of personal, group and nationalist ideology, and to provide a frame for many images from places bounded by frontiers, to homelands in language, symbols, and in the rituals and myths that underlie identity.

THE PURPOSE OF PSYCHIC HOMELAND IMAGES

What then are these images and what purpose do they serve? Clearly, the images will seem as variable as the histories of those who hold them. While some may evoke nationalistic fervor, others will be personal—eccentric, idiosyncratic, creative. While some may reflect real places, others will be abstract, a-temporal, ideological. There is no catalog. We do not yet know what links exist between the dreamer and the dream, nor what meta-themes characterize the images held by particular individuals, groups or nations. Will refugees imagine sanctuary and those with dementia return to a more literal experiential past? Will safety matter as much as continuity of ritual or social group to the survivors of ethnocide? Will democracies use such images as propaganda, while totalitarian states use them to oppress? Are the images constant or do they come and go with the circumstances of time and place? Does the image provide that evanescent sense of belonging when "place" can not? The answers are, as yet, tentative.

Sanctuary and Survival

Among the most powerful of the psychic homeland images is a "fragment" by Herman Hesse.

> A prisoner paints a landscape on the wall of his cell showing a miniature train entering a tunnel. When his jailors come to get him, he asks them 'politely to wait a moment, to allow me to verify something in the little train in my picture. As usual they started to laugh, because they considered me to be weak minded. I made myself very tiny, entered into my picture and climbed into the little train, which started moving, and then disappeared into the darkness of the tunnel. For a few seconds longer a puff of flaky smoke could be seen coming out of the round hole. Then the smoke blew away and with the picture, my person.' (cited in Bachelard, 1969, p. 150)

The passage points to what may be the most compelling use of the psychic homeland—as sanctuary in situations of violence and conflict. Such psychic homelands are a kind of shibboleth, providing passage from conflict or constraint, to refuge or preserve. Hesse's literary fiction evokes the more personal fictions that may permit emotional or even physical survival *in extremis*, and such landscape images have many authors. Lenore Terr (1990) described the dissociation of a child who had been repeatedly victimized. While he was being beaten, he imagined that he was "at a picnic with his head in

Mommy's lap" until he no longer felt pain. Terr described the process as "peeling off feelings from events, by journeying inside the imagination to other places" (p. 89). Such analysis reveals something of the psychological dynamic but still provides little information about the character of the chosen images themselves. Are they familiar or distant, peopled places or places of solitude? The place may be a proxy for the person, as in a poem by ten year old Bosnian refugee, Mujo Mustafic (Schaller, 1995):

> I'm not here and I don't exist.
> There is sunshine and blossoms in my town
> but unknown hands steal its smell of summer and the silk from
>   the *sehar*.[10]
> I'm not here but my soul
> smuggles through every street at night
> and sticks a lily on each buttonhole
> and plants a tree by every house.

Continuity

What is it to *imagine a future for a place* we love when we see none for ourselves? Is it perhaps to imagine oneself saved by binding identity with environment so closely? Does it guarantee some lineage beyond the present moment, like having children to perpetuate our name or character? We give birth to the place itself, its adolescence is ours, its maturity lives on beyond us. Continuity is a bequest, marking our presence and passage. It is our immortality. The power of these narratives lies in the manner in which they reflect our own needs for belief in something that transcends the circumstances in which we live. *We are, as has already been said, a product of the places we remember–but we may survive, as a result of those we imagine.*

Inventing a Future

In 1996, a manuscript was published entitled *In Memory's Kitchen* (De Silva, 1996). It was one of the most improbable books and had had what may be one of the most circuitous journeys of any book ever written. Prepared on scraps of discarded paper and propaganda leaflets by the inmates at the concentration camp at Teresienstadt, it was a book of favorite recipes. Starving and dying, the women struggled to remember and record celebration meals, when they could have had only faint hope that the book would reach their daughters in America. In one particularly painful irony, one author suggests that the cook "let fantasy run free" (p. 52). Did the creation of the book help these women survive? We can not know. Did it provide continuity? Most certainly. But the cookbook was more. It was transformative—of the place and of the person. The propaganda leaflets on which it had been written were themselves transformed into emissaries to another generation in another place and time–like letters that could not be written. They carried a bequest of family and cultural traditions, of ancestry, and lineage, as though these mothers were telling the stories of how they learned to cook: "Blend vigorously . . . Bake it slowly." "Make a strudel dough and stretch it a little thicker than usual." "Out of all one makes a stiff dough . . . One can do everything with it." "Take a large old hen, but do not scald her . . . Bring it cold to the table. It is plentiful and pretty." Reminiscence and imagination are blended until there is little to distinguish them. Breyten Breytenbach (1991, p. 71) in writing of exile said, "Memory, whether apocryphal or not, provides the feeding ground or the requisite space allowing for the outlining of imagination. Imagination is a biological necessity for inventing a future."

Orientation and Iconography

We should not conclude from these fragments, that the psychic homeland is always an escape from present circumstances, nor that it is necessarily composed of reified elements. The psychic homeland may also be a kind of icon, treasured by virtue of its distance from the quotidian and valued for its immutability. Gaston Bachelard (1969) has cited Gladwin's account of the Puluwat islanders who navigate great distances by plotting imaginary islands that are "impossible but necessary." In Western society, myths are built on imaginary star patterns, and the light of the north star carries metaphorical connotations beyond its literal value for orientation. Tuan cites the scholar C. S. Lewis who was overcome with a longing for remoteness and severity, for pure 'northernness,' when he was a child.

> The sadness and sternness of the northern world appealed to
> something very deep in his nature. But he had never lived in

northern lands, nor did he feel the urge to travel northward and confront his personal vision with sensuous experience. He had become infatuated with a landscape through literary and musical means such as illustrations to stories from Wagner . . . (1977, p. 184)

We also conjure up images of real places to act as icons of healing, sometimes without the benefit of direct experience[11] (Marcus, 1990). Such real world images may act as the source and symbol of religious faith (Lane, 1989), or as teacher, or as linchpin in the transmission of culture (Basso, 1996). Organizations like the Nature Conservancy use the image of iconographic places to "save the last great places on earth."[12] In fact it may *require* imagination and projection to create and sustain such places as open land rather than for their *concrete* value in timber, minerals or grazing land.[13] C.L. Rawlins (1992) collects snow samples in remote wilderness areas to test for airborne pollutants. He wrote:

There's a yearning that can be expressed as a place more simply than as a feeling: for beauty, rest, purity, transfiguration. It is easier to think of it as unknown. A knowing love is difficult, like a marriage that persists despite boredom, bitterness and grief. It can be easier to see love's essence in the face of a stranger, passion in a body you've never touched. . . . Contempt for what is close corrodes the heart. . . . Only having abandoned the physical world, can we love "wilderness" more than any real place. . . . What we've been fighting for isn't places, but our souls. (pp. 4–5)

So the imagination of place is critical. The impossible but necessary islands of our imagination are the measure of our faith in the future and our survival—as reminiscence is the means of defining identity. Imagination then, is the lingua franca of religion, the sacred, homeland and utopia. And for the aging, the "vicarious immersion" in distant places provides orientation, coherence and continuity. Imagining "coming home," may be the litmus test of sanctuary *and* survival.

Utopias

Finally, I must distinguish the psychic homeland from utopias. In More's *Utopia* (1516; 1965), which is arguably credited with spawning all subsequent utopian literature, the social, political and economic tenets are thinly veiled social criticism of sixteenth century society and the monarchy (Schaer, Claeys, & Sargent, 2000). The ideal, and therefore static society operated under a detailed system of laws and provided little opportunity for individual choice or pleasure. In contrast, the psychic homeland is generated in individual choice and defined by the individual's design and desire. There is little concern for social equity or socio-political or economic laws, except as the psychic homeland is influenced by nationalism with its potential for xenophobia and racism. While utopias are generally assumed to be positive, psychic homelands may include what Bishop (1989) has described as the paradoxical power of destruction and renewal. Psychic homelands then, may be images of real places or have impossible juxtapositions of time and place.[14] If they are tinted with memory, they are also projected into the future, and their consequences may be benevolent or genocidal. To imagine a place of belonging is to create an alternate identity—to taste freedom or power, be younger or more adult and secure, to escape or dream.

THE FAMILY: A PSYCHIC HOMELAND ALBUM

What, then, are these images that appear as we lift the covers of the family album of (be)longing and desire? I have begun a collection, like clippings in a scrapbook, and like the authors, I will slip from time to time, between past, present and future—between home and homeland, between self and place.

Belonging and Recognition

> Looking back, you are struck by your feeling of having lived for a time up in the air. The sky was rarely more than pale blue or violet, with a profusion of mighty, weightless, ever changing clouds towering up and sailing on it, but it has a blue vigour in it, and at a short distance it painted the ranges of hills and the woods a fresh deep blue. In the middle of the day the air was alive over the land, like a flame burning; it scintillated, waved and shone like running water, mirrored and doubled all objects. . . . Up in this high air you breathed easily, drawing in a vital assurance and lightness of heart. In the highlands you woke up in the morning and thought: Here I am, where I ought to be. (Dinesen, 1972, p. 4)

It is not clear what makes us feel that we have found a place of belonging—the "where I ought to be." It may have something to do with the patterns laid down in childhood (Paterson, 1988), or it may be something in the transcendent qualities of the place itself (Lopez, 1978; Marcus, 1990). It is easy to say that both are relevant; more difficult to understand what specific characteristics in place or person will matter. Is it gender or socio-economic class, hills or meadows that influence what we imagine? We may never find such categories reliable if we reject empiricism for narrative and individual experience, and if we measure accuracy in a kind of recognition, a sense of the "rightness" of the way it feels.[15]

Belonging (and recognition) can come when we recreate places that are familiar because they replicate or transpose the patterns we remember. It may be hard to distinguish these imagined homelands from experienced autobiography except that they are often idyllic and show little of the "messiness" of real life. In a college class, asked to describe their psychic homeland, one student painted a Norman Rockwell portrait of her loving family and her desire to prepare a similar vision for the family she hopes to have.[16] Another spoke of finding home in her boyfriend's arms. My students' dreams were based on reminiscence, recreating what they knew. Some did not think beyond the present moment, recreating the security of their dorm rooms. But others described images that inverted what they saw as they looked over their shoulders at families and identities left behind, substituting happy for sad, healing for hurt, transposing the images on a familiar template. "We moved a lot when I was a kid. I'll live in one place."

The psychic homeland image does not have to reflect the experience of a real place or family to hold power and elicit "recognition." Author and philosopher Kathleen Dean Moore (1999) has described planning a vacation trip to an unfamiliar area of Canada, and as she perused the maps trying to find a place to begin, she suddenly recognized the names of a string of lakes and the way they echoed a familiar lullaby. In discovering these maps, even before she begins to explore these places, she is drawn closer to her mother, to the rituals of childhood, by a place she has never been.

> I know this place as well as I know the house I grew up in. This canoe route is a line from a song my mother used to sing. . . . This canoe route is the background music of my childhood. My mother sang the song softly, a lullaby, as she sat at the foot of the bed and my sisters and I drifted off to sleep. . . . When we were sick,

or lonely, or homesick, this is the song she would sing to comfort us. And now this music has become a dotted line on my map, a place I can find. . . . I will canoe along the line of the song. Then sitting on the edge of Bearskin Lake, I'll sing all the verses I can bring to mind. Quietly, in a voice as uncertain as memory, I will sing to the tuna fish casserole, to the loons, to the white pines, to a woman whose songs had to be enough. (pp. 158–159)

There are important keys here, themes that are echoed often in the literature of the imagination, in the psychic homeland. Moore says she knows the place intimately though she has never seen it. There is an important tie to places and familiar rituals that are now long gone. There is a crucial translation of one image into a metaphor for another—here the music has become a dotted line or representation of place, or even more powerfully, the song and dotted line have become a path to both past and future. Most important, Moore projects a return to an identity-defining place and time, really to another self, and the return can be either literal (by canoe), or metaphorical (by song). These are critical markers of the dreams of place and while others may define the character of their homelands differently, these markers will recur whether the images are of family homes or sacred places, whether of nation-states or utopian worlds—whether the gate[17] through which we pass is language or light, melody or garden blossom. Language will carry the familiar taste of bread baked at home and the smell of the kitchen in the spoken word—*lefsa* or *tortilla*. The light at dusk will carry the sound of evening prayer. The color and sequence of blossom and berry will carry the metaphor of the seasons' passages, and our own. These are the recognizable markers we may seek as we age, as family and rituals become more important, as we are less able to control where and how we live. They have been translated in senior housing as bread machines, or enclosed gardens, or old songs, but it is not clear that such manicured and sterilized collective symbols carry adequate or appropriate personal meaning to "place" us. Can the smell of a bread machine substitute for the kneading of dough and the hours spent in expectation of its taste, and the rituals about "breaking bread" at a Sabbath table? Can the bread machine produce a dough with which one can "do everything" as in the Teresienstadt women's cookbook? Belonging is carried in the layering of people and places, through rituals and the metaphors that describe them—

the place name as lullaby as mother. It is this transformation from the literal to the archetypal that contains the seed of belonging.

In another essay, Moore (1999) expanded the theme, describing the archetypal landscape as home.

> Sometimes I think I am homesick. Sometimes I think that what happens when the landscape seizes me with such sadness is that the moment reminds me of a home I left generations ago, a beloved place I remember in the deepest recesses of my mind. It might be a landscape on an intellectual plane, a Platonic realm of ideas where perfect truth and perfect beauty become one glorious idea that can't be distinguished from love. Or it might be a clean and windswept place, a real place at the edge of water. Maybe something ancient in my mind seeks meaning in the lay of the land, the way a newborn rejoices in the landscape of a familiar face. Maybe I go to the wilderness, again and again, frantically, desperately, because wild places bring me closer to home. (pp. 77–78)

These echoes of the need for wilderness as a remote and sacrosanct image are the "impossible but necessary" islands by which Gladwin's islanders navigate. We also navigate by these images of home. Moore is drawn back to the land by love, by ancestral rituals, by ancient archetypes that carry something of the deepest layers of the persona. She is not drawn in by a specific landscape, but by landscape itself. Norberg-Schulz (1985) has written of the way place "conditions" belonging and personality, defines one's place, literally and metaphorically, and so one's identity. He suggests that even if we are to move somewhere else, the relationship with such a place is always with us. It is place that frames and limits perception, knowledge and even action. It is the taken for granted by which we judge what is different, distinct and foreign—and hence not our place and hence, not our self. The psychic homeland then, may be the projection of this conditioned awareness into the future and it may give us the skills to deal with that which is alien. What Moore has found in wilderness is more than autobiographical reminiscence; it is the archetypal self and the means by which we integrate change—and she is "frantically," "desperately" drawn back.

Paradox: Sanctuary and Struggle

While Moore is drawn to a Platonic ideal, others are drawn to paradoxical images that pair sanctuary and struggle. The late controversial author and academic Edward Said (1999) wrote of his search for identity as a child born in Egypt with an English first name and an Arabic family name, raised in a bilingual house, schooled in a British system, with Christian parents. His highly publicized and debated act in throwing a rock at Israeli soldiers was interpreted as an expression of joy at the prospect of a Palestinian homeland, a place in which the diverse aspects of his persona could at last be unified. Other displaced writers have found no such unity. Andre Aciman's (2000) work is paradigmatic in representing the complexities of the psychic homeland, in delineating the fungibility of time and place for refugees, exiles and the displaced (and, we may presume, the aging).

> Each year the city sees many ex-Alexandrians return and wander along its streets. Like revenants and time travelers, some come back from the future, from decades and continents away, A.D. people barging in on B.C. affairs, true anachronoids drifting about the city with no real purpose but to savor a past that, even before arriving they know they'll neither recapture nor put behind them, but whose spell continues to lure them on these errands in time. The Portuguese have a word, *retornados*, descendants of Portuguese settlers who return to their homeland in Europe centuries after colonizing Africa—except that they are African-born Europeans who return to Africa as tourists, not knowing why they come, or why they need to come again, or why this city that feels like home and which they can almost touch at every bend of the street can be as foreign as those places they've never seen before but studied in travel books. (p. 8)

Nor is Aciman immune from this morphing of time and place. He continues:

> Later that night . . . I think of . . . the young man of fourteen I used to be then, and of myself now, and of the person I might have been had I stayed here thirty years ago. . . . And I think of this imaginary self who never strayed or did the things I probably regret having done but would have done anyway and don't wish to disown; a self who never left Egypt . . . and who, on nights such as these, still dreams of the world abroad and of faraway America, the way I, over the years, have longed for life right here when I feel I don't fit anywhere else.
>
>   I wonder if this other self would understand about him and me, and being here and now and on the other bank as well—the other life, the one that we never live but conjure up when the one

we have is perhaps not the one we want. . . . I had hoped finally
to let go of this city, knowing all the while that the longing would
start again soon enough, that one never washes anything away,
and that this marooned and spectral city, which is no longer home
for me . . . would eventually find newer, ever more beguiling ways
to remind me that here is where my mind always turns, that
here . . . I'll always end up, even if I never come back. (pp. 20–21)

This then, is the fundamental paradox of the psychic homeland
literature. We come to terms at last with the notion that there can
be *no* peaceful accommodation to where we are, or to the world we
wish ourselves back to, or forward to; the one we recognize, or
desire, or design. For some, this acknowledgement may initiate the
struggle to make that notion of "home" real by building it in bricks
and mortar or in policy. For others, it may bring some recognition
that "home," while "devoutly to be wished for," can never be consum-
mated, and we must live on the cusp of longing. We can read the
classic *Wizard of Oz* (Baum, 2000) as a return to sanctuary after
travel, or as the first in a series of adventure stories that presage
the on-going quest for wisdom, strength, compassion and self. Robert
Coles' (1970) work with migrant children is moving testimony to the
desire for a place of one's own, even as these children have given
up the belief that it is possible. One child marvels that he has the
right to a particular chair in the schoolroom. A sharecropper mother
dreams that one of her children will marry and someday settle in a
home of her own, "and never leave it," even as she acknowledges
that it is unlikely. An urban child sleeps with a deodorant bottle
because the label reads "100% safe," and he hopes this talisman
will provide a safe home from the violence of the real city streets
(Garbarino, Dubrow, Kostelny, & Pardo, 1992). What about children,
and their parents, who dream of a homeland that no longer exists?
What about the aging caught in the limbo of refugee camps, nursing
homes, assisted care facilities? What about the aging propped beside
garden paths in places sealed from the outside for their "protection,"
or those remembering a Russia they never knew?

Being Away: Exile

The first imagined state posited here is the foreign land mentally
constructed by all exiles—a land of strangers to which they can
never belong, so they become citizens neither of a past nor a

present land. The mythic homeland, with the further passing of time, increasingly becomes imagined as well, for nostalgia and longing play parts in such cultural constructs. (Del Giudice & Porter, 2001, pp. 2–3)

In their book on the character of imagined homelands, Del Giudice and Porter describe the manner in which oral traditions communicate and teach national identity through notions of utopia they call "dreamworlds." They describe in detail the use of such imagery to "entice and impoverish" and we may see here the potential for development of both the idealized, utopian and xenophobic, genocidal aspects of the psychic homeland. While this chapter does not pretend to be able to address the full implications of the collective notion of homeland, its influence on personal imagery can not be ignored. The Passover seder includes a ritual reference to "next year in Jerusalem" for Zionists and secular Jews alike. Cubans who have settled in Miami to await the fall of the Castro regime say "next year in Havana" whether or not they intend to return. Both Jews and Cubans may be more integrated in their current communities than they would be in their rhetorical homelands, but as has been suggested, Diaspora may become an end in itself. Malkki (1992; 1996) interviewed Hutu refugees in a Tanzanian camp, and found many that rejected settlement options, seeing themselves as a nation in exile with a "moral trajectory" toward the homeland in Burundi. Displacement is a form of "categorical purity" and a way of becoming "more powerful as a Hutu." Ironically the imagined state of Burundi becomes a mere artifact of the "true" nation of exile. Malkki has written: "Now perhaps more than ever before, people are chronically mobile and routinely displaced, and invent homes and homelands in the absence of territorial, national bases—not *in situ*, but through memories of, and claims on, places that they can or will no longer corporeally inhabit" (p. 434).

If there are clear political implications to this, then there are also social implications when we shift our attention to imagination and desire. The UNHCR describes resettlement in the country of origin as its primary goal. There is a parallel assumption that as refugees resettle, they will build a new place identity and place attachments. It is clear however, that the "psychic homeland" can *reduce* integration as immigrants move to homelands that have changed, or places that may be temporary where they settle in enclaves of shared language and nurture notions of ethnic "purity" alongside xenophobic notions of the Other and rhetoric about a return "home." Televised news reports claimed that some Kosovar refugees refused to leave overcrowded camps for a trip to the United States, because they dreamed of returning as quickly as possible to the homes from which they had been expelled. In a moving article on the Lost Boys of the Sudan, Sara Corbett (2001) describes boys and young men who were forced to cross the Sudan, Ethiopia and Kenya in search of safety from wars and the bandits that roamed the African landscape. Some have been resettled in the United States, and the article chronicles their efforts to make the transition.

> Despite the dangers and hardships in camp, not everyone at Kakuma [the refugee camp] applauds the wholesale export of Lost Boys to the United States. Several Sudanese elders in the camp have suggested that the State Department's money would be better spent encouraging peace in Sudan, echoing the philosophy of several human rights organizations that have argued that carefully orchestrated, pre-emptive intervention could stem the tide of displacement worldwide. The elders in Kakuma also worry that once absorbed into American culture, the boys will lose their African identity and with it any commitments to return. Accordingly, a number of the young men arrived in America armed with cassettes of taped lectures from their elders, warning of the myriad dangers they perceived in the boys' future. One afternoon in Boston, an 18-year-old named Jacob played part of his tape for me. . . . He is saying: "Don't drink. Don't smoke. Don't kill. Go to school every day, and remember, America is not your home." (p. 48)

In 2002, 24,000 Sudanese refugees fled violence in the refugee camp in northern Uganda where some of them had lived for as much as 17 years. In 2005, refugees still flee Darfur in the Sudan. Rwandans flee to the Congo, and Burundians flee to Rwanda. The World Food Programme seeks to feed a million and a half people in the wake of the 2004 tsunami in Asia and East Africa. And when this book is on a library shelf, still others will be imagining survival and awaiting return while carrying an image of a beloved place in their heads.

What then *is* the homeland as it is influenced by the collective? Is it some pictorial image that flashes through the head like a life review before dying? Is it language or ritual, religion or mythology? Is it some sense of "otherness" by which we are judged in the cultures that have inherited or housed us? Or is it some sense of being a member of "the chosen people"? There can be no question that the measure of homeland will be taken differently by those inside the culture, and those outside it, by those with power and those without it.

In her eloquent essay on the building of a dam in Gujarat, India, Arundhati Roy (1999) assessed the number of people, displaced by the building of a single "big" dam at 33 million. Considering the lack of alternate job opportunities, transportation and available housing for many of these people, a significant percentage of whom are low caste, the impacts are catastrophic. What is homeland to those whose homes and family histories and livelihoods now lie beneath tons of water? Where is the place they can feel they belong? Or is the imagination of belonging, of a place to settle, a luxury to be denied the poor? It is, of course, the poverty of imagination of planners and government officials that results in projects that give no legitimation or value to a residential population and the power of its imagination of home. We can "cost-out" the loss in arable acres, the need for housing, the jobs lost and gained, but there is no estimate for the loss of the land's stories, the drowning of history on the land, and the loss of home, except perhaps if we measure the cost in terrorism as people kill and die for a place they imagine.

The Language of Familiars

> What was it that stood for home? . . . My homeland was made of something . . . more primary than ideology. Landscapes, certainly, and cityscapes, a sense of place. . . . There was the webwork of friendships and other relationships. . . . But there were also elements less palpable that nevertheless constituted my psychic home. . . . The first great lessons of my uprooting were in the enormous importance of language and of culture. . . . To lose an internal language is to subside into an inarticulate darkness in which we become alien to ourselves. . . . As with language, so with culture. . . . We could hardly acquire a human identity outside it, just as we could hardly think or perceive outside language. (1999, pp. 48–50)

In 1989, Jo-Ann Mort (1999) was on an island in Croatia, where there were no connections to the life she had lived or to familiar land. She says that she began to long for the rhythms she knew, the shapes of words on the tongue, or something taken for granted.

Mort sought a newspaper, a John Wayne movie—for the way he pronounced the words. What she got instead was translation and the occasional British tabloid. These were approximations of the familiar, but there was something missing in the language, the nuance, the rhythm of the expected phrasing. It was not quite home. When Milosevic closed off access to international and local media, all that remained was electronic communication which linked her, for a time, to home and by implication, to freedom, until that too was shut down. The only thing that remained was a web site in cyber-space.

> While television images fade and newsprint crumbles, Web sites remain until their sponsors take them down. . . . While Milosevic silenced radio stations B21 in Kosovo and B92 in Belgrade, they transmitted via the Internet. With . . . software, one could listen to the dissident radio from anywhere in the world, even if it was no longer playing on the radio band. That was too much Internet for Milosevic. Finally, he had to seal off B92 completely, in addition to destroying its radio signal, so that the broadcasts couldn't take place on the internet. But, left as a reminder to the world, if you log on to http://helpB92, you can find this message from the station's director, Sassa Mirkovic: "Radio B92 closed down and sealed off/On Friday, April 2/Struggle Continues, We Shall Never Surrender." The photos of distress on the site are frozen in time (n.p.).

So in the search for the familiar, first it is language that represents "home," but neither translation nor tabloid will do when it is the synesthesia of words that represent cultural memory.[21] For the tourist, the desire for novelty can wear thin after a time, and we begin to seek something that will ground us. A fellow tourist who speaks our language will do, or we write postcards, "wishing you were here," longing for someone to share the experience, or perhaps just to hear the familiar cadences in our head. For Mort, John Wayne has become the symbolic connection, and a technological "fix" has become the channel through which the synesthesia passes—the path between the foreign and the familiar. And as the distance becomes greater between here and home, the path becomes more important, until the path itself becomes "home." And then, when the path is guarded or gone, the signpost to the path becomes home. Breyten Breytenbach wrote, "[Exile] made my mother tongue into a 'homeland,' a moveable feast, indeed a dancing of the bones. . . . It gave a *taste* to words" (1991, pp. 78–79). It becomes easy to find a home, in the language of exile, and as Hoffman suggested, the culture of exile.

What then are the institutions that represent us in exile? If we can not guarantee that we will return to the land, the cityscape, the friends, what holds our place like a bookmark in a book on an unreachable shelf? There is an evocative literature of immigrant populations who have dreamed the nation of America into being, but America also permitted immigrants to dream their homelands into being. In his book on migration to the suburbs, Suarez (1999) described the manner in which immigrant communities built institutions that would not have been available in the places from which they had come. Churches, social clubs, even physical neighborhoods were created to represent patterns that were now long gone or might never have existed—the Puluwat's "impossible but necessary" again.

> In the early years of the century the archdiocese encouraged the establishment of 'national churches' in Chicago. It was more than a spiritual version of 'giving the people what they want'; it was a recognition of national aspirations thwarted back home by centuries of empire and conflict. A glance at a map of Europe would have shown no nation-state called 'Croatia.' But a Croatian church, with mass said in the home tongue, with a vernacular architecture and the adoration of national saints, could create a Croatia of the mind, even thousands of miles away in Chicago. Lithuania and Poland would disappear from the maps of Europe, on and off, but similarly, Poles and Lithuanians could find in the bricks and smokestacks of Chicago a freedom to be Polish, impossible to obtain in Wroclaw and Gdansk; and the Poles built magnificent churches that proclaimed their presence to the rest of the city. (p. 48)

So eventually the representation matters more than the reality— the symbol, the ritual, the memory, the imagination of place that holds us together, helps us survive. Italo Calvino (1972) wrote of the imaginary city of Despina that is accessible only by sea or by camel caravan. The camel driver sees it as a ship, and the sailor, as a camel, and *we* see the homeland we want to see. The Disney town of Celebration has provided a platform to the New Urbanists who have become arguably the most powerful single force in American town planning today. Their principles of small town, low rise, community-based planning will soon be exported across the globe, as American technology, fast food and film culture have been before. Andrew Ross (1999) has quoted the Disney "pitch" for Celebration: " 'There once was a place where neighbors greeted neighbors in the quiet of summer twilight. . . . 'Where children chased fireflies. . . . The movie house showed cartoons on Saturday. The grocery store delivered. . . . Remember that place?. . . . It held a magic all its own. The special magic of an American hometown' " (n.p.). And so we use bricks and mortar to build the psychic homeland as a stage set, and we provide a libretto to guide the audience in singing along: "Oh give me a home where the buffalo roam . . . and where the skies are not cloudy all day."

EPILOGUE

Many years ago, I lived in southern New Jersey, in a rural landscape of sand and pine, with tea colored streams and days of dense fog and roiling fire. I loved exploring its back roads and the mute foundations of long abandoned houses that traced their history to the Revolutionary War. One day, a friend and guide took me down an unmarked sand road and we found ourselves in the "town" of Friendship, not far from Four Corners. The latter was the intersection in leaf rot and pine needles of barely visible sand roads. It had been a major intersection during the Revolutionary War when the local iron ore was made into cannonballs to be used against the British. The town, which may have been built on the ruins of an earlier town was probably built for its proximity to these sand roads, but all that remained in the early 1980s was a single late 19th century structure, its windows long gone, a door off its hinges and an empty, hollow look that left me breathless. Now a name on a map and a haunted house stand for industry, church and home. I wonder whether anyone still dreams of coming home to "Friendship."

Lee Rivlin (Horwitz, Klein, Paxson, & Rivlin, 1978, p. 2) once wrote that our past and present are no longer acquainted with each other as they were for previous generations when 'today and yesterday mixed frequently and familiarly' through the modes of extended families and long-term residence in places. Memory is all we have left to "construct the mosaics of our lives," she said. I am troubled by this notion; there is no sense of the future. As we age, we do not allow ourselves to make choices that have long trajectories—no new careers, no new houses, no pets that might outlive us. We are "honored" for the wisdom of our years and asked to write our memoirs as though we are landmarks on a landscape of the past. And as we amputate the future, as we are asked more about what we remember than about what we dream, we let go of one of the most distinctly human abilities, the one tied to sanctuary and survival—the imagination of coming home.[22]

NOTES

1. Jung et al. (1989, p. 89) describe belongingness as "the quintessential precondition or prerequisite for determining the other senses and feelings of 'homeliness.' "

2. While some dictionaries define "chimera" as a monster, I refer here to a definition of *Webster's Collegiate Dictionary* which also describes a chimera as " . . . an illusion or fabrication of the mind, esp.: an unrealizable dream . . . " (Woolf, 1980).

3. According to Schaller (1995), "In the last decade, an estimated two million children have been killed by war, . . . an estimated four to five million children have been disabled by war, . . . an estimated 12–25 million children have been displaced from their homes either within or without their national borders" (p. 47).

4. I have drawn this "metaphysical loss of home" from the work of Berger, Berger, and Kellner who have suggested that this is the result of the "homelessness" of modern man (Berger, Berger, & Kellner, 1983).

5. There is an extensive literature on the meaning of home. Some of the classic sources include: Bachelard (1969), Rapoport (1969), Cooper-Marcus (1974), Relph (1976), and Altman and Werner (1985).

6. There is an extensive literature on landscape, experience and culture. Among the classic sources are Tuan (1977), Meinig (1979), Jackson (1984), and Groth and Bressi (1997).

7. Proshansky, Fabian, and Kaminoff (1983) have provided a crucial corrective to the self theory of social psychologists in their

emphasis on the role of environment in the development of the individual. They suggest that we have a place-identity defined as a "broad set of positively & negatively valenced cognitions about the physical world which serve to place us, protect us and define attitudes and behaviour" (p. 75). The authors suggest that the place identity influences the way we personalize, communicates place-appropriate behavior, warns us when we are approaching a place of danger, mediates change in the environment, and permits us to distinguish the familiar from the novel environment.

8. Source: *Refugees by numbers—2001 Edition* [on-line]. 2002. Available: http://unhcr.ch-cgi-bin-texis-vtx-home-opendoc.htm?tbl= STATISTICS&id=3d075d374&page=statistics [August 2002]

9. More's term "utopia" is literally translated as "no-place" in an ironic twist representing his implicit social criticism. Others have distinguished between *eu-topias* or positive imagined places and *dys*topias or negative imaginary places.

10. Schaller (1995) translates *sehar* as "A sophisticated expression suggesting that unknown hands are stealing 'the young girl's dowry' and making it impossible for her to get married" (p. 57).

11. Tuan wrote: "A brief but intense experience is capable of nullifying the past so that we are ready to abandon home for the promised land. Still more curious is the fact that people can develop a passion for a certain type of environment without the benefit of direct encounter" (1977, p. 185).

12. Bishop provides an eloquent reminder of the value of imagination in creating the exotic" In one sense, natural landscape does not exist. We inescapably shape the world, even if only with our minds and not our hands. When we shape the world, we create places. . . . It has been said that to be without a relationship to a place is to be in spiritual exile. Humans seem to need such special, even sacred, places. The space under the stairs, or in a corner of a room, so essential in childhood, is echoed again and again in sacred groves, caves, churches and temples. . . . In addition to both the informal respect bestowed by individuals upon their own special places and the collective worship of sites recognized by an entire culture is the grandeur,

but more elusive fascination with faraway places. With these places the fabulous and the empirical merge indiscriminately (1989, pp. 1, 3).

13. The 2003 debate over drilling for oil in America's Arctic National Wildlife Refuge is a case in point. Environmental organizations rallied supporters to block drilling in an area few, if any, would ever see, and the New York Times sent economics correspondent Nicholas Kristof to evaluate what it was that was really being contested. His series of articles laid out the caribou migration patterns and polar bear hunting grounds beside claims of the Bush Administration that the oil reserves would be needed to reduce dependence on foreign sources.

14. Andre Aciman's (2000) brilliant writing carries the reader through a kind of black hole in time. One is never sure whether the memory is in the past or present, reality or fiction. This is the most eloquent model for the time shifting character of the psychic homeland. Aciman calls it "mnemonic arbitrage."

> Not only did I remember, in the girl's studio in Cambridge, a sensation that I had experienced in Rome that evoked Alexandria but, when I eventually did return to Alexandria, in 1995, I caught myself looking at my beloved Mediterranean through tiny side streets only to feel a sudden yearning for West End Avenue, facing the Hudson River through 106th Street—which had become the dearest spot on earth to me, precisely because it reminded me of Alexandria. In Alexandria, I was homesick for the place from which I had learned to re-create Alexandria, the way that the rabbis in exile were forced to reinvent their homeland on paper, only to find, perhaps, that they worshipped the paper more than the land (p. 157).

15. Graham Rowles wrote of the need for "inter-subjective corroboration" or consensual validation in assessing the validity of experiential research. He said "Reductionism impoverishes our sensitivity to the uniqueness and existential meaning of . . . experience. We may become deluded into considering the abstractions as the reality" (1978, p. 175). I use the term recognition here to suggest that we recognize ourselves in the stories of others and that our own stories may prompt insight into our own and others' relationship between place and identity.

16. "The last song I want to play is a song that expresses my psychological home I want to have soon. I want this place to be exciting, filled with love, as was dancing in the kitchen as a child. I want to share this place with someone I love and I want this place . . . to be somewhere where I can practice my medicine and share the skills I have with other people. This place is like a pilgrimage I'm on. Someday I will get there . . . someday . . . "

17. There are echoes of Eliade's (1987) work on the sacred and the profane. He suggests the sacred places we create have a center and a boundary to distinguish them from the profane, with the *axis mundi* as the portal or gate between these realms.

18. In his autobiography, Abba Eban wrote of spending every waking moment that he was not in school with a grandfather who introduced him to the language and traditions of Judaism, until he became so enmeshed with the patterns of Zionism that use of the term "us" evoked images of the Jewish people rather than a smaller family or social unit. "As my grandfather guided me hour after hour through the modern Hebrew literature, my loyalties became linked with more recent dramas—the martyrdoms, inquisitions, massacres and pogroms, and most of all, with the quest for remedy and honor . . . [of] the Zionist pioneers. . . . Before I passed my early teens, I was the captive of a Jewish destiny" (1977, p. 7).

19. Davison wrote "Who says you can't go home again? I'd gone—sort of—and I'd been strangely at ease. Even though I'd never been there before, in person, I knew the famous mantel piece in the living room where they'd all hung their Christmas stockings, the back stairs they'd always sneak up and down to avoid detection. . . . The site was familiar, familial. The rooms looked just the way I wanted them to look. This was not a house, this was home itself" (1980, p. 27).

20. Tan wrote: "I look at their faces again and I see no trace of my mother in them. Yet they still look familiar. And now I also see what part of me is Chinese. It is so obvious. It is my family. It is in our blood. After all these years, it can finally be let go" (1989, p. 330).

21. Adams has written about the government's efforts to assimilate and acculturate Native Americans through the restriction of the use of native languages (1995).

22. Commenting on this chapter, Rowles has noted that "future orientation" is one of the strongest predictors of longevity (a finding from studies of centenarians), and that in recent decades the process of retreating to memories, and the abandonment of a sense of future has increasingly been postponed with an extended life-span. In turn, Chaudhury has noted the value of an acceptance of mortality and the importance of a spiritual phase of life that comes with the latter years. In these comments are the metaphors for the struggle of elders and displaced people—the conflict between concentration on the past and a desire for the future.

REFERENCES

Aciman, A. (2000). *False papers.* New York: Farrar, Straus, Giroux.

Adams, D. W. (1995). *Education for Extinction: American Indians and the Boarding School Experience.* Lawrence, KS: University Press of Kansas.

Altman, I., & Werner, C. M. (Eds.). (1985). *Human behavior and environment: Vol. 8. Home environments: Human behavior and environment.* New York: Plenum Press.

Bachelard, G. (1969). *The Poetics of space.* (M. Jolas, Trans.). Boston: Beacon Press.

Basso, K. H. (1996). *Wisdom sits in places.* Albuquerque, NM: University of New Mexico Press.

Baum, L. F. (2000). *The Wonderful Wizard of Oz.* New York: HarperCollins. (Original work published 1900)

Berger, P., Berger, B., & Kellner, H. (1983). *The homeless mind: Modernization and consciousness.* New York: Vintage books.

Bishop, P. (1989). *The Myth of Shangri-La: Tibet, travel writing and the western creation of sacred landscape.* London: Athlone Press.

Breytenbach, B. (1991, Spring). The Long march from hearth to heart [Special issue: Home: A Place in the world]. *Social Research, 58*(1), 69–87.

Calvino, I. (1972). *Invisible cities.* New York: Harcourt Brace Jovanovich.

Coles, R. (1970). *Uprooted children: The Early life of migrant children.* New York: Perennial Library/Harper and Row.

Cooper, C. (1974). The House as symbol of the self (J. Lang, C. Burnette, W. Moleski, & D. Vachon, Eds.). In *Designing for human behavior* (pp. 130–146). Stroudsburg, PA: Dowden, Hutchinson and Ross.

Corbett, S. (2001, April 1). The Long, long, long road to Fargo. *New York Times,* p. 48ff.

De Silva, C. (Ed.). (1996). *In Memory's kitchen.* Northvale, NJ: Jason Aronson Inc.

Del Giudice, L., & Porter, G. (Eds.). (2001). *Imagined states: Nationalism, Utopia, and longing in oral cultures.* Logan, UT: Utah State Press.

Dinesen, I. (1972). *Out of Africa.* New York: Vintage.

Eban, A. (1977). *An autobiography.* New York: Random House.

Eliade, M. (1987). *The Sacred and the profane: The Nature of religion.* New York: Harcourt, Brace Jovanovich. (Original work published 1957)

Garbarino, J., Dubrow, N., Kostelny, K., & Pardo, C. (1992). *Children in danger: Coping with the consequences of community violence.* San Francisco: Jossey-Bass.

Groth, P., & Bressi, T. W. (1997). *Understanding ordinary landscapes.* New Haven, CT: Yale University Press.

Hoffman, E. (1999). The New Nomads. In A. Aciman (Ed.), *Letters of transit: Reflections on exile and memory* (pp. 35–63). New York: The New Press.

Horwitz, J., Klein, S., Paxson, L., & Rivlin, L. (Eds.). (1978, December). Environmental autobiography (M. Francis, R. Hart, C. Perez, & L. Rivlin, coordinating editors). *Childhood City Newsletter, 14.* New York: City University of New York.

Jackson, J. B. (1984). *Discovering the vernacular landscape.* New Haven, CT: Yale University Press.

Jung, H. Y., & Jung, P. (1989). The Way of Ecopiety: A Philosophic Minuet for Ecological Ethics. In D. W. Black, D. Kunze & J. Pickles (Eds.), *Commonplaces: Essays on the nature of place* (pp. 81–99). Lanham, MD: University Press of America.

Lane, B. (1989, October 11). Fierce landscapes and the indifference of God. *The Christian Century,* pp. 907–910.

Lopez, B. (1978). *Crossing open ground.* New York: Vintage Books.

Lowenthal, D. (1972). Geography, experience and imagination: Towards a geographical epistemology. In P. English & R. Mayfield (Eds.), *Man, space and environment.* New York: Oxford University Press.

Malkki, L. (1992). National geographic: The Rooting of peoples and the territorialization of national identity among scholars and refugees. In G. Eley & R. G. Suny (Eds.), *Becoming National: A Reader* (pp. 434–453). New York: Oxford University Press.

Marcus, C. C. (1990). From the pragmatic to the spiritual: An Intellectual autobiography (Chap. 5). In I. Altman & K. Christensen (Eds.), *Environment and Behavior Studies* (pp. 111–140). New York: Plenum Press.

Meinig, D. (Ed.). (1979). *The Interpretation of ordinary landscapes: Geographical essays.* New York: Oxford University Press.

Moore, K. D. (1999). *Holdfast: At home in the natural world.* New York: The Lyons Press.

More, T. (1965). *Utopia.* (P. Turner, Trans.). Baltimore, MD: Penguin Press. (Original work published 1516)

Morley, D., & Robins, K. (1990). No Place like *Heimat:* Images of home(land) in European culture. In G. Eley & R. G. Suny (Eds.), *Becoming National: A Reader* (pp. 456–478). New York: Oxford University Press.

Mort, J.-A. (1999, Summer). War.com. *Dissent, 46*(3), n.p.

Norberg-Schulz, C. (1985). *The concept of dwelling.* New York: Rizzoli.

Parker, K. (1993). 'Home is where the heart . . . lies.' *Transition, 59,* 65–77.

Paterson, D. (1988). Traditions and memories: Three places of home. *Landscape Architectural Review,* pp. 13–18.

Proshansky, H. M., Fabian, A. K., & Kaminoff, R. (1983). Place-identity: Physical world socialization of the self. *Journal of Environmental Psychology, 3,* 57–83. London: Academic Press, Inc.

Rapoport, A. (1969). *House form and culture.* Englewood Cliffs, NJ: Prentice Hall.

Rawlins, C. (1992). The Meadow at the corner of your eye. *Northern Lights, 8*(1), 4–5.

Relph, E. (1976). *Place and placelessness.* London: Pion Ltd.

Riley, R. B. (1992). Attachment to the ordinary landscape (Chapter 2). In I. Altman & S. M. Low (Eds.), *Place attachment* (pp. 13–36). Human behavior and environment, vol. 12. New York: Plenum Press.

Ross, A. (1999). *The Celebration Chronicles: Life, Liberty and the Pursuit of Property Value in Disney's New Town.* New York: Ballantine Books.

Rowles, G. D. (1978). Reflections on experiential field work (Chap. 11). In *Humanistic geography: Prospects and problems* (pp. 173–193). Chicago: Maaroufa Press Inc.

Rowles, G. (1978). *Prisoners of space?* Boulder, CO: Westview Press.

Roy, A. (1999). *The cost of living.* New York: The Modern Library.

Ryden, K. C. (1993). *Mapping the invisible landscape: Folklore, writing, and the sense of place.* Iowa City, IA: University of Iowa.

Said, E. W. (1999). *Out of place.* New York: Vintage Books.

Schaer, R., Claeys, G., & Sargent, L. (2000). *Utopia: The search for the ideal society in the Western World.* New York; Oxford: New York Public Library; Oxford University Press.

Schaller, J. G. (1995, October). Children, child health, and war. *International Child Health, 6*(4), 45–59.

Schlemmer, L. (1972, December). City or rural 'homeland': A Study of patterns of identification among Africans in South Africa's divided society. *Social Forces, 51*(2), 154–164.

Sopher, D. (1979). The landscape of home: Myth, experience and social meaning. In D. Meinig (Ed.), *The interpretation of everyday landscapes: Geographical essays* (pp. 129–153). New York: Oxford University Press.

Suarez, R. (1999). *The old neighborhood: What we lost in the great suburban migration.* New York: The Free Press.

Terr, L. (1990). *Too scared to cry.* New York: Harper and Row.

Tuan, Y.-F. (1977). *Space and place.* Minneapolis: University of Minnesota Press.

Wickham, C. J. (1999). *Constructing Heimat in postwar Germany: Longing and belonging.* Lewiston, NY: The Edwin Mellen Press.

Wolschke-Bulmahn, J. (1992, Spring). The fear of the new landscape: Aspects of the perception of landscape in the German youth movement between 1900 and 1933 and its influence on landscape planning. *The Journal of Architectural and Planning Research, 9*(1), 33–47.

Woolf, H. (Ed.). (1980). *Webster's New Collegiate Dictionary.* Springfield, MA: G. & C. Merriam and Company.

Yezierska, A. (1991). Soap and water. In W. Brown & A. Ling (Eds.), *Imagining America: Stories from the promised land* (pp. 105–110). New York: Persea Press. (Original work published 1920)

CHAPTER 7

Elderly Migrants and the Concept of Home: A Swedish Perspective

Fereshteh Ahmadi Lewin

The concept of home carries a number of different meanings in every culture. In general, home is conceived of as a safe place, a private sphere, and a place for social life. The concept of home can be given different meanings over the life course, depending on structural as well as group- or individual-related circumstances. Some researchers maintain that home has special significance in the lives of elders because of meanings resulting from length of stay in a single residence, reduced mobility, and the existence of established social networks (Hajighasemi, 1996; Lantz, 1996).

Elders' housing has been studied as a component of their general living conditions (see, for example, Abrahamson, 1993; Gaunt & Lantz, 1996; Herlitz, 1993; Tornstam, 1982). But the meaning of *home* for elders and the components of this concept have seldom been looked at in detail. Scarcity of research on the concept of *home* is especially conspicuous in the case of elderly immigrants. In the majority of investigations of housing and elders, the target group has been elderly natives. Despite the fact that elderly immigrants, especially those from developing countries who are migrating to

Western countries are dependent on having a *home,* perhaps even more than younger ones—not merely as a residence but as a nonmaterial phenomenon, they are given, at best, very little attention in investigations of migration, and, often, none at all.

In this chapter, I discuss why it is important to study how elderly immigrants view the concept of home. I lay down some guiding principles for such a study and present theoretical perspectives that allow us to discover factors influencing how elderly immigrants, with different cultural backgrounds, define their homes. But, first, I briefly review some general perspectives on the meaning of home.

GENERAL PERSPECTIVES ON THE MEANING OF HOME

Informants in many different studies have described the meaning they give to the concept of home (Baker et al., 1987; Csikszentmihalyi & Rochberg-Halton, 1981; Hayward, 1977; Rakoff, 1977; Sebba & Churchman, 1986; Sixsmith, 1986). These descriptions have categorized home as a place of security and control, as a mirror of personal views and values, as an influence and place for change, as both an opportunity for permanency and continuity, as a center for family relationships and friendship, as the center of activity, as a retreat from the surrounding world, as personal status indicator, as a concrete structure, and as a place to own (Després, 1991).

These categories are influenced by many crucial factors including age, gender, personal characteristics, and sociocultural background. For elderly immigrants, we can imagine that variables such as age and immigration characteristics are especially important. Other important variables in this context are arguably elderly immigrants' cultural and social background. These variables—which do not solely reflect individuals' social class of origin, but also factors such as whether they grew up in a big city or a small town—are two of the most important components in the construction of the concept of *home.* We can assume, for instance, that the dimension *home as retreat from the surrounding world* is probably less important for people from a nonindividualistic culture, than for people with backgrounds in more individualistic societies who are likely to perceive this dimension as crucial to their understanding of the home.

Similarly, the category *the home as personal status indicator* can be an important factor underlying how people from distinctive class societies assign meaning to the home. On the other hand, Després (1991) has shown that in societies with relatively small differences among social classes, this dimension is not particularly important. One other key factor is gender. According to some researchers, there is a considerable difference between men's and women's views of home and the significance with which they imbue this construct (Somerville, 1997; Vilkko, 1996). In this regard, the category of *home as center of activity* differs between elder immigrant men and women and especially between elder women and men from developing countries where social and cultural gender differences are more marked than in many Western societies.

It is important, therefore, in studying the concept of home among elderly immigrants, to identify the different factors that affect the meaning given to the concept of home. Three of the most important are identity, culture, and gender.

Home and Identity

Most people perceive their homes as important settings in their lives. It is difficult to cope with the complexity inherent in this perception. The home is a place for important family rituals, practical work, discussions, and other forms of meaningful interaction. Crucial features of the individual's identity are developed in the parental home, either in line with or in opposition to it (Proshansky, 1976).

Nonphysical aspects of a residence represent what we call *home*—as opposed to *house*. The house is where we live, but a home is for the soul. *Home* does not only mean a residence but also mental capacities, emotional relationships and social ties. The home resides at the center of our psyche.

The concept of *home* has multiple origins and is difficult to define. Its symbolic charge is strong. People live in a world of symbols that they themselves have created. The objects they make—their artifacts—express their intentions and meanings. This is, of course, also true of "what is commonly viewed as mankind's greatest and most tangible artifact" (Lantz, 1996, p. 21, my translation), the home. But what do our homes and the things they contain actually mean to us? In answering this question, some scholars emphasize the relationship between the home and identity. According to Lantz (1996, p. 29), the home is part of something he calls the personal sphere. A home is an extension of an individual's very person. According to Redvall (1987), people seek three values in their homes: identity, seclusion, and security. If this is the case—that the home is an integrated part of the individual's identity, then it "cannot be reduced to an apparatus for suiting a number of practical purposes. It is not a housing machine, but instead a complicated fabric of symbols, dreams, ideals and aspirations" (Lantz, 1996, p. 32, my translation).

Home and Culture

The concept of *home* is highly ideologically and culturally charged (Gaunt & Lantz, 1996, p. 1). It has a personal existential charge. The individual's perception of the meaning of a home is, accordingly, a social and cultural construction. The home is constructed from a pattern of cultural processes. It indicates the important boundaries of individuals' and families' private lives and shows how they relate to the larger society. According to Abramsson, Borgegård, and Fransson (2002), habitation includes different aspects. A residence can be merely a physical place, but it can also be part of a person's social, psychological, and cultural security.

Elderly immigrants' ideas about the home have largely been formed by their cultures of origin. Their views have also been affected by life conditions such as class affiliation, social standing, and previous city versus country living. Certain living arrangements, for example, the extended family, are, more common in developing countries. However, elderly immigrants from "developing countries" and especially those from big cities often have already experienced some aspects of modern life in their homeland. In most developing countries, significant changes in traditional forms of living have taken place since the middle of the 20th century. Thus, many elderly immigrants from "developing countries" have experienced sharply contrasting living conditions during different periods of their lives. During their childhood and youth, they lived under more traditional conditions, characterized by extended families and a hierarchical family structure. During middle age and their senior years (for those who were elderly when they immigrated), they have often lived under what could be called "semimodern" conditions, no longer characterized by life in an extended family, but by preserved strong family ties and, thereby, continued customs of social intercourse.

There are some similarities among different elderly immigrants' ideas about the home. But, more important, these ideas clearly diverge among groups and individuals, depending on differences in culture and lifestyle, as well as differences in individual life experiences and experiences of social and economic repression. On the micro-level, we can talk about the diversity of elderly immigrants' social backgrounds as a possible cause of this divergence. On the macro-level, it is more productive to elucidate cultural and sociopolitical differences among elderly immigrants' various homelands and between these homelands and Sweden.

Disparities among different groups of elderly immigrants in their concept of *home* have caused confusion and various types of problems for organizations and authorities working with elders. According to a report from the National Swedish Board of Health and Welfare, "some elderly immigrants desire placement in separate residences along with other elders from the same culture, with the same language and religion, where they can experience a common value system" (Eriksson, 1996, p. 19, my translation). Among other elderly immigrants, there is a repudiation of such group living and identity and an expressed desire to live in their own apartments (Ahmadi & Tornstam, 1996). Hajighasemi (1996) found that none of the elderly Iranians she studied in Sweden were familiar with the idea of group living. Such repudiation or ignorance of group living can lead, among certain groups of elderly immigrants, to refusal to live with their children, despite feelings of loneliness (Hajighasemi, 1996). One possible cause of such an attitude is that the lifestyle of the homeland—framed by development toward a more industrialized society—was no longer based on the extended family, but instead on individual living, a form that came to be perceived as optimal. Another possible cause is that some elderly immigrants have adapted to a Swedish lifestyle (Ahmadi & Tornstam, 1996). This lack of understanding of the disparate, culture-dependent perceptions of the home among elderly immigrants has been revealed in several investigations (Hajighasemi, 1996; Molina, 1997).

Disregarding that *home* can mean different things to different groups not only leads to a general confusion of ideas, but may lead to inappropriate actions (Abramsson et al., 2002). It is also important to recognize that immigrants do not form a homogeneous group. They have different ideas about home, its meaning and function. In order to evaluate how elderly immigrants' living requirements should be met, we need to deepen our knowledge of how they perceive their residence in a holistic sense, e.g., its meaning for them, their preferred forms of living, and how their home-related identities are reconstructed in the new society to which they have immigrated The habitation culture they bring with them to the new country is of considerable interest and importance in this regard.

Home and Gender

Some research shows that gender is an important factor affecting the strategies people use when trying to create a sense of home in a new environment. According to Somerville (1997), one consistent finding seems to be that men have a more uniform outlook on the meaning of the home than do women. Men are more inclined to perceive home in terms of status and achievement, whereas women tend to see it as an emotional retreat or a protective shelter (Rainwater, 1966; Seely, Sim, & Loosley, 1956). There is evidence that women are more involved in the home than are men, and that their benefits from it are greater (Saegert, 1980; Zaretsky, 1986). Somerville (1997) notes that, in the 19th century, the "cult of domesticity" and ideological distinction between different spheres—where women were identified with "the home" and men with "worldliness"—undoubtedly contributed to these gender differences. Similar gender-role patterns can also be observed in many other cultures; in terms of their self-image, women tend to be more intimately tied to the home (Rapoport 1981). More recent research on the home's meaning from a gender perspective has attempted to elucidate how ideological notions of the home are concretely expressed in everyday household chores, for example, in changed uses of the kitchen (Craik, 1989) and in the daily job of caring for the house and those who live there (Hunt, 1989; Mason, 1989). Irrespective of how the meaning of the home is perceived, the foremost conclusion we can draw is that such perceptions are never gender neutral.

What role does gender play in elderly immigrants' perceptions of the home? This is especially relevant given that both elderly men and women spend more time inside than outside the home and that indoor activity constitutes an important part of everyday life for both sexes. Elderly immigrants who have their social and cultural life isolated from the dominant society are even more restricted to home.

One investigation based on elder Finnish men and women's autobiographies shows that in women's autobiographies, the home is closely connected to the family and family life with small children (Vilkko, 1996). The study points out that when women consider the meaning of the home during old age, their interpretative frames include the family. "Living a life of worth in old age means having relatives—children and grandchildren—around one, even in the same house or immediate surroundings" (Vilkko, 1996, p. 6, my translation). This explains why the elderly women in this investigation perceived life in a high-rise apartment as lonely and unnatural. They compared this with their past residential experience, when everyone in the family, irrespective of age, lived under the same roof (Vilkko, 1996).

If we turn to the men in this investigation, they seldom "tell about a cozy family life, about the home's interior etc. when describing their active years. Men described houses and dwelling places from the outside, but only extremely rarely residences they had lived in" (Vilkko, 1996, p. 6, my translation). The men's autobiographies show that they interpret the home in a habitation context. Both women and men view home as a "world" separating them from a real world beyond, although it is also a reflection of the self, albeit viewed from different directions (Vilkko, 1996). Although men did not describe the meaning of habitation during their active years, it is interesting to note that such descriptions appeared fairly often when discussing old age. Aging brings with it a tendency for life to become more restricted to indoor activities. The home as an everyday environment becomes the object of men's reflections; it brings with it children and grandchildren's visits, celebrations, and day-to-day troubles (Vilkko, 1996).

The symbolic meanings of *home* play an important role in how elders appraise their life as a whole. Vilkko shows how expressions such as "to be at home in the world," "to have the world as my home," "to have a home as opposed to a nonhome," and "to be like home" constitute "cultural patterns of thought and expression that are used in life stories when assessing life" (Vilkko 1996, p. 7, my translation). In this way, a comparison between near and far, out and in, known and unknown, comfort and discomfort is shaped. The question is how these metaphorical, meaning-making dimensions coincide with elderly immigrants' gender-specific structures of signification with respect to the home.

HABITATION AND SEGREGATION

For elderly immigrants, the concept of home is largely constituted by the living experiences they carry with them from their country of origin. It is also shaped by experience gathered in the host country through contact with both fellow immigrants and the new society. In this regard, the fact that many immigrant groups live segregated from the host society can be expected to influence their conception of home.

Increasing immigration and higher rates of unemployment have combined to make the problem of segregation a much-debated issue on the political agenda in many Western countries. In Sweden, segregation, one of the most important questions pertaining to the living conditions of the Swedish immigrant population, has been studied for a couple of decades. Early studies were mostly concerned with differences between immigrant groups and the Swedish population, but lately interest in specific immigrant groups has grown stronger among Swedish researchers.

Obviously, there are differences in living conditions between native Swedes and immigrants, but these differences are more pronounced among different immigrant groups (Huttman, 1991; Kemeny, 1987; Murdie & Borgegård, 1998; Social Styrelsen, 1998). New studies of such differences should not be isolated from economic, political, institutional, and demographic development in the country as a whole. For this reason, some researchers (Borgegård, Magnusson, & Özüekren, 1999) point out that it is important to adopt a broader perspective and to work harder to obtain data about different immigrant subgroups. In this way research findings will more constructively aid in the formation of appropriate public policy.

To understand how different immigrant groups define home, we also need to study the housing and living conditions of migrants.

Many different factors affect how immigrants act on the housing market; for example, the timing of their arrival, length of stay, reasons for coming to the new country, success in the labor market, and social integration within mainstream society.

One especially important factor is the cultural values brought to the new country. This factor is crucial to the importance people accord to their places of residence, and how and where they prefer to live (Abramsson et al., 2002). A large proportion of the immigrants who arrived in Sweden during recent decades came from parts of the world that are not only geographically remote but also are culturally quite different from Sweden. Consequently, research about immigrant living conditions is not solely a question of mapping out how different immigrant groups settled geographically or investigating the economic and social reasons for their segregated living and social status. It is also necessary to understand what home symbolizes for different immigrant groups, given their diverse cultural backgrounds and "ways of thinking."

IMMIGRANT HOUSING CONDITIONS

Borgegård et al. (1999) mention that researchers in Sweden often tend to describe immigrant housing conditions from the vantage point of Swedish values, norms, and preferences. For example, it is common to mention that immigrants are overrepresented in the least attractive housing areas of the Swedish urban landscape. The words "least attractive" reflect Swedish values and preferences. Areas where immigrants live are not necessarily the "least attractive" to the immigrants themselves. A study of an area where a large number of immigrants of Turkish origin resided revealed that most of these immigrants did not perceive of the setting as an unattractive area (Borgegård et al., 1999; Özüekren, 1992). On the other hand, Iranian immigrants living in the suburbs of major Swedish towns have been shown to be particularly unhappy about their living conditions and often feel as if they are being stifled in efforts to find housing in higher status areas (Kuusela, 1992; Molina, 1997).

In previous Swedish research, differences in housing circumstances between Swedes and immigrants were explained with reference to "duration of stay in Sweden" and "social and cultural proximity" to Swedish norms and values. It has been claimed that housing conditions are very different among immigrants from cultures that are markedly different from the Swedish culture in that within group cohesion is very strong (Kemeny, 1987). Such differences are seen as diminishing as a function of duration of residence in Sweden (Biterman, 1993; Linén & Lindberg, 1991; Murdie & Borgegård, 1998). "Social distance" has been mentioned as an important causal factor in determining how immigrant households adapt to the housing market (Teeland, 1988). Immigrants with norms and values closer to Swedish norms and values are viewed as being able to more easily integrate into Swedish society. Support for this proposition has been derived from examining immigrants to Sweden from the other Nordic countries, as the construction of their households is similar to the dominant Swedish pattern.

Borgegård, Håkansson, and Müller (1998) observe that when we focus on the geographical dispersion of immigrants during the period 1973–1992, immigrants from Chile and Iran were not more geographically concentrated than were immigrants from other Nordic countries. Turkish immigrants, on the other hand, have come to be geographically concentrated in a few suburbs, depending both on municipal authority direction and a wish to live among fellow countrymen. There has been no substantial migration from these suburbs. On the contrary, the concentration of Turkish immigrants seems to be increasing (Abramsson et al., 2002).

Even though both Turkish and Iranian norms and values differ substantially from those of the Swedish community, these groups show very different patterns of geographical dispersion. Turks claim to enjoy their homes and living areas. They mainly associate within their own ethnic group, with their kin and countrymen. Contacts with the Swedish community are few, even among second-generation Turkish youth. Although Turks live together because they want to preserve their cultural and ethnic identity, Iranians tend to want to have contact with Swedes from a similar social background. For example, it has been observed that Iranians in Stockholm do not live in any particular municipality but rather are spread around the whole Stockholm area (Molina, 1997). The determining factor here is income. Under the heading "demanding Iranians,"[1] Kuusela (1992, p. 108) writes about Iranians' "excessively high demands on housing standard and the location of their homes, and that Iranians want to live in attractive areas where there (are) seldom any available apartments." To Iranians the dwelling is a symbol of family status. They are more likely to be class conscious and to identify with well-educated people like those with an academic degree, and more specifically with the Swedish middle and upper classes, but without being geographically close to the groups with which they identify. Iranians believe this geographical distance to be the reason they have not had the opportunity to establish social ties with Swedes from the upper classes (Abramsson et al., 2002; Kuusela, 1992).

As this example shows, differences in housing circumstances between Turks and Iranians cannot be explained purely by reference to "social distance" from or "social and cultural affinity" to Swedish norms and values or "residential time in Sweden." There is almost no social or cultural affinity between Iranian and Swedish norms and values. Furthermore, the time of residence of Iranians in Sweden is even shorter than that of the Turks!

There is still much to be learned about immigrant housing. To be able to explain the level of integration into Swedish society for each immigrant group in terms of the housing environment, to assess the differences among immigrant groups, and to understand the reasons for these differences, we need to take into consideration the values, norms, and preferences within each group.

HABITATION AND INTEGRATION

Swedish immigration policy has undergone major changes during the last four decades. In the 1960s the stated political goal was to assimilate immigrants into Swedish society. In the 1970s the concept of integration was coined for a new policy. The focus of this policy was that immigrants should have a free choice to preserve their ethnic culture. The government bill on integration (SOU, 1996, p. 55) adds another dimension to the concept of integration: that it is not to be interpreted in just one direction as meaning that immigrants should be integrated into Swedish society, but rather that immigrants and Swedes should be enriched by each other's cultures. This interpretation implies a challenge for all involved. Swedish policy has traditionally been one of general welfare, in which all groups have been treated equally. One of the effects of this policy has been a lack of interest in ethnically based social planning. Instead, all planning has proceeded from consideration of the needs of all citizens rather than special groups. In the light of Swedish immigration policy, new questions are raised concerning how the values of immigrants can best be expressed in general welfare policy. For example, institutional conditions regarding the building of houses and directing housing applicants to special areas might provide the conditions under which integration takes place. That a large number of immigrants live in geographical proximity does not necessarily indicate that they are not integrated into Swedish society. It is possible to be integrated into Swedish society—participating in work, culture, being proficient in the Swedish language, and so on—while at the same time living separately from the Swedes with one's countrymen. Segregation often means associating with countrymen, speaking in one's native language, and preserving native values and norms, thus making the process of integration even harder. Both the positive and negative effects of segregation are well known. There is no reason to discuss them in further detail here. However, it is important to emphasize the effect of community size and cohesion, physical as well as social, and also the importance of social networks (Nyman-Kurkiala, 1999) on individuals' perception of their homes. Just as a decision to move is not entirely individual but must be seen in a collective as well as a societal context (Castles & Miller, 1998), the concept of home is affected by the environment in which one lives.

Defining the concept of integration is a difficult task. The concept has a number of different dimensions: a physical–material dimension including housing and schools; a socioeconomic dimension including income and occupation; and a cultural dimension including language, values, manners, and customs. These different dimensions of the integration process cannot be seen as isolated from each other and need to be appreciated within their interrelated context. For instance, the level of income determines the possibilities one has for decorating and creating a home. In the same way, work opportunities provide a base for living conditions such as choice of housing and community, school and possibilities for participation in leisure and cultural activities. Work, in many cases, still provides the base for pensions and other social transfers. Many older immigrants are no longer working or perhaps have never done so in

Sweden. Studies in Canada (Ley & Smith, 1997) have shown the importance of taking into account the sum income of the whole household or family, because household income might be high even though individual income is low.

This theoretical argument begs a question about how the home relates to other dimensions in the integration process. Is home of central importance to the integration process? Is home a place of refuge when difficulties arise? Is it a base for integration within the larger Swedish society? To what extent is it both?

Much of the research about immigrants and immigrant integration has focused on how individuals and households have changed with respect to various dimensions of integration. Studies focusing on groups of immigrants have shown that some groups are more integrated into Swedish society than others. Indeed, I hypothesize that *the size and geographic concentration of an immigrant group* is central to the process of integration. In this context, Breton (1991) has discussed the process of integration departing both from the personal experience that the individual carries from his or her country of origin, as well as that of the immigrant group to which he or she belongs. He also relates both the individual and the group to the new experiences encountered in the host country. This process has been studied in Sweden by Nyman-Kurkiala (1999), who focused on a colony of Finns from Jakobstad who moved to Gävle and then resettled again after a couple of years. One important factor in studying elderly immigrants' perceptions of home, then, is the role of the entire immigrant group to which they belong in the integration process.

To explore the perception of home in older immigrants, we also need a retrospective analysis of living arrangements so that we can understand how the perception of home has changed over the lifetime. Although the concept of home is made up of personal experiences and expectations, it has also to be viewed in a societal perspective, where structural and institutional factors, on both the national and local level, give rise to possibilities as well as restrictions.

HABITATION AND ELDERLY IMMIGRANTS

The process of aging entails certain distinctive living-arrangement requirements. This fact, in the context of sociopolitical discussion on home-help services and the provision of institutionalized care for elderly people, forces us to take a close look at what we call *home*. How we perceive the home's signification for the elderly can have direct consequences for political debates and policy decisions regarding resource allocation to different forms of care, as well as for elderly people's decisions about their living conditions.

Research on international retirement migration that has dealt with elderly immigrants has primarily focused on issues like quantitative measures of migration flows, assessments of migrants' well-being, reasons for migration, and consequences of migration in the receiving areas (Gustafson, 2001). There has been little research on the meaning of home for this group although some researchers have begun to investigate place attachment and mobility (Gustafson, 2001; Williams et al., 2000). The issue of transnational lifestyles has been an important concept in this context. Gustafson's study (2001, p. 378) among Swedish retirees who migrated to Spain shows that although "the seasonal migration between Sweden and Spain implied a mobile way of life, place attachment also turned out to be an important theme in the analysis of the interviews" (Gustafson, 2001). Here, place attachment involves feelings of being "at home" in one's residence as well as identification with one's home country (Gustafson, 2001). The Swedish retirees, like other elderly Europeans who, because of the prevalence of the welfare state in Europe and as a result of globalization have gained the possibility of migration to the Mediterranean and other areas, have voluntarily chosen to migrate. The reason for their migration is usually to achieve a better life situation by living in a warm climate, by learning a new culture, and by meeting new people. They have usually learned the language of the host country before the migration and know quite a lot about the host country. Interviewees in Gustafson's study "usually expressed an attachment to both countries and regarded such dual place attachment as positive and desirable" (Gustafson, 2001, p. 379). As Gustafson mentions, "seasonal migration and efforts of cultural adaptation in Spain often seems to represent a search for self-fulfillment through individual achievement, and may thus provide a sense of continuity between the migrants working life and their life as retirees" (2001, p. 391). This is not the case for all elderly migrants.

ELDERLY IMMIGRANTS
FROM DEVELOPING COUNTRIES

Many elderly immigrants, especially those from developing countries who left their country involuntary, did not know anything about the country to which they migrated nor about its culture or its language. To such immigrants, migration often means a total disruption of their lives with great dissimilarities between how they used to live in their home country and how they now live in the new country. For this group of elderly immigrants, globalization has not brought continuity but rather disruption.

It is hard to deny that in the postmodern era and with the intensification of globalization, places should be understood also in terms of interconnectedness and process rather than as bounded and self-contained (Massey, 1994). There are, as Gustafson (2002, p. 13) maintains, theories that suggest that "globalization brings along feelings of insecurity and lack of control, which in turn give rise to a search for home, roots and community." One of the outcomes of this development has been the intensified investment of meaning and value in some places, as well as the revival of national identity (Gustafson, 2002). According to some researchers (Bauman, 1998; Castells, 1996), it is primarily the poor and powerless who seek refuge in place attachment and territorial identities. The situation of elderly immigrants from developing countries, especially in Europe, shows that many such elderly immigrants belong in general to the low-income class of the host society (Blakemore & Boneham, 1994; Hjarnoø, 1996; Molina, 1997; Rogers & William, 1992; Social Styrelsen, 1998).

For many elderly immigrants, migration from a non-Western society to a Western country means an intense lack of security and loss of control over important aspects of their lives (Hajighasemi, 1994; Songur, 1996), not only because of their age, but also because of their situation as immigrants, that is, as a result of their "homelessness." Such being the case, housing and the home environment become very important to elderly immigrants.

The number of immigrants in Sweden is now more than one million. At the turn of the year 2001/2002, according to Statistics

Sweden (SCB, 2002), there were 142,655 foreign-born people 65 years of age and older living in Sweden. Compared with statistics for 1990, this is an increase of 59,220 individuals. The number of elderly immigrants will greatly increase during the next few decades, irrespective of future immigration (Eriksson, 1996). For many elderly people from developing countries, the move to Sweden has entailed major changes in habitation. These changes are not only related to their form of housing, but also to lifestyle. Seen in a broad perspective, for many this move has meant a total change in environment.

Elderly immigrants' ideas about what constitutes a *home* (not merely a residence) have generally been formed during their early childhood. Their perspective has later been influenced by the culture and life circumstances they experienced during adulthood (Hajighasemi, 1996). The concept of *home* is constituted by habitation experiences in the homeland, as well as by experiences immigrants have in the new country in encounters with their countrymen and the new society. Thus, it is important to study:

- the habitation cultures elderly immigrants bring with them,

- the possible transformations these cultures have undergone after immigration,

- elderly immigrants' experience of changes in the home environment and the meaning of home that result from emigration in old age or from growing older in a society other than that in which they were socialized,

- the processes through which early habitation history affects abilities to deal with the changes inherent in aging and/or immigration.

ROOTS AND ROUTES

As Gustafson (2002, p. 13) mentions, "With regard to space and place, globalization implies that social and other relations are increasingly stretched out over long spatial distance." It is in this context that in the era of globalization, the meaning and importance of home for immigrants involves two concepts: place attachment and mobility. Furthermore, there are two different approaches to consideration of place attachment and mobility: one values place attachment, place-based community and identity; the other values mobility (Gustafson, 2001).

> Researchers who have adopted the first approach (e.g., Altman & Low, 1992; Hay, 1998) hold that a bond between a place and its residents is important for the well-being of individuals. Mobility is considered a deviation, associated with uprooted individuals and lack of social integration. (Gustafson, 2001, p. 668)

This approach has been criticized for ignoring the effects of increasing mobility and the development of information and communication technologies in postmodern society. Albrow (1996), Calhoun (1991), and Giddens (1991) have stressed the alternative approach, that is, the mobility approach. In this view, place attachment is often, as Gustafson (2001, p. 669) mentions, "interpreted as a defensive reaction of the poor and powerless against contemporary, globalizing forces." If the studied group favored in the first approach is bounded communities, the second approach favors studying very mobile groups.

Although place attachment and mobility tend to be regarded as opposites, some researchers do not accept such a view (Feldman, 1990; Mesch & Manor, 1998). These researchers stress the persistence of place attachment even at times of high geographical mobility (Mesch & Manor, 1998) or in highly mobile societies (Feldman, 1990). Feldman (1990, p. 186), for instance, stresses the "continuity of residential experiences," which is achieved among immigrants who change their residence repeatedly by moving to places that resemble their former home places. These findings are often derived from studies based on investigations of people who belong to higher socioeconomic groups in Western countries, especially in Europe. People who, as natives of welfare societies, have freedom to choose their place of living and to be travelers or tourists. This group has had the opportunity to choose deliberately their own place of residence. These studies have seldom, if ever, focused on poor and/or powerless immigrants.

I suggest that there is a need for new theoretical perspectives for studying the concept of home among elderly immigrants, especially those from developing countries, that is, people who experience mobility not voluntarily or for pleasure, but often involuntarily and with much pain. Taking one step toward this goal, I present how approaches to roots and routes can be applied when studying the concept of home among elderly immigrants, especially those relocating from developing countries to Western countries.

Meanings of home for elderly immigrants need to be looked at by applying not only the concept of place attachment but also that of mobility. As Gustafson (2001, p. 28) points out, the notion of "roots/routes" provides "a new conceptualization of the relationship between place attachment and mobility," which is regarded as a part of a metaphorical system linking people to place (Malkki, 1992). In this context, the concept of roots is considered an expression of emotional bonds with the physical environment (Gustafson, 2001). In addition, it also often contains notions of local community and shared culture. On the other hand, the concept of routes signifies people's mobility, their movements and encounters. Permanent or temporary migration is one of the forms such mobility may take. Roots and routes are not necessarily opposed but rather "intertwined" (Gustafson, 2001). They represent different, but not mutually exclusive, ways of regarding the relationship among people, culture, and place.

Roots and Elderly Immigrant Life Experiences

Different studies have shown that personal experiences are quite crucial for how people perceive the meaning of the home (Anthony, 1984; Steinfield, 1981). Changes in the lifecycle result in a changed outlook concerning the home over time. The wishes of the terminally ill—to die at home and not in a confusing and impersonal hospital milieu—bear witness to the strong feelings and profound intimacy that characterize people's relation to their homes (Gurney & Means, 1993).

When studying conceptions of "home" among elderly people, one has to consider experiences in various stages of their lives that have shaped the meaning and importance of the concept. Migration has come to mean a total change of environment. A theoretical perspective, acknowledging the importance of various experiences in radically different environments and at different stages in life would be useful. The *experiential perspective* is such a perspective. It proceeds from a roots approach and thus emphasizes place attachment and links people to places, identity to territory, and personal experience to the perceived meaning of home.

Crucial to this perspective is the insight that the meaning of the home is specifically connected to experiences that have taken place under different circumstances in time and space, and that this meaning is constantly changing. Experiential methodology (Gurney & Means, 1993), a methodological approach based on the individual's experiences, allows us to investigate issues of emotional security, identity, and private life. We know surprisingly little about such issues with respect to elderly immigrants. This approach does not imply that all explanations can, as a matter of course, be sought primarily at the level of the individual. The intimate relation between individuals and their homes must be analyzed within the framework of each individual's specific political, social, and historical context.

In an experiential perspective, the point of departure is the belief that *home* has multifaceted/multilayered meaning. As Gurney and Means (1993) explain, there are three levels of meaning depending on whether we view the home from a primarily cultural, intermediate, or personal perspective. Home's significance can be traced back to an interaction among these different levels of experience. At the cultural level, home constitutes a topic of political rhetoric, common sayings, myths, and longing. At the intermediate level, it constitutes a commodity that is consumed and produced. At the personal level, it constitutes a profound personal sphere that makes its mark on every individual's life history (Gurney & Means, 1993).

As Table 7.1 shows, according to this model experiences are framed in terms of the three levels of meaning just described. Discussing the *cultural level* in their model, Gurney and Means (1993) focus on how the word *home* is perceived and used in everyday speech. Language is fundamental to a people's culture; so fundamental, in fact, that we might say that a new populace comes into existence with every new language system (Nakamura, 1971). Seen in this light, when studying the concept of home among elderly immigrants, it is crucial to analyze the words that signify *home* in elderly immigrants' native languages. Such an analysis would help us understand their notions of the home (not least their hidden notions) and its meaning. This critical examination of commonly used words for *home* becomes more important when we consider that, in contrast

TABLE 7.1   Home: A Hierarchy of Meanings

Level of experience	Nature of issues
Cultural	Everyday use and understanding of the word "*home*," response structured by peer group, gender, media, etc.
Intermediate	Experience of the state, lending institutions, and local housing market.
	Tenure and class relations.
	Contradiction between this level of meaning and cultural understanding and expectations emerge.
Personal	Important decisions and events in biography that color experience of home in particular ways at different times in the life course.

Note: from: Gurney and Means (1993, p. 126).

to many European languages, not all languages spoken by immigrants differentiate between "home "and "house."[2] This fact has often been neglected in studies on immigrants and their habitation.

In Gurney and Means' model the *intermediate level* focuses on the home's significance and function in a societal perspective. Here, emphasis is put on how people experience the role of the state, credit and loan institutions, the local housing market, legal aspects of housing (forms of ownership vs. renting), and circumstances of class. There is a need for investigation of the extent to which there are contradictions between this level of meaning and that dealing with cultural understanding and expectations.

At the *personal level*, the emphasis is on important previous decisions and events that have been crucial to the individual's later experiences of the home during different life phases. In this light, with respect to studying how elderly immigrants are affected on the personal level by the home's meaning, it seems reasonable to use an autobiographical method of investigation. The reasons are several:

1. An autobiographical perspective on home does not merely deal with changes in residence during the life course, but also with the ideological terminology surrounding the

home—terminology that might be used to explain different phases of life. The autobiography is a "return to the home" (Vilkko, 1996, p. 3). At the same time, as we revisit the past in our thoughts and stories and then return to the present, we organize events, not only from the past, but also in the present. The past melts into the present (Vilkko, 1996.).

2. The autobiography becomes a homecoming, and memories become places we visit. The home is, in this sense, incorporated into the individual's identity. The autobiographical method is therefore important because the autobiography—as a "from home to home" story—mirrors the storyteller's self. An autobiographical method allows us to study the different meanings associated with the home during different phases of the individual's life. In this light, it seems reasonable to emphasize a description of the home, the surroundings, and the general lifestyle, that is, a *home history*. In Gurney and Means' model, this history or "story" is tied to the personal and intermediate levels.

As discussed before, the concept of *home* can be seen in a twofold sense: home as a residence and thereby a source of and environment for daily routines, and home as charged with symbolic meaning, "the home of the mind." The concept of *home history* is used precisely in order to unite these two basic coordinates. Characteristic of the home history is that it "brings out the subjective, intimate and private in meaning making" (Vilkko, 1996, p. 4). It reveals the way in which the "I" and the dwelling places of the life story are interwoven. It shows us how the autobiography is narrated as a "from home to home" story, in which the home, its human relationships, and occupations explain the ego/self. The narrative builds on the relation between time and space, which means that it is possible to follow the changes taking place along the life story's time axis as well as the evolving meaning assigned to the home on the spatial level (Vilkko, 1996).

One of the most important functions of *the home history* is that it links the subjectively lived present with the past. This particular feature is essential in an investigation aimed at studying the concept of *home* among elderly immigrants whose cultural and social past is hardly known.

Routes and the Connection Between Elderly Immigrants' Past and Present Life

The experience of the home here and now is organized such that correspondences and contrasts with the home or homes of the past are revealed. Having a home today that is similar or dissimilar to a previous home can be of importance during old age, particularly for immigrants. Being an immigrant increases people's inclinations to recreate much of their previous way of life by arranging a home milieu reminiscent of earlier milieus from the homeland (Hajigha-semi, 1996). In reality, the "stuff" of home images derives partly from the past and partly from current needs. The question is then: what does *home* consist of, and how can we characterize its diversity? In this regard it is useful to use a phenomenological developmental perspective. Proceeding from a routes approach, this perspective emphasizes mobility as a bridge connecting past to present and the individual's history to his/her future.

The primary interest, in a phenomenological developmental perspective, is to identify the dynamic processes and events that transform a residence, a neutral environment, into a home in the *everyday sense* (Dovey, 1985; Korosec-Serfaty, 1985). The home's signification as permanency and continuity can be interpreted as a process that binds the individual's history to his/her future. This perspective focuses on *the home's signification as an arena for commonplaceness.* In this respect, we can presume that the home constitutes a large portion of the content of an individual's memory, provides the concrete signals that elicit memories, and plays a specific role in memory retention. This perspective is essential in an area of research focused on the home's meaning for the elderly because of the role of the home milieu in memories and the special role of memories in old age.

The feeling of familiarity and routine people develop with regard to how things at home should be also contributes to their experience of feeling at home. Such temporal processes are matters of everyday activities that are coupled to the home and of a recurrent nature. It has been claimed that, with respect to feeling at home, certain dimensions can only be experienced through obvious routines. These meanings have more to do with everyday life and taken-for-granted routines than with thinking (Buttimer, 1978). Another temporal process, through which the home is experienced, is assimilating the home (Dovey, 1985; Korosec-Serfaty, 1985); that is, developing a sense of possession and ownership of the home by investing oneself in it through activities and artifacts. Furnishings, maintenance, and housework bear witness to people's need for assimilating their residence, although this can also be achieved by investing money and physical and/or mental energy.

It is not unusual for elderly immigrants to be forced to change residences several times after coming to their new country. For elderly immigrants in Sweden, a commonly occurring pattern of moves is the following: they live first with their children, are later placed in a temporary residence (one that is usually not particularly agreeable), and then move to a more attractive apartment. The last move can be replaced with various forms of institutional care such as sheltered accommodations, homes for the elderly, or nursing homes, depending on the individual's health. Thus, elderly people who have immigrated to a new society are likely to encounter several obstacles to developing a being at home feeling in their new living environment.

On the one hand, the phenomenological developmental perspective stresses, the relation between the home's signifying a place of permanency and continuity, and on the other hand, the experience of actually feeling at home. The recurring, everyday activities that take place in the home are connected with this signification. They constitute a process in which the individual's history and future are tied together. By applying a phenomenological developmental perspective, we can study whether elderly immigrants have succeeded in developing a feeling of being at home in their living environment after immigration. Moreover, we can clarify what factors might have obstructed or facilitated such a development.

CONCLUSION

In this chapter, the importance of studying how elderly immigrants conceive of home is discussed and some guiding principles for such a study are presented. It is suggested that two appropriate approaches in this context are the roots and routes approaches. In developing these approaches two theoretical perspectives are presented, an *experiential perspective* and a *phenomenological develop-*

mental perspective, which help us discover the factors that influence how elderly immigrants, with different cultural backgrounds, define their home and describe its importance.

NOTES

1. This chapter is based on a study about ethnic segregation in Gothenburg, Sweden. The study involves Turks, Iranians, Finns, and Chileans. Interviews were conducted with immigrants and Swedes who live or have lived in rented apartments in Norra Biskopsgården in Hisingen or in Gårdsten in the suburb of Angered north of Gothenburg.

2. The word "home" in the sense that it is used in the English or Swedish languages does not, for example, exist in the Persian language. "Khaneh," which means "house," derives from the old Persian language Pahlavis word for "room." There is no particular word in the Persian language for "home" in the double sense of a place of residence and a place of symbolic significance. "Homesickness" or "homeland" is not expressed in idiomatic constructions building on the word "home." For example, the word "homeland" is associated neither with the word "home," nor with place of residence. However, the word "family" (khanevadeh) is associated with the word "khaneh" and thus builds on the Persian word for home. The word "khaneman" from the same linguistic root as the word "home", means relation. The word "bikhaneman," which is often used for a homeless person, means a person who lacks both home and family. The idiomatic meaning is a person who does not have anywhere to go. Thus the concepts "khaneman" and "bikhaneman" are logically connected to the concept of family.

   The word "ev," which means "house" in Turkish, can be found in some compounds, such as "evsis," which means homeless. "Ev" is associated with the image of a physical house and means both home and place of residence. However, "ev" cannot be found in compounds such as "homeland." On the other hand, the word "yurt," which means "tent" and refers specifically to the tents of the Turkish nomad, is today often used to denote "homeland." The word is used much in the same way that Swedes use "mother Sweden" as a name for their native country. Today this word is less often used to represent a place of residence. Another interesting word is "ocak," which literally means fireplace but is also used as a word for family. The word traces back to ancient Mongolian fire worship (which in spite of the word has no connection to Persian fire worship). "Ocak" can be used to denote the number of houses in a society in a sentence such as: "In our village there are 50 ocak." The word "ocak" is synonymous to "family" and the state of emotional closeness that is typical of a family. According to some researchers (Redvall, 1987) the word "home" is associated with the three values: identity, seclusion, and safety. An initial hypothesis here is that the word "home" in some languages such as Turkish and Persian is not associated with seclusion or safety but only with identity, and more specifically with family identity.

REFERENCES

Abrahamson, L. (1993). *Boende för äldre: om vanliga bostäder och särskilda boendeformer* (Housing for the Elderly: On Ordinary Residences and Special Types of Housing). Karlskrona, Sweden: The Karlskrona Housing Board.

Abramsson, M., Borgegård, L-E., & Fransson, U. (2002). Housing careers: Immigrants in a local Swedish housing market. *Housing Studies, 17*, 445–464.

Ahmadi, F., & Tornstam, L. (1996). The old Flying Dutchman: Transcending rootlessness. *Journal of Aging and Identity, 1*, 191–210.

Albrow, M. (1996). *The global age: State and society beyond modernity.* Cambridge, UK: Polity.

Altman, I., & Low, S. M. (Eds.). (1992). *Place attachment.* New York: Plenum.

Anthony, K. (1984). Moving experiences: Memories of favorite homes. *Environmental Design Research Association Proceedings, 15*, 141–149.

Bauman, Z. (1998). *Globalization: The human consequences.* Cambridge, UK: Polity.

Baker, M. W., Kramer, E., & Gilbert, G. (Dirs.). (1987). *The Pier 1 Imports study of the American home* (Study No 871925). New York: Louis Harris & Associates.

Biterman, D. (1993). *Immigration housing careers.* Stockholm: Byggforskningsrådet.

Blakemore, K., & Boneham, M. (1994). *Age, race and ethnicity. A comparative approach.* Buckingham, UK: Open University Press.

Borgegård, L-E., Magnussson, L., & Özüekren, A. S. (1999, April). *Integration and housing: The case of the Turks in Sweden.* Paper presented at Housing and Urban Research Seminar, Gävle, Sweden.

Borgegård, L-E., Håkansson, J., & Müller, D. K. (1998). *Concentration and dispersion of immigrants in Sweden, 1973–1992.* Umeå, Sweden: Umeå University.

Breton, R. (1991). *The governance of ethnic communities: Political structures and processes in Canada.* New York: Greenwood Press.

Buttimer, A. (1978). Home, reach, and the sense of place. In H. Idskogius (Ed.), *Regional identity and change in a regional society* (pp. 166–187). Stockholm: Almquist & Wiksell.

Calhoun, C. (1991). Indirect relationships and imagined communities: Largescale social integration and the transformation of everyday life. In P. Bourdieu & J. S. Coleman (Eds.), *Social theory for a changing society* (pp. 95–121). Boulder, CO: Westview Press.

Castells, M. (1996). *The information age: Economy, society and culture, Vol.I: The rise of the network society.* Malden, MA: Blackwell.

Castles, S., & Miller, M. J. (1998). *The age of migration. International population movements in the modern world* (2nd ed.). Hong Kong: MacMillan.

Craik, J. (1989). The making of mother: The role of the kitchen in the home. In G. Allan & G. Grow (Eds.), *Home and family: Creating the domestic sphere* (pp. 48–65). Basingstoke, UK: Macmillan.

Csikszentmihalyi, M., & Rochberg-Halton, E. (1981). *The meaning of things: Domestic symbols and the self.* New York: Cambridge University Press.

Després, C. (1991). The meaning of home: Literature review and directions for future research and theoretical development. *Journal of Architectural and Planning Research, 8*(2), 97–99.

Dovey, K. (1985). Home and homelessness. In I. Altman & C. M. Werner (Eds.), *Home environments* (pp. 33–64). New York: Plenum Press.

Eriksson, T. (1996). *Äldre Invandrare* (Elderly Immigrants). Project report from the National Swedish Board of Health and Welfare. Statens Invandrarverk, Sweden: Norrköping.

Feldman, R. M. (1990). Settlement-identity: Psychological bonds with home places in a mobile society. *Environment & Behavior, 22,* 183–229.

Gaunt, D., & Lantz, G. (Eds.). (1996). Hemmet i vården, vården i hemmet (The home in care, care in the home). *Erstavård Etiska Instituts Tidskrift,* (Special Issue). 4.

Giddens, A. (1991). *Modernity and self-identity: Self and society in the late modern age.* Cambridge, UK: Polity.

Gurney, C., & Means, R. (1993). The meaning of home in later life. In S. Arber & M. Evandrou (Eds.), *Aging, independence and the life course* (pp. 19–131). London: Jessica Kingsley.

Gustafson, P. (2001). Roots and routes: Exploring the relationship between place attachment and mobility. *Environment and Behavior, 33,* 667–686.

Gustafson, P. (2002). *Place, place attachment and mobility.* Göteborg Studies in Sociology No. 6, Department of Sociology, Göteborg University, Göteborg, Sweden.

Hajighasemi, F. (1994). *Invandring på gamla da'r (Migration in old age).* Stockholm: Serie FoU-rapport/Socialtjänsten, Forsknings- och utvecklingsbyrån, Stockholms stad.

Hajighasemi, F. (1996). Hemmet ur äldre iraniers perspektiv (Elderly Iranians' perspectives on the home). *Erstavård Etiska Instituts Tidskrift, 4,* 83–98.

Hay, R. (1998). Sense of place in developmental context. *Journal of Environmental Psychology, 18,* 5–29.

Hayward, J. (1977, February). Psychological concept of "Home." *HUD Challenge,* pp. 10–13.

Herlitz, C. (1993). *Äldre i eget boende: intervjuer bland de allra äldsta och deras anhöriga* (Independent living among the elderly: Interviews with the oldest of the old and their relatives). Falun.

Hjarnø, J. (1996). *Lifestyles of elderly Muslim immigrants.* Esbjerg: South Jutland University Press.

Hunt, P. (1989). Gender and the construction of home life. In G. Allan & G. Crow (Eds.), *Home and family: Creating the domestic sphere* (pp. 66–81). Basingstoke, UK: Macmillan.

Huttman, E. (Ed.). (1991). *Urban housing: Segregation of minorities in Western Europe and the United States.* Durham, NC: Duke University Press.

Kemeny, J. (1987). *Immigrant housing conditions in urban Sweden.* Gävle, Sweden: National Swedish Institute for Building Research.

Korosec-Serfaty, P. (1985). Experience and use of the dwelling. In I. Altman & C. M. Werner (Eds.), *Home environments* (pp. 65–86). New York: Plenum Press.

Kuusela, K. (1992). Valfrihet och tvång i boende (Choice and coercion in housing). In S. Ehn (Ed.), *Så här bor vi* (This is how we live) (pp. 99–116). Stockholm: Building Research Council.

Lantz, G. (1996). Människa, hemmet och tingen (People, the home and things). In D. Gaunt & G. Lantz (Eds.), *Hemmet i vården, vården i hemmet* (The home in care, care in the home) (pp. 19–39). Erstavård etiska instituts tidskrift 4.

Ley, D., & Smith, H. (1997). Is there an immigrant underclass in Canadian cities? *Working Paper 10/97*, Vancouver Centre of Excellence, Immigration (RIIM), Vancouver, Canada.

Linén, A-L., & Lindberg, G. (1991). Immigrant housing patterns in Sweden. In E. Huttman (Ed.), *Urban housing: Segregation of minorities in Western Europe and the United States* (pp. 92–115). Durham, NC: Duke University Press.

Malkki, L. (1992). National geographic: The rooting of peoples and the territorialization of national identity among scholars and refugees. *Cultural Anthropology, 7*, 24–44.

Mason, J. (1989). Reconstructing the public and the private: The home and marriage in later life. In G. Allan & G. Crow (Eds.), *Home and family: Creating the domestic sphere* (pp. 102–121). Basingstoke, UK: Macmillan.

Massey, D. (1994). *Space, place and gender.* Cambridge, UK: Polity.

Mesch, G. S., & Manor, O. (1998). Social ties, environmental perception, and local attachment. *Environment & Behavior, 30*, 504–519.

Molina, I. (1997). Stadens rasifiering. Etnisk boendesegregation i folkhemmet (The racializing of the city: Ethnic housing segregation in the welfare state), *Geografiska Regionstudier, 32*. Uppsala, Sweden: Uppsala University.

Murdie, R., & Borgegård, L. E. (1998). Immigrant spatial segregation and housing segregation in metropolitan Stockholm, 1960–1995. *Urban Studies, 35*, 1869–1888.

Nakamura, H. (1971). *Ways of thinking of Eastern people: India-China-Tibet-Japan.* Honolulu, HI: University of Hawaii Press.

Nyman-Kurkiala, P. (1999). *Att flytta bort och hem igen: Sociala nätverk i kedjemigration* (Leaving the country and moving back home: Social networks in chain migration). Ph.D. Dissertation, Umeå University, Borea förlag, Umeå: Sweden.

Özüekren, S. (1992). *Turkish immigrant housing in Sweden: An evaluation of housing conditions in a Stockholm suburb.* Solna, Sweden: The National Swedish Institute for Building Research: Serie Research report SB 47.

Proshansky, H. M. (1976). *Environmental psychology: People and their physical settings.* New York: Holt, Rinehart & Winston.

Rainwater, L. (1966). Fear and house-as-haven in the lower class. *American Institute of Planners Journal, 32*, 23–31.

Rakoff, R. M. (1977). Ideology in everyday life: The meaning of the house. *Politics and Society, 7*(1), 85–104.

Rapoport, A. (1981). Identity and environment: A cross-cultural perspective. In J. S. Duncan (Ed.), *Housing and identity: Cross-cultural perspectives* (pp. 7–37). London: Croom Helm.

Redvall, C. (1987). *Bostadens estetik. Om relationen mellan människa och bostad (The ethic of housing. On the relation between human being and housing)*. Göteborg, Sweden: Avdelningen för bostadsplanering, Chalmers tekniska högskola.

Rogers, A., & William, H. F. (1992). *Elderly migration and population redistribution: A comparative study*. London: Belhaven Press.

Saegert, S. (1980). Masculine cities and feminine suburbs: Polarized ideas, contradictory realities. *Signs, 5,* 96–111.

SCB (Statistics Sweden). (2002). http://www.scb.se/amne/befolkning.asp.

Sebba, R., & Churchman, A. (1986). The uniqueness of the home. *Architecture and Behavior, 3*(1), 7–24.

Seely, J. R., Sim, R. A., & Loosley, E. W. (1956). *Crestwood Heights: A study of the culture of suburban life*. Toronto, Canada: Toronto University Press.

Sixsmith, J. A. (1986). The meaning of home: An exploratory study of environmental experience. *Journal of Environmental Psychology, 6,* 281–298.

Social Styrelsen (Swedish National Board of Health and Welfare). (1998). Levnadsförhållanden hos fyra invandrargrupper (Living conditions among four immigrant Groups). *Immigrant Project, Report Number 1998:1.*

Somerville, P. (1997). The social construction of home. *Journal of Architectural Research, 14,* 226–245.

Songur, W. (1996). *Äldre invandrare i tre europeiska städer (Elderly Immigrants in Three European Cities)*. Stockholm: Serie FoU-rapport/Socialtjänsten, Forsknings-och utvecklingsbyrån, Stockholms stad, 26.

SOU. (1996). *Sverige, Framtiden och Mångfalden: slutbetänkande från Invandrarpolitiska kommittén* (Sweden, Future and Manifold: Final Report from Government Committee on Immigrant Policy). Stockholm: Serie Statens offentliga utredningar (Government Public Reports).

Steinfield, E. (1981). The place of old age: The meaning of housing for old people. In J. S. Duncan (Ed.), *Housing and identity: Cross-cultural perspectives* (pp. 198–246). London: Croom Helm.

Teeland, L. (1988). Residential inequality in Sweden: A conceptual distinction. *Scandinavian Housing & Planning Research, 5,* 147–154.

Tornstam, L. (1982). Självständigt boende (Independent living). *Working Paper Number 10.* Department of Sociology, Uppsala University, Uppsala, Sweden.

Vilkko, A. (1996). *The home as a meaning-making factor in autobiographies written by elderly men and women*. The 13th Scandinavian Gerontology Conference, Helsningfors, Sweden.

Williams, A. M., King, R., Warnes, A., & Petterson, G. (2000). A place in the sun: International retirement migration: New forms of an old relationship in Southern Europe. *Tourism Geographies, 2,* 28–49.

Zaretsky, E. (1986). *Capitalism, the family and personal life* (rev. ed.). New York: Harper & Row.

CHAPTER 8

Semiotic Use of the Word "Home" Among People with Alzheimer's Disease: A Plea for Selfhood?

Jacquelyn Frank

I want to go home! This expression, as well as others containing the word "home," is uttered frequently by people with Alzheimer's disease. Although an abundance of anecdotal evidence exists on the use of the word "home" by people with Alzheimer's disease, there has been almost no published research investigating the significance of such utterances. This fact is surprising because of the frequency with which caregivers and family members report hearing phrases containing the word "home" uttered by persons with dementia.

As earlier chapters in this book have shown, "home" is a concept with meanings encompassing a variety of dimensions. Of particular significance to this chapter is the notion of home as linked with identity and sense of self. I seek to explore the connections among the meaning of home, sense of self, and unsolicited outbursts involving the word "home" among people with Alzheimer's disease. Using data from qualitative fieldwork, I present a case for use of the word "home" as evidence of Alzheimer's patients as semiotic subjects and suggest that the meaning behind the use of the word relates to the need for a reaffirmation of the "self" among people with Alzheimer's disease.

HOME, SENSE OF HOME, AND THE SELF: LINKS AND CONSIDERATIONS

Home is a concept that is intricately connected to human memory and emotion. Though complex, home can be understood on two primary levels: (1) as a place-based concept related to the physical environment; and, (2) as a symbol representing family, belonging, love, security, and personal identity (Altman & Werner, 1985; Doyle, 1992; O'Bryant, 1982; Rubinstein, 1989; Sixsmith, 1986; Sixsmith & Sixsmith, 1991). The second, more abstract, level represents a *sense of home* (Bulos & Chaker, 1995; Frank, 1999). A sense of home is independent of an actual building or structure; it develops in people over time. As I will argue, this level of home is also strongly associated with selfhood. It is critical to thoroughly examine the symbolic links between identity and home before moving to a discussion of self and home.

Home as a symbol of identity has been well-documented by scholars in a number of disciplines including architecture, anthropology, gerontology, and history (Cooper-Marcus, 1995; Csikszentmihalyi & Rochberg-Halton, 1989; Dovey, 1985; Rapoport, 1995; Rybczynski, 1986; Smith, 1994; Zingmark, Norberg, & Sandman, 1993). According to Brummett (1997), characteristics of home include six important concepts: self projection/self symbol, connectedness/belonging, vessel of memory/vessel of soul, privacy/territoriality, control/autonomy, and choice/opportunity. Each of these concepts reflects an aspect of one's identity. Further illustration of this point comes from Hayward (1977). Hayward identifies nine dimensions of home. Many of these can be closely linked with identity including "home" as a set of relationships with others, as a relationship with the wider social group and community, as a statement about one's self-image and self-identity, as a personalized place, as a place of privacy and refuge, and as a relationship with one's parents and place of upbringing. All of these dimensions can be linked to the complex process of maintaining personal identity. Just as there are different levels to the concept of home, there are also different levels of identity, and "home" encompasses all of these. To further clarify this point, I turn to a brief discussion of the "self."

SELF 1, 2, AND 3

In the past decade, much research has been undertaken to better understand the concept of the self, especially the situations and circumstances in which the self may be compromised (Harris & Sterin, 1999; Herskovitz, 1995; Holstein & Gubrium, 2000; Kitwood, 1990, 1993; Lee & Urban, 1989; Sabat & Collins, 1999; Throop, 2000). It has been proposed that there exist three separate selves within the same person (Sabat, 1998, 2001; Sabat & Harre, 1994). Self 1 represents "the self of personal identity. An individual's continuity with his or her own point of view, displayed in the way a person uses first person pronouns which index, or locate, the speaker in physical and psychological space" (Sabat, Fath, Moghaddam, & Harre, 1999, p. 15). Self 2 is composed of a person's mental and physical attributes and his/her beliefs about those attributes. It "includes not only the current attributes the person possesses, but all the attributes that person has, and will ever have over a life span" (Sabat, Fath, Moghaddam, & Harre, 1999, p. 8). Finally, Self 3 is "the social presentations of selfhood, or social personae understood in terms of the interrelations between people" (Sabat, Fath, Moghaddam, & Harre, 1999, p. 8). Self 3 represents how individuals display Self 1 and Self 2. The most critical point to understand about Self 3 is that it can only exist in relationship with others. These different layers of the self are all critical to the essence of the whole person. When one of these selves is compromised or not acknowledged by others, a person is denied a part of his or her full selfhood (Sabat, 2001; Sabat & Harre, 1994; Sabat & Collins, 1999). It is my contention that the multiple layers of self are reflected in the various meanings of home.

In 1977, Hayward investigated the meaning of home among families in the United States. He found that one of the major dimensions of meaning was *home as self identity*:

Home as self identity centers on the idea that what people call "home" serves as a symbol of how they see themselves and how they want to be seen by others. Thus home may be thought to be a center of one's world, a reflection of one's ideas and values and an important influence on being comfortable and happy with oneself. (Hayward, 1977, p. 12)

This statement illustrates Self 1 and Self 2 as they are represented in the concept of home. Self 1 is shown in the way people express their identity ("I" or "me") through the decoration and presentation of the home—"how I see myself and how I want to be seen by others." Hayward shows Self 2 when he mentions "one's ideas and values." Again, Self 2 encompasses all the physical and mental attributes that individuals have and our beliefs *about* those attributes. For example, "I am caring," "I am loyal," "I have a good sense of humor" and I believe these traits are positive and therefore they make me feel good about myself. Self 2 is woven into our concept of "home" because of our beliefs about what home symbolizes for us ("home is comfort," "home is peace."). Self 3 is also mirrored here in the notion of home as a social relationship. Self 3 is socially constructed and requires the involvement of others in order to fully blossom. The interpersonal aspect of home has been discussed by Smith (1994), Dovey (1978), Brummett (1997), Rapoport (1995), and Despres (1991). For example, Dovey (1978) suggests that "home is a notion universal to our species, not as a place, house, or city but as a principle for establishing a meaningful relationship with the environment" (Dovey 1978, p. 27).

Another example of the multiple dimensions of self within definitions of home can be found in Sixsmith's (1986) study of the meaning of home among 22 postgraduate students. Her research revealed that there are three important modes to the notion of home: the personal, the social, and the physical. Each one of these modes also connects to the various selves described by Sabat. First, there is the personal home.

[It] appears as a profound centre of meaning and a central emotional and sometimes physical reference point in a person's life, which is encapsulated in feelings of security, happiness and belonging. These are not "things" in the sense that a person possesses them, but people are aware of them as essential to their sense of being. . . . This type of total equation of self and home epitomizes the home as a way of "being" in the world. (Sixsmith, 1986, p. 290)

Self 1 is clearly reflected in Sixsmith's explanation of home as linked to one's perspective on the world and placement of "I" and "me" in space and time. The second and third experiential modes of home are the physical and the social. The physical comprises properties such as structure, services, and spatiality. This mode is reflected in Self 2, which comprises attributes (both physical and social) and the person's beliefs about those attributes. The third mode Sixsmith presents is the social mode of home. The social mode consists of the type and quality of relationships with others. Self 3 closely parallels this mode of "home." I believe Sixsmith's discussions of home as representing connectedness and social relationships show the correlation between Self 3 and the deeper level of a sense of home. As Dovey (1978, p. 28) puts this, "to be 'at home' or to 'make oneself at home' is to act naturally, to come closer to one's self."

The multiple dimensions of self and home can be clearly seen through this brief side-by-side examination of these two concepts. Based on my own research I will show that self and home are still strongly connected in people who suffer from Alzheimer's disease. Before engaging in a discussion of home and self in relation to Alzheimer's disease, it is necessary to step back and consider first "home" and then "self" as separate entities in relation to people with Alzheimer's disease. I begin by examining the very pertinence of the concept of home to people with Alzheimer's disease.

HOME AND SEMIOTIC EXPRESSION AMONG PEOPLE WITH ALZHEIMER'S DISEASE

Initially, one might question the relevance or importance of researching the idea of home among people with Alzheimer's disease. Why would one believe that such a concept remains salient in the minds of those with dementia? Further, why should we believe that the use of the word "home" is even applicable for Alzheimer's research? The answer is twofold. First, in spite of the cognitive losses that Alzheimer's disease causes, a sense of home appears to remain in the minds of those with dementia. Based on findings from my 1999 study of three assisted-living residences for people with Alzheimer's in Boston, people with Alzheimer's disease are able to comprehend the concept of home *beyond* a physical place and they are still able to convey what home means to them through personal expressions such as drawings and verbal definitions. Their solicited explanations of home, along with their drawings of what home means to them, illustrate the poignancy connected to this term. Second, psychological research on various memory systems has shown that emotionally significant concepts are retained in the brain much longer, even among those with cognitive impairment (Bradley & Baddeley, 1990; Parkin, Lewinsohn, & Folkard, 1982; Schacter & Tulving, 1994). It has been illustrated in the previous section that the notion of "home" is highly charged with emotion. Although the preceding discussion presents a reasonable argument for someone with Alzheimer's disease maintaining a sense of home, how do we know there is significance in *unsolicited* outbursts such as "I want to go home"? The answer can be found in three domains: automaticity, universality, and semiotics.

Strong evidence for the significance of the unsolicited use of the word "home" can be found in the psychological literature on *automaticity,* which refers to "an automatic mental phenomenon that occurs reflexively whenever certain triggering conditions are in place; when those conditions are present, the process runs autonomously, independently of conscious guidance" (Bargh, 1997, p. 3). Research has shown that the concept can apply to perceptual or meaning-based processes (Bargh, 1996; Isen & Diamond, 1989). In addition, Jacoby, Ste-Marie, and Toth (1993) connect automaticity to familiarity, meaning that our automatic responses to certain stimuli are based on unconscious familiarity with those stimuli. Connecting automaticity to unsolicited outbursts, such as *"I want to go home!"* supports the idea that the word "home" is likely being used automatically by people with Alzheimer's disease because of the term's strong emotional component. The concept of "home" represents love, security, and belonging (all positive symbols). So, why would this word be used automatically by people with Alzheimer's disease in a seemingly *negative* manner? The answer can be found in the *context* in which the phrase is uttered. Automaticity requires a "triggering condition" to occur. In this case the triggering condition for outbursts such as, "I want to go home," are feelings of sadness, frustration, and fear. When someone with Alzheimer's is in this negative emotional state, his or her sense of home kicks in and he or she shouts "I want to go home!" expressing a desire for safety, security, control, and love.

A second piece of evidence supporting the importance of the unsolicited use of the word "home" is its universality. Beyond my research in the United States, which found that phrases such as "*I want to go home!*" or "*Take me home!*" are uttered by people with Alzheimer's disease, preliminary investigation indicates a potential universal use of the word "home" in outbursts made by people with Alzheimer's disease. There is evidence from both Japan and Sweden of Alzheimer's patients repeated use of phrases such as "*I want to go home!*" (Zingmark, 2000; Zingmark et al., 1993, 1995). Additionally, there is significance in the very fact that *home* is the key word in these outbursts. Researchers, family members, and caregivers do not hear those with Alzheimer-type dementia repeatedly say activities they want to do or other places they want to go to, such as "I want to play tennis!" or "Take me to the zoo!" The frequency of the use of the word "home," along with international examples of the use of the word, certainly point to the universal significance of a sense of home and its importance in our lives.

Finally, significance of unsolicited use of the word "home" comes from research on Alzheimer's disease and semiotics. In the past decade, more and more research has been focused on the subjective experience of the person with Alzheimer's disease (Cotrell & Schulz, 1993; DeBaggio, 2002; Downs, 1997; Herskovitz, 1995; Kitwood, 1990, 1993, 1997; Kitwood & Bredin, 1992; Rose, 1996; Sabat, 1998, 2001; Sabat & Harre, 1994; Snyder, 2001). As the subjective perspective of the person with Alzheimer's disease has come to be better appreciated, researchers are coming to understand many new insights about the progression of the disease. One of the milestones in subjective research into Alzheimer's disease has been the realization that persons with Alzheimer's disease should be viewed as "semiotic subjects" (Sabat, 1998, 2001; Sabat & Harre, 1994). Semiotic subjects are defined as "people who can act intentionally in the light of their interpretations of the situations in which they find themselves and who are capable of evaluating their actions and those of others according to public standards of propriety and rationality" (Sabat & Harre, 1994, p. 147). This means that exhibited behavior is not random or irrational because there is an attempt made to communicate meaning to others, even if the behavior or verbalization appears to be incoherent or senseless to an observer. Further, Sabat says that semiotic subjects are also those "whose behavior is driven by the meaning of situations and the ways in which he or she is treated by others" (1998, p. 35). In other words, semiotic subjects are affected by the social context in which they find themselves: It is critical to consider the *context* of the social interaction and the actions of others with whom the person is interacting. Although this idea is potentially very empowering for individuals with Alzheimer's disease and those who study them, the notion of a semiotic subject can also have a major negative impact on the person with dementia. If a person with dementia of the Alzheimer-type is approached harshly or as if he/she is incompetent, the person with Alzheimer's (in the view of semiotics) will respond accordingly. Sabat powerfully explains the scenario as follows:

> If healthy others position someone as defective, confused, and helpless and act out story lines about the afflicted person that emphasize his or her defects, it will be difficult if not impossible for the afflicted person to gain the sort of cooperation needed to construct a Self 3 other than that of "The burdensome, dysfunctional patient." Shortly, others will come to believe that that is all the afflicted person *can* be. (Sabat, 2001, p. 296)

Hence, *how* people with AD are treated can very much determine the quality of interactions they are capable of having. Kitwood (1990) coined a term for the type of treatment described by Sabat: *malignant social psychology.* "Each aspect of the malignant social psychology is, in some way damaging to self-esteem, and tends to diminish personhood; that is why it merits the epithet 'malignant' " (Kitwood, 1990, p. 181). Kitwood (1990) goes on to explain that there are 10 different aspects to malignant social psychology including disempowerment, infantilization, labeling, stigmatization, invalidation, and banishment. Kitwood is careful to explain that the vast majority of people are not purposely being mean or cruel to the person with dementia; rather, "the malignant social psychology is so much a part of the taken-for-granted world of later life that it generally passes unnoticed" (Kitwood, 1990, p. 184). Kitwood elaborates on the reasons why malignant social psychology is so often seen in relation to neurologically impaired older adults. He discusses four associated reasons. First, "many caregivers and service-providers are extremely lacking in their insight" (Kitwood, 1990, p. 184). They care for the person with Alzheimer's disease without being creative about their communication and interactions with the patient. Second, caregivers are overburdened with caregiving responsibilities and cannot take the time necessary for the quality of care that someone with cognitive impairment requires. The third reason for the malignant social psychology relates directly to personhood. Kitwood says,

> there is a tendency not to believe in the sufferer as a person, and so not to treat him or her with the respect that properly accords to persons. At the very least, to be a person is to have the status of a sentient being, to be recognized as having value, and to hold a distinct place in a group or collective of some kind. (Kitwood, 1990, p. 184)

Kitwood points out that often family members or caregivers are heard referring to the person with Alzheimer's disease as "already gone" or among the living dead. Such comments accord the individual with Alzheimer's disease a nonperson status. Fourth, Kitwood claims that there may be unconscious motives behind malignant social psychology, specifically, those related to our own mortality. The malignant social psychology exhibited toward older adults with cognitive impairment may be a way to emotionally distance ourselves from illness, decline, and death.

A critical point to highlight here is that malignant social psychology tends to feed on itself. This is because as the person with dementia is approached and interacted with as "incompetent" or as a "disease visit" then that person will likely internalize this treatment. "As the sufferer is continually invalidated, objectified, etc. he or she loses more and more of that vital contact with others on which personhood depends" (Kitwood, 1990, p. 190). I believe the loss of this vital contact with others seriously compromises Self 3. I return to this issue at the end of the chapter.

THE HOME–SELF–ALZHEIMER'S LINK: EXAMPLES FROM QUALITATIVE FIELDWORK

Now that a foundation has been set for connecting the concepts of home and self with Alzheimer's disease and to the notion of a semiotic subject, it will be useful to turn to some examples from my empirical research. In this section, the voices of those with Alzheimer's disease are presented in order to flesh out the importance of the use of the word "home" as a plea for selfhood. The examples are drawn from two separate studies I conducted on persons with Alzheimer's disease. The first was a study of Alzheimer's residents in three assisted-living sites in Boston, Massachusetts. I examined residents' solicited and unsolicited use of the word "home" through participant observation fieldwork, tape-recorded interviews, resident drawings and feedback from staff and family members. The residents in the study suffered moderate to severe levels of cognitive impairment.

The second study from which data were drawn is a caregiver-needs assessment conducted in central Illinois in the fall of 2001. As part of the assessment, 64 family caregivers were asked about expressions and outbursts containing the word "home" and how often they occurred while under their care. Data from this study are discussed later in connection with an analysis of unsolicited use of the word "home." First, I present findings on solicited meanings of home gathered during the Boston study.

SOLICITED USE OF THE WORD "HOME"

Residents' solicited definitions of home clearly illustrate both a sense of home and the various "selves" presented earlier. During an interview with Murray Isaacson,[1] a moderately impaired assisted-living resident in Boston, Massachusetts, I asked about his interpretation of home. The conversation went as follows:

JF: When you think of home, what do you think of?

MI: I did as I pleased, no obstruction.

JF: What do you associate with the word "home?"

MI: I enjoyed the company (pause) they were very nice to me.

This example clearly shows Murray's sense of home as well as his expression of Self 1. He states, "I did as I pleased" and "I enjoyed the company" through the use of personal pronouns and the expression of his unique point of view, both critical components of Self 1. Murray's Self 2 is exhibited in his perceived feelings of "no obstruction" and the value of personal freedom in his interpretation of what home means to him. His explanation of home, when interpreted in a semiotic manner, also shows an expression of Self 3. When Murray states, "I enjoyed the company, they were very nice to me" he does not directly answer the question that I asked. Because Murray is considered to be a semiotic subject whose responses are meaning-driven, then one can certainly see the connection to the interpersonal nature of Self 3 and how he felt affirmed by those around him in his "home" setting.

Another solicited definition of the word "home" comes from a resident named Evelyn Boyd. On several occasions I asked Evelyn about home. Here are two excerpts from separate conversations.

JF: What does home mean to you?

EB: It means good housekeeping, good food, and good place to sleep.

* * *

JF: What do you think of when I say the word "home?"

EB: I think of my mother. My mother is the one that means everything to me.

Even though Mrs. Boyd suffered from moderate to severe levels of cognitive impairment, her responses exhibit both place-based and abstract levels of home. There is also a relationship aspect to her definition of home that encompasses selves 1, 2, and 3. Evelyn is still able to express her Self 1 with personal pronouns such as "I think of . . . " Her Self 2 is exhibited in her interpretation of what home means to her. Mrs. Boyd voices her values of good housekeeping and good food. Self 3 is demonstrated in the mentioning of her mother. Symbolically, we can see the relationship aspect of home that is also so critical for Self 3.

A third resident, Pauline Einziger, also showed both place-based meanings of home and a sense of home during our interactions. I had multiple conversations with Pauline and had several opportunities to ask her about home. Here are excerpts from three of our conversations.

JF: What do you think of when I say the word home?

PE: My sisters and brothers

* * *

JF: What is the first thing that pops into your head when you hear the word "home?"

PE: The front door being lighted and the back door being lighted.

* * *

JF: What did you like about the home where you grew up?

PE: I loved my mother very much.

Again, both levels of home are expressed in Pauline Einziger's answers as well as the multiple levels of self (including Self 3) and evidence of semiotic expression in order to communicate about what home means to her.

Sometimes, residents' expressions about home were exhibited in ways other than verbal communication. As part of my research I would ask residents of the Alzheimer assisted-living community to draw or illustrate what they thought of when they heard the word "home." I never asked residents to draw *their* home or draw *a* home, simply what they thought of when they heard the word "home." The data from residents' artwork and written communication were extensive and beyond the scope of this analysis. However, I present one resident's response from a drawing session. Olga Subcuni was an assisted-living resident who suffered from severe levels of cognitive impairment. Although she often had difficulty communicating verbally, she would participate in my drawing sessions and would usually be able to explain her artistic response to my queries about home. One day I asked Olga what she thinks of when she hears the word "home." Her response was a poem that she wrote rather quickly. Some of her writing was illegible so I asked her to read me what she wrote. She recited the poem she had written:

> Happy home day and night
> Keep it neat and clean
> Be kind and polite

Again, both levels of home are evident in Olga's poem. She also expresses a clear Self 3 with her statement to "be kind and polite" (hence the relational aspect of Self 3 and home is present).

Interestingly, when many residents were asked to draw or respond verbally, they would not always describe what home means to them. Instead, they responded with poignant, and I believe, semiotic expressions of their feelings. Several times I asked residents "What do you think of when you hear the word 'home?'" Frequent responses to this question were, "I haven't got a home" or "I'm not going home." Powerful statements about home but also quite possibly, about the Self. To examine this point further, I turn to an analysis of unsolicited outbursts containing the word "home" among people with Alzheimer's disease.

UNSOLICITED USE OF THE WORD "HOME"

Unsolicited use of the word "home" was examined in both of my research studies. Both studies reveal critical information about the importance of outbursts containing the word "home" and their relevance to the various levels of the Self. The caregiver-needs assessment asked family caregivers if their relatives ever uttered unsolicited phrases such as "I want to go home" or "Take me home," and if so, how often were they heard. The study revealed that 68% of family caregivers report hearing unsolicited phrases containing the word "home"(Frank, 2002). Further, of those who responded "yes" to this question, 33% reported hearing "I want to go home" (or similar phrases) on a *daily* basis. Another 23% of caregivers report hearing these phrases at least three to five times a week. The data from this study indicate that the vast majority of these expressions were uttered while the person with Alzheimer's disease was *inside his or her own home.* Zingmark et al. (1993) report similar findings from their research in Sweden. They found that people with Alzheimer's were "asking to be taken home when already at home" (p. 15). These results further support the arguments made earlier regarding the universality and automaticity of the use of the word "home" among those with Alzheimer's disease.

Examining unsolicited outbursts from my Boston research reveals several interesting patterns. The first set of examples comes from one of the most outspoken residents I interacted with, Mrs. Rose Kilmore. Rose voiced many statements containing the word "home." It was an almost daily occurrence to witness her walk up to someone in the assisted-living residence and say, "Can you take me home?" or "I'm trying to get a ride home." Some days she would yell her demands to go home, other days she would just seem upset and approach staff or visitors and ask them to take her home.

Mrs. Kilmore's articulations illustrate a common pattern: among the residents, *unsolicited* statements or outbursts containing the word "home" were made universally during times of emotional distress. For example, one day resident Anne Dirklance walked into the activity room of the assisted-living setting and announced to everyone "I don't know where I am, I don't know how to get home and I don't know why you took me here!" Anne's outburst is a clear example of the repeated pattern I witnessed in which the individual with Alzheimer's disease would be in a negative emotional state (either feeling sad, angry, frustrated, or helpless) when he or she would say phrases such as "I want to go home." Mr. Isaacson, Mrs. Boyd, Mrs. Kilmore, and Mrs. Dirklance never cheerfully smiled and joyfully exclaimed, "I want to go home!" Their expressions were only stated in times of emotional distress and usually in conjunction with other agitated behaviors, such as wandering, pacing, shouting, or trying to exit the residence.

I conclude that the residents' outbursts illustrated previously are closely tied to the meaning of the term "home" and its strong relationship to the Self. Home represents relationships, safety, security, control, autonomy, order, and most critically, identity. Therefore, I believe residents' vocalizations such as "Take me home" and "Can I go home now?" are a plea for selfhood. Cognitively impaired residents are searching for validation that they are still full human beings and they are seeking confirmation (through their Self 3) that they can still go "home" (i.e., find their center of identity) and reestablish their full sense of self. Further, the care settings in which many people with Alzheimer's disease reside can further erode the residents' self-identity through the presence of malignant social psychology. The very structure of the "care environment" (with the high level of stress placed on caregivers, and a tendency to sometimes view the person with Alzheimer's as less than a full person) can reinforce different aspects of the malignant social psychology. This occurs through Self 3 interactions that disempower, infantilize, label, stigmatize, and objectify the person with Alzheimer's. The result is that the care environment may inadvertently foster malignant social psychology among its caregivers, further contributing to the disruption in self-identity that results in outbursts such as those described here. This argument is supported through two other pieces of evidence from my research: *where* and to *whom* the person with Alzheimer's disease is speaking when they voice such "home-related" phrases.

First, I tracked the location of residents in the assisted-living community when they would make unsolicited statements such as "Take me home" or "I need a ride home." The data show the highest occurrence of these statements near the kitchen/dining area. This is very interesting considering the kitchen can be seen as symbolic of the center of the home. Possibly the kitchen/dining area triggers an unconscious connection with home (both place-based and more abstract meanings) among those with Alzheimer-type dementia, making it more likely to hear outbursts containing the word "home" in proximity to this very "homelike" area. And reflecting back on my earlier discussion of automaticity we saw that "triggering conditions" (such as standing in the kitchen) can elicit outbursts about home.

Second, and perhaps most crucial to the argument linking self, home, and Alzheimer's is the data I gathered regarding to whom the residents were speaking when they uttered outbursts such as "Take me home!" Every time I witnessed a resident using a phrase containing the word "home" I would write down whom the resident was addressing in his or her statements. My research shows that unsolicited statements containing the word "home" were made almost exclusively to *non*residents (i.e., staff, visiting family members, me). I believe there is great significance to this pattern. My assertion is that residents say, "I want to go home" to staff, family members, or other outsiders because they see those people as *most* able to validate their sense of self during an emotionally difficult time. Residents rarely ever turned to other Alzheimer's residents and uttered unsolicited phrases containing the word "home." Perhaps they carried a cognitive or emotional understanding that these other residents were struggling with the same self-related issues they were and hence could not expect confirmation or support from them. Again, if we consider those with Alzheimer's as semiotic subjects we can conclude that there is meaning behind their behaviors, words, and actions when they approach certain types of people (or more noteworthy, *avoid certain types of people*) when seeking out affirmation of their personhood beyond that of "diseased person."

Based on my research, I do not believe residents are actually saying "I want to go home" with a literal expression of desire to go home with these unsolicited outbursts. Rather, they are tapping into the abstract and emotional significance of home to say "I want to be seen as a person!" "I am scared right now, please validate my personhood!" But, because of the dominant malignant social psychology, caregivers or family members frequently do not comprehend the communication as anything other than literal (I want to *go home*) or a result of their dementia. The result is that persons with Alzheimer's disease do not receive the validation of self they so desperately need. Individuals with Alzheimer's disease need to reaffirm their personhood through Self 3, which necessitates the involvement of other people outside themselves. Sabat and his colleagues support my semiotic argument in their analysis of Self 3 and the person with cognitive impairment.

> The problem each faces is to find someone with whom to construct a Self 3, reflecting the attributes once readily displayed in interpersonal and public interactions, the display of which current disabilities make impossible. In a sense the afflicted person recognizes the following:
>
> 1. I have attributes from my past in which I have taken, and can still take pride—attributes which are still mine.
>
> 2. I have still other attributes that are derived from having Alzheimer's condition and these are sources of embarrassment and signal my decline.
>
> 3. I would prefer to have interactions with others in which they give at least equal weight to (1) and (2) instead of favoring (2) alone, as if (1) no longer exists. (Sabat et al., 1999, p. 27)

My assertion is that when persons with Alzheimer's disease feel alienated, out of place, scared, or unhappy they seek such interaction and support for the Self through their unsolicited statements such as "I want to go home!" In this state of heightened emotion, a critical equation results: *Home=Self.* I believe that home equals self as the person seeks affirmation of Self 1, 2, and 3 through the multilayered nature of home. Home symbolizes love, privacy, security, comfort, connectedness, and identity. The person with Alzheimer's disease needs his or her personhood reaffirmed and he or she does this through the automaticity of using of the word "home." The question now is how this hypothesis can be used in order to improve the lives of those who suffer from cognitive impairment brought on by Alzheimer's disease and to help ensure that self can also equal home? To address this question I turn to the care environment and the "others" with whom the Self 3 interacts.

BEING "AT HOME" WITH ONESELF: THE ROLE OF THE CAREGIVER IN THE RESIDENTIAL ENVIRONMENT

As illustrated throughout this chapter, home is a concept intricately connected to human emotion and personal identity. I have also shown that home is a term that remains important in the minds of those with Alzheimer-type dementia. However, the malignant social psychology unconsciously practiced by many individuals with whom the person with Alzheimer's interacts can and does undermine the individual's personhood and her or his Self 1, Self 2, and Self 3. This scenario raises the question of how researchers, caregivers, and family members can help ensure that the impaired individual can feel at home with this or her "Self?" A possible answer requires a return to the notion of home.

Zingmark and colleagues' research from Sweden can help shed new light on the importance of home when caring for those with dementia. Zingmark and her colleagues investigated the concept of "being at home" among people with Alzheimer's disease (Zingmark, 2000; Zingmark et al., 1993, 1995). Their concern was that people with moderate to severe levels of dementia may not feel at home in their living environments in spite of caregivers' or family members' efforts. One of their research studies examined the experience of being at home among 150 cognitively intact people aged 2–102 years old (Zingmark et al., 1995). The study found that there were a number of interrelated aspects to the experience of being at home. "Common aspects of the experience of being at home identified in all age groups were: safety, rootedness, harmony, joy, privacy, togetherness, recognition, order, control, possession, nourishment, initiative, power, and freedom" (Zingmark et al., 1995, p. 50). Evidence from my own research shows that *these dimensions are represented in the Alzheimer's residents' personal definitions of home*: "I enjoyed the company" (harmony); "my brothers and sisters" (togetherness); "I did as I pleased, no obstruction" (initiative, freedom); "happy home day and night, keep it neat and clean" (order, joy); "good housekeeping, good food, good place to sleep" (safety, nourishment).

An additional finding from Zingmark and colleagues' study was that all 150 participants in the study said that relating to others in a meaningful way was essential to "being at home." This research helps support my earlier contention that expressions involving the word "home" and its meaning help to confirm one's identity through relationship bonds. The question remains how the notion of "being at home" affects those with dementia.

On the basis of her doctoral dissertation research, Zingmark states, "I consider AD in advanced stages as a threat to the experience of being at home" (Zingmark, 2000, p. 30). She came to this conclusion after several years of research in a special care unit for people with Alzheimer's disease. Zingmark and her colleagues reasoned that among people with Alzheimer's disease, "aspects of the experience [of Alzheimer-type dementia] such as order, control, recognition, togetherness, safety, and initiative are affected by memory loss, perceptual problems, agnosia, language disorder, and other problems related to the disease" (Zingmark et al., 1995, p. 60). These aspects of Alzheimer's disease erode the experience of "being at home" for those with dementia.

A third study conducted by Zingmark and colleagues (1993) focused specifically on Alzheimer's residents' feelings of "being at home" and "homesickness" in one special care unit. Because the findings connect so well with my research it is useful to discuss this study in some detail. Zingmark et al. carried out participant-observation research for 20 months in a special care unit in Sweden. Based on residents' expressions about home, the research data were coded and grouped into three major categories or themes dealing with home: "longing for home," "on their way home" and "being at home."

Under the theme of "longing for home" there emerged three subthemes:

(a) longing for the home they used to have
(b) longing for the home they will have (heaven/death)
(c) longing to be at home in the present

Overall, the researchers found that "their [residents] talking about going home was connected to discomfort and restlessness" (Zingmark et al., 1993, p. 12). This finding reinforces my earlier argument regarding the negative emotional state of Alzheimer's residents when they utter unsolicited phrases containing the word "home." Another aspect of longing for home was the occurrence of homesickness.

The researchers explain homesickness to be a state of mind in which one's thinking, feeling, and preference are preoccupied with home. Critically, their research showed that homesickness "appeared when the patients felt uncertain of their own identity" (Zingmark et al., 1993, p. 12). This was reflected in the second theme of residents being "on their way home." "This category covered expressions interpreted as wishes to be at home in the present, combined with an attempt to go home" (Zingmark et al., 1993, p. 13). Residents manifested this homesickness "with clearly and distinctly agitated behavior, e.g., screaming, stamping, swearing, and crying" (Zingmark et al., 1993, p. 13). Of note is the fact that residents *verbalized* an intention to go home in combination with other behaviors (just as they did in my study) and that these verbalizations were unsolicited expressions (just as they were in my study). The theme of "on their way home" was further divided into two subthemes associated with conditions when residents expressed the need, desire, or intention to go home. First, residents would be "on their way home" when they felt overwhelmed. "This theme consisted of an intention to go home in order to escape overwhelming situations . . . when the patients ended up in complicated situations that they could not handle or interpret" (Zingmark et al., 1993, p. 14). I believe this subtheme can be applied to my own research. When Anne Dirklance exclaimed, "I don't know where I am, I don't know how to get home and I don't know why you took me here" she is certainly feeling overwhelmed and wanting to "go home."

Zingmark et al. also found that residents would be on their way home when they felt abandoned. Residents expressed "intentions to go home to escape from being alone, or being with others without being related to them" (Zingmark et al., 1993, p. 14). I believe that this theme can also be applied to my study. As I asserted earlier, people with Alzheimer's disease are using their Self 3 (through outbursts such as "I want to go home") to express their need to be acknowledged as full persons. Zingmark et al.'s findings complement my research and support it by illustrating the importance of the *relational nature* of both Self 3 and home. Residents in the Zingmark et al. study want to "go home" because they feel disconnected emotionally and socially from those around them. Among the Boston residents I studied, Olga Subcuni would clutch her stuffed animal, wander around searching for the front door and ask staff, "Can I go home now?" Evidence of her feelings of isolation is clear.

Shifting to the theme of "being at home," it is useful to first examine the opposite concept of "homelessness." By homeless, Zingmark does not mean being without a dwelling. Instead, to be homeless is "to be absent from a mode of relationship" (Zingmark, 2000, p. 32). Such a homeless state is likely to be experienced by someone with Alzheimer's disease, especially as the disease progresses. Zingmark's study revealed:

> AD is an existential problem of gradual homelessness. . . . During the process of the disease the connection with others . . . becomes disrupted. The relation to one's self is affected by gradually reduced capacity of self-awareness, self-esteem, and self-cohesion. (Zingmark, 2000, p. 32)

I believe Zingmark's findings integrate well with my findings on unsolicited use of the word "home" among people with Alzheimer's disease. I conjecture that the assisted-living residents in Boston voice unsolicited outbursts such as "I want to go home!" when they are feeling upset, disconnected from others, and sensing a loss in their personhood. Integrating the results from Zingmark's work helps me to draw an unequivocal link between home and the Self. I would elaborate further on Zingmark's statements to say I believe that homelessness (or not being "at home") disrupts Selves 1, 2, and 3. All three dimensions of self are affected by the inability to feel at home and result in verbalizations about longing for home or a desire to be "on the way home." Interpreting Zingmark's findings in this manner not only supports the idea that *Home=Self* but equally as poignant, *Self=Home*. When we are not "at home" we are not experiencing our true personhood. In order for Self to equal Home, meaningful interactions with *others* must occur. We need *others* to help validate our selfhood and our sense of home. Among people with Alzheimer's disease, meaningful interactions and "coming home to the self" have the potential to occur only if they are treated as *semiotic subjects* by their caregivers.

Caregivers play a central role in empowering or negating the "personhood" of the Alzheimer's sufferer. How the caregiver approaches someone with Alzheimer's disease in times of distress can not only shape the quality of the interaction, but may also affect the quality of residents' care. This in turn affects the Selfhood of the person with Alzheimer's. Graneheim, Norberg, and Jansson (2001) pose the following provocative question: "Does the nursing care given to people with 'behavioral disturbances' differ according to whether or not the care providers consider the behavior as an expression of meaningful experience?" (p. 17). I believe the answer to this question is most likely "yes" and it poses a *critical* issue for me to examine in future research. I plan to refocus my upcoming research to examine the interactions between Alzheimer's residents and care providers and the responses to exclamations such as "I want to go home!" Also necessary is a shift in the research question to better reflect the relational aspects between caregiver and care recipient and between self and home. Based on my current research findings, I believe future research should address the following question: *Do caregivers respond differently to outbursts such as "I want to go home" depending on whether or not the caregiver is approaching the person with Alzheimer's disease as a semiotic subject?* Woods (1999, p. 37) posits that personhood "is created (or diminished) in the social relationships (usually with caregivers and care workers) around the person with dementia." Consequently, caregivers hold the key to enhancing selfhood among those with Alzheimer's disease. People with Alzheimer's disease are already seeking out affirmation of self through outbursts such as "I want to go home!" and we need to learn to respond to this semiotic expression through our attempts to forge stronger ties with their Self 3. Hence, the need for more research on the interactions between people with Alzheimer's disease and their care providers.

The question now is how to help those with Alzheimer's disease feel at home so that they no longer suffer emotionally and do not continue to shout out "I want to go home!" or plead "Can I go home now?" The answer may rest in a "homecoming" of sorts. In her 2001 study, Norberg speaks of the need for consolation when working with or caring for someone with Alzheimer's disease. She explains that the ancient philosopher Boethius described consolation "as a kind of homecoming: the soul comes home to itself" (p. 49). Norberg believes that people with Alzheimer's disease often need consoling because of cognitive losses, communication difficulties, and emotional frustrations brought on by cognitive decline. Consoling involves a deeper level of caring that truly meets the emotional needs of the person with dementia—not simply his or her activities of daily living or service needs. Norberg's moving discussion of consolation helps to verify the true importance of understanding the *Self= Home* equation:

> Consolation as homecoming seems to be an appropriate metaphor in the care of persons with AD, as their suffering so clearly involves a feeling of not being connected to, among other things, self. (Norberg, 2001, p. 49)

I believe that the type of consolation to which Norberg refers, that of a true "homecoming" to the self can only be accessed through more research and understanding of self (especially Self 3) and its relationship to the malignant social psychology so often used when interacting with people who have Alzheimer's disease. If, as one 16-year-old said, "I feel at home when I can be myself" (Zingmark et al., 1995, p. 55), then we must continue to investigate effective methods of consolation so that we can better validate Selves 1, 2, and 3 among those with dementia. We have to listen to the plea for validation put forth in outbursts such as, "I want to go home!" because it is through the interactive self (or Self 3) that we may be able to help strengthen Selves 1 and 2 among people with Alzheimer's. Someone with Alzheimer-type dementia may no longer have the capability to initiate or assert Self 1 and Self 2 as they would like, but Self 3, because of its interactive nature, can be helped along via *positive* interaction with others. Maybe by focusing on Self 3 in care environments we can begin to enhance Self 1 and Self 2 among those with Alzheimer's disease. But if we do not use Self 3 as a window on which to better understand the experiences of those with Alzheimer's disease (by meaningfully responding to statements such as "I want to go home") then we may further erode the personhood of the Alzheimer's sufferer.

Minimally, if we wish to begin to help restore a sense of personhood among people with Alzheimer's, then family members, caregivers, and friends need to accept and *believe* that "the Alzheimer's sufferer is a person whose fundamental semiotic abilities—to demonstrate coherent intentionality, to give and to construct meaning, and to engage in ongoing relationships—are intact" (Sabat & Harre, 1994, p. 157). And, if we want people with Alzheimer's to feel "at home" then meaningful interaction (through acknowledgment of Self 3) is a prerequisite. As Zingmark's research points out "in all situations in which the patients said they felt at home, they interacted with others (caregivers or family members) in a seemingly meaningful relation. They seemed related to others, and in this nearness, they also seemed related to themselves" (Zingmark et al., 1993, p. 15). We may learn to create a homecoming for people with Alzheimer's disease and help strengthen their full sense of personhood by interacting with them as semiotic subjects and acknowledging the significance of their utterances such as "I want to go home."

NOTE

1.   All names of residents are pseudonyms.

REFERENCES

Altman, I., & Werner, C. M. (Eds.). (1985). *Home environments.* New York: Plenum Press.

Bargh, J. A. (1996). Principles of automaticity. In E. T. Higgins & A. Kruglanski (Eds.), *Social psychology: Handbook of basic principles* (pp. 169–183). New York: Guilford Press.

Bargh, J. A. (1997). The automaticity of everyday life. In R. S. Wyer (Ed.), *The automaticity of everyday life: Advances in social cognition* (pp. 1–161). Mahwah, NJ: Lawrence Erlbaum.

Bradley, B., & Baddeley, A. (1990). *Emotional factors in forgetting. Psychological Medicine, 20,* 351–355.

Brummett, W. (1997). *The essence of home: Design solutions for assisted living housing.* New York: Van Nostrand Reinhold.

Bulos, M., & Chaker, W. (1995). Sustaining a sense of home and personal identity. W. Benjamin, D., Stea, D., & Aren, E. (Eds.). *The home: Words, interpretations, meanings and environments* (pp. 227–239). Aldershot, UK: Avebury.

Cooper Marcus, C. (1995). *House as a mirror of self.* Berkeley, CA: Conari Press.

Cotrell, V., & Schulz, R. (1993). The perspective of the patient with Alzheimer's disease: A neglected dimension of dementia research. *Gerontologist, 33,* 205–211.

Csikszentmihalyi, M., & Rochberg-Halton, E. (1989). *The meaning of things: Domestic symbols and the self.* Cambridge, UK: Cambridge University Press.

DeBaggio, T. (2002). *Losing my mind: An intimate look at life with Alzheimer's.* New York: Free Press.

Despres, C. (1991). The meaning of home: Literature review and directions for future research and theoretical development. *Journal of Architectural and Planning Research, 8,* 96–114.

Dovey, K. (1978). Home: An ordering principle in space. *Landscape, 22*(2), 27–30.

Dovey, K. (1985). Home and homelessness. In I. Altman & C. Werner (Eds.), *Home environments* (pp. 33–64). New York: Plenum Press.

Downs, M. (1997). Progress report on the emergence of the person in dementia research. *Ageing and Society, 17,* 597–607.

Doyle, K. O. (1992). The symbolic meaning of house and home: An exploration in the psychology of goods. *American Behavioral Scientist, 35,* 790–802.

Frank, J. (2002). *Alzheimer's caregiver needs assessment 2002: Final report.* Unpublished report prepared for the Greater Illinois Chapter of the Alzheimer's Association, Bloomington-Normal Office.

Frank, J. (1999). I live here but it is not my home: Residents' experiences in assisted living. In B. Schwarz & R. Brent (Eds.), *Aging, autonomy, and architecture: Advances in assisted living.* Baltimore, MD: Johns Hopkins University Press.

Graneheim, U. H., Norberg, A., & Jansson, L. (2001). Interaction relating to privacy, identity, autonomy and security: An observational study focusing on a woman with dementia and "behavioral disturbances" and on her care providers. *Journal of Advanced Nursing, 36*(2), 256–265.

Harris, P. B., & Sterin, G. J. (1999). Insider's perspective: Defining and preserving the self of dementia. *Journal of Mental Health and Aging, 5,* 241–256.

Hayward, D. G. (1977, February). Psychology concepts of "home." *HUD Challenge,* pp. 10–13.

Herskovitz, E. (1995). Struggling over subjectivity: Debates about "Self" and Alzheimer's disease. *Medical Anthropology Quarterly, 9,* 146–164.

Holstein, J. A., & Gubrium, J. F. (2000). *The self we live by: Narrative identity in a postmodern world.* Oxford: Oxford University Press.

Isen, A. M., & Diamond, G. A. (1989). Affect and automaticity. In R. S. Wyer, Jr. (Ed.), *The automaticity of everyday life: Advances in social cognition.* Mahwah, NJ: Lawrence Erlbaum.

Jacoby, L., Ste-Marie, D., & Toth, J. P. (1993). Redefining automaticity: Unconscious influences, awareness, and control. In A. Baddeley & L. Wieskrantz (Eds.), *Attention: Selection, awareness, and control.* Oxford, UK: Clarendon Press.

Kitwood, T. (1990). The Dialectics of dementia with particular reference to Alzheimer's disease. *Ageing and Society, 10,* 177–196.

Kitwood, T. (1993). Towards a theory of dementia care: The interpersonal process, *Ageing and Society, 13,* 51–67.

Kitwood, T. (1997). The experience of dementia. *Aging and Mental Health, 1*(1), 13–22.

Kitwood, T., & Bredin, K. (1992). Towards a theory of dementia care: Personhood and well-being. *Ageing and Society, 12*(3), 269–288.

Lee, B., & Urban, G. (Eds.). (1989). *Semiotics, self, and society*. Berlin: Mouton de Guyter.

Norberg, A. (2001). Consoling care for people with Alzheimer's disease or another dementia in the advanced stage. *Alzheimer's Care Quarterly, 2*(2), 46–51.

O'Bryant, S. (1982). The value of home to older persons: Relationship to housing satisfaction. *Research in Aging, 4,* 349–363.

Parkin, A. J., Lewinsohn, J., & Folkard, S. (1982). The Influence of emotion on immediate and delayed retention: Levinger & Clark reconsidered. *British Journal of Psychology, 73,* 389–393.

Rapoport, A. (1995). A critical look at the concept "home." In D. N. Benjamin & D. Stea (Eds.), *Home: Words, interpretations, meanings, and environments.* Aldershot, UK: Avebury.

Rose, L. (1996). *Show me the way to go home*. Forest Knolls, CA: Elder Books.

Rubinstein, R. L. (1989). The home environments of older people: A description of the psychological process linking person to place. *Journal of Gerontology Social Sciences, 44*(2), S45–S53.

Rybczynski, W. (1986). *Home: A short history of an idea.* Harrisburg, PA: R. R. Donnelley.

Sabat, S. (1998). Voices of Alzheimer's disease sufferers: A call for treatment based on Personhood. *Journal of Clinical Ethics, 9*(1), 35–48.

Sabat, S. (2001). *The experience of Alzheimer's disease: Life through a tangled veil*. Oxford, UK: Blackwell.

Sabat, S. R., & Collins, M. (1999, Jan.–Feb.). Intact social, cognitive ability, and selfhood: A case study of Alzheimer's disease. *American Journal of Alzheimer's Disease*, pp. 11–19.

Sabat, S. R., Fath, H., Moghaddam, M., & Harre, R. (1999). The maintenance of self-esteem: Lessons from the culture of Alzheimer's sufferers. *Culture and Psychology, 5*(1), 5–31.

Sabat, S. R., & Harre, R. (1994). The Alzheimer's disease sufferer as a semiotic subject. *Philosophy, Psychiatry, Psychology, 1,* 145–161.

Schacter, D., & Tulving, E. (Eds.). (1994). *Memory systems*. Cambridge, MA: MIT Press.

Sixsmith, A., & Sixsmith, J. (1991). Transitions in home experience in later Life. *Journal of Architectural Planning Research, 8,* 181–191.

Sixsmith, J. (1986). The meaning of home: An exploratory study of environmental Experience. *Journal of Environmental Psychology, 6,* 281–298.

Smith, S. G. (1994). The essential qualities of a home. *Journal of Environmental Psychology, 14,* 31–46.

Snyder, L. (2001). The lived experience of Alzheimer's: Understanding the feelings and subjective accounts of persons with the disease. *Alzheimer's Care Quarterly, 2*(2), 8–22.

Throop, C. J. (2000). Shifting from a constructivist to an experiential approach to the anthropology of self and emotion: An investigation "within and beyond" the boundaries of culture. *Journal of Consciousness Studies, 7*(3), 27–52.

Woods, R. (1999). The person in dementia care. *State of the Art for Practice in Dementia, 23*(3), 35–39.

Zingmark, K. (2000). *Experiences related to home in people with Alzheimer's disease*. Umea University Medical Dissertation, Department of Nursing, Umea University, Umea, Sweden.

Zingmark, K., Norberg, A., & Sandman, P-O. (1993). Experience of at-homeness and homesickness in patients with Alzheimer's disease. *American Journal of Alzheimer's Care and Related Disorders & Research, 8,* 10–16.

Zingmark, K., Norberg, A., & Sandman, P-O. (1995). The experience of being at home throughout the life span: Investigations of persons aged from 2 to 102. *International Journal of Aging and Human Development, 41,* 47–62.

CHAPTER 9

Conceptualizing Home and Homelessness: A Life Course Perspective

John F. Watkins and Amy F. Hosier

Home permeates society, and evokes such feelings as belonging, control, comfort, or security whether it involves individuals
or much larger groups of people. Homelands have long been contested within a global arena. Home ownership remains central in
many national political agendas. And the journey home offers rich
fodder in literature and the arts, with novels, poems, songs, and films
consistently employing the idea because of its power in conveying
familiar, immediate, and presumed universal emotions. By natural
extension the idea of being homeless also evokes certain emotions—
despair, isolation, hopelessness, grief—and variably presents such
images as poverty, alcoholism, mental illness, and social deviance.
Just as having and being at home equates with life stability and
some measure of success, being homeless translates into transience,
turmoil, and failure in life.

Home is important, and there is little wonder why scholars have
sought to study notions of home and homelessness. Indeed there
is an extensive literature crossing many disciplines that seeks to
define each concept, characterize people with home and without

home, and identify the individual and social implications of each state of existence. Home and especially homelessness are addressed historically, across cultures, across age, within cities and in rural areas, by gender, and in relation to psychological and social pathologies.

Yet the concepts of home and being without a home remain conceptually vague in scholarship. Home largely tends to be treated as a place, a feeling, and most commonly as a combination of the two wherein the person–environment relationship creates feelings of well-being (Dovey, 1985; Rowles, 2003; Toyama, 1988). Implied is that a disruption in the person or the place causes an attempt to adjust to a new relationship (Rowles & Watkins, 2003). If the adjustment fails, the result is homelessness and an associated "existential despair for the individual" (Carboni, 1990, p. 33). In contemporary homeless research, on the other hand, homelessness occurs when there is insufficient income to afford available housing (Hopper, 1991). Extant literature expresses or implies only a dichotomous option; a person or family either has or does not have a home. Unfortunately, little is known about the mechanisms and processes whereby a person's "sense" of home develops, is maintained, or is reestablished (or not) over time. Where and when does home start? Where and when, if ever, does it end with consequent homelessness? And how does it change in between?

Our central purpose in this contribution is to address these questions by conceptually linking home and homelessness from a developmental life-course perspective. Through this linkage we hope to suggest the following:

- Home and homelessness are not exclusive categories, rather they represent ends of a continuum of possible existential states;

- An individual's state will shift along the continuum through life in response to changes in the person and that person's context or environment;

- Notions of home and especially homelessness must embrace more than a state of permanent residence in affordable housing.

We address these issues, and others, by adopting a life-course view of home as a *life-long process*. Our adoption of life course as a framework (in preference to a life-span approach) intentionally recognizes complex and interwoven influences across spatial scales, ranging from the person to broader society, and across temporal scales, from historical to the immediate, and on to the future. We present and discuss a conceptual model of this process, and then offer brief case studies that exemplify how conditions and events in later life conspire to threaten the sense of home. A basic argument is that the existence and affects of home and homelessness are often obscured by social misconceptions and overly narrow scholarly definitions.

HOME AS PROCESS

"Home is safety." "Home is where I keep my stuff." "Home is where we hang our hats." "Home is where we leave from and come back to." "Home is mine, and nobody else's." "Home is where I am me." "Home is where my family is." "Home is where the heart is." These simple sentences are among the first responses in our research to the question of "what is home to you?" They offer no surprises, and indeed are in accordance with research that has investigated the definitions and meanings of home (e.g., Annlson, 2000; Dovey, 1985; Rapoport, 1995; Sixsmith, 1986; Zingmark, Norberg, & Sandman, 1995). These sentences suggest the importance of shelter, storage and display of valued belongings, a place for self-expression, locus of activity, privacy and control, familial linkage, and emotional freedom as elements of home. Such elements, and others including habituation in place (Marcus, 1992; Rowles, 2000) and memory of personal history (Boschetti, 1995; O'Bryant & Nocera, 1985; Paton & Cram, 1992) provide the foundation on which conceptualizations of home have been constructed.

The fact that first responses in defining home are so varied indicates that individuals express different sets of priorities among elements of home. The reason for such diversity becomes apparent when individuals are asked to explain where their sense of home came from. In our research this has often proved to be a difficult question to field; people tended to know what home is, but they seldom could quickly identify why they knew it.

Continued questioning confirmed that individual definitions of home are rooted in personal history; one's definition of home doesn't just appear but rather develops out of cumulative experiences through life, enduring (but dynamic) memories that may be brought to immediate consciousness (Marcus, 1992; Rowles & Ravdal, 2002; Rowles & Watkins, 2003). Acquiring one's concept of home, then, can be viewed as a life-long process, influenced by relationships with place, ensconced within a social context, and used in preparation for future life transitions and challenges (Bengston, 1978; Gelwicks, 1978; Rivlin & Moore, 2001; Rubenstein & Parmalee, 1992). The sense of home thus assumes a dynamism, shaped by gender, socioeconomic status, marital status, and health status (Fogel, 1992), and with ongoing redefinition across the life span (Hartwigsen, 1987) through exposure to new spheres of influence and through memories of past experiences.

Figure 9.1 illustrates the immediate spheres of influence that affect the developing sense of home through life. Following a simple sequential life trajectory, children are situated within a dependent environment from which they experience an initial sense of home. This environment, and the collection of options available in terms of factors that may constitute a sense of home, is at first quite restricted; it is imposed and frequently reinforced by immediate

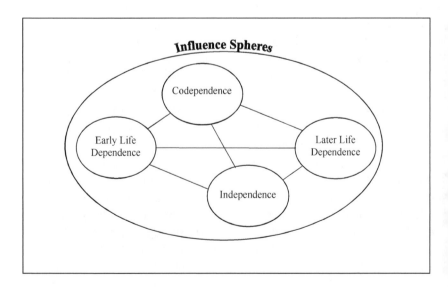

FIGURE 9.1   Influence spheres in the home-development process.

others (e.g., parents or guardians, older siblings). As the child grows, her/his environment expands to include an increasing array of residential place experiences gained directly through personal acquaintances (e.g., a friend's home) and indirectly through exposure to such sources as books, magazines, television, or film. Furthermore, the child's personality and preferences as an individual increasingly develop, and she or he may express certain elements of home within, say, a bedroom or play area. Within the early-life dependent sphere, then, a child's sense of home is largely established and filtered by the influence of others, with nonfamily experiences and individual preferences exerting stronger influences with increased age.

In young adulthood a person eventually leaves the parental home and generally may enter either a state of independence or a state of co-dependence. With independence a person assumes primary decision-making authority over the immediate living environment. Space can be used according to personal preferences; there is freedom to determine what belongings are exhibited and where they are situated, and there is control over how space is allocated between public access (i.e., a living room, kitchen, or other spaces that "guests" are allowed to occupy) and private domain (i.e., a bedroom or master bathroom that are for the exclusive use of the individual or of others by invitation only). Elements of home take on a highly individual quality within this sphere. Early life influences may dominate in the younger years, but the person's own sense continually evolves over time because of the freedom to incorporate preferences emerging from contemporary experiences as an independent being.

Alternatively, a young adult may enter a state of codependence, for example, through a move into group quarters (such as a college dormitory), an apartment or house shared with peers, or through marriage into a shared residence. Although this influence sphere is marked by the need to share control over how elements of home are expressed, it also provides each person an intense experience of alternative senses of home and further opportunity to modify his or her own definition of home. Within this sphere there is active negotiation of how best to accommodate two (or more) individual and evolving perspectives on home within one living space, with negotiation potentially lessening over time as a shared concept of home becomes established.

Eventually a person may need to make a transition to a state of later-life dependence because of declining physical and/or mental capacity. This transition may take several forms, from a move to an institutional retirement, assisted-living, or nursing facility, to a move into the residence of an adult child. The transition may not even involve a physical move at all; an older person may remain in place, but a family member or other caregiver becomes increasingly charged with (or increasingly assumes) decision-making authority for the older person. What is important to recognize is that, unlike early life dependence, a fully developed sense of home will commonly exist in later life dependence, with this sense being a product of a lifetime of experiences. So although one's *image* of home remains, control over the *manifestation* of one's home may become compromised, or even lost, at this stage.

Few people in today's Western world follow such a uniform lock-step progression through the influence spheres as just described. Noteworthy are societal trends of delaying marriage, and of divorce and remarriage. Delayed marriage, for example, will lengthen the time spent under the influence of independence or of codependence in a living arrangement that assures some measure of private space and autonomy. An individual sense of home in such situations becomes more firmly entrenched and, consequently, may make negotiation of the home space more difficult upon marriage. Divorce may result in a move back to the early-life influence sphere in young adulthood, or more generally to independence, with remarriage causing yet another transition to codependent influence, but with a new spouse's sense of home to negotiate. We do not, therefore, propose any fixed trajectory of housing or family formation and dissolution through life. Rather, we suggest that people move among the influence spheres in highly individualized ways, carrying with them and selectively internalizing experiences gained from all preceding spheres as they progress through life. What emerges, and is continually being refined, is the person's own sense of home, a complex collection of attributes having various and changeable priorities depending on the current lived situation.

EXPERIENCED AND IMAGINED HOME

When a person describes her or his sense of home, what we hear is not necessarily a description of the current living environment and situation. Dovey (1985), for example, discusses a yearning for an idealized home and the process of becoming at home. From this we suggest a need to distinguish between the *experienced* home and *imagined* home. The current manifestation of certain attributes of home defines the experienced home, whereas the full complement of prioritized attributes, whether currently experienced or not, defines the imagined home.

Both the experienced and imagined home are products of the life-course influence spheres (Figure 9.2). Each of these, in turn, is affected by external forces (including social/cultural norms, opportunities, and barriers) and internal forces (including personality, anticipations, and expectations). Individuals may be "trained" to accept a particular image of home that has been constructed by society. This image generally may include the 3-bedroom, 2-bath ranch house in the suburbs, with white picket fence and 2-car garage. During early life a child embellishes this basic image with preferences learned from parents for antique furniture, pastel wall colors, and a large and active kitchen. The child was never enamored with the

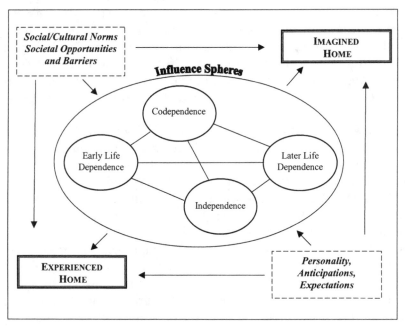

FIGURE 9.2   The experienced and imagined home in the context of process.

cats of the house, however, and instead developed a preference for dogs through experiences at a friend's house. As a young independent adult, the person discovers that living alone is depressing, and the presence of others, perhaps a future family, becomes an important part of the imagined home. Indeed, it is during earlier periods of the life course that the imagined home takes on a prospective quality, incorporating anticipations and expectations of the future (Dovey, 1985; Gelwicks, 1978).

Young and middle-aged adults maintain the prospective view of the imagined home, which now becomes acutely influenced by social forces. Western society promotes home ownership and there is little wonder, in a consumer-driven market economy, why material wealth permeates the imagined home of those striving toward the pinnacle of their careers. Similarly, there is little wonder why the notions of home and homelessness revolve around a built structure and financial security. At the same time, lack of wealth and the means of securing it serve as barriers in the experienced home, and may act to modify the imagined home.

At retirement, the person (at least in Western societies) may choose to move to a new residence. Free of ties to the workplace, the retiree may actively pursue the imagined home, exercising preferences for a different type of house (perhaps even a house with wheels), in a new location. Most retirees stay in place. For these individuals, preferences and anticipations are increasingly employed to modify the experienced home according to the imagined. The spatial extent of home may expand to include the homes of children and grandchildren, ritual places of activity, or favored vacation spots.

Physical declines in old age may result in nursing-home placement. The experienced home is in accordance with societal views of an appropriate home; the person has a semiprivate room that can be decorated and personalized. The imagined home, however, may include the spouse (now dead), socializing with long-time friends and neighbors (now living far away), and the house that was designed and built to accommodate the family's needs and preferences (now sold to qualify for Medicaid). Unlike earlier ages, the imagined home of elders may be retrospective in nature, and the importance of freedom and control may take on much higher priorities in the imagined home as those are the attributes most often sacrificed when elders require increasing levels of care.

THE HOME–HOMELESS CONTINUUM

The experienced home exists from the beginning of life, although this earliest home may be confined to a blanket, a bed, food, and the touch of a parent. Imagined home is an ideal that emerges from experience, both positive and negative, and only takes form when a person has a sufficient experience pool from which to establish preferences and the cognitive capacity to assign values and meanings to experiences. Earlier in life, the person seeks to "become at home" by modifying the experienced home to coincide with the imagined home, which has yet to be fully experienced in life. The imaged home in this case is prospective, but composed of elements from the past that, when combined, may realistically be achieved in the future. A person may also become at home as the imagined home evolves over time; preferences and priorities may change such that the imagined home takes on the attributes of the experienced home. Being fully at home requires conformance of the experienced and imagined home. We would also argue that being fully at home requires maintenance of control over decisions that allow the imagined and experienced home to be modified, or that allow for the fair negotiation of the experienced home in cases of codependence or dependence.

Distinguishing between the experienced and imagined home allows us to conceptualize home and homelessness as a continuum rather than as two exclusive and discrete states of existence. A person's location along this continuum would depend on the degree of conformance between the experienced and imagined home at any point in time. Figure 9.3 illustrates the continuum along the vertical axis. For simplicity we plot the imagined home as a fixed ideal across the life span, although we recognize its dynamic nature and that the "imagined" may change to become either closer to or farther from a relatively static "experienced" home. Each individual possesses a unique life-course trajectory in this continuum. Figure 9.3 represents one illustration, with three alternative later-life options.

During infancy and early childhood the imagined and experienced home are essentially the same. Persons at that young age have yet to develop the cognitive abilities to make value judgments or to think prospectively. We find children of this age, for example, being very resilient when a parent or parents move to a new resi-

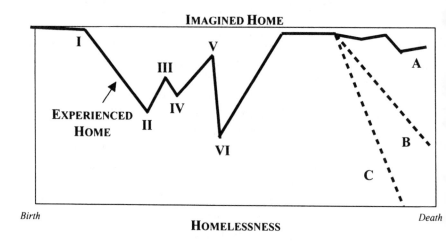

FIGURE 9.3   An experienced home life-course trajectory.

dence. At point I, however, the child is able to attach meaning to elements of her or his environment, to formulate and express preferences, and to react to social trends and pressures. A personalized imagined home takes form that, because of the child's broadening activity space and experience pool, becomes increasingly distant from the parental experienced home in which the child resides.

At point II the person, now a young adult and unmarried, gains independence or perhaps codependence. The opportunity to exercise control and decision-making authority, even jointly with a cohabitant, allows the person to modify attributes of the experienced home to move toward the imagined. Point III represents marriage, a time when both members of the couple increase the importance of certain home attributes (e.g., security, permanence, love, individual privacy) and when negotiation strategies must be modified to accommodate very different imagined homes. Our person's experienced home temporarily moves away from the imagined through point IV as the person adjusts to the shared decision-making authority, however allocated among the couple. Point IV through V suggests a time of converging vision of the experienced and imagined home within the marriage, which has now produced children.

Point V indicates a divorce. The person is essentially forced to move out of the house and away from continued engagement with the children. This one event commonly has a profound effect on the experienced home by taking away a number of key attributes associated with the imagined home. Eventually the person adjusts to the new situation; the experienced home is modified as resources allow, and the imagined home is revised to reflect accepted realities.

Three scenarios are shown in Figure 9.3 to represent possible later life outcomes. Trajectory A illustrates a person who success-fully ages in place. He or she is able to maintain control in the personal environment, and even though certain events, like physical trauma, death of a spouse, or even a residential move, may shift the experienced home away from the imagined, the high level of autonomy and decision-making control allows the person to retain a quality home experience. Scenario B represents an elder who has voluntarily relinquished most of his or her decision-making author-ity. Individual preferences can be expressed, however, and the care-givers generally try to accommodate the preferences if at all possible. Still, the experienced home drifts toward the homelessness end of the spectrum as the person becomes increasingly unable to actively pursue the imagined home. Finally, scenario C represents a situation in which all authority has been stripped from the individual, and the caregivers assume that they know what is best for the person without consultation. The care may technically be sound from a medical perspective, yet the lack of opportunity for the person to actively express her or his self in the environment or to exert any control over the situation results in eventual homelessness.

The home–homelessness continuum across the life course is highly nuanced, and trajectories are as varied as the diversity inher-ent in any population. Two brief case studies, compiled from our life-course research on relocation and spatial experience, help to demonstrate this variability. The studies are derived from tape-re-corded in-depth life narrative interviews involving several sessions and totaling from 5 (Flo) to 17 hours (Ingrid).

THE CASE OF FLORENCE RUCKER

Florence (or Flo) Rucker spent the first 19 years of her life living with her parents, in a well-maintained neighborhood within the Memphis metropolitan area. She completed her education through high school in local schools, and attended a small local college for two years. At college she met the man whom she would marry; Richard was two years her senior. They were wed, and moved first into a small apartment and within a year into their own home, both places located near her childhood neighborhood. Richard worked as a corporate accountant, and Flo was content remaining home and assuming domestic responsibilities.

Flo developed two very important elements of her imagined home during these early years of life. First was a geographic affinity for the Memphis area, and particularly for its older established neighborhood settings. Second was the notion of home as sanctuary. Flo's parents were very giving people, and their house often served as a safe harbor for extended family and even friends during difficult times. Flo's mother played a central role in this service, as matriarch of the home and as counselor to those in need, and Flo modeled herself in such a role later on. Her ability to fulfill this role was fundamental in both her imagined and much of her experienced home through life.

Flo and Richard had two children—a boy, Edward, and a girl, Elizabeth. There would have been more, but Flo experienced two miscarriages in the years after the second child's birth and the couple jointly decided to suspend any further attempts at having children. Flo and Richard were devout and active Christians. They raised their children within the church that Flo and her own parents had long attended. Both children were successful in school and both graduated from colleges located in the northeastern United States Both children would spend their college vacations at Flo and Richard's home.

Church provided an important attribute in Flo's imagined home, serving as a spiritual and moral "code of conduct" in her immediate environment, and providing the closest friendships in her and her husband's lives. They frequently planned dinners in their house with these friends, and also opened their house for small church study and worship groups.

Their daughter, Elizabeth, continued through graduate school, earned her Ph.D., married, and assumed a faculty position at Hunter College in New York. Edward moved to Detroit to assume an engineering position. He eventually married.

Flo and Richard's home was the focal point of holiday celebrations at Christmas and Easter, and each of their now-adult children and their spouses would spend time in Memphis during the summer. Flo and Richard were in their mid-50's when Edward and his wife had the first of four children (each spaced about 2 years apart). Flo and Richard would make occasional trips to Detroit to visit, but their home in Memphis remained the "family" focus.

Richard was diagnosed with lung cancer at the age of 67. Chemotherapy kept him fairly stable for two years, but the cancer eventually metastasized and Richard died at home at age 70, with family, neighbors, and church friends present.

Flo continued to live in the family home, and continued the community-volunteer work that she had started in her early 40's. After Richard's death she also began serving with Hospice, and she increased her involvement in church activities. Her children (and grandchildren) still gathered for holidays, but summer visits became less frequent because of Elizabeth's research commitments and Edward's insistence on "family vacations" with the children around the country.

Richard's death struck a blow to Flo's experienced home. Though she remained active, and even increased her commitments, Flo expressed the feeling that "things just never seemed right after that." Richard was, and remained, a central attribute in Flo's imagined home. In addition, Flo felt a loss in her home as the frequency of visits by her children declined. Still, exceptional physical and cognitive health helped maintain a comfortable sense of her experienced home.

Flo fell and broke her right hip at age 75. She underwent hip-replacement surgery, and attempted to rehabilitate at home. Church friends provided meals, cleaned house, and ran errands during early phases of recovery. They later moved Flo's bed from the upstairs bedroom to the ground-floor study when it became apparent that she would regain only limited mobility. Despite obvious discomfort, she still kept up some measure of volunteer and church activity, although increasingly she contributed through tasks that could be done at home, including administrative bookkeeping and craft making.

By this time, Flo no longer felt "at home." Richard was gone, and she had lost her ability to act in her role as counselor and mistress of an active sanctuary that could serve others. Relocation of her bed to the study represented a big loss. The second-floor bedroom had long been her own private sanctuary in a vibrant household, and both Richard's and her own exclusive domain. Beyond the modest loss of physical privacy—the study was now considered a public space in the house—she keenly felt the loss of emotional privacy.

At age 78, and "moving very slowly these days" Flo fell again and broke her left hip. She endured another hip replacement, but was told by her surgeon that the severity of her osteoporosis, coupled with the fracture and surgical trauma, would likely cause severe mobility limitations. Edward insisted that Flo join his family in Detroit, and after some shuffling of the two children still at home, Flo moved into one of the kid's rooms and the Memphis house was sold.

The situation at Edward's home quickly turned sour. Flo attempted to help in meal preparation and redecoration of the house, which was not well accepted by Edward and his wife, but the biggest conflict emerged from the children. One was tired of "sharing" her room with her little sister, and both were embarrassed to bring their friends home because Flo wanted to greet each friend and talk with them.

After two years in Detroit it was decided that Flo should move in with Elizabeth and her husband, who were now located in Buffalo, New York. Having no children, Elizabeth felt there was plenty of room, and their ranch-style house was located less than 15 minutes from the State University of New York campus (where she worked) in case there was an emergency.

Flo's condition seemed to worsen. Her function declined rapidly to the point that she required assistance toileting, bathing, and often eating. Elizabeth became concerned for Flo's safety, so with Edward's help Flo was admitted to a nursing home. Elizabeth would visit several times each week, and Edward tried to schedule monthly trips to visit his mother.

"Mom is really different," Elizabeth conveyed to Edward at Flo's 83rd birthday party. "I really don't like that home," she continued, "and I don't think they're feeding her enough. Can't you see how gaunt she's become?" Edward agreed and, placing the blame on the nursing home, they together found another facility that promised a higher level of personal care. Flo was transferred, and found herself in a double room shared with a stroke patient. After two weeks she was moved to another room after exhibiting excessive agitation followed by long periods of despondency.

Flo's housing transitions following her second hip fracture are not unusual. Indeed they suggest a high degree of care and thoughtfulness on the part of her children. Regardless, Flo's health trajectory and especially her rapidly growing depression are poignant. Flo's life was essentially her imagined home, and she had long had an experienced home that closely mirrored her imagined. With such a rapidly compromised health status, and the suddenness of losing control over her environment, she had little opportunity and very little help to revise her imagined home. From a societal perspective, Flo was continually afforded the best possible "home." But fundamentally, Flo became homeless while still in her long-time house, and remained homeless through to the end of her life.

THE CASE OF INGRID MILLER

According to Ingrid, "I moved more in my first 16 years than 10 people move in a life time!" Ingrid Miller was born in England into an American military family. Reassignments carried her worldwide, which is not unusual and she did not recall being in one house for more than 4 years at a time until she was well into her 30's. She was an only child, her father was an officer with the Air Force, and her mother was a homemaker and "typical officer's wife." Her early sense of home focused on her mother and the many social activities in the house, regardless of where they lived. For her, home was her family, the anticipation of seeing father again, and the boxes that held all their belongings when they moved, and a good deal of the belongings that never found a place in each new residence.

Ingrid attended two small colleges, both in the Washington D.C. area, before graduating and marrying Sal. She had met Sal during her final year of college. He was at a military social affair with his family, and he and Ingrid had spent most of the afternoon and evening together trying to avoid their parents, and eventually striking up a close friendship. They were engaged within a month and married within a year.

Sal was also military (also Air Force), and with World War II starting, he was away from Ingrid for extended periods of time. Ingrid remained in her parent's home until the war ended and Sal received a permanent staff posting.

It was during the war that Ingrid "began dreaming" of what her imagined home might be like. Permanence of place did not enter the picture at this time, but she emphasized the importance of having a husband nearby on a fairly permanent basis. Like her parents, she too imagined having a very open and social home.

Sal's "permanent" postings turned out to be two to four-year tours that continued throughout most of her adulthood. Sal was initially part of the World War II reconstruction effort, and the couple moved frequently between Europe and Japan until Sal became involved in strategic air base planning and supplies management. This shift in duties brought the couple back to the United States for extended periods, although they continued to change locations frequently between the east and west coasts. Sal and Ingrid had tried unsuccessfully to have children, and despite social pressures eventually accepted their childless state.

Ingrid did not seem regretful of not having children. In fact, she felt like she always had a strong and supportive family in the military. Besides her own and Sal's parents, she viewed their military friends as "family;" there were always children about, and she often shared with childcare duties. Not having a child, however, naturally influenced her imagined home in that her vision did not include any association with children either in her current or prospective thinking.

Furthermore, it was during this period in Ingrid's life that she became increasingly frustrated with the constant packing, moving, and only partial unpacking of her belongings. She was proud of her experiences, of her husband's accomplishments, and of the essence of who she was as a person. Yet she conveyed a sense that her housing never fully reflected the people who lived in it.

Sal retired from the military in 1985, and the couple settled initially in Colorado Springs, Colorado, close to the Air Force Academy. Sal and Ingrid had spoken some of where they might want to live at retirement, and the Academy seemed natural as a means of prolonging access to benefits provided by the military and maintaining connections with military colleagues. But at dinner with friends, the couple with them mentioned a trip they had taken to the Smokey Mountains and their favorable impressions of Hendersonville, North Carolina, just east of the National Park. Within a few months Ingrid and Sal visited Hendersonville and decided, quite spontaneously, to move there permanently.

The move to Hendersonville further confirms the lack of strong geographic influence in Ingrid's imagined home. She said the place just felt right, and the only advantage to its location was the somewhat closer distance to her parents, who had retired outside Cleveland, Ohio. Ingrid's imagined home, in fact, was "someplace where I can finally unpack all our stuff," and where she and Sal could see themselves in the place they lived. Ingrid conveyed that, until Hendersonville, she had never known how "un-at-home" she had always felt. Besides the new opportunity to express herself so fully through her environment, she became aware of how disturbing her footloose life had been. Sal, too, apparently shared these same strong feelings.

Sal died, suddenly, five years after the move to Hendersonville. The death traumatized Ingrid, and at the suggestion of her parents she moved to a small house in the Cleveland area. She welcomed the opportunity to spend more time with her parents, and particularly her mother, who was experiencing declining health at the time. She began volunteering in local service organizations and established a small but active group of friends. Within two years, however, she decided to return to Hendersonville, where she remained until she died.

Ingrid's move back to Hendersonville was an action to move her experienced home closer to her imagined home. She moved to a different house in Hendersonville, but the area itself held intimate meaning for her. The move was a conscious decision to rejoin her husband, admittedly in spirit only. Sal, like Ingrid, had finally identified and lived in their imagined home during the few brief years in Hendersonville, and for the first, and perhaps last time in her life, a fixed location became a critical attribute of that imagined home.

CONCLUSIONS

The case studies present two very different trajectories in the process of developing and maintaining home across the life course. Both Flo and Ingrid established early images of home by virtue of their early life dependence spheres—Flo with a predisposition for a specific place and a particular role in that place, and Ingrid with a more strongly imposed conformance to a highly mobile and necessarily social military lifestyle. Flo successfully negotiated an experienced home through much of her life that closely reflected her imagined home, and not until her later ages and with her infirmities did she finally lose her ability to maintain control over her experienced home. Rapid divergence between the imagined and experienced ensued, and the influence of later-life dependence caused a felt, if not socially identifiable, spiral into homelessness. Ingrid, on the other hand, had a very basic imagined home early in life that was constrained, in part, by the paucity of diverse home experiences gained through her spheres of influence. Her imagined home only became fully developed during later life codependence when she realized the importance of being able to see her self expressed in her living environment. Ingrid was never technically homeless, but she certainly felt, retrospectively, that she had been without a true home for most of her childhood and adult life.

Using a conceptualized process of home, and recognizing home and homelessness as more than two exclusive states of existence, provides richer understanding of the context for decisions made throughout life. Home is, indeed, a powerful force, but it is an ethereal force that is highly individual in nature and as diverse and complex as the people it affects. People develop an image of what home should be for them, with material, geographic, and emotional attributes selected from a wide array of experiences. But what home are they experiencing? How does it correspond with the imagined home? What can be done to bring the experienced and the imagined closer together? Decisions naturally must be made to promote correspondence, and some decisions can be quite difficult, involving job choices, economic standing, marriage or divorce, and even health.

This chapter has not sought to define home or homelessness, two notions that have already been thoroughly, albeit independently, dissected, described, defined, and categorized. Rather, our intent has been to somehow combine these notions in a way that may somehow allow us to begin explaining how we become at home or homeless.

REFERENCES

Annlson, J. (2000). Towards a clearer understanding of the meaning of "home." *Journal of Intellectual and Developmental Disability, 25*(4), 251–263.

Bengston, V. L. (1978). The institutionalized aged and their social needs. In E. Seymour (Ed.), *Psychological needs of the aged: A health care perspective* (pp. 35–38). Berkeley, CA: University of Southern California Press.

Boschetti, M. A. (1995). Attachment to person possessions: An interpretive study of the older person's experiences. *Journal of Interior Design, 21*(1), 1–12.

Carboni, J. T. (1990). Homelessness among the institutionalized elderly. *Journal of Gerontological Nursing, 16*(7), 32–37.

Dovey, K. (1985). Home and homelessness. In I. Altman & C. M. Werner (Eds.), *Home environments: Human behavior, and environment* (pp. 33–64). New York: Plenum Press.

Fogel, B. S. (1992). Psychological aspects of staying at home. *Generations, 16*(2), 15–19.

Gelwicks, L. (1978). Needs, environmental design and health care of the aged. In E. Seymour (Ed.), *Psychological needs of the aged: A health care perspective* (pp. 29–33). Berkeley, CA: University of Southern California Press.

Hartwigsen, G. (1987). Older widows and the transference of home. *International Journal of Aging and Human Development, 25*, 195–207.

Hopper, K. (1991) Homelessness old and new: The matter of definition. *Housing Policy Debate, 2*, 757–814.

Marcus, C. C. (1992). Environmental memories. In I. Altman & S. M. Low (Eds.), *Place attachment* (pp. 87–112). New York: Plenum Press.

O'Bryant, S. L., & Nocera, D. (1985). The psychological significance of "home" to older widows. *Psychology of Women Quarterly, 9*(3), 403–411.

Paton, H., & Cram, F. (1992). Personal possessions and environmental control: The experiences of elderly women in three residential settings. *Journal of Women and Aging, 4*(2), 61–78.

Rapoport, A. (1995). A critical concept of home. In D. N. Benjamin, D. Stea, & D. Saile (Eds.), *The home: Words, interpretations, meanings, and environments* (pp. 25–52). Brookfield, VT: Avebury.

Rivlin & Moore, (2001). Home-making: Supports and barriers to the process of home. *Journal of Social Distress and the Homeless, 10*(4), 323–336.

Rowles, G. D. (2000). Habituation and being in place. *Occupational Therapy Journal of Research, 20*(Suppl. 1), 52S–67S.

Rowles, G. D. (2003). The meaning of environment as a component of self. In M. E. Neistadt & E. B. Crepeau (Eds.), *Willard & Spackman's occupational therapy* (10th ed., pp. 111–119). Philadelphia: Lippincott, Williams & Wilkins.

Rowles, G. D., & Ravdal, H. (2002). Age, place and meaning in the face of changing circumstances. In R. S. Weiss & S. A. Bass (Eds.), *Challenges of the third age: Meaning and purpose in later life* (pp. 81–114). New York: Oxford University Press.

Rowles, G. D., & Watkins, J. F. (2003). History, habit, heart, and hearth: On making spaces into places. In K. W. Schaie, H-W. Wahl, H. Mollenkopf, & F. Oswald (Eds.), *Aging independently: Living arrangements and mobility* (pp. 77–96). New York: Springer Publishing Co.

Rubenstein, R., & Parmalee, P. A. (1992). Attachment to place and the representation of the life course by the elderly. In I. Altman & S. M. Low (Eds.), *Place attachment* (pp. 139–163). New York: Plenum Press.

Sixsmith, J. (1986). The meaning of home: An exploratory study of environmental experience. *Journal of Environmental Psychology, 6*, 281–298.

Toyama, T. (1988). *Identity and milieu: A study of relocation focusing on reciprocal changes in elderly people and their environment.* Stockholm, Sweden: Department of Building Function Analysis, the Royal Institute of Technology.

Zingmark, K., Norberg, A., & Sandman, P-O. (1995). The experience of being at home throughout the lifespan: Investigation of persons aged 2 to 102. *International Journal of Aging and Human Development, 41*(1), 47–62.

PART IV

Creating and Recreating Home

CHAPTER 10

African Reinventions: Home, Place, and Kinship Among Abaluyia of Kenya

Maria G. Cattell

> I have a home in Africa, on the slopes of the Samia
>   Hills . . . [1]
> Grey-blue hazy Samia Hills
> like mother breasts
> roll west to Uganda
> along the red-dust ribbon of road, unfurling to Samia
> and home.

Familiar landmarks whiz by—the gas pump at Ugunja (now electric; a few years ago gas was still pumped by hand) . . . Jera Inn . . . and then, the first sight of the Samia Hills, rolling west to Uganda. My heart dances—I'm nearly home. At Bumala, a busy market town, we leave the blacktop and bump over the red-dust road, past fields of maize and beans and houses roofed with grass or iron sheets. As usual, there are many pedestrians: mamas with babes on backs and loads on heads, uniformed children from school, men on foot and on bikes. They stare, obviously wondering who is this *musungu* (European)? They cannot know I am on my way home.

We reach Funyula. In 1982, Funyula was a weekly open-air market ringed by a band of single-story cinderblock buildings with *dukas* (small shops) offering basic necessities and warm sodas and beer. There was a post office with pay phone (which worked sometimes), a bus stage, the small office of the Chief of Samia Location. In the late 1980s, electricity came and sodas and beer were served cold. By 1999, Funyula had several multistory buildings and was officially designated as an "urban center." In 2004, it has a second ring of *dukas* offering clothing, food, furniture, gifts, hardware and tools, household items, school supplies, battery charging and catering services, videos, access to e-mail and much else.[2] In the 1980s I used to buy peanut butter and jam in Kisumu, 60 miles away. Now you can buy them in Funyula! There is talk that the road will be tarmacked (macadamized) in 2004 and that a small airport will be built on the plain on the other side of the Nangina Mission compound, just up the road from Funyula. People are also buying land in Funyula and constructing houses there, among them JB's older brother Francis, who has land and another house and wife "at home" in Siwongo village.

Speaking of JB, there he is. I jump out of the car into JB's embrace, then step back and ask, laughingly, "What's this? Grey in your beard?" He smiles even more broadly: "I'm getting older. In fact, everyone is getting older." JB is John Barasa wa Owiti (son of Owiti). He calls me "mom." He has come to welcome me home.

We drive on the few kilometers to JB's *dala*, his home in Siwongo village and many more welcomes. I spent two years in Samia, in Kenya's Western Province, from late 1983 until the end of 1985, doing anthropological research on older people in a changing society (Cattell, 1989). Then I was *omukeni*, a visitor or stranger. My many return visits, most recently in 2004, have confirmed my place in JB's family, where my other relationships are defined by this primary one of mother and son.[3] I am no longer a stranger. "Mom, you are almost Musamia (a Samia person)," says JB. Now my heart is content. I am truly home: *mudala*, in the home.

HOME IS PLACE

Suppose I were truly Musamia—what would "home" mean to me? I think I have a pretty good idea. Over the years I have made repeated "day visits" to a number of Samia families and have stayed with other families in their homes, where I live as they do and have had many opportunities to observe and discuss behaviors.[4] Through these experiences I have learned about house construction, the advantages and disadvantages of indigenous and permanent houses, security concerns, gates and fences as social boundaries, the aesthetics of home, sociality and kinship behavior, the life cycle of a *dala*[5] and the life course of its inhabitants, including birth, death, and burial, and much more. I have also learned that Samia people, like most Kenyans and indeed like most Africans—no matter how far they travel—are anchored to a rural home place, the place where they were born or, more commonly for women, the place where they are married.[6]

In 2004, in formal interviews and informal conversations with various Samia people, I heard many times (as I had many times in the past): "Home is the place where I was born . . . where my placenta is buried . . . where my parents are . . . where my father is buried . . . where *emisambwa* (spirits of ancestors) are . . . where I will be buried."

A home or homestead is a *dala* (or *edala*). It is a space with known boundaries, a space that may include one or several houses (*enyumba*) and usually is surrounded by a hedge, occasionally by a fence or wall with a gate, which delineates the outer extent of the home. Many houses are of the indigenous type, with walls of mud from the earth on which the house stands and roofs thatched with locally grown grass. Though size varies, one house is much like another in style. People do not become attached to specific houses, since every 8 to 10 years a mud-and-thatch house must be replaced, with abandoned houses left to return to the earth from which they were made. Items inside, such as photos and calendars hanging on walls, papers stored in boxes and furniture, also tend toward impermanence— they may be reduced to dust by ants and termites. So-called "permanent" houses, built with brick or cinderblock walls and iron sheet roofs, have cement floors to foil termites. Perhaps more sentiment will be invested in houses and their objects as more people build permanent houses—and more are going up all the time.

Home is *mudala*, literally "inside the dala" (*mu-* being a prefix indicating entering into or being inside). Life begins *mudala* and much of life is lived *mudala*, including women's preparation and serving of food, childbirths and childrearing, care of frail elders and sick persons, and much social and ritual activity—though there have been many changes such as children being born in hospitals and spending much of their childhood in schools, and many rituals being carried out in schools, churches, and other external sites. When death comes (and most people die at home), funeral ceremonies are held in the dala and the dead person is buried *mudala*, that is, inside the boundary hedge.[7] Thus home is the physical expression of kinship, the center of social life, and a clearly defined moral space. It is made, by means physical and spiritual, as secure as possible against the "outside" and its many dangers such as other humans and wild animals (Cattell, 2001).

Burial of dead bodies at home is of great importance because a person's spirit wants to be near its body, where it can intervene in the lives of descendants, appearing in dreams or causing illness (though this belief appears to be fading among younger generations). Spirits whose bodies are not buried at home become angry and vindictive. People go to great trouble and expense to return the body of a family member who dies away from home. Or, if the body is unavailable (as may happen in drownings or overseas deaths), a full funeral must be held at home and an object such as a banana or the fruit of a sausage tree (*Kigelia africana*) is buried in place of the missing body. In my 1995 interviews about Robert Wangila (see below), no matter how I pushed them, everyone found it hard to imagine not making every effort to take a body home for burial. But with the long-term downturn in the Kenyan economy since the early 1990s, bodies more often are buried in cemeteries in Nairobi or wherever the death occurred, while at home there is a burial with a surrogate for the deceased's body. As JB told me in 2004: "Carrying a body from Nairobi up to this place [Samia] is damn expensive now. Damn! So if there is not enough money to transport the body, the body will just be buried wherever it is." Thus economic necessity is bringing about change in a deeply held custom.

All this adds up to a concept of home as a particular place marked physically by houses (*enyumba*) and the boundary hedge, socially by the family's daily activities and life rituals (especially burials), and invisibly by the presence of placentas and dead bodies (or their surrogates) in the earth and ancestral spirits hovering in the air around the dala.

IDEOLOGY AND PRACTICE

As I listened to many reiterations of "Home is where I was born . . . where my father is . . . where I will be buried," I realized I was also hearing many anecdotes and seeing for myself in home visits and travels about Samia and Bunyala that, as often happens, people do not always do what they say. Samia today are migrating, moving to new places, creating new homes. Ideology and practice are not always rhyming.

Migration is an old story in western Kenya. In the 19th century and earlier, Samia was in the interlacustrine migration corridor. When elders recite their clan histories, they tell tales of migration, of the movements of clans across the landscape (e.g., Seitz, 1978; Were, 1967). In the 19th century, land was plentiful and people could (and often did) move to gain access to larger or better farming or grazing land or to escape internal conflicts, external enemies; or conditions such as disease, drought, and famine. Land was held and managed communally. Postcolonially, this system was replaced by individual ownerships with official registration and demarcation. At the same time, the population was increasing rapidly. Superficially it would seem that individualized and legalized land tenure and the virtual absence of open land would encourage people to stay where they are. Yet, it seems that contemporary Samia continue to move their homes not only to various destinations in Kenya's cities and in other countries, but also to buy land in other rural areas of Kenya.[8] Within Samia a migration trend is apparent: people are buying land away from their homes, building houses, making new homes. In 2004, I heard stories and saw for myself a number of instances of this mobility.

As we stood outside his house one evening in 2004, JB pointed to Nangina Hill and said: "Up there on the hill—see those lights? A man from Muramba [in Samia] has migrated there with his family. And that other house next to his, that is another man who has done the same thing."[9]

JB's nephew Mase, who was brought up by JB's parents in Siwongo, inherited land from his long dead father in Wakhungu (in Samia) and went there to live when he married a few years ago. But his uncles (father's brothers) in Wakhungu regard him as an interloper and have not been kind to him. Mase is planning to sell his inherited land and buy land in Siwongo to make a new home for himself, his wife and children.

A Munyala woman who worked in Nairobi for many years had no marital home to go to when she retired, as she and her husband had divorced many years earlier. She bought land not far from her (deceased) father's home in Port Victoria and built a house there. Though women, even divorced women, usually are buried in their husband's home, this woman will be buried on her own land. One of her brothers bought land and built a house in Teso District (county), "and he will be buried there."

My daughter Frankline Mahaga (also Munyala) has an MBA from U.S. International University in Nairobi, is a marketing and sales officer with Magadi Soda Company, and has traveled to the United States several times to visit me and to England several times to visit her husband, who has completed a computer studies program and is employed there. Their daughter, Maria Mudidi (Didi), was born in England. In 2004 Frankie and I took Didi, age 2, for her first visit to her rural home in Bondo (her Luo father's home). It is unlikely Frankie and Didi will return often (if ever) to Bondo. Frankie is a city person who rarely visits her own home in Port Victoria. Didi is a city person. Will Didi develop a sense of rural roots?

Imelda Makokha was employed for many years as a cook and housekeeper by the Medical Mission Sisters at Nangina (in Samia). A single mother, Imelda educated her three sons. When she retired, she bought land not far from the Nangina mission compound and built a house. Each son also has his own house, and the family is constructing a brick wall around their dala. This is home for Imelda and her sons, though it lacks a birth history and ancestral spirits—and belongs to a woman. Imelda's son Kizito recently earned a master's degree in the Netherlands. "Whenever I'm comfortable, then I would say that I'm at home," Kizito told me. He hopes to return to Holland to become a university lecturer and expects Holland to be "a new home abroad." His brother Father Peter is an ordained Catholic priest who has been on missions at the Vatican and in the United States and teaches canon law at a Kenyan Catholic seminary. "You can try to make a home wherever you are," said Peter, "but contrary to what Kizito said . . . I would like to stay here in Samia."[10]

Many men remain in their natal homes (and women in their marital homes) throughout their lives, but others are on the move, their homes are on the move, physically, and must be reconstituted as social and moral spaces. With so many examples (though I have no quantitative data to suggest how many people are doing this), I began to wonder: In this landscape full of movement, of people creating new homes contrary to the "rules"—in all this commotion, is the ideology of home helping to provide the sense of rootedness and belonging that would otherwise come from places marked by placentas, fathers and grandfathers?

HOME IS PEOPLE

JB is an agricultural extension agent and a farmer, a man who is very aware of the land, whose daily work brings him in close contact with the earth. His home is on the same land where he experienced most of his childhood, except for a few years in Nairobi, on land he inherited from his father. He is rooted in his place. But he agrees that it is not so much the land that is important. "Home is people," he says. Yes, says Frankline, the woman of the world, "Your immediate family really matters where your home is." Father Peter, the world traveler, the man who in some ways has made the church his home, agrees: "Home is where you have your parents and where you have the children, familiar people. And so home becomes a place where all my problems are solved, where I experience love, the right company, where everyone is concerned about another."[11]

Samia are embedded in extensive networks of both maternal and paternal kin, networks that extend the interactions of families over a wide geographic area. These kin networks of reciprocity and exchange greatly improve a person's life chances. But families are not fixed entities. An individual's claim to family membership is not permanent, not guaranteed by birth or kinship. It must be regularly maintained through exchanges of material goods and services—or you become "lost." Only when one becomes too old and weak to contribute does the obligation relax. Frail elders can "just sit and eat," be cared for by others with no return expected.

Many migrants—even those who spend years outside their home area—make visits home, bring gifts and often, build a house at home, especially as they near retirement (Cattell, 2000). This includes those living far away, such as several of my academic colleagues in the United States (two are Luos, one is a Luyia from Bungoma). These men have lived in the United States for many years but have built houses "back home in Kenya" and return occasionally for visits. From Samia, Patrick Ochwila, whom I first knew in his student days in the mid-1980s, has settled permanently in the United States. In 2003, Patrick went home with plans and money and saw to the building of permanent houses for his parents, brothers, and himself on the family's land. Patrick does not live in his house, his older sister does. But his place is there should he want to claim it in life or for burial.

WOMEN, LAND, AND HOME

In a survey of 200 women and 216 men age 50 and over, which was carried out in Samia in 1985 (Cattell, 1989), I found that nearly all the men (87%) had worked for periods, sometimes for many years, outside Samia, while only 7 of the 200 women had ever been in formal employment and many had never been to any large city. The men had retired back home to land inherited from their fathers. Asked how long they had lived *mudala*, "in this home" (where the interviews were conducted), three quarters said: "I have lived here all my life." Their sojourns in Nairobi or Nyeri or Jinja, whether long or short, were "outside." Only Samia was home, and more precisely, the place of their fathers and grandfathers, where they "really" lived even during long absences.

Women have a different relationship with the land and a different reckoning of home. They rarely inherit or own land (but see Imelda's story, previously described). Instead, they gain cultivation and burial rights through marriage. In the 1985 survey, most women said, "I have lived here many years" or "since my marriage." Women experience a shift in family allegiance and definition of home when they marry. If you ask an unmarried female where her home is, she will most likely tell you the place where her father lives, which is, probably (but not necessarily), the place where she was born and where her placenta is buried.[12] When she marries, a woman moves to her husband's home, the place of his father and ancestors. Ask her then "Where is your home?" and she will name the husband's home. That is where a woman must be buried—though women's burials often are problematic. Where to bury a man is usually a foregone conclusion, but where to bury a woman can be highly controversial (and fairly often is) if there are ambiguities in her marital status or issues about the cause of her death (Cattell, 1992).

The one thing no one wants is to bury a married woman/widow in her father's home, where her spirit might trouble the living in that home. Though even this "absolute" rule can be broken. For example, in 1985 a husband buried his wife outside the boundaries of his homestead (that is, in the wild rather than in the home), thus rejecting her as a wife (Cattell, 1992). In 1995, another young woman's parents buried their daughter in their own home because of disagreements with the "husband" about their daughter's marital status. This followed a court case in which the parents sued, successfully, to get custody of their daughter's body (Cattell, 1999). Since then some people have attributed further deaths in this family to the presence of the daughter's body—and spirit—in the home. Though younger people with doubts about the powers of ancestral spirits seem inclined to think that "if she wasn't happy with [her husband], her spirit wouldn't do that to her parents."

SM OTIENO'S STORY:
WHEN A HOUSE IS NOT A HOME

In December of 1986 a Kenyan criminal lawyer, Silvano Melea Otieno (better known as "SM"), died in Nairobi. His widow, Virginia Wambui Otieno, was preparing to bury him—according to his expressed wishes, she claimed—in a Nairobi cemetery. But her husband's clan intervened. SM died intestate, making no legally binding provision for his burial, and his clan initiated court action against the widow to halt the burial. The clan claimed that SM—like any Luo man—had to be buried "at home." Though Otieno had lived a cosmopolitan life in Nairobi for many years, the clan wanted to bury him at his family home in western Kenya, in Siaya District (county), in the rural village of Nyamila, where his ancestors were buried.

A house, the clan argued, is not a home. Home is where you have constructed a house according to Luo custom, in the place where your ancestors are (Nation Newspapers, 1987; *Weekly Review*, 1987a). Though SM had lived for many years in a house in Nairobi, he had built a house in Nyamila, though he rarely visited it. The clan argued that SM had to be buried in his home (*dala*, the same word as in the Samia language). The case was considered by Kenya's High Court and Court of Appeal. In the end, after 5 months of legal battles, Luo customary law won over Kenyan written and common law. Otieno's body was taken to Nyamila village, where he had established a home according to Luo custom, and buried there on his ancestral lands. On the way, the funeral procession was greeted by thousands of Luos chanting, "*Karibuni nyumbani, karibuni nyumbani*" (Swahili: "Welcome home," literally, "welcome in the house") (*Weekly Review,* 1987b, p. 13).

This case was reported in the international news media and keenly followed by Kenyans, Luos or not (and no doubt many other Africans) throughout the world (see e.g., Cohen & Atieno Odhiambo, 1992; Ojwang & Mugambi, 1989). African and Africanist scholars continue to ponder its many implications, and Mrs. Otieno has written her own account, in bitter disagreement with the courts' decisions (Otieno, 1998). The relevance of the SM burial case here is its reflection of the strength of customs (or culture)—the powerful ideology of home as the place of one's birth, one's father's home, and the home of the ancestors. Burial in such a place unites each individual, in death, with both earth—the same earth from which houses are built and which produces the food people eat—and ancestors. It is a compelling ideology.

WANGILA'S STORY:
WHEN A HOME NEEDS A HOUSE

In the case of SM, the ideology of home was supported by clan action and enforced by Kenyan courts, with the result that SM's body (apparently against his expressed intentions) was buried *mudala*. For another prominent Kenyan, in a case also mediated by Kenyan courts, the ideology was supported but the practice, the practical result of burial in the man's home, was denied because the man, while living, had not actually created the home to which he was entitled. Both these cases, although interesting because of the interplay between cultural ideologies and practices, also highlight another complication: the multiplicity of laws in Kenya (and many African nations)—the laws of legislatures and courts, and the "laws" of custom or indigenous practices.

Robert Wangila was an Olympic gold medalist boxer who died in America in 1994. The return of his body to Kenya set off another court case. The case began with the issue of Wangila's "personal law"—the body of customary law into which he was born, which depended on who his father was. There were three claimants for fatherhood, two from the Kisii ethnic community (to which his mother belonged), and one from Samia. In the end, the court declared that Wangila's father was the Samia man, so Wangila's personal law was that of Samia. But he had never established a legal claim to his father's land nor built a house there to secure his claim to burial rights. He had, in effect, become lost—in spite of his fame. By court order, he was buried in a Nairobi cemetery (Cattell, 1995). Various Samia, in interviews a few months later, disagreed with the court's decision. As an older widow, put it: "A man must be buried *mudala aye* (in his own home). A man cannot be buried at any other place while he's having a home (*dala*)."[13]

HOME, PLACE, AND KIN IN SUB-SAHARAN AFRICA

Throughout sub-Saharan Africa, people engage in labor migration and spend long periods of time as urban dwellers. However, the majority of urban Africans do not entirely break their rural connections, even if the connections become rather tenuous (Gugler, 2002). Rather, they maintain their commitments to people at home and their involvement in family networks that can span considerable distances.

In their new settings migrants tend to reproduce the social structures of their home villages (Smith, 2001), along with developing new coping strategies such as the ethnic associations that provide support to members in other locations much as family would provide support back home. By such processes, Africans are redefining home and family through creating "extended communities" (Berry, 1985) and transforming rural–urban space into a "continuous social field" (Smith, 2000) and local villages into "translocal communities" that reach across continents (Lambert, 2002). Nevertheless, many, perhaps most, migrants plan to retire to rural home places and be buried at home (Gugler, 2002; Møller & Welch, 1990). "Home," the place of the ancestors and of living kin, is an anchor in a world full of movement.

At the same time, home is not always a fixed point, a specific village, a particular homestead. For migrants on the Zambian Copperbelt, home is not necessarily the place of origin of the worker, but rather the place where the returning worker expects to be welcomed by kin (Ferguson, 1999). In northern Zambia, residential choices are very fluid, open to constant negotiation, with whole villages moving from one place to another (Moore & Vaughan, 1994). Indeed, there is great fluidity in some Africans' experiences of home, especially among nomadic and seminomadic pastoralists and foragers. What is home for a nomad? Is it a movable tent (Wood, 1999), a waterhole (Lee, 1979), a rain forest (Turnbull, 1962)? Moke, an old Pygmy, told Turnbull (1962, p. 260): "The forest is our home. When we leave the forest, or when the forest dies, we shall die. We are the people of the forest." For the Pygmies, the whole of the vast Ituri rain forest is a maternal entity that nurtures, sustains, and supports them.

Another set of issues regarding home arises with forced relocations. Under the apartheid regime and its dismantling, with forced removals, a mass rural exodus, and the ensuing development of informal settlements or shantytowns in urban areas, "the lives of a majority of South Africans have been shaped by troubled and ambiguous experiences of localities" (Bohlin, 1998, p. 168). Following construction of the Kariba Dam in the 1950s and flooding of their lands, about 30,000 Gwembe Tonga in Zambia were displaced from their homes and resettled into less fertile lands. It was a bitter experience during which manipulation of kinship ties was the main coping strategy (Colson, 1971). Currently in sub-Saharan Africa there are millions of persons displaced internally and internationally (when they officially become refugees) by conflicts and violence. If and when they return home, how will these displaced persons and refugees experience home?

Even among nomads and other Africans with more fluid concepts of home, there seems to be little trend toward the nonlocalized identities that have been identified elsewhere (Rapport & Dawson, 1998). For most Africans, place remains crucial to identity and to concepts of home and family.

AFTERTHOUGHTS

Writing this piece has been a fascinating exercise. I began with a good understanding of Samia (and other Luyia) concepts of home. But my experiences in Kenya just a few months ago (in February 2004) shook things up a bit. In my previous visits what had seemed to be isolated instances of individuals migrating from their home places, in 2004 seemed more like a somewhat paradoxical trend. The ideology of home as I learned it in my early research persists among Abaluyia. But it persists—and serves perhaps as both comfort and guideline—in the face of growing challenges to its aptness among people for whom place, kinship, and home continue to be of great importance, not only as ideologies but in terms of survival.

Like many other Africans, Abaluyia and other Kenyans are creating continuous rural–urban social fields and translocal communities as they cope with their need for belonging and rootedness and the economic and personal motivations that move them away from the rootedness of their traditional homes. Intergenerational differences are noticeable too, as younger people diverge from their elders in ideas and practices about many things, such as the power of ancestral spirits, the extent of food sharing within a home, and the roles of women. As with so many other aspects of their lives, Kenyans—and Africans generally—are having to reinvent themselves and their ideas about home, place, and kinship.

ACKNOWLEDGMENTS

I am most grateful for the invaluable help over the past 22 years (since 1982) of my Luyia coresearchers, especially my son, John Barasa "JB" Owiti, of Siwongo village in Samia and my daughter, Frankline Mahaga, of Port Victoria and Nairobi. Special thanks to Frankie and JB and their entire extended families for their love and hospitality over the years. Let me especially recognize JB's father, Clement Owiti, who died shortly after my last visit with him in February 2004. May his spirit keep his home safe for his descendants. *Mareba!* Thanks also to the Medical Mission Sisters at Nangina Holy Family Hospital (especially Sr. Marianna Hulshof) and the many pupils and staff at Nangina Girls Primary School (now St. Catherine's), who have welcomed me over the years; and Samia officials, particularly my old friend, Fred Wandera Oseno, Chief of Funyula Divison since 1997. Above all, *mutio muno* to the many people in the Luyia areas known as Samia, Bunyala, and Bungoma (and the Kisumu and Nairobi families of some) who have allowed me to share their lives in various ways. The research was partially funded by the National Science Foundation (grant BNS-8306802), the Wenner-Gren Foundation for Anthropological Research (grant 4506), and a Frederica de Laguna Fund grant from Bryn Mawr College in 1982. I was a Research Associate at the Institute of African Studies, University of Nairobi, in 1984 and 1985.

NOTES

1. A take-off on the opening line of Isak Dinesen (Karen Blixen)'s memoir, *Out of Africa*. The Samia Hills are in western Kenya, just north of the Equator. They are the homeland of Abasamia (Samia people), who are a subgroup of the ethnic community known as Abaluyia (Luyia people), of Bantu origin. Formerly called Samia Location (township), Samia is now officially Funyula Division, though local people still call it Samia, and so do I. Among their close neighbors are other Luyia—Marachi to the east, Banyala to the south—and Luo, of Nilotic origin. The Luyia and Luo communities each numbered around 3 million in the 1999 Kenya census. Though their languages are different, Samia share with Luo various customs and many words, including personal names and the word for home, *dala*.

2. In 1999 no one in Samia had e-mail or cellphones; in 2004, many people gave me e-mail addresses and cellphone numbers.

3. Through my daughter, Frankline Mahaga, I am also a member of the Mahaga family in Port Victoria, in Bunyala, a Luyia territory just to the south of Samia. Banyala are culturally very close to Samia people.

4. My thanks for their many hospitalities to JB Owiti and his wife, Mary Auma, and Regina and Tadeyo Makokha of Siwongo and Bukhulungu villages in Samia, Frankline Mahaga in Nairobi and her grandmother Paulina and father, Joseph, in Port Victoria, and Pastor and Mrs. Ben Wandabwa in Bungoma—with whom I have stayed over the years; and the many other families who have welcomed me into their homes for numerous day visits. They know who they are.

5. A dala expands as sons marry and build houses. When the father dies, sons hive off their own dalas.

6. There are always exceptions. For example, in Ghana older women in matri-
    lineal Ashanti societies may return to their natal homes, sometimes even
    before they are widowed (Stucki, 1992).

7. Although there are cemeteries in Kenya's cities, there are none in Samia,
    so everyone is buried at home. Occasionally persons whose status is
    ambiguous are buried outside the hedge (Cattell, 1989, 1992).

8. In the Eldoret area, in 1985, I visited a settlement scheme (where land had
    been set aside for sale), which was known as "Little Samia" because so
    many of the inhabitants originated in Samia.

9. It was strange to see electric lights shining on the night-dark hill. This has
    come about because people are investing in solar units where there are
    no power lines to deliver electricity to their homes.

10. The third son, Joseph, a social worker at the Nangina Family Helper Project,
    was not present for our discussion. (Interview with Father Peter and Kizito,
    February 15, 2004.)

11. Interview with JB and Frankline, February 8, 2004; with Father Peter and
    Kizito, February 15, 2004.

12. The person's birth and burial of the placenta (*engobi*) at home are im-
    portant but not necessary. John Barasa told me he was born in Uganda
    and his placenta was disposed of there, but "that doesn't make it [Uganda]
    to be my home. [My home is] where my parents originated from." In short,
    his home is in Samia, in Siwongo village, on the land that had been his
    father's. (Interview, February 8, 2004.)

13. Interview with Pamela Silingi, June 20, 1995.

REFERENCES

Berry, S. (1985). *Fathers work for their sons: Accumulation, mobility, and class
    formation in an extended Yoruba community.* Berkeley, CA: University of Califor-
    nia Press.

Bohlin, A. (1998). The politics of locality: Memories of District Six in Cape Town.
    In N. Lovell (Ed.), *Locality and belonging* (pp. 168–188). London: Routledge.

Cattell, M. G. (1989). *Old age in rural Kenya: Gender, the life course and social
    change.* Bryn Mawr College, Ph.D. dissertation (UMI No. 9000504), Bryn
    Mawr, PA.

Cattell, M. G. (1992, November). *Burying Mary Omundu: The politics of death and
    gender in Samia, Kenya.* Paper presented at annual meeting of African Studies
    Association, Seattle.

Cattell, M. G. (1995, November). *Burying who? Samia perspectives on culture,
    gender and identity.* Paper presented at annual meeting of African Studies
    Association, Orlando, FL.

Cattell, M.G. (1999, November). *The daughter who refused to be stolen.* Short story read at annual meeting of African Studies Association, Philadelphia.

Cattell, M.G. (2000, June). *The impact and meaning of migration for older rural Kenyans.* Paper presented at First International Conference on Rural Aging: A Global Challenge, Charleston WV.

Cattell, M. G. (2001, November) *Wild resonances: Intersections of human and animal worlds among Samia, western Kenya.* Paper presented at annual meeting of African Studies Association, Houston.

Cohen, D. W., & Atieno Odhiambo, E. S. (1992). *Burying SM: The politics of knowledge and the sociology of power in Africa.* Portsmouth, NH: Heinemann.

Colson, E. (1971). *The social consequences of resettlement. Kariba Studies IV.* Manchester, UK: University of Manchester Press.

Ferguson, J. (1999). *Expectations of modernity: Myths and meanings of urban life on the Zambian Copperbelt.* Berkeley, CA: University of California Press.

Gugler, J. (2002). The son of the hawk does not remain abroad: The urban–rural connection in Africa. *African Studies Review, 45,* 21–41.

Lambert, M. C. (2002). *Commodities of power: Making migration in a Casmançais community (Senegal, West Africa).* Portsmouth, NH: Heinemann.

Lee, R. B. (1979). *The !Kung San: Men, women and work in a foraging society.* Cambridge, U.K.: Cambridge University Press.

Møller, V., & Welch, G. J. (1990). Polygamy, economic security and well-being of retired Zulu migrant workers. *Journal of Cross-Cultural Gerontology, 5,* 205–216.

Moore, H. L., & Vaughan, M. (1994). *Cutting down trees: Gender, nutrition, and agricultural change in the Northern Province of Zambia, 1890–1990.* Portsmouth, NH: Heinemann.

Nation Newspapers. (1987). Luos have houses, not homes in Nairobi. In Shawn Egan (Ed.), *S. M. Otieno: Kenya's unique burial saga* (pp. 46–52). Nairobi: Author.

Ojwang, J. B., & Mugambi, J. N. K. (Eds.). (1989). *The S. M. Otieno case: Death and burial in modern Kenya.* Nairobi: Nairobi University Press.

Otieno, Wambui Waiyaki. (1988). *Mau Mau's daughter: A life history* (Ed. Cora Ann Presley). Boulder, CO: Lynne Rienner.

Rapport, N., & Dawson, A. (Eds.). (1998). *Migrants of identity: Perceptions of home in a world of movement.* London: Berg.

Seitz, J. R. (1978). *A history of the Samia location in western Kenya, 1890–1930.* West Virginia University, Ph.D. dissertation, Morgantown, West Virginia.

Smith, D. J. (2000, November). *"Home people" abroad: Migration, kinship and community among the Igbo in Nigeria.* Paper presented at annual meeting of the American Anthropological Association, San Francisco.

Smith, D. J. (2001, November). Rural–urban migration and kinship relations in an Igbo community. Paper presented at annual meeting of African Studies Association, Houston, TX.

Stucki, B. R. (1992). The long voyage home: Return migration among aging cocoa farmers of Ghana. *Journal of Cross-Cultural Gerontology, 7,* 363–378.

Turnbull, C. M. (1962). *The forest people: A study of the Pygmies of the Congo.* New York: Clarion Books.

Weekly Review. (1987a, Feb. 6.). The law: When a house is not a home. pp. 5–7.

Weekly Review. (1987b, May 29). The final journey. pp. 8–15.

Were, G. S. (1967). *Western Kenya historical texts.* Nairobi: East African Publishing House.

Wood, J. C. (1999). *When men are women: Manhood among Gabra nomads of East Africa.* Madison, WI: University of Wisconsin Press.

CHAPTER 11

Home, Identity, and Belonging in Later Life: The Perspectives of Disadvantaged Inner-City Men

Cherry Russell

Housing is strongly associated with a range of indicators of well-being in old age. It can have an important impact on the lives of older people not only as a necessity but also through access to wealth stored as equity. Housing can be a crucial factor in determining access to care and to desired lifestyles (Clapham, Means, & Munro, 1993). Housing in old age is most often analyzed as the outcome of housing "careers"—that is, the succession of dwellings occupied over a lifetime (Clapham et al., 1993; Kendig & McCallum, 1990). Researchers have conceptualized the most significant step in this progression as whether or not people ever attain ownership, and if so, whether or not they retain it and eventually pay off their mortgages (Kendig & Neutze, 1999). In Australia, by the time individuals reach their mid-40's to mid-50's more than half own homes outright and one third are purchasers. At ages 65–74, nearly four out of five are outright owners.

The home is widely assumed to have special symbolic and personal significance in later life. Emphasis is placed, in both sociological and policy discourse, on the extent to which older persons are attached to their homes and the social and psychological benefits being "at home" confers. A place of one's own, it is commonly proposed, provides a stable source of security and identity amid the flux and vicissitudes of old age (e.g., Davidson, Kendig, Stephens, & Merrill, 1993; O'Bryant & Nocera, 1985).

Research in different countries (e.g. Davidson et al., 1993; Dupuis & Thorns, 1996; Gurney & Means, 1993; Madigan, Munro, & Smith, 1990; Russell, 1999) has produced broadly similar findings in which the meaning of home reflects "a complex interweaving of the quest for security and identity with the accumulation of assets and other markers of achievement and the transfer of these to subsequent generations" (Dupuis & Thorns, 1996, p. 500). Such an image of home's meaning in practical and existential terms underpins the worldwide policy trend toward care "in one's own home" as the preferred solution in providing for the health and support needs of very old people (see e.g., Daatland, 1997; Dalley, 1988; Gubrium & Sankar, 1990).

Only a partial picture of home in later life emerges from this work. To begin with, most studies reflect the experience of those who have followed majority pathways to old age. Such studies have sought the views of those who are securely housed. Their samples typically comprise elderly owner-occupiers who are mainly married couples or widows living in the family home. A recent interview study in New Zealand is illustrative: all the subjects were home-owners, the majority was widowed women, and about 90% of respondents associated home with either bringing up or being surrounded by family (Dupuis & Thorns, 1996; see also Davidson et al., 1993). Second, extant studies confuse the distinction between "house" and "home" as concepts. The former is a shelter and its fabric, whereas a home does not need to be anything built at all (Rykwert, 1991). As John Hollander puts it, "placing, locating and housing are by no means necessarily homing" (Hollander, 1991, p. 49).

According to Gurney and Means, there are at least three levels of meaning associated with "home": the *cultural*, the *intermediate*, and the *personal*. The *cultural* level is concerned with "the everyday use of the word 'home' and the uncertainties surrounding its definition" (Gurney & Means, 1993, p. 127). At this level, home is the subject of political rhetoric, ideologies, and popular images. At the *intermediate* level, the home is produced and consumed as a commodity, whereas the *personal* level locates the home in the formation of personal biographies. Seen from this perspective, our knowledge of home in old age is largely limited to the experiences of those for whom all three levels converge around an idealized middle–class-life trajectory. In contrast, the men who are the subjects of this chapter are poorly represented in research and policy discourse. They are low-income, unpartnered, nonhomeowning men aged 50+ years living alone in the inner city. Such men pose a particular challenge for services systems that depend on older people having adequate housing and families to provide care for them. At the same time, their occupation of nonnormative households provides opportunity to explore the possibilities and implications of diversity and difference in relation to housing, home, and the relations between them over the life course.

THE AGEING MEN'S HEALTH PROJECT

The Ageing Men's Health Project was a 3-year (1999–2001) ethnographic study conducted in the Local Government Area of South Sydney, a cluster of suburbs on the fringe of the Sydney Central Business District (CBD). Its subjects were men who entered old age with multiple financial, social, and health vulnerabilities. The study sought to elucidate the life pathways of this minority of men outside middle-class suburbs and nuclear families and to examine how they manage their daily lives, what supports are available to them, and what their attitudes and experiences are in relation to the receipt of assistance. The study site afforded a range of habitats for low-income single persons, including private rental accommodation in lodging houses and cheap hotels, public housing, aged-care facilities, and homeless shelters. In addition to conducting some 1,200 hours of participant observation in these and other settings, we recruited a total of 67 men to participate in interviews about their past and present lives. Where permission was given, interviews were tape-recorded and transcribed.[1] These interviews were semi-structured; using open-ended questioning, around the broad topic areas of work, health, housing, family and social networks, and use of supportive services.

The men who participated in the interviews were aged between 50 and 89 years. All were receiving a government pension or benefit, most commonly an aged (29 men), disability support (22 men) or veterans' pension (9 men). The aged pension is set at 25% of average male earnings, currently $184.25 Australian Dollars (AUD) per week, which is 14% below Australia's austere poverty line (Australian Council of Social Services, 2000). Twenty-four of the men had never married or been involved in a marriage-like relationship, 29 reported being divorced or separated (six of these relationships had been de facto), and 14 were widowed (two de facto, including one who had lost a same-sex partner). Just under half of the men had fathered children, though few had remained in regular contact with them. None had a family member available to provide assistance with daily tasks, such as shopping or cooking.

At the time of the interview, 22 of the men were residents of public housing units, 12 occupied single rooms in private lodging houses or hotels, 14 were of no fixed abode, six were "permanent" residents of older emergency shelters, and 13 lived in residential aged-care facilities. Their housing histories did not at all mirror the housing careers characteristic of most Australian men. Home ownership at any time during their lives was relatively infrequent. Only one quarter had at some stage owned or been purchasing a home. By the time they had reached their 40's, when it would be expected that the majority would be on the way to owning their own homes, fewer than 20% had done so and even fewer (12%) had been owners or buyers in their 50's. Although only a dozen interviewees were lodgers when we met them, 35 of the 67 men reported having lived in privately rented single rooms at some point in their lives[2] and most reported considerable housing mobility. As other research (e.g., Crane, 1999; Jordan, 1994; Snow & Anderson, 1993) has shown, such housing histories are characteristic of a particular lifestyle followed by certain men in most of the Western world. They are typically associated—as was the case for many of the men we interviewed—with participation in the secondary labor market of low-skilled, discontinuous, and/or transient work, and often in "masculine occupational communities" that formed around mining, shipping, rail transport, on the wharves, and in most forms of agriculture and pastoral work (Connell et al., 1998; Sommers, 1998). Those who had been home owners at any stage typically had partners and children at the time, and the main reason for relinquishing home ownership was the breakdown of a marriage or marriage-like relationship.

What follows is an account of how such marginal men—those for whom conventional social structures and processes of identity and belonging appear scant or nonexistent—talked about "home." By directing attention to those whose lives have diverged from the normative pathways and lifestyles of middle-class nuclear families, relationships among different levels of meaning can be addressed as an empirical question. At the cultural level of everyday usage, for instance, do the definitions of "home" employed by older people whose living arrangements fail to conform to the idealized view reinforce or resist ideologically dominant understandings? At the intermediate level, it becomes possible to examine the implications of different housing circumstances and transitions for home as a lived experience. Finally, at the personal level, nonnormative households raise questions about the assumed relationship between the identities of older persons and those meaning-making processes of experience and attachment to place, which, it is widely proposed, establish the home as the primary site of identity and belonging in old age (see e.g., Howell, 1983; Rubinstein & Parmelee, 1992).

MEANINGS OF HOME

The interview data include two kinds of talk about home: spontaneous mentions of "home" in talk about various aspects of their past and present lives; and responses to an open-ended question, "Have you ever lived anywhere you would call home?" Through analysis of this talk, it is possible to say something about how these men understand "home" as a cultural construction as well as how—or indeed whether—home was for them a "real and personally meaningful place" (Rubinstein & Parmelee, 1992, p. 140).

Some men defined home as synonymous with a family dwelling. For these men there was a clear contradiction between the cultural ideal and the lived reality. Gregory[3] (aged 54, divorced), for instance, was one of five men who told us he had never lived anywhere he would call home: "Not in the sense like people live in houses with their family all around them. Never had that situation." Others recalled their childhoods as the only time there had been fit between the two levels of aspiration and experience. Talk about one's childhood home often aroused strong emotions, especially among those men who narratively contrasted their past and present situations. For instance:

Interviewer: "Is the place you're living in now 'home-sweet-home'?"

Edward: [short pause] "Oh, I don't know that I'd say that. Home is where you've got family and children. A place of your own. I'm living in a hotel. Day by day. That's not a home. Nothing sweet about it. Just a place to live."

Interviewer: "Have you ever lived anywhere that felt like home?"

Edward: "When I was a kid. That was home. Mum and Dad, John, Paul, and Brody. Lots of space to run around. Get up to mischief. A place to come home to dinner to. Dinner on the table. Your own property. It was family property. Ours to own."

For some divorced and separated men, on the other hand, home had been constituted for a time around a family dwelling in which they were husband and father, and evocation of its loss could still arouse strongly negative emotions. This seems to be especially the case among those for whom relationship breakdown had involved an unwanted loss or diminution of contact with children. In fact, it proved particularly difficult to generate talk about the topic of marital failure. One interviewee, Rover, set limits before the interview began, stating that there were some aspects of his life he was not prepared to discuss. When he inadvertently touched on the topic of access to his former home to see his children he immediately asked that the tape recorder be turned off.

Not all men equated home with the conventional image of a family dwelling. For these men, home was an accomplishment that could occur in a range of accommodation types and in the absence of family relations. As the following responses illustrate, a variety of locations can provide a practical base from which to undertake the routines of daily life and a setting that appropriately mediates identity including public rental as well as nonprivate households, such as homeless shelters, an aged-care facility, and even a car (Rapport & Dawson, 1998). For example:

Interviewer: "So would you call this place (Department of Housing unit) home now?"

David (aged 55, divorced): "Oh, I'm settled here for life now."

Interviewer: "Would you say you've ever lived anywhere that you'd call 'home-sweet-home'?"

Ronald (aged 72, never partnered): "Here" (Aged Care Facility).

Interviewer: "Yeah? What makes it feel like home-sweet-home?"

Ronald: "Well, I like a lot of the chaps here and, um, videos of a night if you want to watch them."

Edwin (aged 72, never partnered): "Well, Bessy [his car] is my home now. Longest time I've ever—longest time I've lived anywhere."

Interviewer: "What makes it like home?"

Edwin: (long pause) "Well, she's mine."

Earl (aged 75, never partnered): "Oh, Hope Hostel (homeless shelter)was my home. . . . You had everything at your fingertips, I suppose. You were satisfied. You wasn't worried because you had everything. I had the shower room and toilet just around the corner. Everything."

Grady (aged 65, divorced): "Oh well, Hope Hostel (was home) I suppose. It was okay. I didn't have to do anything. They changed the sheets and cleaned up the place. I knew everybody there. It wasn't too bad."

Jerome (aged 60, never partnered): "Oh everywhere I've lived was my home. [long pause] I wouldn't call it anything else but that."

Interviewer: "What made the different places feel like home?"

Jerome: (laughs) "That's a hard question."

Interviewer: "It is a hard question."

Jerome: "I couldn't give you an answer."

Overall, then, it seems that there is no single meaning of "home" among these men. Some talked about home as a cultural ideal from which they themselves were excluded by their lack of attachment to family life. Others said they felt, or currently feel "at home" in a range of nonfamilial residential settings. Home was sometimes, but not always, associated with strong positive or negative emotions. At the same time, the interview data provide another kind of insight into the complex association between place, life history, and personal identity that in conventional gerontological discourse tends to be treated as if it were synonymous with "home." The men were asked to evaluate their present accommodation, and their responses suggest that for this group of men the primary source of "place attachment" may not be to a particular dwelling at all.

PLACE, IDENTITY, AND BELONGING

The men identified a limited number of factors as sources of satisfaction or dissatisfaction with their accommodation currently or in the past. These included such things as cost, domestic amenities, privacy, and security of tenure. But by far the biggest single category of talk in this context concerned geographical location. We were alerted to the centrality of the inner-city habitat as a sociocultural as well as geographic space early in the fieldwork by the emphasis that the men placed on ensuring that the researchers understood the geographic location of landmarks, hotels, or other buildings they talked about in their interviews. They would ask if the interviewer knew where certain places were, and if she did not, the men would provide descriptions and directions, which sometimes took up a page or more of transcription.

Frequently, changes in the urban landscape provided the narrative footing for biographical work (Gubrium & Holstein, 1998). Jerome, who had occupied the same room in a lodging house for "10 or 15 years," narratively linked the physical and social changes in his world:

Jerome: "Well, yeah, I've lived in [inner-city suburb] all my life. Yeah. For years."

Interviewer: "Is there anything in particular that keeps you in the area?"

Jerome: "Oh, nothing much. Just because I like the place and nearly all my friends have grown up and got married and moved away and things like that, but I still live here. Half the time you see up the top road there you don't know anyone. It's changed. I used to know a lot of people around here."

The significance of the neighborhood arose in large part from its role as a setting for social connections with other like-situated men. It is commonplace in the literature for homeless or insecurely housed men, particularly drinkers, to be characterized as "undersocialized isolates" (Archard, 1979). Yet in the absence of conventional (i.e., family-based) social bonds, the men still described feelings of connection to others and a sense of belonging that gave meaning to their lives. Consider, for example, how Ronald (above) had narratively linked his definition of the aged-care facility as his "home" with the fact that "I like a lot of the chaps here." This was also evident in the talk of several lodgers, who explained why they had rejected the cheaper option of a public housing unit "out of area." Grady, for instance, had been on the Department of Housing waiting list and had been offered a place. But as he explains:

"I turned one down. . . . It was way out and I wasn't going to go out there. . . . It would be alright if it was near here. That would be OK. I know too many people around here, all my friends, and especially now that I'm less mobile."

Like Grady, Earl had recently been involuntarily relocated from his long-time "home" in Hope Hostel to a lodging house in a different part of the city. He had complained about the poor conditions in the latter and, at the time of interview, was waiting to be transferred to "another place the same [i.e. another lodging house] up there near Hope." He thinks it will be better, and "I know the area too, see." He went on to explain how, in the last 2 months since he moved from the hostel, he had become more aware of the significance of Hope as a social–relational setting:

Earl: "Before, I never took notice of it. People call it loneliness. It's only in the last two months I've taken notice of it. You're on your own. Yeah, that's the hard thing. I still get about. It's something I never took any notice of any more."
Interviewer: "So it must have been difficult then leaving Hope because you would have known a lot of blokes down there?"
Earl: "Oh yeah, yeah. God yes, yeah. You could move about there, you weren't stuck in your room all the time. God yes, yeah. You had company."

Social networks of other like-situated men have been significant in the men's lives in a number of ways. Informal contacts played a central role in recruitment into the spatial and subcultural world of the inner city and continued to constitute most if not all of their meaningful engagement with others. As has been described in detail elsewhere (Russell et al., 2001), men in all accommodation types patronized the area's drop-in meal centers that officially exist to feed the homeless. Although the cheapness of the food was a factor, it was not the only or even most important consideration. As Clive explained: "Put it this way, I don't come here for the meals primarily. I don't. I come here for the people."

DISCUSSION

It is clear from the men's biographical accounts that nonnormative housing "careers" have been shaped within the class structure of Australian society and, more specifically, by the characteristics of the actual work they performed in particular locations and periods of history. During the postwar economic boom, jobs were plentiful and labor was in short supply, particularly in those industries that were heavily dependent on unskilled manual labor. In such a market lack of education and training was no obstacle; on the contrary, as so many of them told us, there were plenty of jobs for the young, strong, and mobile. The nature of the work in turn exposed such men simultaneously to resources (such as on-site accommodation and meals and a ready-to-hand social world of like-situated men) and vulnerabilities (for instance, work-related injury, a masculine lifestyle and culture of "mateship" based around heavy drinking) that offered few incentives or supports for securing a permanent home. At the same time, the cities that the men remained in or "cycled" through provided accommodation appropriate to their (limited) needs. In 1947, for instance, boarding and rooming houses accommodated more than a quarter of Australia's inner-city suburban residents (Kendig & Pynoos, 1996).

When they reach old age such men do not fit neatly into prevailing categories of need and welfare provision. Over recent decades, Australia, like comparable other countries, has implemented a policy of deinstitutionalization of aged-care services. Care "at home" is now the goal for all but the most highly incapacitated elders. Yet access to such care is not equally available to all, with community-based systems having been shown to depend heavily on the availability of secure housing and family caregivers (see e.g., Clapham et al., 1993; Daatland, 1997; Fine, 1999; Hashimoto & Kendig, 1992). As I have discussed elsewhere (Russell et al., 2001), future cohorts of older people are likely to include more rather than fewer men like those who are the subjects of my research: lacking adequate income and housing security, in poor health, and effectively outside an informal system of caregiving. As Keith (1986, p. 395) points out, "if provision of aid continues to be shifted to informal sources, ways of caring for the isolated unmarried will require increasing attention."

Those who study old age and those who make policies or design services for older people have constructed "staying home" as an existential as well as cost-effective solution to the problems of aging. This is because the lived environment is a setting that supports identity and provides a sense of belonging. For these marginal older men I have proposed that it is the inner-city itself, rather than an individual abode within it, that constitutes their primary source of attachment. For such men, the maintenance of identity in the face of aging-related changes—the enactment or representation of "independence and continued competence"(Rubinstein & Parmelee, 1992, p. 139)—takes a distinct and different form, unrelated to dominant cultural constructions of "home" as a private, family-oriented dwelling. If aged-care policies are to respond appropriately to the intense vulnerabilities of these men, ways will need to be found to permit the unconventionally housed to remain at home.

ACKNOWLEDGMENTS

The research on which this chapter is based was funded by the National Health & Medical Research Council of Australia.

NOTES

1. In about 30% of cases permission was not given and extensive notes were recorded instead. Interviews have also been conducted with 19 local service providers though these data are not included here.

2. The proportion may well be higher, given the unstructured nature of the interviews. Some men disclosed more information about their life histories

than others, through choice or, in some cases, because of memory or communication difficulties.

3. Participant names are pseudonyms.

REFERENCES

Archard, P. (1979). *Vagrancy, alcoholism and social control.* London: Macmillan.

Australian Council of Social Services. (2000). *Unemployment benefits now 21–33% below poverty line: New ACOSS analysis* [electronic bulletin board]. ACOSS Media Release. Available: http://www.acoss.org.au/media/2000/mr000113. htm [January 14, 2000].

Clapham, D., Means, R., & Munro, M. (1993). Housing, the life course and older people. In S. Arber & M. Evandrou (Eds.), *Ageing, independence and the life course* (pp. 132–148). London: Jessica Kingsley.

Connell, R. W., Schofield, T., Walker, L., Wood, J., Butland, D. L., Fisher, J., & Bowyer, J. (1998). *Men's health: A research agenda and background report.* Canberra, Australia: Department of Health and Aged Care.

Crane, M. (1999). *Understanding older homeless people: Their circumstances, problems and needs.* Buckingham, UK: Open University Press.

Daatland, S. O. (1997). Welfare policies for older people in transition? Emerging trends and comparative perspectives. *Scandinavian Journal of Social Welfare, 6,* 153–161.

Dalley, G. (1988). *Ideologies of caring: Rethinking community and collectivism.* Houndmills, Basingstoke, Hampshire: Macmillan Education.

Davidson, B., Kendig, H. L., Stephens, F., & Merrill, V. (1993). *'It's my place': Older people talk about their homes.* Canberra, Australia: AGPS.

Dupuis, A., & Thorns, D. C. (1996). Meanings of home for older home owners. *Housing Studies, 11,* 485–501.

Fine, M. (1999, March). *Ageing and the balance of responsibilities between the various providers of child and aged care: Shaping policies for the future.* Paper presented at the Productivity Commission and Melbourne Institute of Applied Ethics and Social Research, 1999 Policy Implications of the Ageing of Australia's Population Conference Proceedings, Melbourne, Australia.

Gubrium, J. F., & Holstein, J. A. (1998). Narrative practice and the coherence of personal stories. *Sociological Quarterly, 39*(1), 163–188.

Gubrium, J. F., & Sankar, A. (1990). *The home care experience: Ethnography and policy.* Newbury Park: Sage.

Gurney, C., & Means, R. (1993). The meaning of home in later life. In M. Evandrou & S. Arber (Eds.), *Ageing, independence, and the life course* (pp. 119–131). London: Jessica Kingsley in association with the British Society of Gerontology.

Hashimoto, A., & Kendig, H. (1992). Aging in international perspective. In H. Kendig, A. Hashimoto, & L. Coppard (Eds.), *Family support for the elderly: The international experience* (pp. 1–14). Oxford, UK: Oxford University Press.

Hollander, J. (1991). It all depends. *Social Research, 58*(1), 31–47.

Howell, S. C. (1983). The meaning of place in old age. In G. D. Rowles & R. J. Ohta (Eds.), *Aging and milieu: Environmental perspectives on growing old* (pp. 97–107). New York: Academic Press.

Jordan, A. (1994). *Going bad: Homeless men in an Australian city.* Melbourne, Australia: Council to Homeless Persons.

Keith, P. M. (1986). Isolation of the unmarried in later life. *Family Relations, 35*, 389–395.

Kendig, H. L., & McCallum, J. (1990). *Grey policy: Australian policies for an ageing society.* North Sydney: Allen & Unwin.

Kendig, H. L., & Neutze, M. (1999, March). *Housing implications of population ageing in Australia.* Paper presented at the Productivity Commission and Melbourne Institute of Applied Economic Research, Policy Implications of the Australian Population, Canberra.

Kendig, H. L., & Pynoos, J. (1996). Housing. In J. Birren (Ed.), *Encyclopedia of gerontology: Age, aging, and the aged* (pp. 703–713). San Diego: Academic Press.

Madigan, R., Munro, M., & Smith, S. J. (1990). Gender and the meaning of the home. *International Journal of Urban and Regional Research, 14*, 625–647.

O'Bryant, S. L., & Nocera, D. (1985). The psychological significance of "home" to older widows. *Psychology of Women Quarterly, 9*, 403–412.

Rapport, N., & Dawson, A. (1998). Home and movement: A polemic. In N. Rapport & A. Dawson (Eds.), *Migrants of identity: Perceptions of home in a world of movement* (pp. 19–38). Oxford, UK: Berg.

Rubinstein, R. L., & Parmelee, P. A. (1992). Attachment to place and the representation of the life course by the elderly. In I. Altman & S. M. Low (Eds.), *Place attachment* (pp. 139–163). New York: Plenum Press.

Russell, C. (1999). Meanings of home in the lives of older women (and men). In M. Poole & S. Feldman (Eds.), *A certain age: Women growing older* (pp. 36–55). St Leonards, Australia: Allen & Unwin.

Russell, C., Touchard, D., Kendig, H., & Quine, S. (2001). Foodways of disadvantaged men growing old in the inner city: Policy issues from ethnographic research. In S. Gauthier, D. N. Weisstub, & D. C. Thomasma (Eds.), *Aging: Culture, health, and social change* (Vol. 10 of the International Library of Ethics, Law, and the New Medicine, pp. 191–215). Dordrecht, The Netherlands: Kluwer Academic Publishers.

Rykwert, J. (1991). House and home. *Social Research, 58*(1), 51.

Snow, D. A., & Anderson, L. (1993). *Down on their luck: A study of homeless street people.* Berkeley, CA: University of California Press.

Sommers, J. (1998). Men at the margin: Masculinity and space in downtown Vancouver 1950–1986. *Urban Geography, 19*, 287–310.

CHAPTER 12

The Image of Nursing Homes and Its Impact on the Meaning of Home for Elders

Elaine Caouette

> Often, a building has a much louder and more honest voice than the men who may talk to us about it and its purpose.—W. Wolfensberger

A LIVING ENVIRONMENT FOR FRAIL ELDERS

The literature on specialized housing for elders in the 1970s was principally focused on supportive housing and on universal design. By the end of the 1980s, the trend was directed toward increasing the efficiency of the care delivered. Emphasis has now changed to the quality of the living environment. This concept is seen as the match between the personal needs of the individual and the capacity of the environment to respond. As a result, the literature in gerontology no longer approaches specialized housing for elders solely in terms of accessibility or functionality, but rather in terms of quality of life. In a study of the psychological well-being of elders, Rousseau and Dubé (1991) summarized the concept of the quality of life. From an objective perspective, it is a multidimensional concept based on measurable elements that are compared to the average population in terms of income, health status, and housing cost. From a subjective point of view, quality of life refers to personal criteria of satisfaction and the way the person perceives his or her own condition. Consequently, quality of life can be evaluated in terms of the concepts of well-being and the satisfaction of elders in relation to their life experiences, self-esteem, identity, and physical/psychosocial well-being.

Studies that approach quality of the living environment in specialized housing rarely mention physical elements of the buildings. They focus on the functionality of the built setting or the quality of life of the residents, but rarely discuss the relationship between both. Howell (1982) noted researchers' ignorance of building traits and the absence of physical variables as omissions in those studies. For example, she stressed that studies on intimacy include variables such as density and the types of regulation, but rarely include notions of spatial dimensions, proximity, storage, or furnishings.

It has become clear that it is essential to investigate nursing homes as living environments when we learn in a study conducted at the University of Montreal that 80% of the residents surveyed do not leave the interior of the establishment, 59% do not leave the floor where their room is situated, and 37% are unable to leave their rooms due to physical restraints (Tilquin & Saucier, 1990). These statistics make it imperative that we investigate the experience of "home" in these institutional settings.

This chapter is based on a study that explored the meaning of "home" for relocated elders with respect to the social and physical images of specialized housing facilities (Caouette, 1995). We first identify changes in the meaning and the experience of home for elders relocated into a private retirement home (rented living units with social activity programs, communal dining room, and other services provided by the administration). With regard to social meanings, we next describe respondents' perception of nursing homes from the perspective of becoming potential future residents. Finally, we investigate preferences regarding the image of nursing homes (public facilities with continuous care provided within the building) and more specifically, which architectural features could facilitate the development of a positive experience of home within those institutional settings.

THEORETICAL APPROACH

Based on a theoretical framework adapted from Després (1991), the principal components of our study are divided into three interrelated themes: *the users, the built environment,* and *society* (see Figure 12.1).

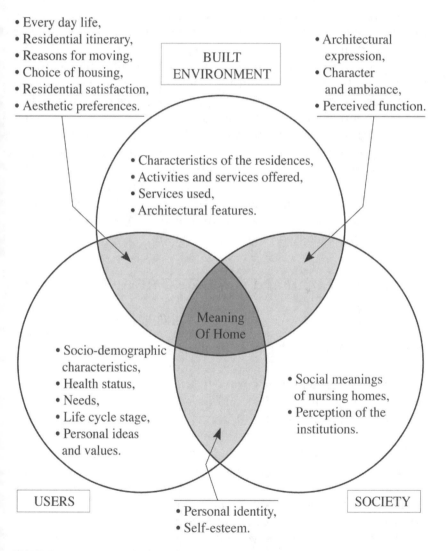

- Every day life,
- Residential itinerary,
- Reasons for moving,
- Choice of housing,
- Residential satisfaction,
- Aesthetic preferences.

BUILT ENVIRONMENT

- Architectural expression,
- Character and ambiance,
- Perceived function.

- Characteristics of the residences,
- Activities and services offered,
- Services used,
- Architectural features.

Meaning Of Home

- Socio-demographic characteristics,
- Health status,
- Needs,
- Life cycle stage,
- Personal ideas and values.

- Social meanings of nursing homes,
- Perception of the institutions.

USERS

- Personal identity,
- Self-esteem.

SOCIETY

FIGURE 12.1   Theoretical approach on the meaning of home for the elderly.

Users are elders relocated to private retirement homes. The *built environment* corresponds to the architectural attributes defining the image of the environment. Finally, *society* concerns the social meaning of these environments as institutions. We are interested in behaviors related to the meaning and the experience of the concept of "home" as influenced by each of these components.

The research format was established from the principal factors revealed in the literature that could influence the meaning of "home" for relocated elders: the personal characteristics of the resident (physiological limitations, self-esteem, residential biography), the built environment that surrounds him or her (architectural features, architectural expression), and the social meaning of this environment (associated image of the establishment, type of housing). Figure 12.1 represents the different factors influencing the meaning of home in a specialized housing facility for the elderly with the interrelated affects of each these factors identified by the intersection of the circles. It should be noted that the relationship to the home experienced by elderly users is well-documented in the literature, but the role of the physical structure and the impacts of its perceived image on that relationship are less well known. These issues will be discussed later in this chapter.

NORMALIZED MEANINGS OF HOME AND OLD AGE

According to a review of literature by Després (1991), "home" in North America refers to a dwelling's physical setting, its stylistic expression, its material structure, its spatial organization, and its neighborhood. "Home" allows one to control his or her environment and assures a sense of security. It offers freedom of action and expresses its resident's ideas and personal values. The experience of home establishes a state of permanence and continuity, which provides a sense of belonging. Home permits us to develop and secure our relationships with family and friends. Home is the center of daily activities; a refuge, a restful and calm sanctuary where one retires far from the daily pressures of the outside world. Home is an indicator of social status. Finally, owning one's own dwelling strengthens a sense of positive relationship to the home.

For our study, various works concerning how elders experience home were consulted. This chapter will not elaborate on these studies, although one is particularly noteworthy. That study, by Tassé (1992), concerns filial relations and the representation of "home." During her research at the Sacré-Coeur Hospital of Montreal, 25 life stories were collected from elders in order to identify what their "last" home meant and determine whether a sense of continuity or rupture modified their appropriation of space. The results suggested that the experience of "home" after relocation is strongly linked to the relationship an individual maintains with other generations of his or her family. The study indicated that the social disengagement expressed by a number of elders after relocation is reflected in the type of relationship to home they have developed with their current dwelling as well as a relationship to home that they have transferred to their descendants.

Three concepts of family bonds were used to describe the rupture or the continuity of this relationship. The "*symbolic transmission of the dwelling*" succeeded when respondents expressed a sense of strong continuity with their new home and the reciprocity of the exchanges between generations seemed to be still very important for them. They continued to have good relations with their children and grandchildren. They were as proud of their children's house as they were of their own former house. For others, "*the abandoned home*" expressed an important rupture of relationships between generations and respondents showed no further interest in emotionally investing themselves in their new "home" after relocation. Finally, the concept of "*function creates place*" indicated a very weak sense of continuity in which the dwelling provided only a functional service. In the functional dwelling, the visits between generations became one-sided; the elders welcomed visitors but they did not desire to visit their children's homes.

SOCIAL MEANING OF LIVING IN AN INSTITUTION

According to Robinson (1985), an institutional environment is a public place that expresses itself with monumental architecture, high ceilings, grand spaces, and landscaping similar to parks. This environment, which usually supports a large number of users, is primarily designed to ensure security. People live in such places temporarily for rehabilitation or because they exhibit antisocial behavior.

In society, we normally work, entertain, and sleep in physically separated places; but institutions create a barrier, which prevents social exchange with the outside world and, ironically, abolishes interior barriers that usually individualize daily activities (Wolfensberger, 1986). Robinson (1994) demonstrated that institutional buildings are "controlled" by the staff; they have their offices near the entrance, whereas the residents live in the most distant rooms in term of accessibility. This spatial separation is an important difference when compared to a residential environment in which the dweller controls the building from the entrance to the most intimate room. These operational definitions of institutions deny the concept of living in a home.

Robinson and colleagues had previously worked on recognition of the architectural elements that evoke an institutional or a residential image. They had formulated a list of architectural features that affect the creation of a "normalized" residential environment (Robinson et al., 1984). The results clearly illustrated a polarity between institutional and residential characteristics. For example, in contrast with an institutional environment, a residential environment offers a diversity of rooms, orientations, types of furniture and windows according to the function of the space.

From these results, Robinson (1985) observed two types of meanings associated with institutional images. The first meaning is the symbolism of residential environments. For example, in an institutional setting, two distinct messages are transmitted to the users: the medical symbolism, "you are sick," and the detention symbolism, "you are supervised." Consequently, to live in an institution means to be sick, dependent, and under surveillance; whereas to live at home means to be healthy, independent, and able to make independent choices. The second type of meaning is the functional aspect of institutional housing. The persons who live there are no longer perceived as "self-sufficient." The building must fulfill the resident's needs. For example, the establishment distributes meals and other services in a communal dining room with commercial equipment, which is necessary because of the number of people who must be served.

According to Wolfensberger and Thomas (1988), a building is highly identified by the service it offers. When one hears the name of an establishment: jail, office building, factory, he or she has in mind a clear representation of the building. As a result, society transfers the building's image to its users. Consequently, it is very important that the building reflects the best image possible. Without falling into environmental determinism, Robinson (1985) concurs in stating that the difference noted between institutional and residential settings not only influences the community's attitude toward the resident but also influences the nursing staff as well as the administrators.

From the principle of "normalization," Wolfensberger (1986, Wolfensberger & Thomas, 1988) elaborated on a program that allows one to evaluate if "the social image" of a building communicates a positive message on values, social status, dignity, social roles, and competence to its residents. He developed a grid that analyzes the features of a building's potential to transmit a positive image. These features are: (1) the history of the building, (2) its aesthetics, (3) the appropriateness of its image to the age of its residents, (4) the similarity of the type of services offered compared to adjacent buildings, and (5) its architectural harmony with the neighborhood.

As a specific example, throughout the history of specialized housing in Quebec, Canada, we can see that the social meaning of a type of establishment is developed over a period of centuries. The first form of public housing in Quebec was created during the era of the French colony by religious communities that welcomed the poor, the sick, and the disabled. These communities founded *Hospices* to attend to the physical well-being, spiritual support, and salvation of the souls of those in need. One witnesses at this time the emergence of a pattern of institutionalization of the "undesirable." Consequently, the use of these "nonfamily" shelters was seen as a sign of disgrace. It was during the era of industrialization that the notion of retirement from an active life first appeared in North America. Lodging houses for indigents also became shelters for disabled, poor, or isolated elders, thus reinforcing the concept of elders as being unproductive. During the years following World War II, medical progress resulted in an increase in life expectancy leading to the considerable expansion of long-term care facilities (Forbes, Jackson, & Kraus, 1987; Zay, 1984).

To eliminate the negative reputation associated with the Hospices, the province of Quebec, at the end of the 1960s, built public nursing homes for elders designated as *Pavilions*. These were conceived as a place of retirement, similar to hotels, and were designed for people with loss of autonomy (Bolduc, Bélanger, & Déry, 1990). In the 1970s, the high costs of these projects led the government to develop public programs of residential care and to create day-care centers for those who were able to remain in their dwellings (Zay, 1984). The nonautonomous elders remained in the long-term care facilities.

Lodging resources available for the elderly were again being modified at the end of the 20th century because of the general aging of the population. The aging of the population presented successive governments with increasing expenditures. As the health system in Quebec is almost exclusively public, the pressure was to develop standardized buildings. In 1992, public nursing homes and long-term care centers were united to create a unique type of public establishments, reinforcing their institutional status. The resulting institutions now provide an environment that is currently closer to a hospital context as the trend is to accept only nonautonomous clientele.

RESEARCH METHODOLOGY

Using structured questionnaires, 25 personal interviews were conducted with independent residents in five private retirement homes. The focus was on private establishments reserved for elders needing services but not continuous care. These residences were selected based on the following criteria: services offered, location in the city, and number of housing units available. Private retirement homes were selected because the respondents had not yet experienced the life and, perhaps, the frustrations of living in a nursing home but had experienced relocation to a specialized housing facility. They were already sensitive to their new social and physical limitations. The interview always took place at the residence of the respondent and, the majority of the time, in the lodging unit itself. Only the respondent was present at the interview, which lasted approximately 90 minutes.

The first part of the interview focused on: (1) reasons for leaving their former dwelling, (2) the locations where they normally had social interactions, (3) the locations where they welcomed their visitors, (4) their involvement in community activities, (5) their current level of residential satisfaction, and (6) the meaning of their previous homes. A section of the questionnaire devoted to daily and weekly activities was directed at verifying the meaning of home as the center of daily activities. Questions were added on what the respondents would consider an ideal home for elders, the changes they would bring to their present retirement home and, finally the perception they had of nursing homes as a potential resident. Later, open-ended questions were used to gauge the respondents' reaction on 11 meanings associated with "home" in relation to their current dwelling, a retirement home, and their former family dwellings (Després, 1991).

During the final part of the interview, each respondent was asked to compare groups of photographs illustrating either the outside or the inside of so-called residential buildings. All of them were identified as alternatives to the traditional image of nursing homes. These illustrations had been selected according to the image projected by the building on a residential/institutional continuum. The interview was completed with questions on the socioeconomic characteristics of the respondent.

In order to validate the questionnaire, two series of preliminary tests were conducted with elders. The questions on the residential itinerary and the meaning of home had to be simplified. For the building photographs, during the preliminary test we assessed if a task of free classification or assessment by level of preference was more valuable than a task of comparison. Some persons become irritated when asked to revisit the same illustration more than one time. Consequently, the task of classification was abandoned in favor of the comparison of pairs. The method did not involve classifying the photographs but rather entailed identifying the most preferred buildings and encouraging commentaries by the participants.

TASKS OF COMPARISON

Twenty-five photographs of Quebec nursing homes were selected representing diverse characteristics such as size, number of stories, outside cladding, and type of windows. A preliminary investigation was undertaken with three persons having schooling in architecture and three other professionals. The principal objectives were to determine which buildings were the most representative of their function and to eliminate bias created by such items as adaptive vehicles or curtains. Although we had not imposed any *a priori* criteria, the six participants principally classified the 25 buildings by using elements related to their function.

Nine of the 25 illustrations of actual nursing homes were retained. In order to ensure representation of the opposite poles of institutional and residential image, nine other buildings were added including student lodging and private retirement homes. With the architectural consultants, the exterior photographs were divided into three series of six photographs according to their place on a residential–institutional continuum. Figure 12.2 presents the retained photographs according to their size and position on a residential-to-institutional continuum.

During the task of comparison, the respondents had to choose the building they preferred in each of the nine pairs. Next, they had to choose their preferred buildings among the three selected photos in each of the series. Finally, we asked them to select their favorite building from among those retained from the three series. The participants' comments justifying their choices were noted at each stage and constituted the principal database for the qualitative analysis.

The comments were classified according to the model of Harris (1975) and to the three elements of our theoretical framework. Finally, we regrouped the comments into more global categories. In order of decreasing importance, these categories were as follows: (1) the architectural features that compose a building, (2) the site of the building and the landscaping, (3) the social significance of the establishment, (4) the perceived and experienced qualities of the building, and (5) personal characteristics.

In order to select the body of interior photographs, we proceeded in essentially the same manner as with the exteriors. We first selected 100 photographs taken from publications or on-site. Then, we asked the panel of six persons to select the most representative photographs of institutional and residential environments. For example, the presence of handrails in a corridor or bench seats in a dining room contributed to the definition of an institutional character (Robinson et al.,1984). Finally, we chose two to three pairs of photos using room types as a category. The interior spaces were

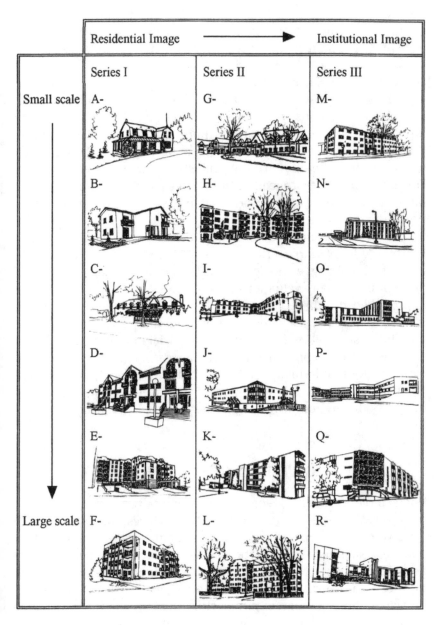

FIGURE 12.2   Images of principal facades.

selected from a sample that represented the living areas. It was essential that the rooms had been used daily by the residents and were along the path of access normally used by a visitor. This encompassed the entry halls; reception desks; corridors; and communal spaces such as living rooms, day rooms, and dining rooms (cafeteria) as well as nurses' stations on the floors, bedrooms and bathrooms.

The photographs of interiors were presented to the respondents in the same manner as the exterior photographs with the exception that there was no comparison among subgroups. This was a result of the fact that the photos did not illustrate the same type of room. For each room, we proceeded to present pairs of photos in which one tended to represent a residential image and the other an institutional image.

Analysis of comments related to the interiors was also inspired by the model of Harris (1975). This model proposes five levels to evaluate a building: ecological, social, operational, experiential, and perceptual. In their evaluation of the interiors, the respondents often approached the three last levels. The operational level related to the efficiency of human occupation and the performance of the building (use of place, factors affecting social interaction, etc.). The experiential level concerned the satisfaction, significance, and lived experience of undertaking activities (ambiance, functionality, etc.). Finally, the perceptual level involved the senses and perception of the built environment (its aesthetic aspects, the character of place, etc.).

PROFILE OF RESPONDENTS

The sample included 19 women and 6 men. All participants, except one, were 70 years of age or older. Of the 25 respondents, 20 were widowed, 3 had separated and 2 lived at the residence with their spouses. Nineteen of the participants evaluated their health status as good or satisfactory. None of the respondents described his or her health as poor. Two persons stated that their health was excellent given their age. Sixteen respondents had lived in their residence for between 2 and 5 years. Only two participants had moved into their current retirement home during the last 6 months.

The sample revealed three types of residential progressions. Of the 20 persons who had been home owners, 8 lived in nonspecialized lodging before moving into their current residence, 4 came from a family residence, and 8 had inhabited intermediate lodging for elders similar to their current specialized residence. Of the five persons who had been renters, two had lived previously in nonspecialized lodging. The other three followed various paths involving primarily specialized lodging.

DESCRIPTION OF THE RESIDENCES

Our sample comprised residences ranging from 16 to 130 units. Services offered were representative of the Quebec market and rental costs were slightly under the provincial average. Figure 12.3 provides a general overview of the residences in the study. In addition to the images of the represented buildings, their principal characteristics, and the number of participants by residence are indicated.

FINDINGS

The principal reasons that the respondents had relocated into a retirement home concerned their daily life in the former dwelling. Domestic activities had become more difficult because of loss of autonomy. The majority of female respondents had left their family dwelling on the death of their spouses, whereas the men vacated because of illness. In the process of choosing their current residence, the respondents attempted to satisfy needs for care, assistance, and, especially, security. They evaluated the services offered, the location of the building, and the independence given to them by the administration.

THE EXPERIENCE OF HOME

Because it requires motivation and demands more time to adapt, the elders were often disinterested in personalizing their new home. They showed a lack of flexibility toward new situations encountered, revealing a rupture between their former residence and their current

I Photo not available	2 to 3 stories 16 units relative cost ($) Sample : 2 respondents	Renovated single family housing Older mixed-use neighborhood, primarily residential.	Bedrooms only, some with sink, communal toilets. Services included : H, M, S, T
II	3 1/2 stories 106 units relative cost ($$) Sample : 7 respondents	New building New residential neighborhood close to a shopping center.	Bedrooms with sinks, some with shared or communal toilets Services included : E, H, M, S, T
III	3 to 4 stories 130 units relative cost ($$) Sample : 5 respondents	Renovated commercial building Center-city	Bedrooms with sinks and private toilets Services included : E, H, M, S
IV 	2 stories 72 units relative cost ($$$) Sample : 6 respondents	New building New residential neighborhood at the exterior limits of the city.	Bedrooms with sinks and private toilets. Services included : E, H, M, S
V	8 stories 65 units relative cost ($$$) Sample : 5 respondents	Renovated old hotel. Center-city	1 to 3 rooms with kitchen and private toilet Services included : E, H, M, S

E	elevator	S	social	Center-city :	Older mixed-use
H	healthcare		activities		neighborhood,
M	meals	T	transportation		primarily commercial.

FIGURE 12.3   Characteristics of the residences in the study.

retirement home. Consistent with the literature, our participants' comments illustrated the temporal process of establishing a relationship with "home." Achieving a sense of permanence, attachment to place and continuity necessitated a period of time that appeared to vary according to health status.

Although the respondents stated that they felt free to act as they pleased in their dwellings, regulations and the presence of the other residents limited their expression of the home as a place offering liberty of action and control. One respondent noted that: "At home, I used to dress as I pleased. Here, I dress better to go out of my room." Others mentioned that it was normal not to feel as free because they now lived "in a community." However, others felt freer now compared to when they had maintained family and work obligations. Further limitations on the experience of "home" were the lack of private rooms, of intimate places, and of usable space within the dwelling. During the relocation, the residents did not enjoy disposing of their possessions; some residents disposed of these items as part of a process of disengagement: "What is the good in keeping my things? I will never return to my home."

It is important to note that the respondents indicated a feeling of isolation associated with changes in the family and social bonds. Their friends had aged and lived too far away to visit. Some of the respondents' children were older than 65, had lost their autonomy, and were unable to visit. It appears that declining health status and the loss of autonomy are still the factors that most modify the relationship to "home" in a retirement facility. Other factors that influenced the quality of the relationship were the participants' residential itinerary (type of dwellings in which they had previously lived—single house, multiplex, etc.), mobility (the frequency with which they had moved), ownership status in the former dwellings (owner or tenant), and changes in family structure such as the loss of a spouse.

Interestingly, it was possible to associate some comments of interviewed residents to the theme of transfer of the dwelling to descendants as identified in the study by Tassé (1992). Indeed, our results suggest that a sense of the "home" as a refuge and a place to create emotional bonds had often been transferred to the children's dwelling. It appeared that the parents' new dwelling was not "emotionally" invested with the same memories and experiences as the family home. The children preferred to bring their parents to their home, where they had created special relationships with their own descendants. The respondents also complained about the impossibility of offering a meal to their family or a resting place to their visitors as they had done in the family residence. Instead of eating in the communal dining room, their children invited them out to a restaurant. The type of relationship developed with descendants was an important dimension of modification of the experience of "home" for the respondents after relocation.

In relation to the sequence of residential occupancies related by the respondents, 11 had already known at least one type of specialized residence before their current retirement home. In comparing their present meaning of "home" to that which had existed in their former dwellings, it appears that this had not changed specifically during their relocation into a retirement facility, but rather at the moment when the elders *"broke from the home."* This expression was frequently used by the respondents; it represented the moment when they moved from the family dwelling, an event mainly associated with the sale of the family house. In French, *"casser maison"* (to break the home) is a strongly representative image expressing the feeling of rupture that occurs in the relationship with the home. Our interviews suggest that, at the moment of the rupture, there is a change in the meaning of home as an indicator of identity and in the social status of the elder. It is not the change in social status that is essentially problematic in the move to a retirement facility but rather a loss of personal identity linked to a transition that occurs as part of the cycle of life. In fact, the move not only confirms a gradual loss of autonomy associated with aging but also results in a modification of identity that undermines the will to invest "emotionally" in the new dwelling.

After relocation, the feeling of belonging somewhere was more strongly related to the residence than to the surrounding neighborhood. Day-to-day activities within the building and a decrease in the use of exterior services reflected a more restricted daily universe. The participants' bedrooms or apartments became the principal places for emotional investment. These places were where they welcomed their visitors, where they retired to be alone—places they could control and personalize.

In summary, the most significant themes in the meaning of home for our respondents were: *permanence and continuity, control of social interactions and the environment, liberty of action,* and *security.* The principal differences between the normalized meanings and those lived by the aged people concerned the home as the *center of daily activities,* as a place encouraging *emotional relationships* as well as a *reflection of identity and personal values.*

PERCEPTIONS OF NURSING HOMES

Although they did not plan to move from their current retirement home, the participants realized that irreversible progress in the residential itinerary of elders might lead to loss of autonomy and consequently the necessity to move into a nursing home. The existence of this practically irreversible progression led us to address the second theme in our research, the respondents' perception of nursing homes. We discovered a conception of the nursing home that was close to the operational definition of institutions as revealed in the literature.

Interviewed residents associated the nursing home with the medical world referring to it as a "place to die" and as a detention type of setting from whence "the severely ill cannot leave." Commenting on his current residence with regard to the function of exterior barriers, one respondent noted that in order to benefit from some services "you have to go out" and "you have the right to leave." An image of de-individualization was associated with nursing homes. Negative images were associated with a large number of residents, a lack of privacy, and an institutional ambiance. As Robinson (1985) had noted, the monumental architecture of the institutional buildings was also an issue. One respondent described nursing homes as "a large building with several stories."

Finally, the respondents considered that, in a nursing home, all activities and all services necessary for everyday life are offered inside the building and under the authority of the nursing staff and administration. The retirement home resembled the nursing home because the services and the regulations were governed by an administration. The primary difference was that the staff members were more available to socialize and that the clientele was more autonomous in the retirement home.

THE IMAGE OF NURSING HOMES AND THEIR ARCHITECTURAL ATTRIBUTES

The final theme studied concerned the architectural features of nursing homes preferred by the respondents. First, we asked about concerns resulting from personal experiences in their current built environment. Following this, we asked respondents to identify preferable elements that should be considered in the future construction of nursing homes. Their comments related to the need of privacy; the importance of accessibility to places that assure physical autonomy; and the desirability of spacious rooms, especially the bedrooms. There was also a focus on the need to design a convivial dining room in preference to the existing commercial-style of dining facilities in which the kitchens are exposed. Also mentioned were the importance of building maintenance, security, natural lighting, and landscaping.

Through comparison of buildings presented as nursing homes, we identified the preferences of the respondents more precisely. Our results indicated that the respondents judged the architectural features of a building based on their personal experiences and their own specific daily activities. In evaluating the exterior, they emphasized the need for several windows and individual balconies. They preferred large galleries at the entrance and landscaping that encouraged walking. Although they liked brick buildings, warm colors, and pitched roofs, they also preferred accessible entrances. Stairs were immediately rejected. They appreciated low-density buildings and fewer floors. Finally, they expressed a preference for articulated physical volumes, ornamented façades, and simple shapes. Additionally, they expressed a desire for a simple building image with a layout, which was clear and easy to understand.

Often, the residents' judgment criteria for assessing the exteriors can be linked with personal characteristics and preferences. Comments indicated that windows are a source of entertainment—providing visual access to the outside world. The respondents stressed features of the front door because it represented contact with the community and the place through which all visitors must pass. Several observations referred to security issues. The building materials should be fire resistant and the size and configuration of the building should facilitate evacuation in case of fire. The building plan should facilitate orientation, because the nursing homes that had been visited by our respondents were described as "large disorienting buildings." Finally, a need for accessibility of the building was mainly associated with the degree to which those visited and assessed were perceived to have physical barriers.

Wolfensberger (1986; Wolfensberger & Thomas, 1988) encouraged architectural expression that emphasized the cultural significance of buildings. Respondents in our study effectively associated a function with an illustrated building through its general architectural expression. When the respondents indicated a dislike for luxurious congregate housing while preferring simpler buildings with an older style and a residential character, they were making a reference to the value of their traditional living environment. They rejected buildings with an institutional style reminding them of religious or corporate buildings. They disliked buildings with a public character. These findings can be interpreted in terms of the concept of home because they clearly refer to an *indicator of identity and social status, reflecting the ideals and personal values* of the buildings' occupants.

In their assessment of interiors, the respondents insisted on the presence of a reception desk in the hall, as well as the presence of chairs in a waiting area. The nurses' station on the rooms' floor was similarly perceived as providing for functions of security and entertainment. On the other hand, the nurses' station seemed to be the place most often associated with an institutional environment. For public rooms such as the dining room, day room and living room, the respondents were looking for comfortable seats arranged in small groups. They preferred brightly colored rooms with large windows and additional artificial lighting in order to help compensate for their reduced sight. Public rooms had to be welcoming, simple, and family-like. Corridors were the places to exercise and socialize, particularly during the winter season. They should be well lit, allow for the personalization of the resident's entry door, and facilitate orientation to the rest of the facility. The respondents also requested functional features, such as handrails and chairs for resting. They preferred single bedrooms with furniture, windows, and decorative elements with a residential character. The whole ambiance should give a spacious, comfortable, and welcoming atmosphere. Finally, essential features of the bathroom requested were storage, accessible sanitary equipment, and a counter.

In general, the respondents judged the building differently depending on whether they were evaluating the exterior or the interior. On the one hand, they attempted to respond to the question of the character of the environment by emphasizing residential exteriors. On the other hand, they wanted to satisfy their functional needs and looked for interior amenities consistent with their personal concerns for accessibility. The respondents preferred density and a size sufficient to offer the necessary services to satisfy their needs. Although they would relocate for the services, they did not want a building that was representative of traditional long-term care facilities. Rather, there was a preference for a pavilion-like architecture, pitched roofs, usable outside places (galleries, balconies, and landscaped areas) and an orientation toward safety. Findings regarding the comparison of exteriors are summarized in Figure 12.4. In sum, the findings encouraged the conceptualization of an attractive building, with a variety of furniture adapted to loss of autonomy while emphasizing simplicity and intimacy—a family atmosphere similar to that usually found in a "home."

CONCLUSIONS

Although we have looked for continuity between residential and institutional environments, the illustrations available in design guides and planning trade magazines transmit an image of comfort indicating what we may call "the bourgeois way." In contrast, the respondents in this study preferred amenities associated with a Quebec cultural context—a country house where the family reunion and informal discussions were held in the kitchen. Conscious of the realities of the community aspects of specialized housing facilities, the respondents did not search for a truly typical family setting. They were instead searching for the "image" of their former living environment.

During the course of the interviews, we learned that the personal characteristic of *users* most affecting their relationship with home was their attitude relative to health status and degree of autonomy. We sensed a process of disengagement with their previous home the moment they experienced a loss of autonomy—a moment often

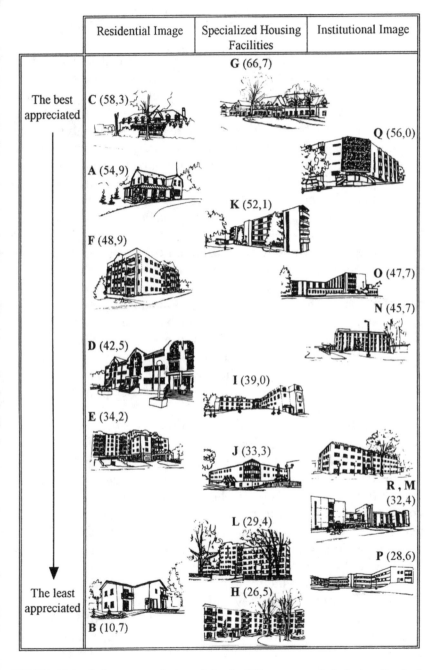

FIGURE 12.4   Relative popularity of the buildings presented during the task of comparison.

associated with departure from the family residence. The expression *casser maison* was very representative of the sense of rupture that the respondents felt.

Concerning the *built environment*, the physical limits of residents' identification of home were essentially restricted to the bedroom. They were more limited with respect to the residence and the neighborhood. On the one hand, a positive relationship between the users and the built environment reflected the home viewed as a place offering security. Indeed, security was a constant preoccupation in all parts of the interviews. On the other hand, negative aspects of the relationship included the difficulty in developing a sense of belonging in a specialized residence where the administration established rules and regulations. This became a limiting factor in acting freely or modifying one's place. The home as a refuge where we retire, or a place we control was limited to the bedroom. For the less autonomous residents, the center of daily activities was limited to the residence. The residents were also constrained by limited available space. They had to leave behind many of their meaningful possessions and were prevented from having a defined space in which to receive family members or visitors. Finally, the home that permits one to develop and secure relationships with family and friends was very different in the environment of a nursing home. The home was experienced in the context of social bonds and not of familial bonds.

We arrive then at the relationship between the *users* and the *social meanings* of nursing homes. The perception the residents had of nursing homes was representative of the operational definitions surveyed in the literature. We sensed a strong resistance to perceiving a nursing home as a potential home. Relocation into an institution could be seen as a second rupture because one must have a major loss of autonomy in order to be admitted. Several questions remain to be answered. What are the consequences of relocation into an institution where medical care is omnipresent? Can the nursing home become a place that residents control, within which they can achieve privacy and within which they can create bonds?

As noted previously, the operational definition of institutions leads to the position that residents are no longer functionally self-sufficient. They must be served because they can no longer function normally in everyday life. This social perspective helps us understand the preference of respondents for specialized housing facilities with a hotel-like character. Several respondents expressed their willingness to come and "rest" in a retirement home and be served as in a hotel. The hotel signifies a well-deserved rest, a reward, just as the institution signifies the disengagement of families or the incompetence of the residents; a disgrace in the face of society. It is interesting to note that the most preferred building type, representative of an ideal nursing home in this study, was in fact a real hotel. The hospitality design image seemed to be a successful adaptation for the respondents.

It is important to understand the origin of the respondents' perception of nursing homes. This generation had visited their grandparents in the former *Hospices*, their parents in the *Pavilions* of the 1960s, and their friends in more contemporary nursing homes. It will be worthwhile to explore the relationship with "home" that the future generations will develop in parallel with the evolution of architectural preferences, changes in residential mobility, and the emergence of new family structures.

We have previously discussed the indicators used by researchers to evaluate the living environment of relocated elders. Several of these indicators are intended to encourage a positive experience of the home. Perhaps one could judge the quality of life or the quality of the living environment by evaluating the quality of the relationship developed with the place as "home." By sensitizing designers, legislators, medical staff, and administrators to notions of home, one might encourage recognition of nursing homes as real-life living environments. We must understand that architectural design can effectively create a positive image of one's environment and facilitate successful integration of the concept of home into the daily lives of residents of retirement residences and nursing facilities. A physical environment that is socially valued would provide an image of security through the use of its materials, its height, and its accessibility. It would transmit a positive image to its residents through its simplicity, its density, its spatial articulation, and its residential-like architectural elements. Finally, and most essentially, it would value the identity and the social status of each future resident because, often, the building has a *much louder and more honest voice* than its users.

ACKNOWLEDGMENT

This study was made possible through a scholarship from the Canada Mortgage and Housing Corporation (CMHC) and from the AFDU-Quebec Foundation.

REFERENCES

Bolduc, M., Bélanger, L., & Déry, A. (1990). *Les services socio-sanitaires aux personnes âgées en perte d'autonomie: la nécessité d'un virage. Social-health services for older people losing their autonomy: the need for change.* Québec, Canada: Ministère de la santé et des services sociaux du Québec.

Caouette, E., (1995). *La relation au chez-soi des personnes âgées en résidences spécialisées et leur perception de l'image des centres d'accueil. Older persons' relation to their home in specialized residences and their perception of the image of community centers.* Mémoire de maîtrise, Faculté d'architecture et d'aménagement: Université Laval.

Després, C. (1991). The meaning of home: Literature review and directions for future research and theoretical development. *Journal of Architectural and Planning Research, 8*(2), 96–115.

Forbes, W. F., Jackson, J. A., & Kraus, A. S. (1987). *Institutionalization of the elderly in Canada.* Toronto: Butterworths.

Harris, R. S. (1975). *A model for designers.* School of Architecture and Allied Arts: University of Oregon, Eugene, Oergon.

Howell, S. C. (1982). Built space, the mystery variable in health and aging. In A. Baum & J. E. Singer (Eds.), *Advances in environmental psychology: Environment and health* (pp. 31–48). Hillsdale, NY: IEA.

Robinson, J. W. (1985). Architectural settings and the housing of older developmentally disabled persons. In M. P. Jaricki & H. M. Wisniewski (Eds.), *Aging and developmental disabilities: Issues and approaches* (pp. 391–400). Baltimore, MD: Brookes.

Robinson, J. W. (1994). The question of type. In K. A. Franck & L. H. Schneekloth (Eds.), *Ordering space: Types in architecture and design* (pp. 179–192). New York: Van Nostrand Reinhold.

Robinson, J. W., Thompson, T., Emmons, P., Graff, M., & Franklin, E. (1984). *Towards an architectural definition of normalization: Design principles for housing severely and profoundly retarded adults.* University of Minnesota: Center for Urban and Regional Affairs, Minneapolis-St. Paul, Minnesota.

Rousseau, J., & Dubé, M. (1991). *Étude du réseau de support social, du système de croyances et du milieu de vie comme déterminants du bien-être psychologique chez les personnes âgées. Study of the social support network, of belief systems and of living environment as factors of the psychological well-being of older people.* Université du Québec à Trois-Rivières: Conseil québécois de recherche sociale.

Tassé, L. (1992). *Transmettre son espace de vie: Filiation et représentations du logement chez les personnes âgées. Transforming living space: Link and representations of lodging of older people.* Communications de la 5e Conférence internationale de recherche sur l'habitat, Montréal.

Tilquin, C., & Saucier, A. (1990). *Synthèse de: L'alourdissement des clientèles placées dans les programmes offrant des services de longue durée. Équipe de recherche opérationnelle. Synthesis of: The heaviness of clients placed in programs offering long-duration services. Team of operational research.* Université de Montréal, Ministère de la Santé et des Services sociaux.

Wolfensberger, W. (1986). *The principle of normalization in human services.* National Institute on Mental Retardation, Washington, D.C.

Wolfensberger, W., & Thomas, S. (1988). *PASSING: Programme d'analyse des systèmes de services. Application des buts de la valorisation des rôles sociaux.* Les communications Opeil inc.

Zay, N. (1984). Analyse critique des politiques et des institutions québécoises concernant les personnes âgées. *Sociologie et sociétés, 16*(2), 105–118. *Sociology an societies.*

PART V

Community Perspective on the Meaning of Home

CHAPTER 13

On Community As Home: Places That Endure in Rural Kansas

Carolyn Norris-Baker and Rick J. Scheidt

> For a place to exist—there must be a stability to its
> social institutions and a historical record in its physi-
> cal environment . . . those places are inhabited by peo-
> ple who know where they are and who they are; they
> have the hold that any personal relationship has—the
> chance for meaning.—P. Stegner

Three interrelated constructs—place attachment, place
identity, and place dependence— contribute to the sense of place
in the communities Stegner describes. Place identity is one aspect of
cognitive self-identification in relation to the environment, whereas
attachment involves individuals' emotional or affective linkages with
the environment, and place dependence describes the perceived
strength of connection with specific places and their behaviors (Giuliani & Feldman, 1993; Jorgensen & Stedman, 2001; Stokols & Shumaker, 1981). Although there is ongoing debate about the ways in
which these constructs are defined and measured, as well as the
interrelationships that exist among them, we will adopt some of the

constructs as put forth in Altman and Low's edited volume: *Place Attachment* (Altman & Low, 1992; Giuliani & Feldman, 1993). We will consider place attachments to be complex concepts that involve inseparable blends of affect, cognition, and practices, physical settings, people, and temporal qualities, which provide a basis for communal as well as individual aspects of identity (Brown & Perkins, 1992; Low & Altman, 1992). As we discuss the small rural communities we have studied, we will consider the ways in which such concepts can be applied in this context, and describe some of the diverse processes and consequences of responding to change: sustaining community, protecting community identity, reframing community, accepting a dying community, and letting go of community.

COMMUNITY CONCEPTS OF ATTACHMENT AND IDENTITY

We believe that place meaning and identity shape and are shaped over time not only by our individual selves, but also by our communal selves and cultures. Each person's dwelling rests within a larger context that contributes to the experience and meaning of home— the neighborhood, the community, and the regional culture (Hummon, 1995; Rowles, 1981, 1987; Rowles & Ravdal, 2002; Scheidt & Norris-Baker, 1999). As McHugh and Mings (1996, p. 530) state, "The concept of 'home' is geographically elastic." Furthermore, the dynamic processes of forming and transforming place attachments occur within the framework of life-span development that includes not only current bonds with place, but past bonds and interactions of the two as well (Rubinstein & Parmalee, 1992).

Long-standing attachments to dwellings many extend to the broader community context and its settings (Boschetti, 1990; Fried, 2000; Golant & LaGreca, 1994; Norris-Baker & Scheidt, 1994; Rowles, 1981; Rowles & Ravdal, 2002). For many older individuals, it may be hard to disentangle interwoven memories of home and of neighborhood (Toyoma, 1988). As Kevin Lynch wrote many years ago, "We take delight in physically distinctive, recognizable locales and attach our feelings and meanings to them. They make us feel at home, grounded" (1976, p. 23). In a cultural sense, people's shared emotional and affective meanings for a place can provide the basis for both individual and group understanding of and relation to an environment (Low, 1992, cited in Giuliani & Feldman, 1993). Community provides a social-symbolic basis of this broader identity, in which one belongs "not only to a place, but in its institutions and with its people" (Fitchen, 1991, p. 253). However, as Hummon (1992) points out, it is important to recognize that strong emotional attachment to community may take different forms, depending on individual variations in sense of place, and that although shared bonds to neighborhood, community, region, type of environment [urban, rural], or even nation are important for many people, it is not a universal phenomenon (Feldman, 1996; Hummon, 1995). Emotional attachments and meanings attributed to communities may vary greatly and change over time.

The complexity of a construct that incorporates multiple aspects of people–place bonds involving individuals, groups, cultures, and social relationships with places varying in scale and extended across time mandates an ecological, transactional viewpoint. Transactional frameworks "emphasize the reciprocal or bi-directional nature of people–environment relations—individuals not only take steps to respond to their environmental conditions but also take steps to influence and restructure their surroundings" (Stokols, 1995, p. 825). Phenomena are studied as "holistic unities composed simultaneously of people, psychological processes, the physical environment, and temporal qualities" (Werner, Brown, & Altman, 2002, p. 203). Thus, a transactional view mandates the understanding of temporal aspects as integral to attachment and the exploration of processes involved in adapting to transitions in place and place attachment over the life cycle of both people and communities.

Here, Gustafson's (2000) triangular framework for meanings of place may also be useful. This conceptualization locates place meanings within anchor points of self (personal meanings developed over an individual's life course), others (relations with and perceptions of), and environments (physical, symbolic, or historical). These interconnected points form a conceptual map within which self–others (social relationships and sense of community), others–environment (atmosphere or character of a place), environment–self (knowledge of the environment and opportunities to shape it), and self–others–environment themes can be located. At the heart of the triangle, where the tri-part themes lie, are community-level meanings such as citizenship, anonymity, and traditions or festivals.

CHANGING COMMUNITIES

We know that the affects of transitions in place, whether of long or short periodicity, can vary greatly. The experience of transition in communities (whether by relocation choices or changes within the community itself) can involve social relationships, shifts in roles and status, and even the community's acceptance of new residents (Cuba & Hummon, 1993; Hummon, 1992, 1995). Cuba's (1989, 1992, 1995) research in Cape Cod communities has provided us with insights about processes of disengagement and resettlement that involve reinterpreting past place identities and changes in the roles one fills in community settings. Some changes can be anticipated in ways that result in minimal disruptions of place attachment, whereas other events such as natural disasters may cause disruptions so great that people must strive to find threads of continuity and stability in their lives (Brown & Perkins, 1992). Coping with loss of attachments and developing new ones may be mediated in some ways by opportunities for planning and control of the relocation and for retaining some form of bond with past places. The affects of community change, whether rapid or gradual, can transform the bonds between people and places, with consequences for the well-being of the community and of its residents.

Understanding the roles of changing community and regional meanings and identity in the lives of older adults is essential for multiple reasons. First, "striking changes in the nature of community attachments develop over the adult life course as functions of individual and community processes" (Fried, 2000, p. 194). The length of the life course (and thus potentially the longer length of residence in a community) may enhance the potential for strong bonds to form among place, self, and community identity. "Longtime residence can . . . create a sense of autobiographical affinity with the space beyond the home" (Rowles & Ravdal, 2002, p. 88) and cumulative layers of meaning within certain places may enhance their significance (Rowles, 1993). Second, differential impacts of individual life, community events, and experiences outside the community [as in McAuley's (1998) findings regarding racial segregation and discrimination] may influence bonding. Thus, among older adults, community meanings and identities and their importance should be expected to vary both between people and over time. Residents also may evaluate changes in communities in different ways depending on age or length of residency (Cuba, 1992; Fitchen, 1991; Rowles, 1990). Third, attachment to places may foster independence and competence among older adults (Rubinstein & Parmalee, 1992), potentially influencing the ability to continue to reside in a small community with limited services.

Fourth, attachment to places can be strengthened when long-term group affiliations and identity are based on race, ethnicity, socioeconomic class, or culture (Giuliani, 1991). This premise is supported by recent research on small Iowa towns, which identified higher levels of community attachment and involvement in community activities in more homogeneous (less ethnically diverse) towns (Rice & Steele, 2001). It is possible that social pressures toward uniformity within a small community may be one mechanism for reducing points of conflict in the belief that "united we stand but divided we fall." Community culture (or that of an identifiable subgroup within the community) can provide a milieu, including aspects of the physical and social environment, in which late-life developmental changes can be experienced safely and in a psychologically healthy way, supporting needs for community, security, and self-continuity through cultural components (Gutmann, 1992). On the other hand, deculturation may deprive older adults of this enfolding cultural environment, which buffers the stressors of developmental changes. The salience of these cultural factors should be greatest in locales where cultural homogeneity has existed for an extended period of time (McAuley, 1998). Finally, older adults often take the roles of culture-bearers, attempting to preserve and pass on to the next generations the community values and systems of idealized objects that are their culture.

CASE-STUDY APPROACH

The examples we will use as springboards for considering some conceptual issues in community attachment and identity are drawn from experiential field research we have conducted in a variety of small rural towns in Kansas, each of which has a large proportion of older adults. Although some of these communities struggle with economic decline, others are more economically stable but are culturally diverse. These case studies were based largely on observations gathered through open-ended interviews with key informants. Additional data were gathered through informal structured conversations with other residents, participant observation, identification of some of communities' behavior settings, and archival research. Our approach (Scheidt & Norris-Baker, 1990) incorporates the contextual view of environmental stress developed by Aldwin and Stokols (1988), with aspects of behavior setting theory (Barker, 1987), especially as extended by Wicker (1987, 2002). It is a community's behavior settings (or what Fried terms "role places"—regularized settings for activities and interactions) that "dominate a sense of community identity rather than the purely physical qualities of the places themselves" (Fried, 2000, p. 195). Thus, we believe our approach offers a way to describe community sentiment and identity within the context of a pattern of dynamic, interrelated changes in individuals and the places where they live.

Another concept we have found helpful in considering these issues is that of a community covenant (Norris-Baker & Scheidt, 1993). Schroeder (1980), who first proposed the concept, believes that each community's individual character was related to tenuous, informal agreements among a plurality of residents about what was most important to the town. These covenants are dynamic, responding to events, traditions, and sociocultural milieu as well as individual leadership, and may be embodied and read in symbolic messages visible in the community. Their embodiment in the physical milieu of the community helps convey these cultural messages to long-time residents as continuity and validation of their beliefs, and to new residents and visitors as guidance about community expectations. An example of a covenant that relies primarily on ethnic identity is found in a community that identifies itself as "The Czech Capitol of Kansas." It expresses its group identity through many physical symbols, including the Czech-language welcome sign at the entry to town, colorfully painted windows throughout the small business district, the transformation of the old opera house into a Czech museum, and the permanent sign in the city park advertising the annual Czech festival. The role of ethnicity as culture in shaping this community identity is intentional, and is recognized as an asset for the town.

SUSTAINING COMMUNITY

In some small communities we have explored, one aspect of their covenant seems to be cooperative resilience. In these communities, response to local threat or disaster is a social phenomenon, especially if what is perceived as a core element of the community is affected. One example from our earlier research comes from a town where the only café in town burned, leaving no place for community residents to gather and socialize. The response was immediate; a member of the community purchased a vacant fast food restaurant 30 miles away, and had it moved to the site of the former café. Fewer than 6 months after the fire, the café was reopened and serving its community. A more recent example of this kind of commitment to sustain one's community comes from another town about 75 miles west of that community. According to a report of the Associated Press (2002), residents of this town of 500, which lost its only grocery store to a fire in late 2001, have not only raised money to help rebuild it, but are helping with its construction as well. The story quotes a community leader who said, "If you don't have a school you don't have a town. If you don't have a store, you don't have a town" (p. A3). Six months after the fire, the store is reopening at three times its former size, thanks to the commitment of the owners, to whom the community has always been "home," the local construction company, which is working at break-even pay, and the countless hours of volunteer efforts. Such resilience is unlikely without a strong community covenant that fosters a sense of community attachment and dependence among residents.

PROTECTING COMMUNITY IDENTITY AND DISTINCTIVENESS

Sometimes, the physical expressions of a community's history and covenants may be threatened because the ways these places and symbols sustain cultural meanings and attachment go unrecognized until they are threatened or lost. Increasingly, local governments and planning professionals are attempting to identify and preserve the environmental features believed to contribute to the character/

culture of communities. A recent quantitative case study by Green (1999) explored some of the psychological and physical aspects involved in residents' perceptions of the character of a small seaside town that was rapidly being transformed by tourism and growth. His results suggested that a positive character image was associated with aesthetically pleasing natural landscape features, built landmark features, and settings that provided opportunities for social interaction. Features that residents identified as incompatible with the town's character, many of which were newly constructed buildings using standardized designs (supermarkets, housing, etc.), were associated with negative meanings.

In many of the towns we have studied, preoccupation with community survival and periodic natural disasters such as tornados, floods, and fires, have made systematic planning a moot point. In fact, for some of these communities, new construction of any kind would likely be associated with positive meanings reflecting future prospects for the town. At the same time, landmarks in the built environment often are at risk because of lack of awareness and neglect. Here, we can recount the example of a financially successful older businessman who returned regularly to visit the town of his childhood. He was successful enough that he decided he wanted to move a special boulder from the side of the highway near the community where he grew up to a place of honor in his own back yard 150 miles away. The boulder had special significance for him because it had saved his father's life by providing him a place of safety to climb onto when there was a cattle stampede. As the boulder was being hoisted onto a flatbed truck, another man from town drove up and challenged him—What right did he have to take public property? When our interviewee explained that he had obtained permission from the state highway department, the other man told him he really wished he wouldn't take that rock, because his father had escaped a cattle stampede by climbing on it, and the place was special to him. He inadvertently was depriving the community of what was a shared but unidentified community icon. As this example suggests, even when communities are preoccupied with what seem more pressing economic and social issues, we need more systematic strategies for identifying places with shared meaning as well as for sustaining community covenants and the symbols that embody them.

At the same time, we need to better understand the ways in which the distinctive qualities of settings or buildings contribute to a community's "character," and the meaning such uniqueness may hold for different residents. Our example comes from a family-owned Mexican café in a very small town. The son decided that the best way to reflect the family's sense of pride in both the success of their business and their Mexican heritage was to have the nicest looking building on the main street. He worked hard to improve the appearance of their building—first by adding a covered entry porch onto the street, then a new sidewalk, then benches, while still maintaining the proud display of an American flag, Aztec medallion, and religious icons in the café window. With each improvement, other Anglo-owned businesses in the community followed suit—to the extent that the town has new sidewalks, streetlights, and bought all the identical benches that a hardware chain had stocked throughout the state! Although the appearance of the town's main street benefited greatly from the family's initiative, the unspoken goal of the Mexican family, to have a distinctive building that visibly symbolized their pride in their heritage, was thwarted by the other business owners.

REFRAMING COMMUNITY

Community celebrations support both community identities and social relationships (Manning, 1983), as well as provide a mechanism through which to sustain the enculturating milieu, which Gutmann (1992) believes is so critical for the well-being of older residents. Werner and colleagues (2002) suggest that celebrations provide both opportunities and obligations for people "simultaneously to validate their uniqueness as well as their membership in different social groups" (p. 204), strengthening group bonds and cultural identities. Engaging in such celebrations, together with remembering similar events, helps people feel "supported by and bonded with . . . other social groups, as well as feeling attached to the familiar settings that support these celebrations" (p. 104).

Many small rural communities hold an annual community celebration, with older residents typically taking key roles as culture-bearers. If we think in terms of community covenants, we might label this the Brigadoon Covenant, an idealized community culture that some towns bring briefly to life from past memories, but which leaves a legacy in the culture and environment of the present. These celebrations provide opportunities to reminisce in ways that both cherish the past and create a sense of continuity with the historic community and rural culture. They may provide the impetus to preserve or memorialize valued places or embodiments of the culture, either in reality or in symbol, as an expression of the covenant. Examples range from the gaily painted windows of the Czech community to the memorialization of a former church building by the placement of its bell tower and a gravestone in the local cemetery, to the volunteer-constructed monument outside the community building in a "ghost town," incorporating remnants of what had been the landmark buildings of the town. The celebrations also draw in generations of families whose ties to the community are tenuous, creating opportunities to acculturate them. The specific focal point—whether it is the Czech Festival, a Fiesta to celebrate Mexican Independence Day, Ol' Settlers' Day in the "ghost town," a Memorial Day event, or Emancipation Day in an "all-Black" town like Nicodemus, Kansas, seems less important than the existence of an annual celebration that brings children, grandchildren, and former residents back into community life. These community reunions and celebratory events and the functions they serve are not unique to Kansas; they can be found in other small towns throughout the Midwest, as described in Taylor's (2001) study of older African American residents living in a small Indiana community.

At the same time, some of the celebrations, like the Czech Festival, provide an impetus for tourism and for looking not only to the past but also to the future. The community's adoption of an identity as the official Czech capitol of Kansas, together with local recreational amenities and proximity to an interstate, has led to proactive marketing of the community. When older residents not of Czech heritage were asked how they felt about the way in which ethnicity is embedded in the physical and social milieu of the town, their universal response was: "It's OK, because it's good for the town—we have a good time with it." This response seems to bring together the desire to have rural culture survive by use of whatever strategies available with the ability to accept different meanings of ethnicity as community culture and as group membership.

ACCEPTING A DYING COMMUNITY

In other situations, the threats to a community may be easily recognizable and beyond the control of individual residents. Loss of meaningful environmental settings or landmarks may shape residents' feelings of attachment, permanence, and continuity (Brown & Perkins, 1992; Scheidt & Norris-Baker, 1999). Some older residents in the small towns we have studied question who will die first—themselves or the town—and they are unsure of the winner. Any time they leave what in many cases are modest but comfortable dwellings, the community that engulfs them is one of deterioration and even decay. Some of these residents may not experience this dichotomy if they engage in selective mental reframing of these places. They may be able, as Graham Rowles discovered in his studies in Appalachia, to "retain the meaning of the places of their lives in the face of radical transformations in these environments by continuing to vicariously inhabit them as they were in the past" (Rowles & Ravdal, 2002, p. 95). Testimony to this response can be found in old photographs of the communities and their valued places prominently displayed in many homes.

LETTING GO OF A COMMUNITY

"In a sense, the environment(s) one inhabits remain as a testament to one's life" (Rowles & Ravdal, 2002, p. 87). One of the dysfunctional aspects of place attachment can be "when the desire to cling to the fragments of a home which has been physically or socially destroyed persists against all possibility of living there again" (Fried, 2000, p. 202). When changes occur slowly, over several years, it may be difficult for life-long residents to judge the actual extent of the entropy that propels community degradation. "Letting go" may occur equally as slowly. In the absence of social and economic capital, some residents use the last reservoir of human capital—their own talents—in poignant efforts to revivify declining communities. In one small town, for example, a retired couple worked diligently to restore an old two-story house in order to convert it into a bed-and-breakfast, failing to realize that without minimal services and natural sites of interest, few outsiders would be attracted to use it. In another, two middle-aged sisters—returning to the declining Midwestern town of their younger days—purchased and almost single-handedly restored two old homes, dedicating rooms in one to various family members. Although the town continues to lose vital service settings, they search for a theme that might attract groups of out-of-towners to use a local building as a meeting place or retreat center. The activities of these individuals have become a part of the local community culture, earning them near-heroic status in the eyes of other residents.

The closing of a café in the same town illustrates how the process of "letting go" can, from a community perspective, be more healthfully anticipated and grieved. The café was run for almost 50 years by the same owner-operator. As other businesses along Main Street disappeared, multiple behavior settings sprouted at the café in response to continuing community needs. In addition to serving "the best [and only] hamburger in town," the café served as a video rental outlet, a mini-quick shop (e.g., selling candies, over-the-counter drugs), an informal meeting place, community bulletin board, and a bus stop for children on winter mornings. Closing of the café was necessitated by the owner's desire to retire, the status of her husband's health, and the failure to find a local buyer. News of the imminent closing was well-announced in the local newspaper, by word of mouth, and on town fliers advertising the auction of its components (e.g., silverware, plates, chairs, videos, appliances, signs, bottles), as well as the building itself. The weekend auction was well-attended by both local and out-of-town residents. Aware it was dissolving into the remembered past, local residents carefully sorted through three flatbed trucks loaded with café artifacts, seeking, as one resident put it, "something I can remember this place by," to symbolize a panoply of meanings.

Public auctions in small declining towns serve important community functions for those who strive to distinguish the way things were from the way things will be now. There are few other shared rituals that mark this experience when places are extinguished. Dana (1965), describing his maiden sea voyage in *Two Years Before the Mast*, recalls a crewman falling from his perch atop the mast of a sailing ship, plunging directly into the dark Atlantic. Boats were lowered and shipmates rowed back and forth in a ritualistic, futile search, while discussing at the same time the disposition of his shipboard belongings. Like the sea search, the auction-day process itself constitutes a psychologically "overloaded" occasion, allowing the community to recognize the passing of the setting, and to redistribute objects, including the building itself, which made up its identity as a community focal point. For some, such objects now become important touch and sight points for organizing the array of memories from the remembered past. Rowles and Ravdal (2002) articulate this well, noting that:

> The ability to derive and sustain meaning, both through place making and through the recollection and integration of the places of our lives within our persona, is a source of support and may be related to well-being in old age. In the artifacts we accumulate and the places we possess (even if only in our consciousness) we define who we are (p. 106).

CONCLUSIONS

Though rural communities share many common outcomes produced by changes in both rural and global economies, there are clear distinctions among them that affect the targeting of interventions designed to improve the viability of the community environment and the quality of life of older residents. These include consideration of local leadership potential, the viability of a critical mass of community-level resources weighed against the severity of acute and chronic risks to and losses of economic, social, human, and natural capital, the particular point in the cycle of place decline, as well as life-course differences among those who may seek change (Flora, 2000). We have offered selected strategies for place therapies elsewhere (Scheidt & Norris-Baker, 1999). Most recently, there is a serious push to introduce broadband technology into rural areas to stimulate local and regional economic activity and to provide more adequate holistic health care for older residents via voice, video-conferencing, and other data services (Rural Access to Technology, 2000). Some programs specifically target caregiver assistance in rural areas (Buckwalter & Davis, 2002). Other rural programs use communication technologies to connect "virtual communities of communities," allowing them to learn survival techniques from each other (Rural America at the Crossroads, 1991). A growing trend toward community development and training to meet the needs of older residents is exemplified by the Elder Friendly Communities Project (Austin et al., 2002). This project involves an assessment of community supports for elders, as well as assets, capacities, and needs of elders and their families in order to provide environments that allow residents to age-in-place more successfully. A similar program in Kansas, the "Lifelong Communities Initiative," is designed to prepare select communities, through collaboration among local leaders, businesses, organizations, and government agencies, to develop and implement plans for enhancing the quality of life for elders.

Whether this initiative will create a form of triage, with resources focused only on communities with the greatest potential leaving others to decline unsupported, remains uncertain. Even in the best of circumstances these interventions will not bring much aid to small rural communities in the most remote (e.g., nonadjacent Standard Metropolitan Statistical Area) counties. Recent dramatic declines in state tax revenues will only exacerbate the challenges these communities face. Many small communities will undoubtedly continue to whither, gradually becoming little more than rural neighborhoods, consisting of single-family dwellings with few, if any, supportive services. Robert Anderson, in the screenplay of his autobiographical film, "I Never Sang for My Father," states that "death ends a life. But it does not end a relationship." Increasingly, older residents of remote declining communities may cling to the meanings of a personal and shared past, remaining attached to and continuing reminiscent relations with places and people that survive only in memory. The long-term consequences of these actions on their well-being remain unknown.

REFERENCES

Aldwin, C., & Stokols, D. (1988). The effects of environmental change on individuals and groups: Some neglected issues in stress research. *Journal of Environmental Psychology, 8*, 57–75.

Altman, I., & Low, S. (1992). *Place attachment.* New York: Plenum Press.

Associated Press. (2002, 14 June). Town works together to replace grocery. *Manhattan Mercury* (Manhattan, Kansas), No. 109 ed., sec. A, p. 3.

Austin, C., Flux, D., Ghali, L., Hartley, D., Holinda, D., McClelland, R., Sieppert, J., & Wild, T. (2002,June 25). *A place to call home: Final report of the Elder*

Friendly Communities Project. Available: http://www.gov.calgary.ab.ca/community/publications

Barker, R. G. (1987). Prospecting in environmental psychology. In D. Stokols & I. Altman (Eds.), *Handbook of environmental psychology* (pp. 1413–1432). New York: Wiley.

Boschetti, M. (1990). Continuity and change in century old farm houses. In R. Selby, K. Anthony, C. Jason, & B. Orland (Eds.), *Coming of age* (pp. 139–146). Oklahoma City, OK: Environmental Design Research Association.

Brown, B., & Perkins, D. (1992). Disruptions in place attachment. In I. Altman & S. Low (Eds.), *Place attachment* (pp. 279–304). New York: Plenum Press.

Buckwalter, C., & Davis, L. L. (2002, June 25). *Elder caregiving in rural communities.* Administration on Aging: Implementing the National Family Caregiver Support Program. Available: http://aos.gov.carenetwork/issue-briefs0302/Fin-Buckwalter-Davis.html

Cuba, L. (1989). Retiring to vacationland. *Generations, 13,* 63–69.

Cuba, L. (1992). Aging places: Perspectives on change in a Cape Cod community. *Journal of Applied Gerontology, 11*(1), 64–83.

Cuba, L. (1995, November). At home in many places: Multiple place identities in older and younger migrants [Symposium]. In R. J. Scheidt & C. Norris-Baker (Organizers), *Place transitions: Implications for the well-being of native and transitory community-based elderly.* Symposium conducted at the 48th Annual Meeting, Gerontological Society of America, Los Angeles, CA.

Cuba, L., & Hummon, D. (1993). Constructing a sense of home: Place affiliation and migration across the life cycle. *Sociological Forum, 8,* 547–572.

Dana, R. H. (1965). *Two years before the mast: A personal narrative.* New York: Harper & Row.

Feldman, R. (1996). Constancy and change in attachment to types of settlements. *Environment and Behavior, 28,* 419–445.

Fitchen, J. (1991). *Endangered spaces, enduring places: Change, identity, and survival in rural America.* Boulder, CO: Westview Press.

Flora, C. (2000). Measuring the social dimensions of managing natural resources. In D. Fulton, K. Nelson, D. Anderson, & D. Lime (Eds.), *Human dimensions of natural resources management: Emerging issues and practical applications.* St. Paul, MN: Cooperative Park Studies Program, Department of Forest Resources, University of Minnesota.

Fried, M. (2000). Continuities and discontinuities of place. *Journal of Environmental Psychology, 20,* 193–205.

Giuliani, M. V. (1991). Toward an analysis of mental representations of attachment to the home. *Journal of Architectural and Planning Research, 8,* 133–146.

Giuliani, M. V., & Feldman, R. (1993). Place attachment in a developmental and cultural context. *Journal of Environmental Psychology, 13,* 167–274.

Golant, S., & LaGreca, A. (1994). Housing quality of U.S. elders: Does aging in place matter? *The Gerontologist, 34,* 803–814.

Green, R. (1999). Meaning and form in community perception of town character. *Journal of Environmental Psychology, 19,* 311–329.

Gustafson, P. (2000). Meanings of place: Everyday experience and theoretical conceptualizations. *Journal of Environmental Psychology, 21,* 5–16.

Gutmann, D. (1992). Culture and mental health in later life revisited. In J. Birren, R. B. Stone, & G. Cohen (Eds.), *Handbook of mental health and aging* (2nd ed., pp. 75–97). New York: Academic Press.

Hummon, D. (1992). Community attachment: Local sentiment and sense of place. In I. Altman & S. Low (Eds.), *Place attachment* (pp. 253–279). New York: Plenum Press.

Hummon, D. (1995, March). *Place attachment: Observations on multiple ties to home, community, and region* [Symposium]. In R. Feldman & M. Fried (Chair), Functions and Dysfunctions of Place Attachment. Symposium conducted at the 26th Annual Meeting, Environmental Design Research Association, Boston.

Jorgensen, B., & Stedman, R. (2001). Sense of place as an attitude: Lakeshore owner's attitudes toward their properties. *Journal of Environmental Psychology, 21,* 233–248.

Low, S., & Altman, I. (1992). Place attachment: A conceptual inquiry. In I. Altman & S. Low (Eds.), *Place attachment* (pp. 1–12). New York: Plenum Press.

Lynch, K. (1976). *Managing the sense of a region.* Cambridge, MA: MIT Press.

Manning, F. E. (1983). *The celebrations of society: Perspectives on contemporary culture performance.* Bowling Green, OH: Bowling Green University Popular Press.

McAuley, W. J. (1998). History, race, and attachment to place among elders in the rural all-Black towns of Oklahoma. *Journal of Gerontology: Social Sciences, 53B*(1), S35–S45.

McHugh, K. E., & Mings, R. C. (1996). The circle of migration: Attachment to place in aging. *Annals of the Association of American Geographers, 83,* 530–550.

Norris-Baker, C., & Scheidt, R. J. (1993). Community covenants: An indicator of sustainable small town habitats. In E. G. Arias & M. G. Gross (Eds.), *Equitable and sustainable habitats.* Oklahoma City, OK: Environmental Design Research Association.

Norris-Baker, C., & Scheidt, R. J. (1994). From "Our Town" to "Ghost Town?" The changing context of home for rural elderly. *International Journal of Aging and Human Development, 38*(3), 99–120.

Rice, T. W., & Steele, B. (2001). White ethnic diversity and community attachment in small Iowa towns. *Social Science Quarterly, 82,* 397–407.

Rowles, G. D. (1981). The surveillance zone as meaningful space for the aged. *The Gerontologist, 21,* 304–311.

Rowles, G. D. (1987). A place to call home. In L. Carstensen & B. Edelstein (Eds.), *Handbook of clinical gerontology* (pp. 335–353). New York: Pergamon.

Rowles, G. D. (1990). Place attachment among the small-town elderly. *Journal of Rural Community Psychology, 11*(1), 103–120.

Rowles, G. D. (1993). Evolving images of place in aging and 'aging in place.' *Generations, 17*(2), 65–70.

Rowles, G. D., & Ravdal, H. (2002). Aging, place, and meaning in the face of changing circumstances. In R. S. Weiss & S. A. Bass (Eds.), *Challenges of the third age: Meaning and purpose in later life* (pp. 81–114). New York: Oxford University Press.

Rubinstein, R., & Parmalee, P. (1992). Attachment to place and the representation of the life course by the elderly. In I. Altman & S. Low (Eds.), *Place attachment* (pp. 139–165). New York: Plenum Press.

Rural access to technology: Connecting the last American frontier. (2000, October 5,). Hearing before the Subcommittee on Technology of the Committee on Science, House of Representatives (One Hundred Sixth Congress, Second Session), Serial No. 106-104.

Rural America at the crossroads: Networking for the Future, OTA-TCT-471. (1991, April). U.S.Congress, Office of Technology Assessment. Washington, DC: U.S. Government Printing Office.

Scheidt, R. J., & Norris-Baker, C. (1999). Place therapies for older adults: Conceptual and interventive approaches. *International Journal of Aging and Human Development, 48*(1), 1–15.

Scheidt, R. J., & Norris-Baker, C. (1990). A transactional approach to environmental stress among older residents of rural communities: Introduction to a special issue. *Journal of Rural Community Psychology, 11*(1), 5–30.

Schroeder, F. (1980). Types of American towns and how to read them. *Southern Quarterly, 19,* 104–135.

Stegner, P. (1992, September–October). Where the heart is. *Audubon,* pp. 40–41.

Stokols, D. (1995). The paradox of environmental psychology. *American Psychologist, 50,* 821–837.

Stokols, D., & Shumaker, S. A. (1981). People in places: A transactional view of settings. In J. Harvey (Ed.), *Cognition, social behavior, and the environment* (pp. 441–488). Hillsdale, NJ: Lawrence Earlbaum.

Taylor, S. A. P. (2001). Place identification and positive realities of aging. *Journal of Cross-Cultural Gerontology, 16,* 5.

Toyama, T. (1988). *Identity and milieu: A study of relocation focusing on the reciprocal changes in elderly people and their environments.* Unpublished manuscript, The Royal Institute of Technology, Stockholm, Sweden.

Werner, C. M., Brown, B. B., & Altman, I. (2002). Transactionally oriented research: Examples and strategies. In R. B. Bechtel & A. Churchman (Eds.), *Handbook of environmental psychology* (pp. 203–221). New York: Wiley.

Wicker, A. W. (1987). Behavior settings reconsidered: Temporal stages, resources, internal dynamics, context. In D. Stokols & I. Altman (Eds.), *Handbook of environmental psychology* (pp. 613–653). New York: Wiley.

Wicker, A. W. (2002). Ecological psychology: Historical contexts, current conception, prospective directions. In R. B. Bechtel & A. Churchman (Eds.), *Handbook of environmental psychology* (pp. 114–126). New York: Wiley.

CHAPTER 14

The Influence of Neighborhood and Community on Well-Being and Identity in Later Life: An English Perspective

Sheila M. Peace, Caroline Holland, and Leonie Kellaher

Very few people live in complete isolation from others. Consequently, any real understanding of the meaning of home has to include a consideration of the material and social consequences of location. In this chapter we turn to issues of neighborhood and community in relation to older peoples' living places. As people relocate, emigrate, and repatriate, and more and more elders live in global communities, our discussion must acknowledge the different scales of geographical context of many people's lives. Our starting point is the near-home environment, which stretches typically from the dwelling-place to a point at which the home-dweller feels that he or she has left his or her own neighborhood. As we will describe, definitions of this area and of communities vary. Our discussion assumes that the experience of neighborhood includes the materiality of places, the social construction of meaning, and the effects of individual and group biographies on reactions to place. To illustrate our current understanding of neighborhood and aging, we go on to describe findings from our recent study, "Environment and Identity in Later Life: A Cross Setting Study."

COMMUNITIES AND NEIGHBORHOODS

What do we mean by communities? According to Taylor, Barr, and West (2000), most communities can be defined by two dimensions: (1) the characteristics of their members' (including, for example, beliefs, economic status, activities), and (2) the common interests that tie members together (such as cultural heritage, social relationships, political power base). Etzioni (1995) talks of "social webs" of people who know one another as persons and help maintain "civic, social, and moral order" (p. 248), and Bourke (1994) suggested that community might include elements of identification with a particular neighborhood or street, a sense of shared perspectives, and some reciprocal dependency. Communities are not primarily about location; diasporic religious and cultural communities are a case in point. As people claim (or are claimed to have) belonging to some communities, they are implicitly excluded from others on grounds that might include race, class, culture, or economic status (e.g., Alibhai-Brown, 2000; Ratcliffe, 1999). Nevertheless in different situations individuals may align themselves with different groups and to varying degrees. For example, the same man might identify himself in one place as a Yorkshireman, in another place as a retired professional, and in yet another place as a British Muslim. Status and roles within communities are not static. Inclusion and exclusion within community can also be affected by aging and by the ways in which people build and draw on social capital. Self-identity in later life involves dealing with change against a background of continuity. Sometimes this involves maintaining or increasing engagement, sometimes it means letting go or withdrawing.

But communities can and often do relate to specific neighborhoods; proximity helps, through constant reinforcement, to maintain links. Furthermore, for some people, including many older people, the reality is that face-to-face interactions with other people are confined to the neighborhood if not the residence itself. During the mid-20th century, community studies in Britain examined particular working-class neighborhoods (Rosser & Harris, 1965; Young & Willmott, 1957) and identified characteristics such as the sense of belonging to a social group, the centrality of mother–daughter relationships in family networks, and the mutual aid offered among people as key elements of community (Bornat, 2002). Do these characteristics still exist? In 1994 and 1995 Phillipson and colleagues (2001) re-visited the locations of some of these earlier community studies and showed how despite diversity and variety in family and household change, both social support through the family and engagement within locality remain important to the well-being of older people.

Neighborhoods are geographical areas with personal and social meaning related to the materiality of the environment. Taylor and Brower (1985) describe them as those environments most proximate to individuals' homes in which interest and control are shared among households. Nevertheless, this shared zone probably includes many subareas that are private, semiprivate, and semipublic. For example, in the English study we will describe, the semiprivate front gardens of individual houses contrast with the semipublic lawns in front of retirement apartments.

People sometimes define one neighborhood by reference to others, and in some circumstances neighborhoods may be formally organized for social, political, or developmental activities. The boundaries of neighborhoods, especially as experienced by individuals, are not simple. They can include fixed elements (such as railway lines or main roads) but they can also be diffuse and vague. For the purposes of studying identity and well-being, we defined the reach of an individual's neighborhood as extending from her or his own front door to the limit of relative familiarity and "insiderness" in the public spaces around the individual's home. The extent of this area varies, partly in relation to mobility, but whatever the size of a person's effective neighborhood we can conceive of a gradient of interest and control tapering away from the intimacy of the home base. Disability or frailty may steepen this gradient, resulting in spatial contraction (Rowles, 1978); here technologies—for example, mobile phones, affordable and easy to manipulate mobility aids, and passive infra red lighting—may have an ameliorating effect. On the other hand, in neighborhoods experiencing violent crime or other turbulence, the gradient may be steep for almost everybody. We suggest that the rate of neighborhood change, as well as its nature, is crucial to whether people can feel in control. Rapid change can disrupt the congruence between personal identity and the place identity that is an important part of attachment to neighborhood.

Moving around the neighborhood, people negotiate and interpret it as they engage with the various elements it presents, in varying degrees of complexity. The material environment itself might be simple and composed of few elements, or it might be highly complex, with some aspects presenting barriers to social engagement. For some people, aging entails a heightening of the sensual impact of the micro environment as material elements such as ground textures, changes in level, and physical barriers become more problematic. Transportation in and out of the neighborhood is an issue for many. Some people, especially current older generations of women in Britain, have never had independent access to a car, and as men and women age they are increasingly likely to give up driving, so that moving out beyond the neighborhood requires accessible public transportation, taxis, or the help of others. The sense of control over movement/mobility can be crucial to self-esteem.

The complexity of social environments also varies from place to place. For example, the range of socioeconomic classes present or the combination of minority ethnic groups and the extent to which these groups are integrated or segregated differs among communities. At all stages of life, people constantly edit their understanding of the social environment and construct a network of relationships for themselves based on opportunities and constraints on their own participation. In 21st-century Britain the context for these networks is an increasingly complex society with generally smaller households, geographically dispersed families, more people living alone for extended periods including later life, and a tendency toward privatism rather than collectivism in social activities.

Interpreting the neighborhood also carries a time dimension. Collective memories and narratives about elements within the neighborhood contribute to the insiderness of people familiar with neighborhood histories. This can be seen, for example, when long-term residents refer to places by historic or arcane names, or give directions by referring to landmarks that have been removed. At the same time, individuals have their own recollections of events-in-place. Familiar places, especially those with which people have long-standing involvements, can support older people in a number of ways. These include underwriting an "entitlement" to place by virtue of co-history of habitation; giving the security of knowing other people/ being known by other people, even if only by sight; and the confidence of knowing how to handle the material environment—good places to cross the road, public lavatories, shortcuts, safe routes, and places to avoid. Memories alone are not enough. People also need current knowledge about their neighborhoods to be able to negotiate and interpret them. One of the problems with other neighborhoods is the uncertainty about interpreting their spaces. Familiarity can give confidence if the wisdom of place is respected.

What people actually do within their neighborhoods in part relates to life stage (as, for example, with school-gate socializing, fund-raising coffee mornings, or evenings in the local pub). It also relates to opportunities, expectations, and the extent to which people feel accepted (and unwatched), or fearful or anxious when out and about. For some older people, security concerns can result in an involuntary disengagement from the neighborhood. Others find a solution in what has been described as the "integrated segregation" of communities of older people (McGrail et al., 2001). But such communities, in recreating a secure internal neighborhood, may also reinforce the "otherness" of older people relative to the wider population (Laws, 1997; Phillips et al., 2001). The tension between comfort and discomfort in neighborhoods has emerged as an important theme in understanding older peoples' constructions of home.

ENVIRONMENT AND IDENTITY
IN LATER LIFE STUDY

How are we to find out how the community/neighborhood environment influences the way older people feel about the places and spaces in which they live? This question formed one of the objectives of "Environment and Identity in Later Life: A Cross-setting Study" funded by the Economic and Social Research Council in Britain as part of the Growing Older Programme (1999–2003) (Peace, Kellaher & Holland, 2003). The project is one of 24 research studies that aim to rethink how we understand the quality of life of older people at the beginning of the 21st century.

The research focuses on environment in its widest definition, encompassing the dwelling in which the person lives; the external environment surrounding that dwelling, which may be enclosed or open; the street-life of the neighborhood and community in which it is located; and beyond, to a wider, less tangible environment that may be known or unknown, built or natural, and yet forms a part of how the person interprets the world.

Finding a way of encompassing this scope of environment led us to adopt an ethnographic approach to the research. Initially, two criteria were crucial to the study: (1) location and (2) dwelling type. We chose three different locations in which to undertake this study: metropolitan/urban, small town/urban/suburban, and rural village environments. We worked within a 70-mile radius of the Open University headquarters in Milton Keynes, England: in the north London Borough of Haringey; the town of Bedford, Bedfordshire; and villages and small towns within the southern part of Northamptonshire.

Having chosen our locations we began at the level of the collective. Although we knew that we would want to develop individual case studies about people and their individual environments, we also wanted to hear from groups of older people within each location. Therefore we began by running a series of nine focus groups with three to eight older people in each. Two of the groups were assembled specifically for our discussion, and the other seven consisted of "naturally occurring" groups that included two social/luncheon clubs; a Mothers' Union (Christian) group; a sewing circle; a Black oral-history group; a men's billiards group; and a (Sikh) cultural community group. Of the nine groups, four were all-White British and Irish; three were mixed race; one was all-Black-Caribbean, and one was all-Indian. Two of the groups were all-male; four were all-female; and three were mixed gender. The sessions were led by one or more of the researchers, depending on the number of older people who had accepted our invitation to talk about environment and identity, and they were audiotaped for later content analysis. They were held in local venues, either the group's own regular meeting place or, in the case of the specially convened groups, in the community rooms of a friendly local minister and a sheltered housing scheme. In describing some of the results from the study, we look first at issues about neighborhoods and communities that arose in these focus groups before going into more detail about three of the individual case studies.

GROUPS TALKING ABOUT NEIGHBORHOOD AND COMMUNITY

Participants in the three research locations did not communicate with each other directly but they did see newsletters that covered the essence of the discussions at the other sites. Briefly, these discussions centered on the communities that people were comfortable with (for practical purposes this often coincided with locally based networks of "friends" and "neighbors"), problems with the social and material neighborhood, the effects of change, and ideas about improving the quality of neighborhoods.

Belonging

The participants agreed that they liked to feel they "belonged" and "were known" locally. For some people who had been feeling isolated, the new community they found in sheltered housing was able to meet this need. People in this situation tended to mix mostly with other older people, although they valued their contacts with younger relatives and friends. Others defined their community as "like-minded people"; or as people who understood things much as they did: This group often recognized religious faith groups or, in the case of people whose first language was not English, their own language community.

Insecurity

Problems were described as largely emanating from the behavior of people in the neighborhood who were not part of the respondents' particular communities of standards, values, and expectations. Some of these problems were particularly acute for the city-dwellers: they included direct harassment from landlords or other residents; noisy music and inconsiderate or aggressive behavior; mess, untidiness, and vandalism in flats and in the street; crime, especially crime related to drugs; lewd or other unacceptable activities in public places; excess traffic and street noise, litter, and street disturbances. Although some respondents ascribed these problems, in part, to the increasingly multicultural composition of their neighborhoods, most felt that the main problem was with younger people, including children and young families as well as teenagers and young adults.

Connections

For most people, moving to another neighborhood was not an option. Moving to a new area or community was regarded as one of the biggest challenges. People who had relocated in later life described working hard to get to know people by taking part in activities and clubs and being open to conversations with new acquaintances. Sometimes people's circumstances had changed unexpectedly—for example, when they lost their husband or wife, when they became seriously ill or disabled, or when having moved to be near a child, this child had moved away. In these situations, it mattered very much to respondents that they felt connected to their local communities and had the energy to engage.

Movement

Transportation was an issue for respondents in all of the research locations. Specific problems with transportation included getting to and from places on foot, given the poor state of pavements and the busyness of roads; getting on and off buses; and the unreliability of buses. There were also issues about using taxi services and relying on other people for rides, including having to fit in with the schedules of other people (this included dial-a-ride and other ride services) finding people to offer rides, and admitting to age by using these strategies. Participants who still had cars (and some people who had given them up) felt that having a car was a lifeline because it enabled them to go out and provided independence, but there were concerns about risk and adaptability and when and how to make the decision to give up driving.

In dealing with all these changes, access to information and to authorities and agencies able to make an impact was considered to be crucial. Experiences of response from the police and local authorities varied. Some people felt that their problems were not taken seriously, and that they were not listened to as much as younger people. Some participants also thought it was very important to have a community center or some kind of communal space, like a park or a village green where people could meet. The support of others was valued. Notwithstanding the problems of public order and vandalism in some public spaces, people who lived in flats where they would not see or talk to their neighbors on a regular basis felt that this was particularly important.

Being part of a community made the respondents feel more secure that they could get help if they needed it. Some people thought that there came a stage in life during which a person had to decide to settle and make wherever one lived, one's home for life. This meant different levels of involvement with the neighborhood. In general, people were more concerned about the quality of the neighborhood where they lived now than the place with which they originally identified. As one migrant from India to Bedford put it, "My roots are there, but my branches are here."

INDIVIDUALS TALKING ABOUT NEIGHBORHOOD AND COMMUNITY

The aim of the study was to be inclusive and to hear from people who lived in all kinds of dwellings from apartments in social housing schemes to privately run residential-care homes. Although the emphasis was on "mainstream" private homes in regular communities, we wished to break the divide between studies of people living in "ordinary" and in "special" housing where care is formalized. The study did not include people in nursing homes, where care issues are paramount.

Discussions in the focus groups were used to develop a schedule for subsequent interviews, including a "Facets of Life" wheel prompt (see Figure 14.1). In the form of a spinning wheel, this tool sets out for the researcher and the respondent the derived domains of investigation in eight segments. It allows the respondent to co-man-

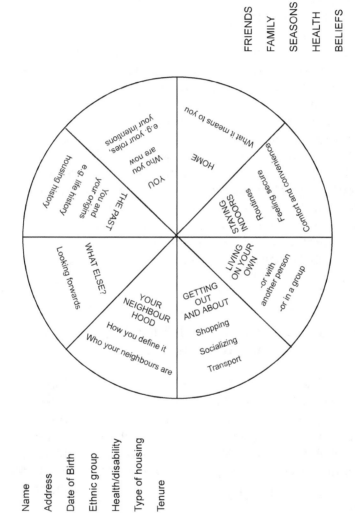

FIGURE 14.1 The "Facets of Life" wheel.

Name

Address

Date of Birth

Ethnic group

Health/disability

Type of housing

Tenure

FRIENDS

FAMILY

SEASONS

HEALTH

BELIEFS

age the interview, exploring the issues indicated in the eight segments on their own terms while being aware in advance of the foci of the research. The eight areas under consideration were:

- Self (who are you now?; roles);

- The Past (origins, life story, housing history);

- Home (what it means to you);

- Staying indoors (routines, comforts, convenience, security);

- Getting out and about (shopping? socializing? transportation?);

- Neighborhood (where is it? what does it mean to you? who are your neighbors?);

- Living with (alone; with another person; in a group); and

- What else? (including future plans and projects).

The "wheel" was used as a prompt for informal discussion as part of a suite of data-gathering/creating tools. This protocol was used in case studies with 18 respondents in each location with ages ranging from the early 60's to early 90's. For each of the respondents we compiled a dossier containing interview transcripts/data from the "wheel" prompt, a housing-history profile, responses to quality-of-life questions from the Housing Options for Older People (HOOP) schedule, basic respondent and accommodation characteristics, health and financial data, local area mapping, and commonly used questions relating to relatively stable personality traits. Photographs were taken at most of the dwellings. Data from the transcriptions were subject to content analysis for the development of key themes.

Initial analysis indicated key aspects of neighborhoods that might influence their enjoyment by older residents. We expect these categories to be refined and expanded by further analysis. The most obvious factors were:

1. the material complexity of the neighborhood: including such elements as the diversity of housing, street layouts including parking places, the variety of uses of public spaces, and the availability of accessible transportation;

2. the level of urbanization: rural, semirural, suburban, urban, metropolitan;

3. the social heterogeneity of the neighborhood community including the mix of race/culture, age, wealth, class and so on;

4. material affordances: the barriers/aids to mobility such as traffic flow, street gradients and curbs, levels of dilapidation and vandalism;

5. the situation relative to proximate neighborhoods; whether up- or down-market, routes in and out, and the amount of contact with the wider area; and

6. organizational factors: including the degree to which governance is locally devolved; the provision of health and welfare services; and recreational facilities.

To illustrate how these factors presented in the data from individual interviews, we describe here sections from three of the cases. "Max" lives in the historic town of Bedford (population approximately 73,500*). "Dolly" lives in the Northamptonshire town of Burton Latimer (population approximately 7,000*), and "Roy" lives in Haringey, a metropolitan and multicultural Borough in north London with a population of over 220,000.*

Max

One of the youngest respondents was Max, aged 62, who lived on the third floor of a 20-storey apartment block. Nine years previously, while involved in a difficult divorce and financial settlement, he suffered a stroke, leaving him without the use of one arm, and with restricted mobility. Within a few months Max had lost his marriage, his home, his job as a lawyer, and his health. Eventually the local authority offered Max the tenancy of a two-bedroomed flat, and he began to reconstruct his life and his sense of identity, becoming a committee member of the residents' association.

> I have got gradually better over the years with walking, but I still can't use this right hand. I try and run my life so that I know what I want, so I do things. I tidy up, try and keep things

---

*2001 population estimates.

clean. I go into town on Tuesdays so I have got my life more or less settled. I do try and keep myself active and know what I am doing. At the moment I lock up downstairs—we have got a communal room and toilets and we close the toilets at about 4.30–5.00 p.m., and I have got the keys, it makes me feel official.

Basically, my neighborhood is these flats. I feel secure here. I suppose it helps knowing everybody and they all know me. I mean, a lot of people say "Hello Max" because I have got my photograph downstairs, because of the committee you see, I am chairman. It gives me a bit of confidence and it means a lot. And they are very nice to me; you know I am really lucky.

I am in quite a lot, but I have a lot of things to do. In the communal room downstairs we have books and jigsaws, I like jigsaws. That little owl up there—I got that for losing at whist. But they do things like that—they got me that, a little ornament with three owls, one is upside down on its head, it says, "Nobody is Perfect." It makes you feel really wanted, part of a family; that is what I always think. One lady, her son was moving and he gave me a load of stuff. A lady from one of these flats gave me a kettle. I have got two warm coats, loads of shirts and I have got long sleeve shirts if it gets really cold, so I am alright.

I walk around [to] the church next door OK, if it is wet I don't walk on the grass, I don't take chances, I go around the long way. But as I say, there is always somebody who will go with me. But I don't go out on my own at all. You know if it is dark you can't see what you are walking on, so I don't bother. I like Bedford because we have got "shop mobility" so I just go downstairs and get a lift in their bus and so I can get about the town now. And I know most of the people in the library, I go quite a bit. We have got the river here, and with all the greenery around the flat it is lovely. I have got a bird box on my balcony. I have blue tits in. But that is about all I do.

Although not native to Bedford, Max had already settled in the town before the stroke and was active within his (then) middle-class neighborhood. Since the stroke, his day-to-day activities had become more focused on the apartment block where he was member of the social committee. A rather uninviting building from the outside, the block was set back from the main road among mature trees and alongside an old church with a community hall. From inside the flat, the view through leafy branches gave Max great pleasure. The flat was full of representations of owls—photographs, ornaments, on plates—many of which had been given as gifts by people who knew about his love of these birds. To get out beyond the immediate area around the apartment block required transportation and assistance, so Max had centered his life around supporting and helping to create the community of neighbors within the block. Recovering from his stoke, Max discovered that downshifting to a lower-status neighborhood was not a major issue. For him, the materiality of the neighborhood was paramount in allowing him to remain socially active. Living in an apartment block with a communal entrance and activity rooms, rather than a street of detached houses, enabled him to engage with people in ways that minimized the effects of his disabilities and emphasized his usefulness. The combination of "urban" access to organized facilities and the "rural" vista from his window suited him perfectly. Max died following a further stroke in 2002.

Dolly

Dolly, age 78, had lived for the last 14 years in a small bungalow owned by the local authority and purposely built for elders in a street of similar houses. She was born in the nearby town of Northampton and moved to the much smaller settlement of Burton Latimer when she married in 1947:

> You used to walk down the street and you knew everybody . . . I mean there was just the high street and a few streets off it, and the new estate up Spinney Road where we lived, I mean it wasn't a very big place at all. And there were one, two, three . . . four shoe factories, three clothing factories. People used to come into Burton to work. I mean you could pack your job up in the morning and get another one in the afternoon; there were so many places to work. Nobody went out of town to work, you didn't need to. But then of course one after another they were closing factories, and the shoe factories all closed. And that were it, we were only left with the Weetabix [factory] and a few little bits of pieces of factories so quite a lot of people have to go out of town to work.

> Most of us here lived up at Spinney Road. Those houses were pulled down, and I think these bungalows were built at the same time as the posh houses, and . . . the council took them over and bought them because they had got to get people out of Spinney Road. The majority of us were getting older by then because we all went up there as young families with young

children, you know. There is only about three who have moved in since, because people only move out of here if they die. Anybody else who comes, everybody is made welcome you know, and everybody knows everybody, and we all help each other. It is nice.

When we came to Burton we had our own police station, a police sergeant and three constables, all in Burton. Now we have got nothing. I mean it is absolutely ridiculous, and there is no good ringing the police because they just don't get here. We were sitting outside one day waiting for our taxi to pick us up, and these two policemen came walking up the street. It was in the summer, I know they had got the shirt sleeves . . . you know. And I said, "Good lord! I wish I had a," and so they said "why?" and so I said "I can't remember the last time I saw one policeman in Burton, but two of them! Has somebody been robbing the bank?" I mean they were laughing. And I have not seen any since, and that was last summer.

. . . And I must admit that hill coming up here, you know . . . my husband said "they only put the old folk up the hill to get rid of them quick" I mean he always did say that, bless him. You come home now with a bit of shopping, and oh crikey, you start at the bottom and it gets worse and worse. I must admit that is why we have a taxi a lot of the time because of getting up that hill with shopping.

Well I suppose you can say I am a Burtoner folk now (laughs) I think I have been here long enough now, yes.

Dolly's identity as a "Burtoner folk" is of a particular kind—the old guard of inhabitants who remember the town as it was: small, self-contained, and communally-minded. She was fairly unusual among the respondents in believing that Burton belonged to her as much as she to it. Most of the respondents had relocated several times in their lives and almost all said that they now identified themselves with the place they lived to the extent of not really wanting to live somewhere else. The reasons given for this sense of attachment usually included effective networks of local support (kin, friends, neighbors) and familiarity with the material environment. However, the respondents were generally more reticent about claiming complete "belonging," which for many retained connotations of a "born and bred" sense of insiderness. Dolly also recites the commonly held view that neighborhoods have suffered over time from the dissolution of locality-based communities as the structure of society becomes more fragmented, more people work and socialize outside the area, and local government functions become centralized and uprooted from local neighborhoods. Like many married women of her generation, Dolly had never learned to drive and most of her activities were still locally based. She attributed many of the disadvantages of living in Burton (inadequate public transport and policing, insufficient recreational activities) to the centralization of Burton's affairs to the nearby larger town of Kettering. Nevertheless she found the small size and relative lack of complexity and homogeneity of Burton to her taste.

Roy

Aged 68 at the time of his interview, Roy had lived in an apartment in a large sheltered accommodation scheme for about 6 years. He was born in India and at the age of 18 left his wealthy family to travel to a university in Britain, a move that became permanent. After two marriages (one to a woman from India), a serious motorcycle injury and several relocations, Roy found himself living alone in a run-down London apartment. Because of his multiple health problems, the local authority offered him the tenancy of a sheltered apartment after he retired. Roy is coping with partial paralysis as a result of an old thigh bone fracture, high blood pressure, diabetes, and kidney and heart problems. These conditions strongly affect his relationship with places:

> I have to think twice. For example, I can't go back to India now for the fear that if I am not feeling well I may not come back alive. Because you have to be very confident about medical attention wherever you go. The other thing is staying somewhere . . . a day trip is alright, but more than that, you have got to think about toilets and all sorts of things.

Roy manages by having friends and children of old friends take him shopping and do the carrying. In return he will do paperwork for them—he likes to feel that he can do something in return. His one-bed apartment is crammed with books, ornaments, and surplus quantities of goods he buys in bulk; hence reducing the need to go out shopping. He needs to park his car very near to the door that leads to the elevator to his flat. For example, once he could not park right outside and bad weather set in. He couldn't manage to walk to the car as it was slippery underfoot. This caused him to be housebound for 4 days.

Roy also sees himself in transition between two communities. He feels he would no longer be able to live in his Indian birth place because he has adopted the values and standards of the English community, and has settled within his present neighborhood, where he feels secure. Yet he maintains communication with Indian culture through having piped Indian television, which he watches, alongside British television, and he talks of feeling in limbo:

> The thing is Sheila, to be truthful, many people like us here who after being here for such a long time, if you go to India we are out of place there because India has evolved and developed in a different direction and a different way to the way we have done here. In other words we have got British values; it is not only the language but other things as well about law, standards, and other things. They have their own standards and way of life. And we are out of place there. We don't belong there, you see. And that is why . . . and sometimes at odd times we feel we don't belong here, so we are in a limbo sort of thing, you get that feeling. But most of the time I feel this is my home. . . . We take part in politics, we back a football team, we do everything that any British citizen would do, which when you go to India we are foreigners. And it stands out a mile.

For Roy the material attributes of his adopted neighborhood and access to health services had become critically important as he tried to maintain his independence. The social mix within the housing scheme was a bit of a problem for him but he could retain a sense of social engagement through the "virtual" Indian community and by getting out in his car. Of the three respondents discussed in this chapter, Roy was the least emotionally attached to his immediate neighborhood but he acknowledged that its location suited his needs very well.

A LOCAL FUTURE FOR OLDER PEOPLE?

Many countries face change brought about by globalization, environmental change, changing social structures, increasing longevity and declining birth rates, and developments in forms of communication and technologies. Yet the neighborhood continues to be a significant point of attachment to society for most older people. It provides a context for and a bridge between the intimacy of the dwelling place and the wider public domains of township/county/state/country— with which all people might identify at some level, but not really know. No longer being able to go out independently is a critical stage in identity construction because, without the wider contexts that lie beyond the dwelling, the home itself becomes diminished as a source of identity construction. Continued capacity to engage with "the other" is represented by neighborhood in a way that the immediate domicile cannot demonstrate or provide.

Given that individuals react differently to their environments, can we begin to identify the kinds of neighborhoods that are most likely to help older people to remain socially engaged at whatever their chosen level? How inclusive can the locality of neighborhood be for people in later life? Although some older people can still rely on support from within neighborhoods as seen in Phillipson et al.'s (2001) studies of Bethnal Green, Wolverhampton, and Woodford, this is not the case for many. What are their future options? We have seen in the "Environment and Identity" study that alongside trans-spatial engagements with family and wider communities through technology (telephone/television/internet), for many (most?) older people, *actual* engagement in material and social neighborhoods is still essential to well-being and self-identity. As an aspect of older people's housing need, neighborhood has been relatively underemphasized: Yet it is clear that, as people age and become more focused on home, the salience of neighborhood increases. In Britain, most people as they age remain in "regular" neighborhoods rather than move into collective retirement communities. It remains one of the great challenges of our aging society to make those neighborhoods good places in which to grow old.

REFERENCES

Alibhai-Brown, Y. (2000). *Who do we think we are? Imagining the new Britain.* Buckingham, UK: Open University Press.

Bornat, J. (2002). *Unit 2, Communities and Networks, Open University Course: 'Care Welfare and Community.'* SHSW, Open University, Buckingham, UK.

Bourke, J. (1994). *Working class cultures in Britain 1890–1916:* Gender, class and ethnicity. London: Routledge.

Etzioni, A. (1995). *The spirit of community: Rights, responsibilities and the communitarian agenda.* London: Fontana Press.

Laws, G. (1997) 'Spatiality and age relations'. In A. Jamieson, S. Harper, & C. Victor (Eds.), *Critical approaches to ageing and later life.* (pp. 90–101). Buckingham, UK: Open University Press.

McGrail, B., Percival, J., Foster, K. with Holland, C., & Peace, S. (2001). Integrated segregation? Issues from a range of housing/care environments. In S. Peace & C. Holland (Eds.), *Inclusive housing in an ageing society: Innovative approaches* (pp. 147–168). Bristol: Policy Press.

Peace, S. M., Kellaher, L. & Holland, C. (2003). Environment and identity in later life: A cross setting study, end of award report L480254011, Swindon, U.K.: Economic and Social Research Council.

Phillips, J., Bernard, M., Biggs, S., & Kingston, P. (2001). Retirement communities in Britain: A 'third way' for the third age? In S. Peace & C. Holland (Eds.), *Inclusive housing in an ageing society: Innovative approaches* (pp. 189–214). Bristol, UK: Policy Press.

Phillipson, C., Bernard, M., Phillips, J., & Ogg, J. (Eds.). (2001). *The family and community life of older people.* New York: Routledge.

Ratcliffe, P. (1999). Housing inequality and 'race': Some critical reflections on the concept of 'social exclusion.' *Ethnic and Social Studies, 22*(1), 1–22.

Rosser, C., & Harris, C. (1965). *The family and social change: A study of family kinship in a South Wales town.* London: Routledge & Keegan Paul.

Rowles, G. D. (1978). *Prisoners of space? Exploring the geographical experience of older people.* Boulder, CO: Westview Press.

Taylor, M., Barr, A., & West, A. (2000). *Signposts to community development* (2nd ed.). London: CDF Publications.

Taylor, R. B., & Brower, S. (1985). Home and near-home territories. In I. Altman & C. M. Werner (Eds.), *Home environments* (pp. 183–212). New York: Plenum Press.

Young, M., & Wilmott, P. (1957). *Family and kinship in East London.* Harmondsworth, UK: Penguin.

CHAPTER 15

Growing Older in Postwar Suburbs: The Meanings and Experiences of Home

Carole Després and Sébastien Lord

THE GRAYING OF THE POSTWAR SUBURBS

The suburbs—housing, streets, amenities, and residents—are aging. Analysis of 1996 Census data for the Quebec City metropolitan area reveals an astonishing portrait of this area that is very different from the young family neighborhood image typically associated with suburbia (Morin, Fortin, & Després, 2000). There are now more elders in the suburbs than in central neighborhoods of the city (Morin, 2002). By 1996, in the neighborhoods developed between 1950 and 1975, only 3 of every 10 dwelling units were inhabited by nuclear families; 40% of children were older than 18. There were no significant differences in these statistics among rented or owned dwellings, detached houses or apartments. One of every five residents was 60 or more years old; and of these, half had already reached their 70's.

The suburbs in the Quebec City metropolitan area were originally planned for young nuclear families with car-oriented lifestyles. Application of strict zoning regulations permitted large sectors of one-story detached houses (ranch houses or bungalows), cores of rental apartment buildings located along major arteries, and commercial strip malls. Today, most streets have no sidewalks, and public transportation is infrequent and inefficient. Schools and churches are closing, and sports facilities (for example, baseball fields) are underused or have not been adapted for an aging population.

To what extent will these suburbs fit older adults' eventual loss of functional autonomy and vehicular mobility?[1] Which architectural and urban transformations could help accommodate senior suburbanites' changing needs? How could governments, elected officials and policymakers support the adaptation of these suburbs? Before addressing these questions, it is necessary to consider elderly residents' needs and residential aspirations.

HOUSING ASPIRATIONS
OF SENIOR SUBURBAN HOMEOWNERS

As part of an extensive research and action program pertaining to the retrofitting of postwar suburbs (Fortin, Després, & Vachon, 2002), we conducted detailed in-person interviews with 56 homeowners, aged 65 to 82, living in the first ring of Quebec City's suburbs.[2] Slightly fewer than half were older than 75. Two thirds lived with their spouse, and among these, half were childless couples. Eight had at least one 25-year-old son or daughter living with them, whereas two lived with a tenant or boarder. Thirteen seniors, including 11 women, were living alone.

In general, these seniors were healthy, mobile, and socially integrated; they had a positive experience of home. When asked about future residential aspirations, the majority wanted to grow old in their present house (84%). Only severe loss of autonomy and health problems would make them consider moving. A minority of seniors was attracted to other housing arrangements. If required, most would choose a nursing home, preferably either in their neighborhood or in a more central district, as shown in Figure 15.1 (for more details, see Després & Lord, 2002).

To interpret this profound desire to age in place, we turned to the concept of "home." Beyond housing satisfaction and needs,

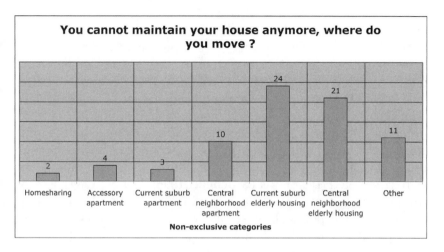

FIGURE 15.1   Residential preferences of elders if faced with the necessity of moving.

emotional meanings and past residential experiences may be a major factor accounting for seniors' attachment to suburban housing and lifestyle.[3] In the next section of this chapter, the dimensions of the meaning and experience of home are first presented, followed by a discussion of seven specific dimensions that help understand the high priority that these suburban elders put on aging in place.

THE CONCEPT OF HOME

Since a literature review published by Després (1991) over a decade ago, an extensive literature (articles, books, and collections of essays) has developed on home (e.g., Benjamin, Stea, & Saile, 1995; Birdwell-Pheasant & Lawrence-Zuniga, 1999; Chapman & Hockey, 1999; Marcus, 1995). It is not our intention to proceed with an exhaustive review of this material in this chapter. Rather, we will use the research conducted at the École d'architecture of Université Laval in Québec City in the last 10 years to present a perspective on this concept.

From 1992 to 1996, we studied a turn-of-the-century neighborhood of Quebec City. The dominant housing type was the terraced

apartment house called a triplex (Figure 15.2). We purposely explored dimensions of the meaning and experience of home, which,
at the time, were underreported. First, specific attention was given
to the *neighborhood scale* in order to overcome a dominant emphasis
on the dwelling unit (Després & Larochelle, 1997). Second, to better
understand the influence of time in the experience of home, specific
attention was paid to *residential biography* and residents' *length of
residence* (Després & Larochelle, 1998). Third, to evaluate the influence of the built environment on the experience of home, in-depth
urban and architectural analyses of *housing type* and *urban form*
were completed (Després & Larochelle, 1996; Vachon, 1994). Finally,
we took into account the influence of *cultural norms* by looking at
the ideological, political, legal, and economic contexts that gave
birth to the neighborhood and its housing, and how they evolved.
Specific attention was paid to the evolution of advertisements for
housing and municipal housing regulations, from 1909 to 1992 (Després & Larochelle, 1998; Vachon, 1994).

Differences in relationship with the dwelling and to the neighborhood were found among three generations of residents: the *pioneers*,
who moved into the neighborhood while it was under construction
in the 1920s, 1930s, and 1940s; the *resistance*, who moved in during
the suburban expansion in the 1950s and 1960s (while inner-city
neighborhoods were in decay); and the *urbanites* who selected the
neighborhood after 1975, after government revitalization programs
were created. Attachments to the neighborhood differed greatly:
older people were attached to their parish; the middle generation,
to their neighborhood; the new generation, to the broader city.
Residential biographies added another fundamental dimension in
understanding differences and similarities in experiences of home.
Family roots, networking, and support in the neighborhood played
an essential role in defining people's emotions toward their home.
In relation to the urban and architectural typology, all residents
were fond of the urban lifestyle associated with their specific block
pattern, streetscape, and triplex type. The large individual balconies
providing the façades of the apartment houses were still used by
the younger generation of residents for sitting and relaxation, and
appreciated as a way to take part in the neighborhood's street anima-
tion and urban life.

Following this study, we embarked on a broad research and
action program aimed at retrofitting postwar suburbs. The bungalow

FIGURE 15.2   Typical street and triplex buildings in turn-of-the-century neighborhood of Quebec city.

(or ranch-style house) is the housing type that replaced, chronologically, the terrace flat apartment house described previously during the economic boom that followed World War II (see Figure 15.3). Several residents of terrace flat houses remembered the suburban exodus, during the 1950s, of local landlords, shop owners, professionals, and the upper-middle class.

The first survey was conducted by Thierry Ramadier, and consisted of 63 homeowners in Duberger, a postwar suburb of Quebec City. Again, the influence of *length of residence* and *personal biographies* was investigated in relationship with people's representations of the city, the suburb, and of their neighborhood, this time using mental mapping as the main survey tool. Two generations of suburban dwellers were interviewed: (1) pioneers, who had been living an average of 34 years in their neighborhood; and (2) more recent dwellers, who had been in their neighborhood for an average of 12 years (Ramadier, 2002; Ramadier & Fortin, 2004). Both groups shared the symbolic meanings associated with the presence of nature, greenery, and mature trees in their neighborhood, as well as an appreciation of the quietness, calm, and social peace of their suburban setting. Several respondents, even among the youngest residents, had a network of family and friends living close by, or at least knew acquaintances they enjoyed as good neighbors.

Beyond the similarities between the two groups, more recent dwellers saw the functional character of their neighborhood as something more important than did the pioneers. The central location of their suburb in relation to the larger metropolitan area and its accessibility from and to major arteries, highways, and employment cores were often mentioned. The meanings and experiences of the house and of the neighborhood were influenced by the homeowners' vehicular mobility in the metropolitan area (Richer, 1999). Although the meanings of home for the older generation of residents had to do with anchoring and identity, those of the younger generation seemed more influenced by the physical (functional) and geographical characteristics of their setting. Accessibility and mobility were important dimensions of a positive experience of home (Bénali, 2000). The location of the house was part of a strategy to reconcile work, family life, and leisure. Even though the architectural form and style of the bungalow did not necessarily fit younger residents' image of a dream house, its location provided them with a central

FIGURE 15.3   Typical low-density suburban street and bungalow house in Quebec City.

and accessible location, as well as with a calm, green, and physically mature community.

Following this first survey, we conducted 173 interviews with bungalow homeowners. Among these were 56 seniors whose responses will be examined in the next section. Two analyses, building on Ramadier's insights, were completed to explore our previous findings in more depth. In the first analysis, suburbanites' social and spatial representation of the city and the suburb were studied in relationship to the concept of settlement-identity (Brais & Luka, 2002; Luka, 2001).[4] In the second, a typology of mobility patterns was defined and examined in relation to residents' social life and community involvement (Daris, 2002, 2003).

Once again, people's experiences and emotions toward home were very much related to their *residential biography* and *length of residence* in the neighborhood. Luka (2001) compared the discourses of 18 respondents of a noncentral suburb with 18 others living in two suburbs that possessed continuity with the historical district and inner-city neighborhoods. Even though most respondents appreciated the quiet, pleasant, and green character of their neighborhood, their perception of city life and setting differed. Luka identified a multiplicity of settlement-identities among suburbanites, identities located on a continuum between urban and rural: Some residents were identified as urban-oriented suburbanites, whereas others were more rural-oriented. Individuals' residential biographies are very important to understanding their identity. Indeed, although some older respondents had moved from the countryside to the suburbs in the 1950s, others had left crowded and underserviced inner-city neighborhoods. For the former, the suburban location is the ultimate compromise to not living in the country; for the latter, it is the compromise to not living in the city. This can be useful for understanding seniors' openness to moving closer to a more central neighborhood.

In her analysis of the typical weekday mobility itinerary of 95 residents living in two postwar suburbs, Daris (2002) identified different types of suburbanites according to their mobility patterns and orientation toward community. Her research emphasizes that *vehicular mobility* and the use of the larger metropolitan area by residents should not be overlooked while trying to understand the meanings and experiences of home in contemporary suburban living. According to Daris (2002), *cosmopolitan* persons, who have geographically spread out social relations and actions, display a more generic kind of attachment toward their neighborhood. On the other hand, *localist* residents find most of their social and functional needs satisfied in their neighborhood, and consider their local community as the locus of irreplaceable resources.

From our ongoing research, we have identified 29 dimensions of the meaning and experience of home, which we classified in more general categories: psychological, social, economic, material, temporal, and space-time dimensions (Table 15.1).

THE MEANINGS AND EXPERIENCES OF HOME OF SUBURBAN ELDERS

What does home mean for elders living in postwar suburbs? Seven dimensions of the meaning and experience of home, listed in italics

TABLE 15.1   Dimensions of the Meaning and Experience of Home Classified in Six General Categories

Home as . . .

Psychological dimensions	**Economic dimensions**	**Temporal dimensions**
Mirror of the self	Ownership	*Familiar setting*
Place to personalize	Financial investment	*Attachment and*
Personal control	Savings and	*memories*
Physical and psychological security	inheritance	**Space-time dimensions**
Physiological and phys-	Affordable housing	Anchor
ical comfort	**Material dimensions**	*Center of daily life*
Social dimensions	Network of urban	*Territory of mobility*
Locus of socialization	places	Settlement-identity
Privacy and refuge	Urban territory	Proximity and accessi-
Indicator of social status	Services and commercial facilities	bility
Desirable social composition	Nature and greenery	
Access to human resources	Housing type	
	Space around the house	
	Safety and universal accessibility	
	Personal belongings	

Table 15.1, were found to be of particular relevance, at both the house and neighborhood scales, to interpreting senior suburbanites' aspirations to remain in place: (1) home as physical and psychological security, (2) home as locus of socialization, (3) home as indicator of social status, (4) home as familiar setting, (5) home as attachment and memories, (6) home as center of daily life, and (7) home as territory of mobility. Each of these dimensions is discussed below.

Home as Physical and Psychological Security

Home is a place where one feels secure, both psychologically and physically. This dimension of home is very important to an understanding of seniors' experiences of the suburbs. Security is understood in four major ways. First, security is *feeling protected from physical aggression*. In general, the suburbs are perceived as safer than the city. The fact that suburbs are low-density, quiet, homogeneous, and "have a good reputation" contributes to this perception of safety: "People have a good level of education . . . I don't know, it's part of living with civilized people, we feel safe. There're all quiet older people or else well-raised young people." Length of residence in the neighborhood also plays a major role: the neighborhood and the neighbors are well known; the presence of familiar people is reassuring: "I am used to living in this neighborhood; I have been here for 50 years, more than that . . . I know everybody; there is nothing to worry about." Although respondents have reported robberies, either in their house or in the dwelling of a close-by neighbor, they nonetheless feel safe in their house. Several own an alarm system: "I am not afraid; we have an alarm system." At night, however, the absence of good lighting contributes to people's feeling of insecurity, and influences their willingness to go out. For older women, the presence of a husband, or in one case, a dog, contributes to their feeling of security.

Second, security is *being protected from accidents and injuries*. Seniors are afraid of injuring themselves, which, in old age, may imply severe loss of autonomy and a long healing period. Because most suburban streets have no sidewalks, seniors feel less safe about walking because of cars driving by, often too fast: "Here it is a street that connects with all the others. It's terrible; people drive at 80 km/h." Wide and unmarked suburban crossroads are more difficult to cross with weakened legs, impaired hearing and poor vision. Interestingly, the few existing sidewalks are not considered fully appropriate because they constantly have changing elevations because of multiple driveways. In addition, the lack of lighting influences people's willingness to go out at night.

In winter, seniors feel less secure about going out by foot and by car; ice and heavy snowfalls are reasons to stay at home: "When it's slippery, I don't like that. When it rains and it's icy, I do not like to go out." However, driving is considered easier in suburbs compared to the city because "there is less traffic." For most respondents, taking the bus is not an option: the bus stop is too far, the waiting period too long and shelters too rare: "At my age, I can't take the bus anymore; I'm not enough mobile. To take the bus, it's complicated. It's far to take the bus. A long walk to go and a long one to come back." Moreover, the presence of young people has made several feel insecure. In crowded public places, seniors are afraid of being hurt: "In the Old City, there're all kinds of people, you get pushed and shoved around."

In the house, respondents feel well-protected from injuries. The one-level floor plan of the bungalow makes it fully accessible with no stairs to get into or out of the house or to access bedrooms; trips to the basement are occasional and not a necessity. Some respondents have had their house modified with special technology to improve their autonomy and mobility. Moreover, they are confident their house is well-maintained: "I know my house. I built it myself. I know the electrical system, the heating, the plumbing, the roof . . . I am not worried."

Third, the feeling of security is enhanced by the *ability to reach out for help*. This is very much related to respondents' health. Seniors living with a husband or wife know that they can count on each other for help. The presence of neighbors, friends, or family close by comes next as a source of confidence. To be known in one's neighborhood is reassuring: "If something was to happen to me, there's always somebody around on whom I could count." Informally, people care and watch over each other. A few respondents' houses are connected with their Local Center for Community Health through telecare equipment: "I had an alarm system installed even though I don't use it." Having access to a car and a driver is also reassuring as most medical services are far away. The thought of losing this privilege is frightening to most seniors.

Finally, seniors' perception of security is linked to *home owner-ship*. Not only their status of homeowner, but also the fact that their mortgage is entirely paid-off makes people feel secure about their financial future. Keeping their bungalow is also considered an affordable housing option: "That's why we decided to stay; it does not cost more than buying elsewhere. . . . It's still the place where it cost the least to live." Taxes and maintenance fees are low compared to what a rental apartment or an apartment in an elder housing complex would cost on a monthly basis.

Home As Locus of Socialization

For several respondents, the house has become the locus of their socialization. If they don't go out as much, for reasons discussed previously, they entertain at home. The house gave them the opportunities to have their children, grandchildren, relatives, as well as friends and neighbors visit:

> That's why I don't want to move into a seniors' home: we can't have people over as we wish.

> I can have people over here; we can eat outside, nobody bothers us.

> We have a nice yard, we have flowers; our grandchildren play ball, run and build an ice castle in it in winter.

Staying in a bungalow also permits the possibility of having company over for various lengths of time, as often as wanted; it is the freedom to entertain when and how one wants. The elders like the possibility of having their children and grandchildren stay overnight when visiting. Some have even kept the original bedrooms intact for this purpose. Most seniors do not consider their bungalow as too spacious. On the contrary, all the rooms are used either on a daily basis or for special occasions, even if only a couple of times a year, such as at Christmas or for birthdays:

> When the children are home, we have three televisions . . . they get videotapes for the young ones to watch them in the basement. All rooms are occupied.

There is a room for all of our children when they come to visit us, if we are too many, some sleep in the basement, it is heated.

The house as the center of socialization questions the belief that elders, because they go out less frequently, are isolated and do not socialize much. Moreover, telecommunications keep seniors in touch with outside life. They have regular, if not daily, telephone conversations with children, friends or relatives: "Our children (. . .) often call to ask how we're doing."

Home As Indicator of Social Status

The house and the neighborhood reflect in large part the past residential and personal choices of seniors: "I always dreamed of owning a house." or "We were not happy in an apartment with a lease; always obligated to ask for heating . . . we were not at ease, we were anxious to become owners." Maintaining homeownership not only reflects enduring values and lifestyle, it contributes to seniors' positive self-image, preserving their social status as autonomous and independent persons. Breaking up with one's house is acquiring the status of a socially dependent person: "I hope to stay healthy longer . . . to be autonomous. My spouse thinks the same way. We hope one day, we will just fall off of our chair and that will be it."

Ownership of a detached house in a low-density neighborhood—the American dream—is a source of pride associated with status in society. It is very much linked, in older suburbanites' discourse, to the expression of identity, values, and tastes. It has to do not only with the house itself but also with the type of neighborhood in which it is located. Some seniors refer to it as belonging to a privileged social class: "I would not want to live with—I don't want to seem pretentious—cheap people; here, all people are like us, well-off people."

Home As a Familiar Setting

The familiarity of seniors with the house, the neighborhood, and a network of regularly used roads and places is another crucial dimension of their positive experience of home. Most of our respondents (43 of 56) have been in their current house for more than 30 years:

"If I had to leave, I think that I would be very sad. I feel good here; I am used to this place."

At the urban scale, they are familiar with the street network and with the location of services and commercial facilities. They know where to go without having to think too much. Beyond their familiarity with the physical setting, they have established, over the years, a social network of merchants and clerks (in restaurants, banks, groceries, dry cleaning, post offices, etc.), as well as neighbors who, for the most part, have not moved: "Everybody knows me, I know everybody."

At the scale of the house, familiarity with the rooms, domestic objects, and personal possessions is seen as very positive: "It is my house, my furniture, my things. I have been here for 46 years." Older residents know where things are and how to move about, which contributes to staying active in and around the house. Holding on to their bungalow is thus maintaining not only their social and physical environment but also their daily habits and routines.

With the acuity of the senses diminishing in old age, as well as cognitive deficits (including memory loss) as a predictable source of loss of autonomy, it is easy to understand that maintaining seniors' routines, social networks and physical surroundings can contribute positively to their feeling of comfort and security. In fact, several seniors question their capacity to adapt to a new residential environment. Instead, they show tenacity and a remarkable capability to adapt and hold on to their home despite autonomy problems:

> We'd like to keep our things, our habits, our neighbors . . . as long as we can keep a fairly good quality of life in our house. Taking into account our weakness, our age, our diminishing health and capacities, we would still like to stay here.

Home As Attachment and Memories

Senior suburbanites are very much attached to their home:

> I never felt like moving. I feel comfortable here; my life is and has been here and I will continue it as long as possible. When I can't anymore; I'll sell it or give it away.

The number of decades spent in the house and in the neighborhood is very much related to emotional attachment to their physical as well as to their social environments: "Next year, we'll have lived here for forty years. . . . You get used to a neighborhood; it would be difficult to leave." Because most residents bought their houses in the 1950s and 1960s, they have developed friendly relations with their neighbors and have grown old with them.

The respondents' residential biographies help us understand their attachment. Slightly more than half had their house built or purchased it new. A large number had selected their neighborhood in continuity with their former residential experience: for some, a member of their household had grown up in the neighborhood; for others, the house belonged to a member of their family; finally, several had rented an apartment in their current neighborhood or close by before buying their house:

One of my brothers lived on the next street.

This house belonged to a relative; one of my aunts lived here. It is an inheritance.

We had a house in the same neighborhood. When we went from seven to two people in the family, I sold the other house and moved here.

After 30 to 40 years of residency, the house has become a witness to important steps in the family life cycle, to memorable events, to economic sacrifices, and physical efforts to maintain and improve it: "We've been here 46 years, a house filled with memories, built for us and that we love" or "I worked 20 years at night, two jobs to own a house." It has become, along the years, a museum for the family patrimony, a safe for meaningful possessions. The house is also seen as a financial investment that is finally starting to pay off. It was an early desire for most respondents to have a house free of mortgage for their old age:

We liked the idea to be stable, to become homeowners, to have our own house to raise our children.

It's a security, a possession that we have kept despite everything, and that we find again at the end of our lives. We have a house that we have well-maintained, and as such, we have recouped our investment.

Home As Center of Daily Life

Growing older often means a reduction in the scale of the environment used outside the house. Obstacles (physical, climatic, and psychological) between the house and urban places beyond its threshold can limit seniors' mobility: "With my legs, I have problems. I can still get around but only to a certain point." Moreover, retiring often means more time in the house for domestic activities that are completed at a slower pace. This reduction in home range is not necessarily perceived as negative: "We are both very busy. We would not have time to work outside the house anymore. That is why we stay here. If it was not like that, it would kill us."

For several seniors, maintaining a house is seen as a way to stay active and healthy:

> You know, you have to keep moving . . . because, for sure, the old age will get the better of you. Maintaining a house has its inconveniences but the more you move, the better it is.

However, they are aware that moving around the dwelling is becoming harder every year, as the following quote from the same respondent exemplifies: "I feel it is harder and harder to accomplish all there is to do, but we will keep up the efforts for a while. When we can't anymore . . . we'll see."

Daily activities, routines and leisure occur more around the house; its use is thus maximized:

> I feel like staying alone in my house for a while. Alone, you know, to really take advantage of my house. When you have somebody, you always pick up, cook for others. Alone, I feel really good. I am a lucky woman: 82 years old, healthy and able to drive.

> When I stopped working, that's what we wanted: be at home, take care and enjoy our things.

> I have my workshop downstairs and lots of things.

As discussed earlier, seniors' sensory and cognitive acuity is or will eventually be diminished. With the help of a familiar environment and established routines, the probability that they can remain autonomous is thus much higher than if they were to relocate.

For about half of the respondents gardening was a significant leisure activity:

> We have a little garden in the backyard, we mow the lawn, trim our cedar hedge; it keeps us busy and improves the house.

> I have a vegetable garden that I maintain even though I have somebody cut the grass for me. I weed the garden everyday for an hour or more; that's a real job.

Some have had to give up gardening because of physical limitations: "Maintaining the garden is becoming a burden. I did that for years. In summer, I was never bored." Reading, television, card-playing, crossword puzzles, knitting, and painting are the most often mentioned indoor leisure activities.

At the scale of the neighborhood, seniors talk about their dances, bowling, or card games. If we exclude shopping activities, going outside the neighborhood for leisure is rare. It is reserved for cultural activities such as concerts, plays, or else for those who have a cabin or a seasonal house to visit.

Seniors are much more mobile when it comes to shopping. Shopping is not the only reason to go to the mall. It is often an opportunity to go out with friends or to meet with them: "I go to the Carrefour [shopping mall]; I meet with the older gang; I chat with a couple of them. I go around eight and I come back around ten."

Home As Territory of Mobility

Although the majority of older suburbanites are less mobile than their younger counterparts, most use their car on a daily basis and enjoy it. The majority have developed strategies to drive after or before rush hour on known routes and several avoid busy highways. Most undertake at least one outing a day to run errands. Some are quite mobile. Others prefer to shop near their houses, but complain about the lack of commercial facilities or the closure of local stores (groceries, hardware store) and their relocation to large malls and big-box retailing facilities. Driving to these facilities is seen by some seniors as stressful and tiring: it often requires the use of highways as well as a lot of walking from the parking lot to the store and in the store itself: "I don't drive so far . . . I don't like large boulevards. At my age, I find that dangerous."

Faced with the thought of losing their driver's license, most respondents foresee a drama: "Losing my drivers' license, I can't imagine that. It would be like having my two legs cut off." Losing their license could radically modify their routines. They would have to depend on their children, relatives, friends, and neighbors, or use taxis. Several older women already depend on their husbands for mobility: "I go by foot; my husband takes the car." Some of the older women living alone are already experiencing this situation. They can spend entire days without going out. However, they do not seem to suffer. They count on their children, friends, or acquaintances to visit them, and run errands for or with them. Some live alone without an automobile: "I do not own a car anymore; I sold it to my son . . . My son runs my errands." Using public transportation, or the thought of using it, makes most seniors feel vulnerable or tired. Only four seniors in our sample use the bus services and most others consider this transportation option their least favorite. Taxis are favored over buses when seniors cannot drive or if a ride is not available from relatives or acquaintances.

CONCLUSIONS: ADAPTING POSTWAR SUBURBS?

Older suburbanites' experiences of housing and neighborhood help understand their aspirations to grow older at home. Several meanings of home identified for various populations and in different social contexts are reinforced by a larger concentration of activities in and around the house and, often, by reduced mobility. The feeling of security and familiarity toward the residential setting, the socially respected homeowner status, and the freedom to travel about the entire urban territory are important dimensions of seniors' positive experience of home. As long as they are healthy and mobile, as is the case for the majority of seniors, problems remain minor. In the next 15 to 20 years, however, the loss of autonomy and the incapacity to drive for a large proportion of older residents could seriously affect their experience of home. Could the retrofitting of postwar suburbs facilitate a positive experience of home? How can suburban layouts, originally conceived for cars, be modified to accommodate less independent and less mobile elders? Several avenues emerged from extensive consultation about the future of Quebec City suburbs, coordinated by the Interdisciplinary Research Group on Suburbs (GIRBa, in French; e.g., Després & Lord, 2002; Vachon & Després, 2002).[5] They are presented in relationship with the seven critical dimensions of the meaning of home for elderly discussed in the previous section.

One important dimension of seniors' positive experience of home is the feeling of *physical and psychological safety.* In Quebec City suburbs, the repairing over the next 10 to 15 years of streets built in the 1950s and 1960s offers several possibilities: street pavement width, currently between 10 to 15 meters, can be reduced for safer pedestrian crossing; sidewalks and appropriate lighting, added to provide a clear distinction between pedestrians and cars and safer walking; rest areas and shade trees, inserted for comfort at regular intervals on streets; and emergency phones, installed for increased safety. Finally, pedestrian crossings should be clearly marked on pavement and streetlights added for the visually impaired.

To respect seniors' *attachment* to and desire to grow older in their house, neighborhood, and community, services that could contribute to increasing their autonomy and independence need to be put in place. Our interviews have revealed that Quebec's elders are either not well-informed about home-care services available to them or have a negative perception of them. People taking care of older relatives, friends, or neighbors often have difficulties locating all the support they need for dependent elders. In this respect, small-scale homecare centers, centrally located for high visibility and easy access, should be favored over larger establishments and should be allowed by zoning regulations in residential sectors. Municipalities could provide strategically located pieces of land for this purpose, for instance, an underused recreational field or school.

Zoning regulations also need to be modified to allow for the addition of accessory apartments to single-family houses. Our experience has taught us that, in 9 cases out of 10, this type of apartment is planned to house a child, a close relative, or, to a lesser extent, a nurse or a tenant. It provides elders with help and increased security. Finally, to serve elders suffering from more severe loss of autonomy, suburban nursing homes should be allowed by zoning regulations in single-family residential sectors to respect seniors' desire to remain within a familiar social and physical environment.

Home is the *center of daily life*; it is even more so for seniors spending more time in and around the house. Because the rooms of most suburban houses built in the 1950s and 1960s are frequently on only one floor, it is easier for residents with reduced mobility to maintain their daily routine and to adapt their homes for wheelchair accessibility. At the neighborhood scale, the development and consolidation of small community nodes should be encouraged to provide services and commercial activities within walking distance of the residents. At the urban scale, innovative public transportation should be further developed to maintain seniors' access to more distant commercial and cultural facilities.

In many cases, allowing older residents to remain in their house is a way to maintain home as the *locus of socialization*. Being able to entertain with children and grandchildren and to have them sleep over on special occasions constitutes an important part of respondents' socialization. In this respect, apartments and rooms in senior housing should be planned to accommodate comfortable socialization with family and friends. Accessory apartments, as discussed previously, should be encouraged to favor intergenerational exchanges. The addition of senior and homecare centers could provide less autonomous residents with occasions to mingle with younger retirees. Finally, well-located and small-scale public places and commercial nodes would offer opportunities for socialization with friends and neighbors. Zoning regulations should allow for all the above proposals.

Remaining a homeowner is often an indicator of *social status* for older suburbanites. Not only is homeownership socially and financially enviable, it also projects an image of independence and autonomy. For instance, an 80-year-old woman living alone in her house is looked at with respect while a senior moving out to an elder-care facility is perceived as fragile and weak. This being said, if all homeowners were thinking about selling their house in the near future, there would be an insufficient number of young buyers, on the one hand, and a paucity of specialized housing for seniors, on the other hand. It is thus to everybody's advantage to keep suburban homeowners in their houses. This is also often the least expensive housing solution as most seniors have already repaid their mortgage. Even though this is not the first motivation to remain in their house, the fact that homeownership is cheaper than specialized seniors' facilities is acknowledged. Even the entire cost of building a new accessory apartment would cover only 3 to 5 years of rent in an elderly home. Consequently, grant programs should be developed and fiscal advantages offered to encourage and facilitate the adaptation of houses to seniors' needs and the addition of accessory apartments.

Finally, as previously noted, home is a *territory of mobility*, providing the possibility for most senior suburbanites to use their car to travel as they please in the metropolitan area. In most suburbs, concentrations of single-family houses and of commercial activity are located far from each other and linked by highways and commercial strips. Several strategies could help lower car dependency. First, the permeability of the street network needs to be increased to reduce walking distances from one destination to the other; this could be done by inserting pedestrian paths or new street segments where possible, in the middle of blocks. Second, public transportation has to be adapted to elders: routes and frequencies should go beyond the dominating city–suburb bus routes and rush-hour services; the number of universally accessible buses needs to be increased; additional transit stops and shelters with seating, emergency phones, and lighting should be added; services such as a "taxibus" to bring elders to the nearest transit stop need to be developed. Finally, zoning regulations could allow commercial uses on strategic streets in single-family neighborhoods to help elders reduce their dependence on their car.

Helping to implement these urban and architectural solutions is our next challenge! This is a task that will require transdisciplinary collaboration.

NOTES

1. The province of Quebec's Ministry of Health and Social Services predicts that the demand for elder care and services will greatly increase by 2011. Already, the waiting lists for certain services are long. Even though homecare is being promoted, financing, staff, and technical support are lacking. In the geographical context of suburbs, implementing and rationalizing homecare is made even more difficult because the travel distances between clients are greater than those in urban neighborhoods.

2. A significant number of suburbanites were between 55 and 64 years old; their discourses will be analyzed in the context of Sébastien Lord's upcoming doctoral dissertation.

3. In is particularly important to consider the higher life expectancy of women compared to that of men (81 compared with 75 years) (ministère de la Santé et des Services sociaux du Québec, 2000). In 1996, in the province of Quebec, 63% of women aged 65 years old or more lived alone compared with only 27% of men. For those over 80 years of age, this percentage climbs to 86% (Milette, 2000).

4. The city/suburb distinction has been well documented in the work of Roberta Feldman (1990, 1996) at the University of Illinois in Chicago.

5. Because we are writing from an architect's and planner's perspective, we will focus on architectural and urban proposals although community-based initiatives are as important in a global support system aiming at increasing elders' ability to stay in their houses and communities as long as possible.

REFERENCES

Benali, K. (2000). *Les représentations spatiales et l'attachement du quartier chez les résidants de Duberger* (Spatial representations and neighborhood attachment of Duberger residents). Essai en design urbain. École d'architecture, Université Laval, Quebec, Canada.

Benjamin, D. N., Stea, D., & Saile, D. (Eds.). (1995). *The home: Words, interpretations, meanings and environments.* Abington, UK: Avebury.

Birdwell-Pheasant, D., & Lawrence-Zuniga, D. (Eds.). (1999). *House life: Space, place and family in Europe.* Oxford, UK: Berg.

Brais, N., & Luka, N. (2002). De la ville à la banlieue, de la banlieue à la ville: Des représentations en évolution (From city to suburbs, from suburbs to city: Representations in evolution). In A. Fortin, C. Despres, & G. Vachon (Eds.), *La banlieue revisitée* (Suburbia revisited) (pp. 151–180). Quebec, Canada: Nota Bene.

Chapman, T., & Hockey, J. (Eds.). (1999). *Ideal homes: Social changes and domestic life.* London: Routledge.

Daris, A. (2003). *Une perspective sociale des comportements de mobilité des résidants des banlieues anciennes de la région de Québec* (A social perspective on older suburbs' residents mobility). Master's thesis, Université Laval, Quebec, Canada.

Daris, A. (2002). Mobilité et vie sociale: Entre le quartier et l'ailleurs (Mobility and social life: The neighborhood and the larger community). In A. Fortin, C. Desperes, & G. Vachon (Eds.), *La banlieue revisitée* (Suburbia revisited) (pp. 213–232). Quebec, Canada: Nota Bene.

Després, C. (1991). The meaning of home: Literature review and directions for future research and theoretical development *Journal of Architectural and Planning Research, 8*(2), 96–115.

Després, C., & Larochelle, P. (1996). Modernity and tradition in making of terrace flats in Québec City. *Environments by Design, 1*(2), 36–49.

Després, C., & Larochelle, P. (1997,July). Le rapport à la rue des résidants du Vieux-Limoilou (The relation to the street of Old-Limoilou residents). In B. Krantz & D. Vestbro (Eds.), *Evolving environmental ideals, changing ways of life, values and design practice* (pp. 412–427). Proceedings of the 14th IAPS Conference: Stockholm, Sweden.

Després, C., & Larochelle, P. (1998). L'influence des trajectoires résidentielles et des normes culturelles d'habitat sur les significations et les usages du Vieux-Limoilou. (The influence of residential biography and housing cultural norms on the meanings and uses of Old Limoilou). In Y. Grafmeyer & F. Dansereau (Eds.), *Trajectoires familiales et espaces de vie en milieu urbain* (Family biographies and life spaces in urban settings) (pp. 43–71). Lyon, France: Presses universitaires de Lyon.

Després, C., & Lord, S. (2002). Vieillir en banlieue. (Aging in the suburbs). In A. Fortin, C. Despres, & G. Vachon (Eds,), *La banlieue revisitée* (Suburbia revisited) (pp. 233–258). Quebec, Canada: Nota Bene.

Feldman, R. (1990). Settlement-identity: Psychological bonds with home places in a mobile society. *Environment and Behavior, 22*, 183–229.

Feldman, R. (1996). Constancy and change in attachments to types of settlements. *Environment and Behavior, 28*, 419–445.

Fortin, A., Després, C., & Vachon, G. (Eds.). (2002). *La banlieue revisitée* (Suburbia revisited). Quebec, Canada: Nota Bene.

Luka, N. (2001). *Suburbia revisited: Images and meanings of postwar suburbs in the Quebec City metropolitan region.* Master's thesis, Université Laval, Quebec, Canada.

Marcus C. C. (1995). *House as mirror of self.* Berkeley, CA: University of California Press.

Milette, C. (1999). *Bien vivre avec son age: revue de literature sur la promotion de la sante des personnes agees* (Live well while aging: Literature review on elderly health promotion). Quebec, Canada: Ministere de la Sante et des services sociaux du Quebec, Direction generale de la sante publique.

Ministere de la Sante et des services sociaux du Quebec. (2000). *Sante au Quebec: Quelques indicateurs* (Health in the province of Quebec: Some indicators). Quebec, Canada: Ministere de la Sante et des services sociaux du Quebec.

Morin, D. (2002). Les banlieusards et les temps changent. (Suburbanites and times are changing). In A. Fortin et al. (Dir.), *La banlieue revisitée* (Suburbia revisited) (pp. 73–122). Quebec, Canada: Nota Bene.

Morin, D., Fortin, A., & Despres, C. (2000). À des lieux du stéréotype du banlieusard: Les banlieues de Québec des années 1950 et 1960 (Miles away from the suburban stereotypes: Quebec City's 1950 and 1960 suburbs). *Les Cahiers de Démographie, 29*, 335–356.

Ramadier, T. (2002). Centralité et banlieue depuis le quartier Duberger. In A. Fortin, C. Despres, & G. Vachon (Eds.), *La banlieue revisitée* (Suburbia revisited) (pp. 213–232). Quebec, Canada: Nota Bene.

Ramadier, T., & Despres, C. (2004). Le territoire de la mobilite et les representations d'une banlieue vieillissante de Quebec (The territory of mobility and representations of an aging suburb in Quebec City). *Reserches sociogaphiques.* 45(3), 521–548.

Richer, J. (1999). *La mobilité des résidants de Duberger* (The mobility of Duberger residents). Essay in urban design. École d'architecture, Université Laval, Quebec, Canada.

Vachon, G. (1994). *Histoire, développement et forme du quartier Limoilou à Québec.* (History, development and form of limouilou neighborhood of Quebec.) Mémoire de maîtrise (Master Thesis), Université Laval, Quebec, Canada.

Vachon, G., & Despres, C. (2002). Réaménager le territoire des banlieues: Propositions urbaines et architecturales. (Retrofitting postwar suburbs: Urban and architectural proposals). In A. Fortin, C. Despres, & G. Vachon (Eds.), *La banlieue revisitée* (Suburbia revisited) (pp. 259–286). Quebec, Canada: Nota Bene.

PART VI

Leaving Home: Commentaries

CHAPTER 16

On Using "Home" and "Place"

Amos Rapoport

I suspect that I have been asked to write this brief commentary in the role of a devil's advocate, probably because of my criticisms of the terms "home" (Rapoport, 1995b) and "place" (Rapoport, 1994a). I will, therefore, not deal with other aspects of the book. I will emphasize "home" because it plays a more important role and appears in the title. Because the two articles are contemporaneous and parallel, what I say also applies to "place" (which is a primary theme in this book).

On the (reasonable) assumption that not everyone will rush out and read the two articles, I begin by summarizing the most important criticisms.

1. It is important to use clear and unambiguous concepts; "home" and "place" are not unambiguous.

2. Even when attempts are made to clarify these terms, they remain extremely vague, ambiguous, unclear, and used in many, and inconsistent ways.

3. Terms must be usable and operational.

4. The usage of the terms does not go much beyond popular use.

5. The terms are highly subjective and emotive.

6. "Home" is meant to go beyond "dwelling," yet is often used as a synonym for "dwelling."

7. There is a circularity: "home" is often defined in terms of "meaning of home."

8. Physical aspects that might help design are often neglected.

9. There are well-established concepts in environment/behavior studies that can, and should be used; this helps in synthesis and theory building.

I will, therefore, first evaluate the book in terms of my earlier criticisms and, second, evaluate my criticisms in terms of this book, that is, over 10 years later. I will ask two questions: (1) Could the book have achieved its goals without the use of "home" "place?" and (2) Could it then have been better?

THE POPULAR/FOLK USAGE OF "HOME" AND "PLACE"

It needs to be admitted that it is often difficult to discuss certain topics without using these terms because they are so much a part of ordinary language. We thus say: "This is a nice place," "It's nice to be home again," "I like staying (or being) at home," "I'm going home tomorrow," "This is like no other place I know," and so on. This is probably why a 1991 series of advertisements for Smirnoff vodka is titled "Home is where you find it" and described as "a place where we feel comfortable . . . defined by family and friendship . . . where we find laughter and contentment." It concludes that "many of the places we find Smirnoff feel like home." Examples include a wedding and a bar (on the value of analyzing ads see Rapoport, 1990b). Note how close this is to many definitions used in the book.

A number of chapters emphasize the unconscious (or "automatic") use of "home." Thus, from chapter 3 it is clear that "home" has meaning for lay people. That meaning, or rather the different meanings that apply to dwelling, inner city, family need to be discovered. Similarly, from chapter 8, it is clear that for Alzheimer's patients the link with their dwellings when they were well is important.[1] As one would expect, they use the available folk term "home." In that sense the term is diagnostic—it draws attention to certain important points of people's relations with certain important settings.[2] It then becomes useful to analyze that use and its meanings, and the researcher's task it to clarify and operationalize these terms. That task is impossible if one merely uses the term, that is, there is a conflict between "folk" and scientific usage. Thus, rather than using everyday language one needs to develop a scientific research terminology—the public's use is only a starting point.

In research terms one needs to know, first how "selfhood" and "personhood" themselves can be analyzed (their attributes, roles, importance, etc.) and, second, how they are related to the dwelling, the situation, settings, furnishings (semifixed features) and other people (nonfixed features). Similarly, the important needs and wants for "safety, rootedness, harmony, joy, privacy, togetherness, recognition, order, control, possession, nourishment, initiative power and freedom" (chapter 8, this volume, p. 187). After dismantling and operationalizing these rather vague terms one needs to identify which attributes of environments elicit these feelings (in whom, under what circumstances or contexts, etc.), and hence underlie (or constitute) the folk usage of "home."

The point is made (chapter 1, this volume, p. 10) that " 'home' immediately captures popular imagination (as opposed to settings, 'house,' 'dwellings,' 'housing')" and that this makes it "highly potent for methodological purposes." I would argue, however, that is precisely what makes it unsuitable for research and theory building. Which of these positions is valid needs investigation.

Terms like "home" are part of what have been called "folk theories," and in science there has been discussion whether such theories can be "fixed" to become scientific theories, or whether they need to be replaced. In physics, folk theory was wrong and was replaced. In psychology there is an ongoing debate about this. In my view, scientific terms do not need to "capture the popular imagination" (chapter 1, this volume, p. 10). On the contrary—a scientific term needs the detachment and objectivity needed in research. Moreover, as I argued in my original criticism, scientific terms require clear operational definition and the precision and clarity needed to enable distinctions to be made among things (cf. Rapoport, 1990c). It follows that the lay use of "home" needs to be *interpreted*, analyzed systematically and rigorously across many groups to determine what underlies its use (and that of "place") and to identify its attributes.

In the 12 years since I first presented my criticisms, and the decade since publication, this has not been done. As I "predicted" then, and will try to show later, the use of "home" and "place" does *not* clarify; instead, it often leads to vague, romantic, and difficult-to-understand terms and passages. In Lakatos' terms this has proved a "degenerating research program" (Rapoport, 1990a Revised edition Epilogue, 1997a, 2000a).

THE USE OF "HOME" AND "PLACE" IN THIS BOOK

I now turn to the question of whether the book could have achieved its goals without the use of these terms, that is, whether their use adds anything. To answer this, I did what I have done previously for publications using semiotics (Rapoport, 1990a)—I have replaced every use of "home" *throughout the manuscript* with "dwelling," "residential environment," "habitation," "residential setting," and so on, and "place" with "setting," "locale," "milieu," "location," and so on. In most cases this proved quite easy, especially in those chapters that did not really rely on these terms (and, in many of which, significantly, "home" is frequently used with quotation marks), but it always proved possible to replace them.

I first give some "randomly" selected examples (from what would otherwise be another book length manuscript!) in which words in [ ] replace "home" and "place," and show that nothing is lost. I will then try to show that, in fact, something is gained.

Chapter 1, p. 9: "diversity of [settings]" is perfectly clear, and is an example of what I call the system of settings (Rapoport, 1990d, 2005) (which is also the case in many other chapters).

Chapter 2, p. 24–25: "The immediate [residential] environment is the primary living space in old age; both in terms of the time older people spend in [their dwelling] as well as the [settings] where many activities occur. It is a well-documented finding that aging coincides with a reduction in action range [corresponds to my "home range" in Rapoport (1977) and elsewhere], especially during very old age. . .-.Older people spend more time [in the dwelling]. . . . Observational data have also shown an age-related tendency for environmental centralization inside the [house (or "dwelling" if apartments are included)] especially around the most favored [settings in the dwelling]. These [settings] which can be found . . . typically [have certain attributes]" (these can be determined and listed; comfort, good views, and location are mentioned).

Chapter 2, p. 59: "most people do not consider their [dwellings] to be just space, but turn them into [settings] with personal significance."

Chapter 3, p. 47: "[Many elements, including the dwelling], [settings] therein and personal objects [have a mnemonic function and lead to culturally specific routinized behavior] (cf. Rapoport, 1990a).

In *Chapter 4*, not only is every use of "home" easily replaced by "dwelling" or, in some cases "setting," but in some cases people themselves use "house"!

Chapter 7, p. 145: "Nonphysical aspects of a residence represent what we call home as opposed to house. [A dwelling involves psychological responses of the residents and their affective relationships with friends, family, and kin, that is, it is a center of social networks.]" (Compare with original cited later regarding the negative effects of using "home").

Chapter 7, p. 149: "Aging brings with it a tendency for life to become more restricted to indoor activities. The [dwelling] as an everyday environment [becomes more important.]"

Chapter 8, p. 172: "[The dwelling] can play a dual role for people: [it is a particular physical setting that also communicates meanings related to] family, belonging, love, security, and personal identity [—i.e., it is intricately connected to human memory and emotion]."

Chapter 10, p. 219: The discussion of Africa does not need "home." In fact, the Tswana have 3 dwellings: city, village, and cattle station. Which is "home?" Which camp is "home" for nomads where mobility is critical and being settled destructive (Rapoport, 1978). If "home is where the heart is," how does this relate to the physical milieu or location? There are also problems in the case of cyclic migration, common in Africa (e.g., Weisner, cited in Rapoport, 1990a). In the conclusion "home" can be eliminated without losing any of the important ideas, such as the importance of kin and social networks, mobility, extended community, continuing social fields, and so on.[3]

Chapter 11, p. 230: "[The affective meaning (or evaluation) of the dwelling] reflects a complex interweaving."

Chapter 12, p. 251: "Nursing home" is less of a problem because it represents a well-known and described building type or type of living environment. This also applies to "funeral home."

Chapter 12, p. 254: "[A dwelling] allows us to control his or her environment and assures a sense of security. It offers freedom of action and expresses its residents' ideas and personal values . . . it is an indicator of social status. Finally, owning one's dwelling (in the original!) strengthens the sense of personal relationship to [it (or 'that dwelling')]."

In *Chapter 14*, "home" is used only nine times (excluding "residential care home" (= nursing home), which is a building type), and "place" is also used in relatively few places. In these few cases, "residential locus" or "residential setting" for "home," and "locale" or "setting" for "place" would do. In fact, neighborhood, community, setting, house, flat, bungalow, dwelling type, and location are all used in this chapter and in the title. On p. 301: "How are we to find out how the community/neighborhood environment influences the way older people feel about the [settings] and spaces in which they live?"

Chapter 15, p. 317: "The Meanings and Experiences of [habitation (or dwelling).]"

Chapter 15, p. 318: "In general these seniors . . . had a positive experience of their [residential settings]. When asked about future *residential aspirations* (!) the majority wanted to grow old in their present *house* (!) (84%). . . . A minority of seniors were attracted to other *housing arrangements* (!) (emphases added).

Chapter 15, p. 318: "Once again, people's experiences and emotions toward [their current residence (or dwelling)] were very much related to their *residential biography* and *length of residence* in the neighborhood."

Chapter 15, p. 325: "What does the [residential setting; habitation or dwelling] mean for elders living in postwar suburbs? Seven dimensions of the meaning and experience of home, listed in italics in Table 15.1, were found to be of particular relevance, at both the house and neighborhood scales, to interpreting senior suburbanites' aspirations to remain in place: [The residential settings (or dwelling)] (1) as [a provider of] physical and psychological security, (2) as locus of socialization, (3) as indicator of social status, (4) as familiar setting, (5) as attachment and memories, (6) as center of daily life, and (7) as [a] territory of mobility."

Now, more briefly, I show that the use of "home" (and "place") has negative consequences. The examples that follow show the confusion and vagueness I originally criticized. It also seems to me that those chapters that used "home" and "place" least were the most successful. For example, chapter 11 makes its points with a minimal use of "home" and it almost seems that the term is being used as a "Procrustes bed," the material being forced into it. I have already referred to chapter 14.

In *chapter 2*, p. 26, there is the same confusion I originally criticized. "Little is known about the meaning these elders were able to invest in their homes after these transitions, and how their meaning of home compared." There is a major gain in clarity by using "dwellings" for "home" and "the meanings those had for them" for "their meaning of home."

Chapter 1, p. 9: "These attempts have added two somewhat neglected aspects of home or place," which implies their equivalence and is confusing.

Chapter 3, p. 48: "Three questions provide a framework from which to consider self across disciplines: What comprises the self or how is self defined? What are the "essential" components of the self? And what are the ways in which the self is known and made known, the architecture of the "she" or "he," and the "I," the "me" and the "mine." I must admit that (1) I do not know what that means and (2) I fail to see how that helps improve living environments for the elderly.

Similarly, I find that I do not understand *chapter 8*, p. 191: "consolation [is] a kind of homecoming, the soul comes back to itself." Moreover, surely science has replaced ancient philosophy and this leads to the use of vague, emotive, and ontologically suspect and empirically intractable categories such as "soul," "higher self," and "narrated self"; to what seem to be just words: "disembodied," "displaced," "journey in self-realization," "coming home"; to mysticism and romanticism; it ultimately leads into the thickets of postmodernism, narrative, language theory, and other questionable directions away from scientific research.

There is a reluctance to turn mysteries into problems (to paraphrase Chomsky cited in Pinker, 1997, p. ix). There is also a neglect of the most recent research findings. One example is the neglect of the recent explosion of research in cognitive science, neuroscience, cognitive neuroscience, evolutionary psychology, and so on, which bears on memory and the self, for example, Dennett (1995, 2003), Pinker (1997, 2002), and the work of Gazzaniga among many others.

This mind-set also leads to the use of unexamined assumptions. Consider just one—the importance of "home." Thus, chapter 8, p. 192: "I feel at home when I can be myself" can happen in many (or any) settings: in a hotel room, a plane (immersed in a book), in a ship's cabin on the Amazon or in Patagonia, in a living room, soaking in a hot bath, in the country, by a glacier, on a mountain peak, in a forest or desert, and so on. The role of the dwelling (or any other setting) needs to be established, needs analysis and empirical and theoretical support. The question is: Which settings have which roles, how important a role, what kind of role, for whom? And so on.

In many chapters the "home" is asserted or presupposed, rather than established as existing or useful in research. Thus "the centrality of home in life experience (chapter 1, this volume, p. 12) assumes what needs to be proved before one can proceed. Thus, chapter 1, p. 15) "if experience of and emotional experience with home shapes the evolution of self." That is a big "if;" also, that "experience of home is associated with defining, maintaining, and recreating self-identity" needs to be demonstrated; it can be occupation, religion, group membership, locale, and so on and on. These are all assumptions or hypotheses as is the statement that home is the "center of our 'psyches' " (chapter 7, this volume, p. 145). For example, Margaret Mead in her autobiography *Blackberry Winter (1972)* makes the point that her base, center, and locus, which gave her a sense of continuity, her "point of centering" (chapter 1, this volume, p. 3) was her office at the American Museum of Natural History in New York.

Chapter 13, p. 280, defines "place attachments" to be "complex concepts that involve inseparable blends of affect, cognition and practices, physical settings, people and temporal qualities." Thus, in an otherwise useful chapter, we find that the use of "place" implies an inability to study or research: if one cannot dismantle one cannot study. But, in fact, one can always analyze and dismantle, and there is an immediate contradiction: Just listing the various components, in effect, begins the process of analysis and dismantling.

The most important negative impact of the use of "home" and "place," however, is on the possibility for unification, synthesis, and generalization and, above all, theory building—already the weakest part of Environment–Behavior Studies (EBS) (Rapoport, 1997a, 2000a). The fact that most chapters can be understood and interpreted in terms of more widely used EBS concepts means that such opportunities are lost. As one example, chapter 4 can be fully interpreted in terms of settings (the best developed concept in EBS) and their "furnishings" (i.e., semifixed features). This includes their mnemonic functions (Rapoport, 1990a, 2005). At the same time, meaning, as a most important function is neglected, as is the distinction between different levels of meanings and manifest and latent function. Meaning is added, as it were, rather than emerging "naturally" (Rapoport, 1990a, 2000a, 2005). The fact that there are different meanings—individual, group, cultural, as a result of "filters" (Rapoport, 2005, Fig. 19) is neglected, yet it bears on a number of other chapters that discuss a variety of subgroups of elders, that is, that age alone does not define groups. The whole argument can be expressed in terms of environments as organization of space, time, meaning, and communication, forming cultural landscapes consisting of systems of settings, and made up of fixed and semifixed features that communicate different levels of meaning. This would integrate chapters among themselves, with the EBS literature as a whole and with many other disciplines (Rapoport, 2000a, 2005). It would also help with building explanatory theory.

Such reinterpretation could be done for (almost) every chapter. Consider chapter 3, which is probably furthest from my position. It could be greatly clarified and integrated by using the recent cognitive science literature regarding memory, the "self" etc., and concepts such as dwelling, culture and its components and expressions (Rapoport, 2000b, 2005, Figs. 43–45), systems and systems of settings, activity systems, and so on and on. Nor is "language theory" (p. 51) needed. As for chapter 4 (another link) it is better to refer to settings and their semifixed features, which communicate meanings nonverbally (Rapoport, 1990a). Similarly for semiotics (chapter 8, this volume, p. 176). That people act in accordance with their interpretation of the situation is a key to the important mnemonic role of settings, and is a nonverbal communication process. Moreover, as already mentioned, like "home" semiotics can be eliminated, without loss, from much of the *useful* "semiotic" literature. Again, integration would be facilitated, not only with EBS, but with another discipline—cognitive science (through frame-script theory (Rapoport, 1990a, pp. 235–239).

CONCLUSIONS

In answering the questions posed at the outset, I conclude that neither "home" nor "place" are needed and the goals of this book could have been achieved, and achieved better, without their use. I had hoped that I could modify my original criticism and that these terms had been made operational and became useful. Unfortunately, that is not the case. None of my criticisms have been addressed, let alone answered, nor have the suggested alternatives been explored.[4] Overall, the terms do not provide a useful conceptual framework for the (useful and interesting) material of this book.

Three individual chapters (chapter 2, Figures 2.1 and 2.2 and Table 2.1; chapter 12, Figure 12.1 and chapter 15, Figure 15.3) begin to try and operationalize "home" explicitly, by dismantling, that is, trying to identify its attributes. *But it is not needed even then.* Thus, in chapter 2 (in the Table) "meanings of home" can be replaced by "attributes of environment" (neighborhood, dwelling, space, settings, etc.) and how these elicit particular affect, meaning, preference, and so on (see Figure 2.1). In chapter 15 (in Figure 15.3), "home" can be replaced by "dwelling" in column 1, and "places" by "settings" in column 2 (which is then equivalent to my "system of settings"). Thus, while dismantling (as usual) can be helpful, and these and other attempts are a way forward (especially if used in the same way, with the same dimensions/attributes by all), it would be even more useful to drop the terms.

In this book there is no attempt to do the same for "place." Such attempts have, however, been made by several doctoral students in architecture at the University of Wisconsin—Milwaukee, who explicitly tried to respond to my original criticisms. Thus, Imamoglu (2002) responds by defining "place" explicitly (p. ii) as "a socially constructed, purposive and meaningful living environment created by the integration of people, physical environment and program." This, however, is precisely how *settings* are defined! Imamoglu specifies that multiple settings are usually involved, but this has been discussed for many years now (Liu, 1994; references to LeCompte, Bechtel, etc., in Rapoport, 1977; cf. Rapoport, 1990d, 1994b, 2005). Finally, "place type" is not needed—building type, facility type, and so on, are more than adequate.

In an undated article written at the Department of Architecture, University of Wisconsin, Milwaukee ("Place, Narrative and Relationship: A New Approach to Place Attachment") related to his 1996 dissertation, Childress responds by trying to come to an "overarching" definition of "place" condensing the many explicit or implied definitions into 11 recurring themes, that is, deriving a list of attributes. Although potentially useful as an approach (and one I have often used) in none of these is "place" needed; "setting" seems adequate and, if not, many other terms are available: milieu, locale, location, and so on. As in this book, I was able easily to replace the term and also to show that clarity improved. The loss of possible consilience because of the wide use "setting" (possibly the best-developed concept in EBS) is major.

A recent item in the *New York Times* ("Metropolitan Diary," Feb. 16, 2004) describes what many of its advocates would regard as important about "place" by using one of my suggested terms— "location."The first paragraph of Maureen Kurtz's entry says: "Locations hold memories. I often pass the block on the West side of Broadway between 68th and 69th Streets. To most people this is a place [folk usage] without meaning. To me it is the magical location of the whale." In fact, a meaningless place is contrasted with a magical meaningful *location*!

A number of chapters (2, 7, 11, and 12 among others) discuss the shrinking of the home range with aging. Many years ago, in passing, Doxiadis suggested that at birth our environment is restricted to a bassinet, then expands, and often, with old age shrinks, once again, to a bed. An important qualification is that the maximum extent varies (with education, lifestyle, gender, income, etc., as well as age). This can be generalized in one diagram (Figure 16.1).

This can be related to my home range–territory model (Rapoport, 1977, Figure. 5.6), and also the embedding of the dwelling (as a system of settings) in the neighborhood and settlement (Rapoport, 2005, Figs. 7 and 8). More generally, the significance of settings beyond the dwelling, of neighborhood, settlement, and locale (discussed in many chapters) and of social networks can be discussed and understood in these terms (Rapoport, 1990d, 1997b, 2000b). These generalizations, made possible by the use of "standard" terms rather than "home" and "place" relate to the general theme of increasing criticality, whether with the shrinking home range and reduced competence of the elderly, of immigrants or other populations, for example, in conditions of rapid culture change, the importance of the residential environment settings increases (Rapoport, 1978, 1983a, 1983b). This, once again, helps to integrate many bodies of literature, domains of EBS and other disciplines, and to build theory. It also adds cultural, subcultural (group), lifestyle, health, income, and other variables to age in this case and in dealing with groups in all cases [and such groups tend to be *small* (cf. Pagel & Mace, 2004; Rapoport, 2000b, 2000c, 2005)].

This book provides important data, which can be interpreted in terms of the conceptual system described briefly, and combined with all of EBS and beyond (Rapoport, 1997a, 2000a, 2005). In my terms, the central message of this book is that various attributes of the environment are important generally, and especially for certain more vulnerable populations, including the elderly. In other words, in Environment Behavior Research generally environmental quality and human characteristics interact both through their effects and through choice (Rapoport, 1995, 2005). This will clearly play a role in any EBS explanatory theory and will be facilitated by dispensing with "home" and "place." This can be summarized in a diagram that I propose as an alternative to "home" and "place" (Figure 16.2).

A.   Dwellings are types of built environments and, as organizations of space, time, meaning, and communication they form parts

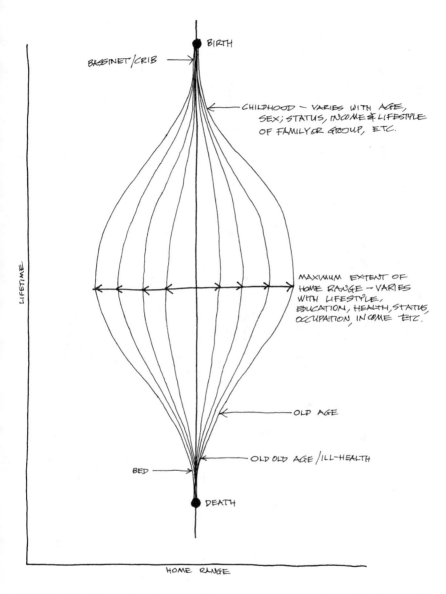

FIGURE 16.1   Generalized extent of home range incorporates shrinkage with old age and other attributes.

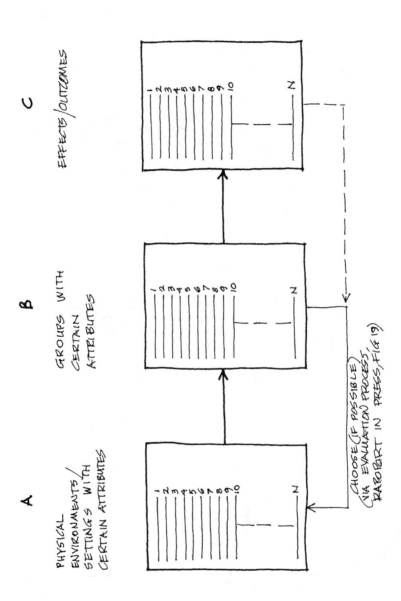

FIGURE 16.2   Alternative to use of "home" and "place."

356

of cultural landscapes (regions, cities, parts of cities, neighbor-hoods, towns, villages, etc.). These consist of systems of set-tings (within which systems of activities take place) and are composed of fixed and semifixed features. All of these can be identified and described, and can be characterized by certain attributes (or characteristics), using the general approach of dismantling (Rapoport, 1983c, 1992a, 1992b).[5]

B.   Certain groups prefer and chose these environmental attributes and, in any case are affected by them in various ways. These various effects depend on the attributes of these groups, and these can also be identified and listed. Multiple attributes define relevant groups, which tend to be *small* (cf. Pagel & Mace, 2004; Rapoport, 2000b, 2000c, 2005), so that age alone is not enough to define a group—detailed attributes are needed (e.g., values, ideals, lifestyle, activity systems, social and kin relations and networks, cohort effects, status, and so on). Many chapters implicitly support this position (e.g., 2, 5, 7, 8, 9, 11, and 13). As pointed out previously, the importance of certain settings for certain groups (as in this book) can be interpreted in terms of increased criticality resulting from Lawton's concept of re-duced competence (Rapoport, 1983a) as well as reductions in home range—in both of which aging plays a crucial, but not the only, role.

C.   Depending on the attributes of the environments in question (A) and the groups involved (B), the environments will (or may) elicit certain behaviors, affect meanings, preferences, provide particular (specified) supportiveness, serve needed mnemonic functions, and so on.

Figure 16.2 can then be used to describe the content of this book (e.g., Table 2.1; Figure 12.1; Figure 15.3, etc.). It also provides a way to analyze, understand, and make operational the terms "home" and "place."What is called "home" in popular (folk) usage (and "feeling or being at home," "sense of home," "meaning of home," "coming home," etc.) is some type(s) of relationships between some (specified) subset of (A) for group (B) with its specified attributes, leading to a particular (specified) set of outcomes (C). This could be applied to *any* type of environment—in the case of the present book, domestic, and institutional settings for the elderly (e.g., Robinson, 2004). Although dismantling is certainly a way of operationalizing "home" (and "place"), those terms are not then needed.

The proposed alternative also allows for incorporating concepts such as choice (of environmental quality, neighborhood, locale (e.g., location in a city), dwelling, system of settings, social environment, for example, population type and so on and on (Rapoport, 1985, 2000b, 2005). Furthermore, by changing the attributes of settings (A) and of user groups (B), the process can be generalized to all EBS: housing, offices, hospitals, nursing homes, schools, laboratories, streets, parks, neighborhoods, and so on—even space stations and undersea habitats (Rapoport, 1997a, 2000a). This would not only enable, but encourage integration and synthesis with other EBS literature and with other disciplines. It would also encourage generalization and theory building.

Thus, from my perspective, using "home" and "place" represents a *loss*.

NOTES

1. This is also the case, in other chapters, for other people's links with neighborhood, village, small town, inner city, suburbs, etc.

2. In the case of chapter 8, it also necessary to record the "unsolicited use" of other words, of *all* utterances and to determine the percentage of the use of "home," as well as the contexts in which all utterances are used.

3. These findings also link to chapters 11, 13, 14, and 15, among others, which do not need "home" either.

4. The many, and inconsistent ways in which "home" is used, so that it can really mean anything one wants it to mean, reminds me of Margaret Masterson's criticism of Kuhn's use of "paradigm" in the first edition of *The Structure of Scientific Revolutions* (1962), which, she showed was used in 20 different ways (in later editions Kuhn did reduce it to *1* use). I wonder how many uses of "home" and its cognates a thorough analysis would discover in this book.

5. This also redresses a certain neglect in this book of more specific physical aspects of built environments. The attributes of (A) can also be used as components of environmental quality profiles (Rapoport, 1990, 1995, in press), which describe what in chapter 12 (this volume, p. ___) is called "the quality of the living environment."

REFERENCES

Childress, H. A. (1996). *Landscapes of betrayal, landscapes of joy: Curtisville in the lives of its teenagers.* Doctoral dissertation in architecture, University of Wisconsin—Milwaukee.

Dennett, D. C. (1995). *Darwin's dangerous idea (evolution and the meanings of life).* New York: Simon & Schuster.

Dennett, D. C. (2003). *Freedom evolves.* New York: Viking.

Imamoglu, C. (2002). Toward an understanding of place schema: Societal and individual-level representations of assisted living, Doctoral dissertation in architecture, University of Wisconsin—Milwaukee.

Kuhn, T. S. (1962). *The structure of scientific revolutions.* Chicago: University of Chicago Press.

Liu, C-W. (1994). From old town to new city: A study of behavior settings and meanings of streets in Taiwan, Doctoral dissertation in architecture, University of Wisconsin—Milwaukee.

Mead, M. (1972). *Blackberry winter: My earlier years.* New York: William Morrow and Company.

Pagel, M., & Mace, R. (2004). The cultural wealth of nations. *Nature, 428,* 275–278.

Pinker, S. (1997). *How the mind works.* New York: W. W. Norton.

Pinker, S. (2002). *The blank slate (the modern denial of human nature).* New York: Viking.

Rapoport, A. (1977). *Human aspects of urban form.* Oxford, UK: Pergamon Press.

Rapoport, A. (1978). Nomadism as a man–environment system. *Environment and Behavior, 10,* 215–246.

Rapoport, A. (1983a). Development, culture-change and supportive design. *Habitat International, 7,* 249–268.

Rapoport, A. (1983b). The effect of environment on behavior. In J. B. Calhoun (Ed.), *Environment and population (perspectives on adaptation, environment and population)* (pp. 200–201). New York: Praeger.

Rapoport, A. (1983c). Environmental quality, metropolitan areas and traditional settlements. *Habitat International, 7*(3/4), 37–63.

Rapoport, A. (1985). Thinking about home environments: A conceptual framework. In I. Altman & C. M. Werner (Eds.), *Home environments (Vol. 8 of human behavior and environment,* pp. 255–286). New York: Plenum Press.

Rapoport, A. (1990a). *The meaning of the built environment (rev. ed.).* Tucson, AZ: University of Arizona Press.

Rapoport, A. (1990b). Indirect approaches to environment-behavior research. *National Geographical Journal of India, 36*(1/2), 30–46.

Rapoport, A. (1990c). Defining vernacular design. In M. Turan (Ed.), *Vernacular architecture (paradigms of environmental response)* (pp. 67–101). Aldershot, UK: Avebury.

Rapoport, A. (1990d). Systems of activities in systems of settings. In S. Kent (Ed.), *Domestic architecture and the use of space* (pp. 9–20). Cambridge, UK: Cambridge University Press.

Rapoport, A. (1992a). On cultural landscapes. *Traditional Dwellings and Settlements Review*, 3(2), 33–47.

Rapoport, A. (1992b). On regions and regionalism. In N. C. Markovich, W. F. E. Preiser, & F. G. Sturm (Eds.), *Pueblo style and regional architecture* (pp. 272–294). New York: Van Nostrand-Reinhold. (paperback edition)

Rapoport, A. (1994a). A critical look at the concept 'place.' *National Geographical Journal of India, 4*(1–4), 31–45.

Rapoport, A. (1994b). Spatial organization and the built environment. In T. Ingold (Ed.), *Companion encyclopedia of anthropology: Humanity, culture and social life* (pp. 460–502). London: Routledge.

Rapoport, A. (1995a) Environmental quality and environmental quality profiles. In A. Rapoport, *Thirty-three papers in environment-behavior research* (pp. 489–512). Newcastle, UK: Urban International Press.

Rapoport, A. (1995b). A critical look at the concept 'home.' In D. N. Benjamin (Ed.), *The home: Words, meanings and environments* (pp. 25–52). Aldershot, UK: Avebury.

Rapoport, A. (1997a). Theory in environment–behavior studies: Transcending times, settings and groups. In S. Wapner, J. Demick, T. Yamamoto, & T. Takahashi (Eds.), *Handbook of Japan–U.S. environment–behavior research (toward a transactional approach)* (pp. 399–421). New York: Plenum Press.

Rapoport, A. (1997b). The nature and role of neighborhoods. *Urban Design Studies, 3*, 93–118.

Rapoport, A. (2000a). Science, explanatory theory and environment-behavior studies. In S. Wapner (Ed.), *Theoretical perspectives in environment-behavior research: Underlying assumptions, research problems and methodologies* (pp. 107–140). New York: Kluwer Academic/Plenum.

Rapoport, A. (2000b). Theory, culture and housing. *Housing, Theory and Society, 17*, 145–165.

Rapoport, A. (2000c). On the size of cultural groups. *Open House International, 27*(3), 7–11.

Rapoport, A (2005). *Culture, architecture and design.* Chicago: Locke Scientific.

Robinson, J. W. (2004). *Architecture of institution and home: Architecture as cultural medium.* Doctoral dissertation in architecture, Delft University of Technology, The Netherlands.

CHAPTER 17

Home As Paradox

Kim Dovey

In assessing all that we have learned in recent decades about the concept and experience of "home" one of the key insights is surely what a tantalizing concept it is; how little we know and how far we are from getting to the "bottom" of it. Although there remains a certain frustration at the ambiguities that persist, at the slippages of meaning, my sense is that this is the nature of home and the source of its great interest. If we examine the literature base on theories of "home" as reflected in this volume, we find that it begins primarily in phenomenological geography in the 1970s (Buttimer, 1980; Relph, 1976; Tuan, 1977) and then expands into environmental psychology and "environment–behavior" research from the mid-1980s after the publication of Altman and Werner's (1985) edited volume *Home Environments*. A fine review article by Despres (1991) summed up the work of the 1980s and a great deal more has been published since (Benjamin, Stea, & Saile, 1995; Groat, 1995). Over this time we have learned a great deal about the meaning of "home" as a place of security and order, an order that is at once spatial and social. The experience of "home" is also a form of ontological security with a crucial connection to constructions of "self" and the question of "spirit" (Marcus, 1995). It is a mirror or symbol of the self, a place where social and cultural identities become expressed and stabilized. The experience of "home" is largely unselfconscious and unrecognized until threatened; distinguished in this regard from the much more conscious "sense of place." It is a mode of dwelling that Heidegger terms *zuhanden*, the world of everyday engagement, contrasted with the *vorhanden* mode of detached contemplation (Heidegger, 1962). The meanings of home are established by repetition and memory; in a marvelous phrase by Freya Stark it is: "a place where every day is multiplied by all the days before it" (quoted in Tuan, 1977, p. 144). Home is an experience that repeats, a "refrain" that gains depth over time and may become more intense as we age.

A common thread in this research is the attempt to explore the experiential dimensions of "home" through qualitative research techniques in which the semistructured interview has been the most fruitful of methods. Yet one thing that has become clear is that the experience of home is largely unselfconscious; indeed it is in part defined by a profound sense of familiarity that we take for granted until it is threatened. Although interviews may unearth the "taken for granted" and subconscious, they may not. To what degree does the interview privilege the conscious effects of dislocation rather than the "taken for granted" experience? In William James' terms, to what degree is one studying the "me" ("my home") rather than the "I" ("I am at home")? The danger lies in reducing the topic to its researchable aspects and then finding that we have missed the point. This is not to suggest that interviews are not an appropriate method; merely that they may not be enough. Research on "home" opens up a philosophical abyss for which there can be no easy solution. This is linked to the slippages in meaning between "house" and "home"; between home as spatial and social; between home as house, neighborhood, landscape, city, and nation.

STORIES

One of the lessons evident in many chapters of this volume lies in the value of particular stories or narratives that emerge from interviews. Stories open windows onto particularities and contingencies in the experience of home. Although they are not dependable or reliable in terms of building a knowledge base, they often generate insights to further work and expose ambiguities. Stories often have a potent capacity, not just to move us, but to unsettle assumptions and to provoke a re-thinking. One that sticks in my mind is about the man in Kansas who wanted to claim and move a public boulder (which saved his father's life) as a memento, before discovering that the boulder had the same significance for others (Norris-Baker & Scheidt, chapter 13, this volume). This story reminds us of the role of seemingly insignificant places and landmarks as cognitive "hooks" for potent memories, and that such meanings often do not surface until threatened. It raises questions about the possibility of transferring the meanings of home from place to place as it exposes one of the key ambiguities of "home" as a conception that is at once both private and public. And in doing so it raises the most important question of all—what happens when conflicting conceptions of home intersect in the same place?

In a rather different story, the 2003 film *House of Sand and Fog* explores such a theme through a narrative wherein two quite different conceptions of home compete for the same house. Because of a bureaucratic mistake, a Californian woman is evicted from the house she inherited from her father. The new owner is a former Iranian military leader in exile, desperate to recreate a new sense of home in the same house. The power of the film derives in part from a reversed allegory with the situation in Israel/Palestine—the home is at once a house and a world, both local and global; and any resolution is uneasy. These local/global tensions are also apparent in the 2004 film *Goodbye Lenin*, a comic story that portrays an aging woman whose familiar sense of "home" in East Berlin has collapsed along with the Berlin Wall while she was in a coma. In the attempt to protect her from the shock of capitalism, her loving son constructs her apartment as an illusion of the ideal socialist state—an illusion she plays along with when she realizes that his desires are also being met. To what degree is the treatment of the aged, the desire to give them or place them in a "home," based on illusion, stereotype, paternalism, and a need to see the elders safely contained? This film also illustrates what Bachelard (1969) calls "intimate immensity"— the potent ways in which small and intimate spaces can evoke a whole world or a life. And this is rarely more apparent than in the intimate spaces of elders.

Moving to a more local and factual drama, I recently attended a public meeting about urban development in my own neighborhood in suburban Melbourne, Australia. Led by actor Geoffrey Rush, a number of mostly middle-aged and elderly residents added their voices of opposition to what was perceived as "inappropriate development." They each spoke with passion of how long they had lived in a neighborhood where the sense of "home" and "character" was now under threat. Yet there was no clear development proposal and this threat remained vaguely defined by terms like "inappropriate," "high-density," and "overdevelopment." Although these threats may become real, this self-conscious proclamation of home as neighborhood character and community was based on an imagined threat. I was also struck by the paradox that as residents age—and as household size shrinks along with the capacity to drive and to look after a large garden—their best chance of remaining in the neighborhood lies in the development of new and denser housing types. Pedestrian access to community facilities and public transportation are keys to a sense of community for elders and they depend on at least medium urban densities. The paradox is that some of the changes necessary to provide a sense of "home" in later life may be subject to fierce resistance in the name of preserving a sense of "home."

Finally, in an ancient story, Tantalus of Greek myth was accused by the gods of acquiring knowledge humans should not have; he was punished by standing up to his neck in water with fruit hanging above him. Every time he tried to eat or drink, the fruit blew away and the water level sank. To be "tantalized" is to see what we desire only to have it vanish when we seek it. Bauman (2001) uses this story as a window onto the burgeoning desire for an experience of "community." "Community," like "home," is taken for granted. The quest for "community" tantalizes, suggests Bauman, because the experience cannot survive the moment of self-consciousness.

> Once it starts to praise its unique valor, wax lyrical about its a pristine beauty and stick on nearby fences wordy manifestos calling its members to appreciate its wonders and telling all the others to admire them or shut up—one can be sure the community is no more . . . a community speaking of itself is a contradiction in terms (Bauman, 2001, p. 12).

From this view the quest for "community" and "home" are after effects of their vulnerability and loss. The quest creates what Bauman terms "peg communities," "homes" as places for hanging provisional identities. The paradox of community is the paradox of home; both home and community are the "doxa" of everyday life, which become something else ("para-dox") when we turn them into subjects of research and contemplation. As our faith in the protection of the state declines, safety is sought in home, neighborhood, and community as a stranger-proof voluntary ghetto (Bauman, 2001, p. 114).

THEORIES

Stories have a capacity to open up the ambiguities and contradictions of the experience of home but the task remains to research and to rethink it. My sense is that this task is best served by a broadening of the theoretical frameworks within which research questions are developed, to include a range of theorists whose work remains largely outside the current literature on "home." I want to start with the suggestion that the concept of "home" has been wrongly conflated with the idea of "essence." The search for deeper meaning can easily embody the premise of a closure of meaning and identity as somehow fixed and immutable. Alternatively the experience of "home" can be approached dialectically, as the product of conflict, contradiction, and the play of difference. What if the tantalizing ambiguities of home are linked to its authenticities? As Berger (1992, p. 216) puts it: "Authenticity comes from a single faithfulness, that to the ambiguity of experience." The ambiguities of home, the experiences that won't stabilize, can be where one finds authenticity. The paradox here is that the idea of home as a quest for essential, deep, and unchanging meaning can have a conservative, stabilizing, and even paralyzing effect on formations of identity.

One of the fundamental dialectics of home is the inside/outside dialectic, founded on the distinction between "home" and its "other." This can be linked to what Douglas (1966) long ago theorized as an opposition between purity and danger; a place of purity, strongly identified with the human body and the social body, is defended by socially mediated (yet universally prevalent) spatial rituals. Key examples are the symbolic rituals associated with bodily orifices and passage across them—food, sex, and ablution. Such rituals identify a zone of purity and order while ritually defending the body against the perceived dangers of difference. This dialectic is embodied in the built environment that mediates the penetrations of "otherness" into our lives; it keeps "difference" and "dis-ease" at bay. The inside/outside dialectic becomes ordered along the lines of closed and open, safety and danger, home and journey, familiar and strange, self and other, private and public. Practices of "entering" bodies and buildings are universally given ritual meanings about social identity and threats to it. The inside/outside dialectic structures the lifeworld with boundaries and thresholds, all strongly linked to the construction and protection of identity—it structures social relations between insiders and outsiders; between identities and differences.

The theories of Deleuze and Guattari (1987) are interesting in this regard since they generally involve a privileging of the journey, the "flow of desire," the "line of flight" and "nomadic" modes of dwelling over a stable sense of home. Their interest is in identity formation, in "becoming" rather than "being." Within this conception the experience of "home" is like a refrain:

I.   A child in the dark, gripped with fear, comforts himself by singing under his breath. . . . Lost, he takes shelter, or orients himself with his little song as best he can. The song is like a . . . calm and stable center in the heart of chaos.

II.   Now we are at home. But home does not preexist: it was necessary to draw a circle around that uncertain and fragile center, to organize a limited space. . . . The forces of chaos are kept outside as much as possible.

III. Finally one opens the circle a crack, opens it all the way, lets someone in, calls someone, or else goes out oneself, launches forth. One opens the circle not on the side where the old forces of chaos press against it but in another region, one created by the circle itself. . . . One ventures from home on the thread of a tune. (Deleuze & Guattari, 1987, p. 313)

This passage outlines a process of establishing the sense of home as a "calm and stable center" that keeps the forces of chaos at bay. Yet this circle finally cracks open in a way "created by the circle itself." This is the dialectic of inside and outside, of home and journey, of identity and difference. Without a secure ontological center there is no journey, no acceptance of difference. Although the subject here is a child in the process of identity formation, how different is this at the other end of the lifecycle? Has the refrain of home become fixed and determined to repeat endlessly until death? Or does one continue to venture forth "on the thread of a tune?" The usefulness of such theory lies in its focus on flows of "desire" as the flows of life itself.

The work of Giddens on constructions of identity is interesting in this regard. Based in Heideggerian notions of being-in-the-world coupled with Erikson's theories of ego-identity, Giddens (1990) argues the importance of "ontological security" in identity formation. Closely linked to the phenomenology of "home," ontological security is a confidence in the continuity of self-identity, strongly linked to the built environment as the place where such identities are produced and performed. The home is a protective cocoon, a way of seeing as much as an enclosure, which brackets out aspects of our world that would otherwise engulf us and cause paralysis of the will (Giddens, 1991). Giddens suggests that globalization and modernity have transformed the very tissue of everyday experience—the home is infused to its core with local/global tensions. This does not signal a loss of "home," rather it is the end of the closed local home-place where singular identities are linked to semantic and spatial enclosure (Giddens, 1990). The creation of mock-historic "homes" based on a retreat to a false history, a synthetic "past" of the harmonious community, is not so much a creation of home as a nostalgic symptom of homelessness.

The concept of "home" as unselfconscious experience, as everyday practice, and as ontological security has a strong congruence with Bourdieu's notion of the *habitus*. As Bourdieu (2000, pp. 142–143) puts it:

> The agent engaged in practice knows the world . . . without objectifying distance, takes it for granted, precisely because he is caught up in it, bound up with it; he inhabits it like a garment (*un habit*) or a familiar habitat. He feels at home in the world because the world is also in him, in the form of habitus.

This sense of home as *habitus* suggests that the experience of home is strongly enmeshed in practices of social power; the *habitus* conflates a "sense of place" with a "sense of one's place." The *habitus* as home is an ideological formation where practices of power are driven underground in a kind of "silent complicity" in which: "The most successful ideological effects are those that have no words, and ask no more than complicitous silence" (Bourdieu, 1977, p. 188). Bourdieu is also well-known for his conceptions of social and symbolic capital. Social capital is popularly known through the ways that cohesive social networks with high levels of trust are linked to a strong sense of "community" and high levels of engagement in public life (Portes, 1998; Putnam, 1995). Networks of social capital are often spatially embedded in pedestrian networks, social settings, and valued places. Yet for Bourdieu the production of social capital is also the reproduction of social class. The sense of home as a retreat to a community of like-minded people is not necessarily benign. The home place also becomes what Bourdieu terms "symbolic capital"—a form of symbolic distinction that establishes and stabilizes social distinctions among people (Bourdieu, 1984). The real-estate market refuses to use the word "house" because it doesn't carry the symbolic capital of "home." The meanings of "home" are thus formed in discourse and one of the opportunities for research would seem to be in combining discourse analysis with more traditional methods of research. These two dimensions of home, as symbolic and social capital, are not separate. All places establish forms of both social cohesion and of social distinction.

To conclude here with any sense of closure would undermine my purpose. Yet in the sense that the idea of home is identified with the return or the refrain, I will return to the idea that the desire for home, like the desire for community and authenticity, cannot approach closure without destroying what it seeks. At one level the quest for home is often driven by an essentialist desire to stabilize identity and exclude difference. Yet it does not follow that this quest can be conflated with such exclusion. The dialectic is always two sided—constructions of home are equally a product of homelessness and the unhomely. There are no roots without journeys. As the role of memory increases and that of the journey declines with age, to what degree do we acquiesce in the idea that the identity of the elders is fixed and finished? To what degree do we accept the idea of home as a closure of place experience and to what degree are we institutionalizing the closure of life? The elders who are most alive are those whose sense of home is neither fixed nor finished.

REFERENCES

Altman, I., & Werner, C. (Eds.). (1985). *Home environments*. New York: Plenum Press.

Bachelard, G. (1969). *The poetics of space*. Boston: Beacon.

Bauman, Z. (2001). *Community*. Cambridge, UK: Polity.

Benjamin, D., Stea, D., & Saile, D. (Eds.). (1995). *The home*. Aldershot, UK: Avebury.

Berger, J. (1992). *Keeping a rendezvous*. Harmondsworth, UK: Penguin.

Bourdieu, P. (1977). *Outline of a theory of practice*. London: Cambridge University Press.

Bourdieu, P. (1984). *Distinction*. London: Routledge.

Bourdieu, P. (2000). *Pascalian meditations*. Cambridge, UK: Polity.

Buttimer, A. (1980). Home, reach, and the sense of place. In A. Buttimer & D. Seamon (Eds.), *The human experience of space and place* (pp. 166–187). London: Croom Helm.

Deleuze, G., & Guattari, F. (1987). *A thousand plateaus*. Minneapolis, MN: University of Minnesota Press.

Després, C. (1991). The meaning of home. *Journal of Architectural and Planning Research, 8*, 96–155.

Douglas, M. (1966). *Purity and danger*. London: Routledge & Kegan Paul.

Giddens, A. (1990). *The consequences of modernity*. Stanford, CA: Stanford University Press.

Giddens, A. (1991). *Modernity and self identity*. Cambridge, UK: Polity.

Groat, L. (Ed.). (1995). *Giving places meaning*. London: Academic Press.

Heidegger, M. (1962). *Being and time*. New York: Harper & Row.

Marcus, C. C. (1995). *The house as a mirror of self*. Berkeley, CA: Conari Press.

Portes, A. (1998). Social capital. *Annual Review of Sociology, 24*, 1–24.

Putnam, R. (1995). Bowling alone: America's declining social capital. *Journal of Democracy, 6*, 65–78.

Relph, E. (1976). *Place and placelessness*. London: Pion.

Tuan, Y. (1977). *Space and place*. Minneapolis, MN: University of Minnesota Press.

CHAPTER 18

New Horizons on Home[1]

Maria D. Vesperi

The front-page headline was unambiguous and direct: "Wanted: smart, young adults." The accompanying story by Robert Trigaux, a business writer for the *St. Petersburg Times*, detailed a recent national study that ranked the Tampa Bay region 47th among 50 large metropolitan areas when it came to the concentration of residents under age 35 (Trigaux, 2004). First-ranked Austin-San Marcos, Texas boasted 18.2%, compared to the 12.7% who reside in Tampa-St. Petersburg-Clearwater. Tellingly labeled "The Young and the Restless: How Tampa Bay Competes for Talent," the study was commissioned by local business leaders who were concerned that the retirement of baby boomers would leave them with a depleted workforce. Austin and Atlanta, Trigaux warned, "enjoy populations flush with young adults." In contrast, young people were leaving Tampa Bay after college for "other metro areas perceived as better job markets or simply more interesting places to live."

Trigaux summarized the study's conclusions about the amenities that young, educated adults value in a city. These include: "A sense of place and history that includes distinctive shops and restaurants. A clean and safe downtown that is alive and serves as a social center." High among the worries articulated in local focus groups were the perceived lack of a unified identity for the region, the dearth of activity in Tampa's downtown and concern about finding suitable mates. In other words, many of the young adults surveyed were not just seeking good employment opportunities; they were hoping to find the ingredients they regard as critical for making a region home.

Striving hard for an upbeat note, Trigaux identified several business-community initiatives designed to make the area more competitive as a residential choice for young adults. He stressed that local leaders were aware of the challenge and eager—if not desperate—to reline the nest in ways that would attract a youth migration. Elsewhere in the piece, Trigaux referred to the problem as a "Darwinian search for youth," reinforcing the link between demographics and community survival in a fiercely competitive urban environment.

Courting youth so openly can be a rather shameless topic, so like many who discuss it, Trigaux began this way: "With baby boomers starting to retire and a labor shortage on the horizon . . . " Reference to the sheer demographic weight of the baby boom generation has become standard in debates about age. A nod to objectivity has allowed negative bias in discussions of the "new old" to take shape without challenge. Although touted as a market opportunity by many, baby boomers have also emerged as a threatening demographic group in discussions of aging. Beyond the obvious issues of cohort size and the resulting strain on health care and Social Security, new issues are beginning to register on the social agenda. Discussions of housing, employment, and consumer spending among this population often emphasize the depletion of resources for younger groups rather than the potential of healthy, well-educated retirees with discretionary incomes to make significant contributions to their communities.

Newspaper coverage of "home" was once confined to real-estate listings and practical columns about how to build bookshelves, cure moldy basements, and keep wallpaper seams from curling. Today's papers offer full home and lifestyle sections, fat with advertising inserts and reports on trends such as "nesting" and "downscaling." Yet, even when boomers are acknowledged for their collective purchasing power, there are worries about how much time they count as leisure and how they plan to spend it. For example, some trend-watchers point to the upswing in second-home purchases and travel among older boomers. Others fear that these same trends will prompt boomers to ignore the ad-heavy Sunday paper or cancel it altogether. Writing for *Editor and Publisher*, Lucia Moses cites this dire warning from demographer Peter Francese: "That 55- to 65-year olds will be the fastest growing age group in the next four years sounds good because they're also among the biggest spenders on newspapers. But they're also the most likely to own second homes where they will spend more weekends out of reach of their home-town paper" (Moses, 2003). Whether boomers are traveling abroad or just upstate, these trends suggest that tomorrow's retirees may be less engaged in civic life than their predecessors. They may be desirable to a community as consumers of goods and services, but not as reliable producers of the values and spirit that give places texture and infuse them with meaning.

It is not surprising that much of the current discussion about today's elders and the graying of the baby boomers is focused on economic influence. Age deserves more representation in the media, the argument goes, because older people have money to spend. We should be careful what we wish for, however. How constructive is the potential for niche marketing as a defining image? Is it enough? Or even, as a jaded observer might ask, is there any other kind? The image of old age as a healthy, wealthy, self-absorbed time of life may be no better fit for the majority of people than the model of frail dependency it has superceded. It is certainly no better as a source of the moral authority one needs to exert agency on the world and to participate actively in civic life.

The relationship between aging and place is most often ap-proached from the perspective of the situated self. Elders work to accommodate some changes in health status, income, and social support while resisting others, a process that can be identified and plotted as continuity or disruption of personal experience. Research-ers want to know what happens to older people when they age in place, or when they don't. A larger, and in some ways more urgent question might be: What happens to places themselves when long-term residents modify or sever ties to home?

As young adults filled the work force and the suburbs after World War II, the guarantee of steady, if modest, retirement incomes paved the way for the Sunbelt migration and for the establishment of the nursing home industry. Ironically, at the moment when social scientists were exploring the idea that biological and social aging were interdependent, widely variable across cultures and, hence, malleable, U.S. society at-large was becoming fully socialized to the belief that chronology is destiny. The assumed inevitability of frailty, role loss, and senility combined with new patterns of age-based residential segregation for elders and young families alike to promote the stereotype of retirees as frail, disengaged burdens on community rather than as community resources.

Age segregation in housing has increased radically since Robert Butler focused on its negative impact in his seminal article, "Ageism: Another form of Bigotry" (1969). Butler introduced the term "ageism" to public consciousness by questioning the civic benefit of policies that relocated the elderly poor from age-heterogeneous neighborhoods to age-segregated public housing. "I do not want my children to grow up in an isolated neighborhood, knowing neither the realities of old age nor the meaning of racial heterogeneity," he wrote. Subsequently, the Reagan–Bush era heralded an ongoing shift away from the emphasis on aging as a social welfare problem and toward a focus on healthy, active seniors with stock portfolios and independent lifestyles. Instead of reinvesting in their communities, however, many well-off retirees contributed to an acceleration of the trend toward homogenization by age and class. Age-segregated housing, once the refuge of the elderly poor, was newly touted as an upscale choice for healthy retirees who could buy "freedom" from long-established familial and civic ties.

Anthropologist Setha Low (2003) has documented the dramatic proliferation of gated residential developments and their popularity among diverse age and income groups, and the trend is continuing to accelerate. Low notes, "In areas such as Tampa, Florida, gated communities account for four out of five home sales of $300,000 and over" (Low, 2004).

Most of today's gated communities are no more than walled housing developments with recreational perks such as swimming pools and golf courses. Because schools, stores, and places of worship are located outside the walls, residents still have the opportunity—and the obligation—to engage in public life. There are exceptions, however. Sun City Center, a self-contained, age-restricted municipality near Tampa, was still a novelty in the mid-1980s when Frances Fitzgerald traveled there to do research for her 1987 book, *Cities on a Hill*. In a state that had long been viewed as a bellwether for age-related trends and baldly speculative approaches to real estate, the sprouting of an instant town based on age segregation was still noteworthy. Fitzgerald was writing about communities of choice, from San Francisco's Castro district to the followers of a well-heeled guru in Oregon. Sun City was different. Rather than a place made unique because of the people who were drawn to live there, it was a unique place designed to draw people, and perhaps to remake them.

Fitzgerald saw Sun City this way: "The lakes are artificial, and there is hardly a tree or a shrub or a blade of grass that has any correspondence to the world just beyond it. . . . From there, you can look out at a flat brown plain that used to be a cattle ranch. The developer simply scraped the surface off the land and started over again" (1987, p. 204).

Sun City was a raw, new place for new people, the newly retired. These were citizens who, as Fitzgerald described, were living on a "chronological frontier," the frontier of so-called "active retirement." Fitzgerald (1987) accurately identified the "active retirement" concept for what it was, a marketing tool for developers such as Sun City founder Del Webb. THE TOWN TOO BUSY TO RETIRE read a billboard along Fitzgerald's route to the community, which was relatively isolated in the early 1980s.

Too busy doing what? Marketing strategies suggested answers, and imagination filled in the details: playing golf, indulging passions for a wide range of hobbies and engaging in civic life with a self-selected sample of new best friends. "It's the people who sell the houses, not the real estate agents," one informant told Fitzgerald.

Twenty years later, Sun City Center is no longer geographically isolated but it remains a community apart among a rapidly growing sector of private communities. I recently spent a day in one such "new place," Celebration, Florida, along with four other anthropologists from several universities across the country. We had our separate reasons for being there: three of us were urbanists, one was an archaeologist who worked uncovering ancient cities and the fifth, a doctoral candidate, was developing a specialty in consumer credit and consumption patterns. Yet, comparing notes at the end of the afternoon, we were all struck by the way the community was promoted and embraced as *an active choice to purchase civic engagement* in the perceived absence of such opportunities in society at large. One resident, clearly a baby boomer, described the community as "like on the television shows in the 1950s," and, later, as like the childhood she herself remembered from that time. Celebration is not age-restricted and we did see some young families. It is, however, an expensive community by Florida standards and well beyond the reach of most young families.

Sun City and Celebration, with their emphasis on intentional community, are actually models of *dis*engagement from the perspective of the larger society. Every well-educated, well-employed, or successfully retired citizen who withdraws to the "safety" of a private enclave is simply no longer available to public life as a mentor, a first-base coach, a member of the city council. And although older people can continue to make public contributions as long as their health and personal circumstances allow, private engagement is solely conditional on the continuing ability to pay for the privilege. Celebration was founded in 1994, "a product of the affluent Clinton years," as one anthropologist in our group observed. The residents of Celebration and similar private communities are only as "safe" as their bank accounts.

The cumulative effect of age segregation has been to restrict and impoverish public dialogue about the increasing presence of older people in 21st-century communities. A key question for scholars concerned with the cultural construction of aging is whether boomers will break free of existing stereotypes or ultimately reinforce them. Will tomorrow's retirees be viewed as community-based mentors with time and experience to share, or as selfish consumers who are draining the legacy of future generations? There is evidence to suggest that tomorrow's retirees will be less civic-minded (Prisuta, 2004; Putnam, 2000, 2003). At the same time, there are hopeful precedents. Savishinsky (2000) found many examples of new civic engagement and the blossoming of avocations in his ethnographic study of 26 individuals from pre-retirement through the early retirement years. Large-scale answers will depend on a realignment of the infrastructural mix of social policy, economic reality and public opinion that has generated popular stereotypes about today's elders.

Attention to these issues and to long-term trends in community-based volunteerism has led to initiatives aimed at keeping the newly retired actively involved in civic life. For example, the Harvard School of Public Health has joined with the MetLife Foundation to explore new models for social interaction, problem solving, and constructive engagement for the baby boom generation. They have issued a report that calls on communities to identify specific social problems, invite older people to participate in solving them,and create "bridge" jobs between work and retirement for those who cannot afford to volunteer (Harvard-MetLife Foundation, 2004). More than three decades after Robert Butler accurately identified age segregation as the loss of a cultural legacy, attention to the gradual but profound dislocation of older citizens from heterogeneous communities has become even more vital to the realization of what "home" can mean at all stages of the life cycle.

NOTE

1. Portions of this commentary are adapted from Vesperi, M.D. "Forty-nine plus: Shifting images of aging in the media" (2004), in *Reinventing aging: Baby boomers and civic engagement.* Cambridge, MA: Center for Health Communication, Harvard School of Public Health; and Vespri, M.D. "Changing Images of Retirees in the Media," a presentation to the Harvard-MetLife Foundation Conference on Baby Boomers and Retirement: Impact on Civic Engagement. Cambridge, MA, October 9, 2003.

REFERENCES

Butler, R. (1969). Ageism: Another form of bigotry. *The Gerontologist* 9, 243–246.

Fitzgerald, F. (1987). *Cities on a hill.* New York: Touchstone.

Harvard-MetLife Foundation. (2004). *Reinventing aging: Baby boomers and civic retirement.* Cambridge, MA: Author.

Low, S. (2003). *Behind the gates: Fear, security and the pursuit of happiness in contemporary America.* New York: Routledge.

Low, S. (2004 April). *The politics of fear: The ethnography of gated communities.* Plenary presentation to the Society for the Anthropology of North America conference, "Containment and Transgression: Global Encounters with North America at the Twenty-first Century," Atlanta, GA.

Moses, L. (2003). Sunday will never be the same. *Editor and Publisher Online.* Available at http://www.editorandpublisher.com/editorandpu.../articledisplay.jsp?vnucontent_id=195319

Prisuta, R. (2004). Enhancing volunteerism among aging boomers. In *Reinventing aging: Baby boomers and civic retirement.* Cambridge, MA: Harvard University and the MetLife Foundation.

Putnam, R. (2000). *Bowling alone: The collapse and revival of American community.* New York: Simon & Schuster.

Putnam, R. (2003, October). Generations and life cycles in civic engagement and social capital. Presentation to the Harvard-MetLife Foundation conference on Baby Boomers and Retirement: Impact on Civic Engagement. Cambridge, MA.

Savishinsky, J. (2000). *Breaking the watch: The meanings of retirement in America.* Ithaca, NY: Cornell University Press.

Trigaux, R. (2004, May 20). Wanted: Smart, young adults. *St. Petersburg Times,* pp. 1A, 1D, 5D.

CHAPTER 19

Leaving Home

Graham D. Rowles and Habib Chaudhury

> We shall not cease from exploration
> And the end of all our exploring
> Will be to arrive where we started
> And know the place for the first time.—T.S. Eliot

Our journeys invariably start from home. At the end of the journey, it is to home that we return once more. And so, at the end of the sojourn that has been this book, we return to the place where we started and ask ourselves and you (the reader)—to what extent do we now know *home*? We suspect answers to this question will be as diverse as our readers. Our hope is that, like all good explorations, the journey has posed at least as many provocative and worthwhile questions as it has answered. Although the tantalizing ambiguity of home remains, we believe that some of the basic dilemmas of investigating and harnessing the concept have been brought into sharper focus.

As Cattell (Chapter 10) so clearly reveals, for most people, coming home is a pleasant experience. We are embraced by the familiarity of a "place," whether it be a physical location, a network of relationships, or a state of being, in which we feel secure, supported, valued, in control, and at one with the world. But staying at home, for all its often taken-for-granted benefits of familiarity and comfort, can become stultifying. Indeed, as Dovey points out (Chapter 17), being at home comes into consciousness and assumes meaning only in relation to being away. After a time, we become restless and feel the urge to venture forth once more, to explore the world beyond the threshold. Paradoxically, in so doing we come to better define the home we cherish, because we become more familiar with the alienation and discomfort of it's "other"—not home. Life involves an ongoing tension between wanting to remain within the known and familiar—being at home, and an imperative to venture forth and reach out into an unknown that is both exhilarating and foreboding— being away from home (Balint, 1955).

In leaving home once more to find home, where should we venture? First, it is important to acknowledge and to work on reconciling the dichotomy of two cultures of home that coalesce around opposite poles of a continuum. One culture views home in very concrete terms—essentially as a physical structure, a dwelling or place of residence sited in a particular location and having certain physical accoutrements. Home is the geographical hub of our comings and goings—our transactions with a physical setting. From this perspective, home is best understood within the paradigm of classification, typology, singular definitions, and measurable variables.

The other culture views home from a phenomenological perspective as a visceral sense of being in place. From this perspective, home is more an experienced than an observable phenomenon. We can feel at home when we are alone in a familiar setting and experience a profound sense of being at one with our environment. We can feel at home when we are with a particular group of people—a social definition of home. And we can experience, or at least anticipate, a spiritually transcendent sense of home as being part of a universe where material and spiritual worlds intersect and where, when we die, those who acknowledge an afterlife will go "home" to our God or to Mother earth as a part of the endless cycle of life. Each of these manifestations and understandings of home, from the most concrete to the most ethereal, is legitimate.

On the most fundamental level, the extremes of the two cultures reflect a tension between positivist ("scientific") perspectives on home and its phenomenological ("experiential") expression. The two cultures are brought into sharp contrast in the opposing commentaries of Amos Rapoport (Chapter 16) and Kim Dovey (Chapter 17). On the one hand, Rapoport suggests that, as presently construed, the term "home" is unscientific and so ill-defined that it serves to obfuscate rather than clarify, and so is of little value to planners and architects as they seek to design environments for our elders. He urges formal definition and consistent use of terminology that will facilitate the cumulative development of a verifiable body of knowledge on the topic. In contrast, Dovey argues for elaboration on nuance and celebration of the ambiguity and tantalizing presence and intimacy of a phenomenon considered to be at the core of human existence and part of life's eternal quest, which is ultimately, almost by definition, impossible to pin down.

There is a need to reconcile the two cultures and, at the same time, to move beyond the limitations of merely developing and elaborating on typologies of the characteristics of home. This will require progressing beyond anecdote, description, and classification. It will require a focus on investigating the complex and intricate ways in which different expressions of home overlap, feed into each other, and evolve over time. To provide some examples of research questions focusing on such overlap: What are the perceptual mechanisms and processes that link specific environmental-design features to the development of an emotional sense of home? To what extent do items of furniture and cherished possessions provide physical cues and become tools in the creation and maintenance of a sense of home? When we feel "at home" with a group of neighbors or members of our community of interest, to what extent is such a sense nurtured and stimulated by a responsive physical environment, designed to stimulate and facilitate social interaction, and foster a sense of community? How does the environment condition our creation of home? Alternatively, to what extent is our manipulation of the environment an essential component of the creation of home? To what extent is the development of home a transactional process? At the same time, in seeking greater insight into home, how do we accomplish this while heeding Dovey's (Chapter 17, p. 364) warning of the "danger that lies in "reducing the topic to its researchable aspects and then finding that we have missed the point"?

As we leave home once more in the paradoxical quest to find home, we believe that success may result from a combination of probing ever more deeply some of the questions explored in this book, addressing key questions that have been ignored in the previous pages, answering new questions that have been introduced by our contributors, and opening our eyes to new and unexpected manifestations of the phenomenon. First, additional phenomenological inquiry is needed into the essence of home. Is a need for home—at least in some form—a universal human phenomenon? Building on the analyses of Rubinstein and Medeiros (Chapter 3) and Rubinstein (Chapter 6), how does a sense of home relate to the development of the self? To what extent is home an individual versus a social construction? Making such philosophical and empirical questions especially challenging is the problem of measurement. How do we transcend the dangerously beguiling complacency of anecdote? Can we progress beyond warm fuzzy feelings? Is there a systematic way in which sense of home might be measured? How do we meaningfully integrate "measurable" variables with the intangible aspects of meaning of home to gain a more holistic understanding? In this book, the measures introduced by Oswald and Wahl (Chapter 2) and Peace and her colleagues (Chapter 14) offer possibilities that merit further elaboration and assessment; but neither allows us to capture the emotional depth of the concept—what home feels like.

Second, it is important to devote more attention to exploring the geographical elasticity of home (McHugh & Mings, 1996)—to probe differences in the nature and meaning of home on different spatial scales. Our home is, at the same time, the apartment where we live, "our" neighborhood, "our" community, and "our" homeland. The work of Norris-Baker and Scheidt (Chapter 13), Peace, Holland, and Kellaher (Chapter 14), and Després and Lord (Chapter 15) provides important insight on different expressions of home on the level of community. However, we know little about the manner in which home is differentiated and reconciled by the individual when he or she simultaneously considers being "at home" on the level of the dwelling, the immediate neighborhood, the community, and the nation. Community perspectives on the meaning of home for older adults span a diverse and complex set of topics that include home as a symbol of social and cultural structure, affective aspects of community, social networks in the neighborhood, contested meanings of home as a place for caregiving, community identity, community as a place to "age in place," sustaining community through maintenance of collective heritage and memories, cultural variations of meanings of home and community within the home–community continuum, and so on. Although this topic of community issues in home environments gets formal attention in one section of this volume, it deserves a volume of its own.

Third, it is essential that we begin to focus more directly on temporal dimensions of home. Extending the contribution of Oswald and Wahl (Chapter 2) and Watkins and Hosier (Chapter 9), how does home develop and change over the life course? How do people develop a sense of home—from infant affinity for the mother's breast, to the comfort of the crib, to the childhood security of the backyard, to the adolescent territorial home of our neighborhood, to our sense of community as home? To what extent is our sense of home modified during relocations that occur during the life course? Do we recreate home with every move in a predictable manner? How do we deal with severance from a familiar home? In short, how does home evolve over the life span in parallel with an individual's changing personal capabilities and identity and environmental circumstances?

Fourth, there needs to be further inquiry into the cultural and cross-cultural issues of the meanings of home to older adults. As cities in North America and throughout the world become increasingly culturally diverse, the promises and challenges of between- and within-group frictions, harmony and commonalities in perspectives on home and community become increasingly important in envisioning and planning the meaningful coexistence of diverse cultural groups. The insights of Mazumdar and Mazumdar (Chapter 5) provide a fascinating glimpse into the world of Indian culture. Their chapter clearly demonstrates the importance of culturally based variants in the expression of home? Although we have included studies from five continents—Europe, Africa, North America, Australia, and India—in this volume we have barely scratched the surface of critical cross-cultural similarities and differences in the experience and manifestations of home. Why, for example, is there such a strong imperative in most cultures to be returned home for burial? (Cattell, Chapter 10; see, also Rowles & Comeaux, 1986, 1987). Creating a corpus of comparative international studies that embraces the full array of nomadic and sedentary cultures, less-developed and Western cultures, and rural and urban societies, presents an exciting challenge.

Fifth, moving to the more concrete world of design and dwelling characteristics discussed by Caouette (Chapter 12), Sherman and Dacher (Chapter 4), and in Rapoport's commentary (Chapter 16), how do different architectural and residential designs and configurations nurture or preclude the development of a sense of home? Does a building's façade influence its potential to become home through the messages it conveys? To what extent do items of furniture, the way in which dwellings are decorated and life-history-affirming cherished possessions shape elders' conceptions of home? Here we move into consideration of very practical issues. Although there is much anecdotal material on the importance of our home and much literature on the negative consequences in terms of morbidity and mortality resulting from its involuntary loss, there has been very little work on the relationship among specific design features, the creation and maintenance of a sense of home, and well-being.

Sixth, consideration of essentially positive aspects of the experience of home must be counterbalanced by research on those whose experience of home is filtered through circumstances of disadvantage and conflict—the alienated, displaced, and homeless. Manifestations of such circumstances are provided in this book by the contributions of Lewin (Chapter 7), on the problems faced by immigrant elders in Sweden, in Russell's description of the non-dwelling-based meaning of home to inner-city men in Australia (Chapter 11), and in Frank's (Chapter 8) poignant consideration of the separation from and quest for home of institutionalized persons with dementia. Each of these chapters provides powerful reinforcement for our contention that concern with the meaning of home is far more than merely an intellectual exercise and that, on many levels, issues pertaining to the concept have critical implications for physical and emotional well-being and even for survival. We must develop deeper understanding of what it means to be homeless, to be a stranger in a strange land, or to be separated from one's self through dementing illness. But beyond developing such sensitivity, we must vigorously investigate the personal, social, economic, historical, and political conditions that lead to these states. We must contribute insight to resolving the tensions that arise when competing views of home generate conflicts over place ranging from neighborhood disputes to international warfare. Such investigation will be potentially of great value in developing effective diplomatic, policy, programmatic, and interpersonal-level interventions to improve quality of life and well-being on scales ranging from the local to the global.

Seventh, a particularly important need with respect to studies of both home and homelessness is the development of theory. In this volume we see initial steps in this direction in several chapters. For example, both Oswald and Wahl (Chapter 2) and Despres and Lord (Chapter 15) provide a heuristic framework identifying and differentiating domains of the meaning of home. The need for developing models that explore the complex relationship between home as experienced versus home imagined and aspired to is clearly demonstrated by Russell in challenging the universality of traditional forms of home ownership as the basis for defining the concept (Chapter 11). An important step in providing more sophisticated theoretical understanding of the relationship between home and homelessness in life-course context is offered by Watkins and Hosier (Chapter 9). But we still lack a dynamic integrated theory that effectively links the experience of being at home with the physical, social, and psychological correlates of that feeling.

Finally, a number of our contributors including Oswald and Wahl (Chapter 2), Cattell (Chapter 10), and Norris-Baker and Scheidt (Chapter 13) suggest that it is important to look to the future and to consider changing conceptions and significances of home in relation to community lifecycles (Norris-Baker & Scheidt, Chapter 13), social and environmental change, societal evolution, and the evolving political economy of aging. Cattell (Chapter 10) provides insight into changing cultural conceptions of home, starkly revealed during her recent trip back to Kenya, which appear to be associated with a contemporary globalization of the lifestyles of younger African cohorts. Vesperi's thoughtful commentary (Chapter 18) begins to take us in this direction in a Western context by posing provocative questions with respect to what home will mean in the context of the changing demographics and economics of society. New questions regarding the nature of home in communities with acute anticipated labor shortages of young people or more highly mobile cohorts of less place-based baby boomers (two facets of changing community demographic and social profiles), attendant changes in patterns of engagement in civic life, and changing views of the role of elders in society may lead to threats to the very survival and integrity of the intergenerational community as home, at least as we construe the phenomenon today. As Vesperi (Chapter 18, p. 375) ponders: "What happens to places themselves when long-term residents [custodians of history and culture] modify or sever ties to home?" Are contemporary societal changes placing us at risk of becoming alienated and homeless because of our failure to adequately consider one of the core quests of humanity—the search for home?

REFERENCES

Balint, M. (1955). Friendly expanses—Horrid empty space. *International Journal of Psychoanalysis, 36*, 225–241.

Eliot, T. S. (1943). Little Gidding V. In *Four quartets*. London: Faber & Faber.

McHugh, K. E., & Mings, R. C. (1996). The circle of migration: Attachment to place in aging. *Annals of the Association of American Geographers, 83*, 530–550.

Rowles, G. D., & Comeaux, M. L. (1986). Returning home: The interstate transportation of human remains. *Omega: Journal of Death and Dying, 17*, 103–113.

Rowles, G. D., & Comeaux, M. L. (1987). A final journey: Post death removal of human remains. *Tijdschrift voor Economische en Sociale Geografie, 78*, 114–124.

Index

Springer Publishing Company

Qualitative Gerontology
A Contemporary Perspective
Second Edition
Graham D. Rowles, PhD
Nancy E. Schoenberg, PhD, Editors

This second edition examines recent trends in the application of qualitative methodologies and the emergence of new qualitative techniques such as focus groups, studies of personal histories, and the use of photography. Chapters include discussions of critical and feminist perspectives, practice issues, ethical issues, and the contribution of qualitative research to the progress of science.

Contents:

2001   312pp   0-8261-1335-4   hardcover

11 West 42nd Street, New York, NY 10036-8002 • Fax: 212-941-7842
Order Toll-Free: 877-687-7476 • Order On-line: www.springerpub.com